RADICAL ABOLITIONISM

Anarchy and the Government
of God in Antislavery Thought

RADICAL ABOLITIONISM

Anarchy and the Government of God in Antislavery Thought

by LEWIS PERRY

Cornell University Press / ITHACA AND LONDON

First published 1973 by Cornell University Press.
Published in the United Kingdom by Cornell University Press Ltd., 2-4 Brook Street, London W1Y 1AA.

International Standard Book Number 0-8014-0754-0
Library of Congress Catalog Card Number 72-12913

Printed in the United States of America by York Composition Co., Inc.

Librarians: Library of Congress cataloging information appears on the last page of the book.

For Curtis

Contents

Preface

Henry David Thoreau tells us, on the first page of *Walden,*
that he requires "of every writer, first or last, a simple and sincere
account of his own life, and not merely what he has heard of
other men's lives." Beyond question my book does discuss topics
that are echoed in the controversies and passions of our own
time—topics such as pacifism, anarchism, and interracial violence—and I would not quarrel with anyone who said that it
tells of the present condition of its author as well as of actors
in the past. My book is concerned, nonetheless, with what I have
learned of other men and women—the abolitionists—and it must
stand on its own as an essay in intellectual history. Although I
have spoken briefly of the modern relevance of abolitionism in
an epilogue, my major purpose has been to understand some of
the meanings of pacifism and anarchism for the abolitionists
themselves.

A few autobiographical comments may help to clarify the
problems with which the book is concerned. It was begun at a
point in my education when I had just finished coediting *Patterns of Anarchy: A Collection of Writings on the Anarchist
Tradition.* The research for that book plainly indicated that the
United States had its own anarchistic tradition, with a distinctive
emphasis on individual "self-ownership." Some interpretations
attributed this tradition either to European influences or to the
legacy of Thomas Jefferson. But it seemed likely that anarchism
had received important definitions in the antislavery movement

before the Civil War and that it was, in fact, only one of many
attempts in American history to escape the perils of "slavery."
Therefore I decided to undertake a study of what I understood
to be the anarchistic wing of the antislavery movement—that is,
the often criticized followers of William Lloyd Garrison. Most
standard works on abolitionism recognized that some Garrisonians were attracted to anarchistic ideas, a fact which was generally treated as sad, ridiculous, or deplorable. In the prevailing
scholarly view, anarchism was "extraneous" to abolitionism and
symptomatic of the dementia of a handful of New England abolitionists. Thus it could not be taken seriously. But I wanted to
know more about the reasons abolitionists gave for linking antislavery to anarchism, and I wondered whether anarchism might
not have been a thoughtful response to the problem of slavery,
as understood by abolitionists. There was some encouragement
for this inquiry in the writings of Louis Filler and John L.
Thomas (and soon there would be more in the writings of Aileen
Kraditor and Bertram Wyatt-Brown). It may have been an advantage, though it could suggest misleading analogies, that at the
time of my research the civil rights and antiwar movements were
debating issues similar to those that had once vexed abolitionists,
particularly the issues of violent means and political action. Certainly in a time of bitter interracial conflict it did not seem outlandish to read an abolitionist's claim that to abolish slavery by
violence or governmental force would be to invite centuries of
continuing violence and coercion.

The original manuscript, after six years and frequent revisions,
developed into this book. I still believe there was a doctrinal link
between antislavery and anarchism, and it still seems false to
label anarchism as extraneous or demented. On the other hand,
I no longer believe that there was an anarchistic wing—that is,
a few identifiable anarchists—in the antislavery movement. I
would argue that certain of the most basic ideas honored throughout abolitionism turned out in experience to have anarchistic
implications. In explaining why slavery was evil and intolerable
(a conviction which theoretically might have been presented

in a variety of ways), abolitionists described slavery as a type of authority forbidden by God: the slaveholder interfered between God and another moral agent, the slave, and thereby placed himself in the sinful position of contending against divine sovereignty. Abolitionism contained an implicit vision of utopia in which man would be rescued from the domination of other men and would respond directly to the governance of God. This vision might never have become problematical if abolition had swiftly succeeded, but such was not the case. Faced with violence from Northern mobs, the indifference of Northern churches, and repeated compromises by the federal government, some abolitionists asserted that other forms of authority shared the essential sinfulness of slavery. Besides attacking slavery, violence, institutional religion, and human government, they occasionally tried to establish new, noncoercive styles in human relationships. This quest led them to new departures in religion, community life, marriage, spiritualism, and even political parties. But the quest was so varied and inconsistent that it would be difficult to define an anarchistic wing of abolitionism. We are on safer ground, I think, in taking note of the importance of the problem of authority in antislavery ideology and then in recognizing a wide range of attempted solutions to that problem in the lives of abolitionists.

The book is not an apology for the abolitionists. Despite my insistence that anarchism was neither extraneous to antislavery nor the outcome of personal dementia, it is true that the intellectual commitments that led to anarchistic thinking proved to be a source of confusion in the 1850s. The trouble was not that a few abolitionists tried to foist a consistent anarchistic ideology on their brethren in reform. It was that anarchism was too often blended with political desire, and utopian thinking was too often harnessed to the machinery of secular reform societies. A recurrent theme of this essay is the failure of abolitionists to examine forthrightly the relationships between anarchism and the millennium, on the one hand, and political change and secular reform, on the other. In any case, by the mid-1860s there were few alternatives to accepting the identification of the cause of the slave with the causes of the Republican Party and the union army.

I have entitled the book *Radical Abolitionism*, a term which once referred to the beliefs of a small group of reformers led by William Goodell. The beliefs of Goodell and his friends are analyzed (and further study of the strategy and tactics of political abolitionism would surely be welcome), but I have used the term in a larger sense than they might have accepted. It is not my purpose to argue that one faction of abolitionists, for better or worse, was more "radical" than others. I am interested in the varied types of radicalism which developed out of abolitionist ideas once it became evident that the institution of slavery would not be swiftly or easily abolished. Both Goodell and Garrison, along with numerous others, offered related versions of antislavery radicalism, even though the disagreements among them were often extremely unfriendly. In view of my title, it may also be relevant to observe that several historians have recently suggested that all abolitionists, to the extent that they believed in racial equality, were "radical," even if unwittingly so, because slavery and prejudice were fundamental to the American power structure. This book emphasizes attitudes toward authority rather than toward race, but the radicals whom I discuss would usually have agreed that the abolition of slavery presupposed a revolution in power relationships in America. Racial equality was not the end of their radicalism, but it was central to their beliefs.

One question has been raised by various persons who have looked at my manuscript or heard me talk about it. Do I dishonor the abolitionists by stressing the cultural backgrounds of their antislavery commitment and underscoring the importance of the problem of authority in their own lives? I do not believe so. Apparently the question arises from the feeling that slavery was wicked enough in itself to explain all opposition to it and that more complicated accounts of antislavery thought make the abolitionists seem insincere. The question may have its source in the attempts of historians in the 1960s to restore the good reputation of the abolitionists after decades of unsympathetic treatment. But surely our growing awareness of the horrors of slavery and racism in the American past does not require us to portray all white advocates of the cause of black men as the children of light. Such a requirement would serve our need to understand the past no better than the single-minded search for racism in abolitionist thought which new styles in liberalism may make fashionable. The book itself may show that I am generally sympathetic to a wide range of abolitionists: although I do not see their lives as simple responses to the evils of slavery, I think it is important that they often managed to devote their lives to giving reasoned accounts of that evil and to ending it. If they saw connections between slavery and other instances of unjust authority in the modern world, then they are at least partially cleared of the contemporary charge that they were insensitive to oppression and suffering in the North. I see nothing wrong in their belief that their own liberation was part and parcel of the liberation of the slave. Even if I did, when a belief of that sort had significant implications in antislavery thought I would still be obliged to pay attention. For example, I think that abolitionists failed, by and large, to envision much of a role for the slave in the ending of slavery and that this failure tended to confound their reactions to the tests of violence in the 1850s and 1860s.

It may be helpful to suggest how the logic of the essay is carried out in the nine chapters below. The first two chapters serve as prologue and introduction; they place abolitionist radicalism in the contexts of American history and historical writing and explore the intellectual backgrounds of some of the key ideas of abolitionism. Chapter III discusses the origins and ideology of the New England Non-Resistance Society, the most famous expression of anarchistic thinking in the antislavery movement. I argue that nonresistance was based on a number of inconsistent or inadequate formulations which were twisted and refined in the subsequent history of abolitionism. Chapter IV examines a species of religious radicalism known as "come-outerism" which accentuated some of the most extreme ideas of abolitionists. The fifth chapter, on the other hand, surveys the attempt of Adin

Ballou, a nonresistant of conservative temperament, to build a community which would stay in good order and yet remain free of sinful coercion. Chapter VI analyzes some radical elements in the Liberty Party and political abolitionism. My contention here is that while many nonresistants became increasingly political in the 1840s, political abolitionists were often trying to devise versions of politics that were uncorrupted by expedient appeals to temporal power. The seventh and eighth chapters are concerned with variation and confusion among abolitionist radicals: the former considers various attitudes, found especially in the 1850s, toward law, community, spiritualism, and marriage; the latter traces the accommodation of most nonresistants to violence before the Civil War. Although I believe that much of radical abolitionism had been silenced—or silenced itself—before the 1860s, I suggest in Chapter IX a few ways in which it survived, but with considerable change of form.

I am glad to have this opportunity to express my gratitude for several grants and fellowships. A grant from the Social Science Research Center at Cornell University enabled me to travel and pursue some of the initial research for this book. Two fellowships —the George C. Boldt Fellowship from the Department of History at Cornell and a New York State Regents Fellowship for Doctoral Study—were also very helpful. Later I was aided in my research and writing by a grant from the Committee on Research and Creative Activity at the State University of New York at Buffalo and by a summer fellowship from the Research Foundation of the State University of New York.

Historians frequently thank librarians in their prefaces, but until I had done my own research I had never appreciated how crucial the help of librarians can be in the completion of a book. I am particularly grateful to Mrs. Constance Clark of the Bancroft Memorial Library in Hopedale, Massachusetts. I would also like to thank the staffs of these libraries: the New-York Historical Society; the Cornell University Libraries, especially the Rare Book Room; Lockwood Memorial Library of the State Univer-

sity of New York at Buffalo, especially the Interlibrary Loan
Service; the Brown University Library; the Boston Public Library, especially the Rare Book Department; and the Harvard
College Library, especially Houghton Library. Certain quotations
from Henry Clarke Wright and Bronson Alcott were found in the
collections in the Houghton Library, as the footnotes indicate,
and are used by permission of the Harvard College Library.

I also appreciate the permission given by Little, Brown and
Company to quote from *The Journals of Bronson Alcott*, edited
by Odell Shepard (Boston, 1938). In addition, the editors of two
scholarly magazines have permitted me to incorporate into this
book portions of my articles which they had previously published.
My thanks go to the editors of *Church History* for allowing me
to use parts of "Adin Ballou's Hopedale Community and the
Theology of Antislavery" (September 1970) in Chapter V, and
to the editors of the *American Quarterly* for allowing parts of
"Versions of Anarchism in the Antislavery Movement" (Winter
1968, Copyright, 1968, Trustees of the University of Pennsylvania) to be used in several chapters of this book.

If I were to meet Thoreau's requirement of an autobiographical narrative, I would give much space to the many friends, colleagues, and counselors who have aided my continuing education
and growth. A full list would be impossibly long, and a few
words cannot do justice to my feelings of gratitude even to those
whom I am able to mention. My greatest intellectual debt is to
David Brion Davis of Yale University, who read the manuscript
three times in early drafts and who each time encouraged me to
believe that the project was worthwhile. I have been cheered by
his friendship and inspired by his example, and my book has
greatly benefited from his criticism. My debt is also great to
Maurice F. Neufeld of Cornell University, who has helped me
both as teacher and friend. While working with him I came to
love history, and his close commentary on several early drafts
helped me to rewrite this book. At a point when I was uncertain
where to go next in my revisions, the manuscript was read by
David A. Hollinger, my colleague at the State University of New

RADICAL ABOLITIONISM

Anarchy and the Government
of God in Antislavery Thought

I

Tolstoy's Discovery

After Leo Tolstoy renounced his literary career in order to adopt Christian pacifist beliefs and a peasant's style of life, he had opportunities to talk with two of America's leading reformers: William Jennings Bryan and Jane Addams. He found Bryan "remarkably intelligent and perceptive," but Bryan was astounded by the extreme rejection of violence and government to which Tolstoy was led by the teachings of Jesus. The American asked what should be done in the case of "a brigand who kills or violates a child." The novelist replied that in seventy-five years he had encountered "that fantastic brigand" only in argument, while he had seen "millions of brigands" enabled to harm the children of working people through the institutionalized right to do violence to their fellows. Bryan broke out in genial laughter, conceding, as Tolstoy thought, "that my argument was satisfactory."[1]

The two men liked each other. Tolstoy later made it known that, as long as the United States had a government, he thought its president should be someone with the anticapitalist and antimilitarist sympathies of Bryan.[2] But cordial as this friendship may have been, Tolstoy's social theories were of dubious appeal

---

[1] Leo Tolstoy, "Introduction to a Short Biography of William Lloyd Garrison," trans. Aylmer Maude, *Tolstoy Centenary Edition,* XX (London, 1935), 579.

[2] Aylmer Maude, *The Life of Tolstoy: Later Years* (New York, 1910), p. 638. Cf. Paul W. Glad, *The Trumpet Soundeth: William Jennings Bryan and His Democracy* (Lincoln, Neb., 1966), pp. 30–31.

to the political advocates of the American farmer. Although Tolstoy devoutly believed that the best life was on the land, he also condemned striving for material wealth, migrating away from the family, and expecting improvement to come from government. He is often considered the outstanding philosopher of modern Christian anarchism.[3]

Even though Tolstoy's agrarianism and his Christianity had little in common with Bryan's, there was one branch of American reform to which he might perhaps have spoken effectively. Preaching that urban squalor could not be abolished unless the well-born identified themselves with the displaced poor, Tolstoy might have made a favorable impression on the sentiments of settlement workers. To be sure, some of the profits from his last novel, *Resurrection*, were sent to Hull House, Chicago's famous haven for oppressed immigrants. And Jane Addams recalled that *What Then Must We Do?* was read with excitement by urban reformers. Yet she also remembered irritation at Tolstoy's contempt for "benevolence" as a solution to social problems, impatience with his emphasis on personal righteousness at a time when Americans were struggling to extract a social message from Christianity, and discomfort at his insistence that art and culture resulted from class exploitation. In addition, American reformers attributed Tolstoy's disdain for economics to the ignorant backwardness of his country.

Jane Addams' interview with Tolstoy was less genial than Bryan's; he criticized the superfluous material wasted on her sleeves and bluntly called her an absentee landlord. She concluded that this kind of uncompromising moral radicalism, even though the Russian was a man of peace, could be the source of more hostility than the pragmatic and flexible outlook of her fellow Americans.[4] On the basis of Tolstoy's encounters with Bryan

---

[3] George Woodcock, *Anarchism: A History of Libertarian Ideas and Movements* (Cleveland, 1962), pp. 222–235, discusses Tolstoy as a pillar of the anarchist tradition. Tolstoy declined to call himself an anarchist and applied the term only to those who projected violent change.

[4] Jane Addams, "Introduction," *What Then Must We Do?*, Tolstoy

and Addams, it would be easy to conclude that his type of pacifistic anarchism was as alien to America as the incendiary doctrines that immigration laws were then being devised to prohibit. It was too spiritual for the interest groups and too individualistic for benevolent groups.

Tolstoy himself was surprised to discover American antecedents of his ideas. After his efforts to live according to the Bible led him to repudiate government, he learned that American abolitionists had anticipated his religious views a half-century earlier. Following the publication of *My Religion* in 1884, one of the sons of William Lloyd Garrison wrote to him about the striking similarity between the views in that book and those once espoused by the great abolitionist.[5] Thinking that the validity of his Christianity would be confirmed if other sincere men had reached the same understanding independently, Tolstoy sought further information about the New England Non-Resistance Society, the organization through which Garrison had reiterated Jesus' injunction not to return evil for evil.

Information was scarce. Tolstoy wrote:

How little is known in regard to the question of non-resistance may be gathered from the fact that the younger Garrison . . . in answer to my inquiry whether any society for the defense of the principles of non-resistance was yet alive and possessed adherents, wrote me that, so far as he knew, the society had dissolved and its members were no longer interested, while at this very time Adin Ballou, who had shared Garrison's labors, and who had devoted fifty years of his life to the teaching of the doctrine of non-resistance, both by pen and by tongue, was still living in Hopedale, Massachusetts.

<hr>

Centenary Edition, XIV (London, 1934), vii–xiii; Jane Addams, *Twenty Years at Hull-House* (New York, 1961), pp. 191–199; Maude, *Tolstoy: Later Years*, pp. 524–526.

[5] Lyof N. Tolstoi, *The Kingdom of God Is within You* (New York, 1899), p. 4. Garrison's sons do not mention the correspondence, but their lengthy footnotes indicate the similarity of their father's perfectionism to Tolstoy's; see Wendell Phillips Garrison and Francis Jackson Garrison, *William Lloyd Garrison, 1805–1879: The Story of His Life Told by His Children*, 4 vols. (New York, 1885, 1889), III, 12–13. Hereafter cited as Garrisons, *Garrison*.

Judging from the historical obscurity into which nonresistance had fallen in America as elsewhere, the Russian wondered whether the world was determined to ignore the message of the New Testament.[6]

Tolstoy was pleased with a chance to correspond with the forgotten American, Adin Ballou. He translated several of Ballou's works into Russian, and in 1889 and 1890 the two men exchanged letters on points where their opinions differed. But Ballou was extremely bitter and argumentative, and the correspondence became rather unfriendly. Ballou died shortly afterward.[7] Tolstoy was never able to satisfy his own curiosity concerning the rise and fall of nonresistant anarchism in America. Nevertheless, the discovery of Garrison and Ballou plainly held great significance for him, and he referred to the antebellum Americans frequently. They were associated in his mind with the excitement of his own conversion, "the spring of my awakening to true life." In addition, they testified to the existence of a radical tradition of Christian believers whose convictions differed from those of the institutional churches and states. Nonresistance was a universal expression of Christianity with a history going back at least as far as the Reformation and, ultimately, to the life and teachings of Christ. This tradition had received some of its most enthusiastic statements in America before the Civil War. Tolstoy urged Americans to rediscover the writings of Garrison, Ballou, and Henry David Thoreau.[8]

Although Tolstoy could not learn much about the disappear-

---

[6] Tolstoi, *Kingdom of God*, pp. 11, 19.

[7] Count Leo Tolstoy and Rev. Adin Ballou, "The Christian Doctrine of Non-Resistance . . . Unpublished Correspondence Compiled by Rev. Lewis G. Wilson," *Arena*, III (Dec. 1890), 1–12.

[8] *Tolstoy's Writings on Civil Disobedience and Non-Violence* (New York, 1967), pp. 377, 129, 5, 241, 304. After World War II, when Martin Luther King began his pilgrimage to nonviolence, though not of course to anarchism, he read widely and was inspired by Gandhi and possibly by Tolstoy, but he seems to have been unaware of the native precedents of the abolitionists. Cf. King, *Stride toward Freedom: The Montgomery Story* (New York, 1964), chap. 6; William Robert Miller, *Martin Luther King, Jr.* (New York, 1969), pp. 26–35, and *passim*.

ance of nonresistant anarchism in America, he surmised that radical pacifistic doctrines must have been discarded in the belief that they encumbered the cause of the slave. Because the country evaded those doctrines, it marched into a fratricidal war which ended the particular form of coercion known as slavery but left a hideous pattern of interracial violence and injustice. This pattern could be effaced, in Tolstoy's view, only by returning to the principles which Garrison and Ballou had tried to teach. One thing Tolstoy understood perfectly from his own anarchistic perspective: Garrison's followers had been inclined toward anarchism not in addition to hating slavery but because they hated slavery. He made the connection succinctly:

Garrison, a man enlightened by the Christian teaching, having begun with the practical aim of striving against slavery, soon understood that the cause of slavery was not the casual temporary seizure by the Southerners of a few millions of negroes, but the ancient and universal recognition, contrary to Christian teaching, of the right of coercion by some men in regard to others. . . . Garrison understood . . . that the only irrefutable argument against slavery is a denial of any man's right over the liberty of another under any conditions whatsoever.[9]

One of Tolstoy's most anarchistic works was entitled *The Slavery of Our Times*.[10] An enlarged definition of slavery came to him as naturally as the open-ended definition of brigandage he had used in conversation with William Jennings Bryan. He was not interested in the reform of a few narrowly defined institutions; he was a perfectionist to whom social justice meant nothing less than the eradication of sin from human society. All men, he preached, must renounce violence and coercion and in that way give their support to the kingdom of God. From this viewpoint he made the exciting discovery of the kinship of his beliefs with those of American abolitionists; it seemed obvious that an anti-slavery movement should have been pacifistic and anarchistic.

[9] "Biography of Garrison," pp. 577–578; Tolstoi, *Kingdom of God*, pp. 10–11.

[10] New York, n.d., *c.* 1900. See Appendix below on "European Anarchism and the Idea of Slavery" for discussion of this work.

ii

Tolstoy's unsuccessful search for information occurred when American interest in abolitionism was still fairly strong. The union had been saved, the slaves emancipated. Abolitionism was regarded as evidence of the moral superiority of the victorious North. But union troops and governmental actions had ended slavery, and the Republican Party held a pre-emptive claim on the legacy of moral superiority. Therefore, old hostilities of Northerners against abolitionists were largely forgotten. There was also slight reason to recall that prominent abolitionists had once said that the union should be dissolved, had insisted that slavery must be ended by moral suasion rather than by force, had argued bitterly against the virtue of political parties, and had even assailed human government as unchristian. What little recollection there was of nonresistance and other radical aspects of the antislavery movement—and Tolstoy learned there was very little—was pleasantly subsumed under the heading of "The Eccentricities of Reformers." While harboring some folly and lunacy, the movement had existed mainly to give voice to the "Northern Conscience."

In the twentieth century, historical writing on the abolitionists has become more professional, detached, and critical. Historians, sometimes with clearly Southern sympathies, have presented unfavorable critiques in which the abolitionists appear as neither conscientious heroes nor harmless eccentrics—they were incendiaries and fanatics. The reformers have sometimes, of course, received gentler treatment. But until recently a proabolitionist viewpoint has tended to require that the legitimacy of Garrison and other radicals within the movement be denied or ignored. A favorable historian may write, for example, of "the war which abolitionists had long hailed as the necessary *modus vivendi* for direct action against slavery." The same historian chooses to describe the formation of the Liberty Party in 1840 as practically the origin of the Republican Party.[11] This interpretation strongly

[11] Dwight Lowell Dumond, *Antislavery Origins of the Civil War in the*

resembles that of the late nineteenth century: the virtues of abolition were the virtues of war and Republicanism. It excludes
those reformers who opposed war and politics from the good faith
of the movement. Vain and impractical, they tried to impose their
extraneous commitments upon the antislavery crusade. There is
in this view no room for Tolstoy's insight that some abolitionists
felt inclined toward anarchism precisely because of their devotion to the cause of the slave.

Recent scholarship has yielded sympathetic appraisals of antislavery radicalism. In modern America it no longer seems obvious
that one must be demented or conceited to oppose war and denounce the American political system; perhaps this is why we
can reread Garrison and his followers with greater sympathy.
Because previous criticisms of their impracticality and fanaticism
were so immoderate, the most important attempts to revise our
estimate of them have stressed their tactical astuteness. "The perfectionist, no-human-government doctrine was, of course, a vision
of the millennial future," Bertram Wyatt-Brown has pointed out;
but what should be appreciated is "its pragmatic effect" of keeping a diverse group of people united and uncompromising in
pursuit of their common antislavery goal.[12] Aileen S. Kraditor
has similarly cleared Garrison's reputation of the charges of fool-
ishness and narrow-mindedness by illuminating the distinction
"between Garrison's opinions as a nonresistant and the tactics he
thought the abolitionist movement (as a coalition of adherents of
many philosophies) ought to pursue."[13] These are welcome cor-
rectives to our knowledge of antislavery; no future study of the
Garrisonians need adopt a defensive tone.

This book will not emphasize Garrison's pragmatism or his

United States (Ann Arbor, 1959), p. 113; Dwight L. Dumond, *Antislavery: The Crusade for Freedom in America* (Ann Arbor, 1961), p. 297.

[12] Wyatt-Brown, *Lewis Tappan and the Evangelical War against Slavery* (Cleveland, 1969), pp. 270–271.

[13] Kraditor, *Means and Ends in American Abolitionism: Garrison and His Critics on Strategy and Tactics, 1834–1850* (New York, 1968), pp. 105–106, 158, and *passim.*

tactical soundness, but instead will explore his millennial vision
and his nonresistance. Nor will its focus be mostly on Garrison.
In pursuing the radical strain within antislavery, it will follow
the careers of a diversity of reformers, some of whom were indifferent or even antagonistic to the gospel as preached at Boston.
Opposition to slavery depended on visions of the universe that
could flower into numerous versions of anti-institutionalism or
anarchism. In spite of this variation, however, it can be argued
that it is difficult to understand antislavery properly without taking account of its anarchistic offshoots.

iii

Since this book concentrates on the two decades before the Civil
War, it may be helpful to outline a certain amount of background
information. Slavery, regarded with complacency throughout
much of the history of Western civilization, became acutely troublesome after the mid-eighteenth century, a period, according to
David B. Davis, which "brought an almost explosive consciousness of man's freedom to shape the world in accordance with his
own will and reason."[14] Once the Revolution had deepened
America's commitment to the enlightened ideal of liberty, human
bondage presented an obvious and painful incongruity. The institution gradually vanished from the Northern states where ideological considerations were not outweighed by the presence of
great numbers of Negroes.[15] At no time after the Revolution
could antislavery ideas be totally dormant, and yet the nation's
prejudice had deeper roots than its libertarian philosophy. The
end of slavery in the South, where Negroes were present in large
and growing numbers, was postponed indefinitely. Antislavery
eventually came to mean that blacks should be freed only as they
could be colonized in areas remote from contact with whites.

[14] Davis, *The Problem of Slavery in Western Culture* (Ithaca, 1966),
p. 485.
[15] The best study of this process is Arthur Zilversmit, *The First Emancipation: The Abolition of Slavery in the North* (Chicago, 1967).

And effectively this meant that slavery would not be ended at all.[16]

The American Colonization Society, the organization most successfully blending dislike of slavery with fear of free Negroes, claimed the support of respectable and patriotic citizens (it continued to attract some conservative reformers long after the Civil War).[17] Men of less compromised sympathy for the slave, like the tireless Benjamin Lundy, struggled against disheartening resistance and occasionally faced hard questions concerning their loyalty to basic social institutions. In 1823, Lundy hailed the secession of antislavery Baptists in Illinois from their denomination and the founding of a new sect named the Friends of Humanity. "Come out from among them, come out from among them," was his response.[18] The cry to "come out" from corrupt institutions would be raised many times in succeeding decades.

In the 1830s the American Colonization Society began to meet powerful criticism. That decade saw the emergence of a "new breed" of abolitionists—*immediate* abolitionists, as they were called—who argued that the obligation to create a moral society required that the sinfulness of bondage be acknowledged and the institution of slavery be eradicated without delay. The outstanding leaders of this new movement, though united in their evangelical militance, followed diverse walks of life. Theodore Dwight Weld, as restless as he was charismatic, had been an itinerant lecturer before experiencing conversion in front of the great revivalist of upstate New York, Charles Grandison Finney;

[16] See Winthrop D. Jordan, *White over Black: American Attitudes toward the Negro, 1550–1812* (Baltimore, 1969), pp. 542–569.

[17] See Edwin S. Redkey, *Black Exodus: Black Nationalist and Back-to-Africa Movements, 1890–1910* (New Haven and London, 1969), pp. 73–149. A recent work stressing the sensitivity of the colonizationists to the problems freedmen would face in a hostile, white world, rather than their racism, is George M. Frederickson, *The Black Image in the White Mind: The Debate on Afro-American Character and Destiny, 1817–1914* (New York, 1971), pp. 6–27.

[18] Merton L. Dillon, *Benjamin Lundy and the Struggle for Negro Freedom* (Urbana, Ill., and London, 1966), p. 75.

thereafter, Weld traveled in Finney's band of disciples and served as an agent of societies for social reform. As an abolitionist he perfected the style of the itinerant agitator. More settled and solemn were the Tappan brothers, Lewis and Arthur, whose organizational talents had helped to bring them prosperity as New York merchants. Arthur donated huge sums of money to antislavery and secured the support of other benefactors; Lewis lent his administrative skills to the national enterprise in New York. The best-known abolitionist was William Lloyd Garrison, a printer from an impoverished Baptist family who had tried several editorial jobs before discovering the iniquity of the Colonization Society. In 1831 he published the first issue of *The Liberator*, the newspaper through which he would denounce enemies or false friends of the slave and broadcast the gospel of immediate abolition, however his reading of that gospel changed, every week until 1865. Garrison's editorial vehemence gained him the special affection of Northern black abolitionists, whose opposition to the colonizationists had been drowned out in previous decades. But only three Negroes sat with the sixty whites at the meetings in December 1833 which launched the American Anti-Slavery Society.[19]

The new society brought together those who were willing to set themselves against the prestige of colonizationism and brave the violence of American anti-Negro feelings. As "gentlemen of property and standing" saw in the new radicalism an intolerable threat to social order and middle-class people imagined the horrors of racial "amalgamation," mob violence erupted in nearly every region of the North.[20] In addition to the animosity it aroused, the movement was seldom harmonious within itself. Arthur Tappan and his merchant friends distrusted Garrison from

[19] Benjamin Quarles, *Black Abolitionists* (New York, 1969), pp. 18–25, and *passim*.

[20] For an informative study of the social composition of abolitionism and antiabolitionism, see Leonard L. Richards, *"Gentlemen of Property and Standing": Anti-Abolition Mobs in Jacksonian America* (New York, 1970).

the outset; in fact, they had been reluctant to join a national society. Among New Yorkers there was division between those who cared to run the society economically and those who were impatient for ever greater propaganda campaigns.[21] Would important interests be offended if antislavery expressed itself too radically?

The subsequent history of the American Anti-Slavery Society was defined by controversy. If women spoke from abolitionist platforms with a status equal to that of men, would not potential friends of abolition be driven away? What would be the impact on public opinion if religious mavericks seemed to represent the movement? There was irreconcilable conflict between conservatives, to whom slavery was a singular evil to be eliminated from the basically sound American society, and others who saw slavery as merely the most horrible symptom of America's deep-seated sinfulness.[22] Abolitionists were also divided by the stubborn resistance of influential institutions to their message. What program would be effective against the insensitivity of political parties, the lack of concern on the part of benevolent and charitable societies, the unwillingness of great denominations to chastize Southern members, and the failure of most Northern ministers to join the movement? The original plan called for the conversion of the slaveholder: he would see the sinfulness of his ways and emancipate his slaves *immediately*. No one expected mass conversions of this sort to occur overnight, but the tiny minority meeting in 1833 demanded nothing more and nothing less. Swifter results were anticipated in the North. Ministers would see the light and would instruct their congregations on the iniquity of slavery. Prominent laymen, religious organizations, and political parties would begin to rebuke slaveholders for their sin. When these hopes proved unfounded, abolitionists could either defect from the cause or proceed to new forms of dissent. Divergent styles of religious radicalism started to come between

[21] Wyatt-Brown, *Lewis Tappan*, pp. 107, 112.
[22] Kraditor, *Means and Ends*, pp. 8–9, makes some extremely useful distinctions among the various factions.

them. Political innovation was similarly divisive; while some abolitionists moved toward third-party politics, others extended their indictment of slavery to encompass a general denunciation of all government as they knew it. And there were abolitionists who labored to experiment with new communities, separating true Christians from the corrupt world.

Disagreement within the American Anti-Slavery Society was accompanied by intolerance. Schism finally became irreversible at the 1840 convention when the Tappans led a walkout of delegates offended by the inclusion of women on the executive committee. A short-lived rival organization, the American and Foreign Anti-Slavery Society, was quickly formed. Garrison and his followers had already created the New England Non-Resistance Society to express their developing radicalism. James Gillespie Birney emerged as the leader of another faction which, having failed to rid the original antislavery society of the taint of non-resistance, had organized the Liberty Party earlier in 1840. In the following decades abolitionists often turned onto their own divergent organizations the hatred which they had once been united in aiming at the colonizationists. According to some historians, the antislavery effort may not have actually been weakened, for various means of expression were now available and everyone could find his own appropriate activity.[23] But one thing is certain: the antislavery movement was sundered.

Schisms and new departures in the national movement meant that local societies and individual writers and lecturers became more important than ever. Few, if any, discarded the original belief that slavery was a sin and ought to be abolished immediately. In a way, it was only after the divisions of 1840 that the full meaning of that belief was open for exploration. The sundering of the movement may not have been beneficial to the advance of antislavery sentiment among the unconverted. Once the question of unity was obsolete, however, the task of intellectual dis-

[23] See, for example, Quarles, *Black Abolitionists*, p. 54; Wyatt-Brown, *Lewis Tappan*, pp. 199–200.

covery and redefinition of first principles was made easier. The 1840s would be a fertile period in abolitionist thought.

iv

In nineteenth-century memoirs, where the details of abolitionism faded into the glorious legacy of the triumphant North, it was necessary to allude to the quirks of the reformers. Some abolitionists wore the bloomer costume, bathed in icy water (afterward rubbing their bodies till they glowed), ate faddish diets, had the bumps on their skulls analyzed by phrenologists, or, more tragically, entrusted the health of their families to what seem to have been quack doctors. Charles C. Burleigh and James Russell Lowell grew beards in a period when it was unconventional to do so. We are told that Burleigh also "dressed like a tramp"; at one antislavery gathering his brethren hired a tailor to steal his filthy white duck pants and leave him "fresh pepper-and-salt habiliments."[24] Abolitionists delighted in conventions on novel subjects and could debate almost interminably to promote their special projects.

The idiosyncrasies of reformers do not justify refusal to take their main contentions seriously. A distinction must surely be made between peculiarities of dress or habits and intellectual or religious commitments. It can be shown, furthermore, that comparable enthusiasms seized contemporaries who were not reformers. (Stonewall Jackson, for example, governed his body according to strict principles of water cure that would have awed the most zealous reformer; and in social situations his concern to keep his alimentary canal straight required him never to cross his legs or incline his back.[25]) It is always too easy with hindsight to sort out truth from error, science from pseudo-science, and to criticize the benighted convictions of actors in an earlier era.

[24] Thomas Wentworth Higginson, *Contemporaries* (Boston and New York, 1899), p. 331; Henry B. Stanton, *Random Recollections* (3d ed., New York, 1887), p. 71.

[25] Frank E. Vandiver, *Mighty Stonewall* (New York, 1957), pp. 48–53, 85.

When all these points are admitted, however, antebellum reformers may still seem to us to have been exceptionally given to eccentricity. A brief discussion of the problem of eccentricity may provide clues to the character of antislavery radicalism.

Both Henry B. Stanton and Thomas Wentworth Higginson addressed the subject forthrightly in their autobiographies. It was possible, after the war, to approach the subject with greater tolerance than before. Stanton left this vivid description of a Boston convention:

There was a representative array on the front seat, near the platform. First was Garrison, his countenance calling to mind the pictures of the prophet Isaiah in a rapt mood; next was the fine Roman head of Wendell Phillips; at his right was Father Lampson, so called, a crazy loon—his hair and flowing beard as white as the driven snow. He was the inventor of a valuable scythe-snath, and invariably carried a snath in his hand. His forte was selling his wares on secular days and disturbing religious meetings on Sunday. Next to Lampson sat Edmund Quincy, high born and wealthy, the son of the famous President Quincy [of Harvard]. Next to Quincy was Abigail Folsom, another lunatic, with a shock of unkempt hair reaching down to her waist. At her right was George W. Mellen, clad in the military costume of the Revolution, and fancying himself to be General Washington, because he was named after him. Poor Mellen died in an asylum.

Clearly, we are not considering frivolity or irresponsibility; this kind of eccentricity had a serious and sometimes tormented personal dimension. "The terrible strain put upon the human intellect in those old Anti-Slavery days," wrote Stanton, "turned some light-headed persons' brains."[26] Stanton was not inclined to pass judgment on any faction of the movement. Their lives had not been ordinary. The goals to which they had been committed were exalted, their expectations stupendous. The opposition they met was potentially baffling. It was not difficult to see how the noble and eccentric could have sat side by side.

[26] Stanton, *Random Recollections*, pp. 69–70.

Higginson, in his essay, "The Eccentricities of Reformers," argued: "This tendency of every reform to surround itself with a fringe of the unreasonable and half-cracked is really to its credit, and furnishes one of its best disciplines." All reformers disrupt the settled rules of peace and order in their societies; all risk being called insane. Humility and self-control were to be gained from tolerant association with those who have gone farther and lost their balance.[27] There was a feeling of kinship, of a common language being spoken. Perhaps they were all fools for Christ. They all hoped for a millennium in which the settled rules would be altered. This did not mean, however, that efforts should not be made to keep the unkempt and compulsive from ruining the work of the movement. It did mean that, just as Father Lampson was able to devise a useful scythe-handle, Abby Folsom and George W. F. Mellen could sometimes contribute sensibly to the noisy dialogue within abolitionism.

Higginson also reports on a prevalent phrase, " 'the Sisterhood of Reforms,' indicating a variety of social and psychological theories of which one was expected to accept all, if any."

This I learned . . . through the surprise expressed by some of my more radical friends at my unacquaintance with a certain family of factory operatives known as the "Briggs girls." "Not know the Briggs girls? I should think you would certainly know them. Work in the Globe Mills; interested in all the reforms; bathe in cold water every morning; one of 'em is a Grahamite."[28]

Though aware of the element of gullibility in the catholic interests of reformers, Higginson too went on to embrace much of the "sisterhood." Once a person had decided to live according to one unpopular reform, he was obviously susceptible to conversion to the next. Many reforms did suggest the adoption of a new style of individual life as well as promising the general re-

[27] Higginson, *Contemporaries*, p. 329.
[28] Higginson, *Cheerful Yesterdays* (Boston and New York, 1898), pp. 119–120.

tailoring of society. Part of the romantic quest of American reform, in fact, was to discover new styles of Christian life suitable
to the coming of a regenerated world. In these chapters the meaning of abolitionism will frequently be interpreted in the light of
that quest. As John L. Thomas has indicated, antislavery could
easily be viewed as "the core of a complex of general reform."[29]

The most often quoted essay on antebellum eccentricities is
Ralph Waldo Emerson's "New England Reformers." Starting with
the insight that reform often meant the secession of truly religious people from the confines of institutional Christianity, Emerson elaborated the irony in the tendency of reformers to redirect
their discontent, once reserved for the churches, onto one another. Jealous of their own independent judgment and mistrustful
of all authority, they hatched an abundance of projects for removing error and coercion from the world; "the fertile forms of
antinomianism among the elder puritans seemed to have their
match in the plenty of the new harvest of reform." Emerson's
tone is sometimes disdainful. He himself did not wish to enlist
in the reforms, but he conceded that the movements reflected the
best spirit of the age. They upheld "the sufficiency of the private
man," and their most persuasive modes of action were "original"
and flowed from "the whole spirit and faith" of individuals.[30]

Antislavery convictions often inspired a quest for spontaneity
and originality. The burden was on the abolitionist to rescue himself from enslavement. If this common quest was even dimly recognized, the reformer could sympathize with his fellows who lost
their minds and could appreciate the discipline that came from
tolerating eccentricity. Sober-minded abolitionists, of course, merit
more attention than the deviants they tolerated. On the other
hand, we should understand that for all but the conservative
abolitionists, especially after the schisms of 1840, it was not sim-

[29] Thomas, "Antislavery and Utopia," in Martin Duberman, ed., *The
Antislavery Vanguard: New Essays on the Abolitionists* (Princeton, 1965),
p. 248.
[30] Brooks Atkinson, ed., *The Selected Writings of Ralph Waldo Emerson*
(New York, 1950), pp. 449–468.

ply the black man in the South who had to be freed. The movement offered liberation to the abolitionists who joined it. For
abolitionsts, as for Tolstoy, an extended definition of slavery was
desirable. In seeking to save themselves from the slavery of this
world they were apt to journey very close to anarchism.

II

Slavery and Anarchy

At the end of May 1839 a steamboat carried a group of abolitionists back to New England after an especially strife-ridden
convention of the American Anti-Slavery Society. Getting away
from the formal meetings and the continual maneuvering for control of the society made it possible for the abolitionists to argue
more temperately. "Those who had denounced each other's
principles, in no measured terms, could meet each other face to
face and treat each other as brethren."[1] A debate was set up between Henry C. Wright, the most anarchistic of antislavery radicals, and Orange Scott, a political abolitionist whose attitude toward nonresistance may accurately be described as loathing.

The adversaries had much in common. Both were middle-
aged: Wright had been born in 1797, Scott in 1800. Their parents
had been poor. Both had risen to become ministers in good
standing in the evangelical churches of Massachusetts, Wright
as a Congregational pastor in West Newbury and Scott as presiding elder over Methodist ministers around Springfield. Each
had been inspired by William Lloyd Garrison to convert to the
doctrine of immediate abolition; the conversion of each had put
him on a collision course with his own denomination. Both had
joined the famous seventy agents of the American Anti-Slavery
Society whom Theodore Weld trained in 1836.[2]

[1] The account is Henry Wright's in the *Non-Resistant,* June 1, 1839, p. 2.
[2] On Scott, see Donald G. Mathews, "Orange Scott: The Methodist
Evangelist as Revolutionary," in Duberman, ed., *Antislavery Vanguard,* pp.

Although they now represented opposing factions in the anti-slavery controversy, signs of their common background could be heard in their debate. Wright advocated the doctrine of nonresistance: "Human government is just as necessary as sin—no more." Men should submit to divine government rather than continue on the ruinous course of presuming to govern one another. "All attempts of men to govern men," Wright asserted, "by prisons, whips, chains, swords and guns, have ended and must end in anarchy and blood." If he was an anarchist, it was because he despised slavery and anarchy and saw them connected. Scott, in his rebuttal, depicted what he thought must be the consequences of nonresistance: "Disorder, licenti[o]usness, misrule, concubinage, slavery, anarchy, carnage and general slaughter."[3] His interpretation of the government of God led him to politics. But through his list of imagined horrors, no less than Wright's, walked the specters of slavery and anarchy.

The purpose of this chapter is to furnish a preliminary explanation of the eruption of anarchistic tendencies in the abolitionist movement. The stubborn refusal of American institutions to heed the message of immediate abolition helps to explain why some abolitionists should have grown more radical, but it does not explain why that radicalism should have been anarchistic. The debate between Wright and Scott illustrates the two principal themes of this chapter: first, that a conceptual relationship between slavery and anarchy may have worked to point a movement against slavery in anarchistic directions; and second, that this abstract possibility came alive in the course of evangelicalism's struggles with the problems of divine sovereignty and the moral accountability of man in America.

We should first notice that no abolitionist, and no American for that matter, called himself an anarchist in the 1840s or 1850s. Even critics who accused abolitionists of fomenting chaos and

---

71–101. The only useful study of Wright appears in Louis Billington's unpublished M.A. thesis, "Some Connections between British and American Reform Movements 1830–1860," University of Bristol, 1966.

[3] *Non-Resistant*, June 1, 1839, p. 2.

bloodshed coined terms such as "political individualism" to describe them.[4] The term "anarchism" must be clarified and used carefully, even though scornful historians have regularly applied it to the views of Garrison.[5]

The problem of defining anarchism is tackled skillfully in a recent analysis of the philosophy of Pierre-Joseph Proudhon, the French anarchist who was a contemporary of the abolitionists. Alan Ritter suggests that the first ingredient of anarchism is the belief that the violence and coerciveness of government mean that it is evil. He reminds us that this belief is not unusual: "Luther, for instance, described political rule as 'the fastening of wild and savage beasts with chains and bands . . . so that they must needs keep peace outwardly against their will' and found fault with it for doing so." But Luther maintained that government was a necessary evil since the world would "always" be unchristian. A second ingredient of "unequivocal anarchism," therefore, is the belief that no government is necessary. Ritter observes, furthermore, that Rousseau also shared the belief that government is evil but did not call for its abolition because of his great respect for law. In Ritter's summary of his thought, "Government is indeed an enchainment, but if men are chained by laws, their bondage is salutary." The counterexample of Rousseau, who thought government could be limited, yields a third ingredient of anarchism: "antipathy toward law."[6]

There is no need to secure the title of "unequivocal anarchism"

[4] George Frederick Holmes, "Theory of Political Individualism," *De Bow's Review*, XXII (1857), 133–159.

[5] Dumond, *Antislavery*, p. 297; John L. Thomas, *The Liberator: William Lloyd Garrison* (Boston, 1963), pp. 5, 232–234, 412; Eugene D. Genovese, *The World the Slaveholders Made: Two Essays in Interpretation* (New York, 1969), p. 224. Recent studies by Bertram Wyatt-Brown and Aileen Kraditor (see above, Ch. I, nn. 12, 13) tend to minimize the descriptive value of the term for Garrison.

[6] Ritter, *The Political Thought of Pierre-Joseph Proudhon* (Princeton, 1969), pp. 101–104. The quotation from Luther may be found in John Dillenberger, ed., *Martin Luther: Selections from His Writings* (Garden City, N.Y., 1961), pp. 370–371.

for the Garrisonians, and yet Ritter's analysis helps to clarify the issue. Henry Wright certainly believed that government was evil. Was it necessary? Wright argued that it was no more necessary than sin—and, unlike Luther, he did not believe that the world would *never* be Christian. The troublesome question is whether his view can be described as "antipathy to law." Wright was a champion of God's law which, he thought, should not be confused with the coercive laws of human governments, however limited. God's law operated through voluntary obedience to Him. In Wright's thought, then, all three ingredients of anarchism may be detected.

Henry Wright thought of himself as a servant of the Almighty, not as an anarchist. Because all societies seek to maintain order and suppress disorder, the term "anarchist" had been used opprobriously for centuries. Proudhon in 1840 was probably the first reformer to consent to call himself an anarchist.[7] He did not influence American abolitionists in this or any other way, but a look at his reasons for calling himself an anarchist will further clarify the relevance of the term to abolitionism. Proudhon was deliberately paradoxical—anarchy, he insisted, was the secret of order. "*Anarchy*" did not mean that society should be without principles and rules; it meant only the absence of sovereigns and laws backed by coercion.[8] He anticipated the emergence of laws of a higher validity than those by which governments control mankind. These evolving higher laws would resemble contracts except that they would not be influenced or enforced by the power of outside authorities. Such laws would develop naturally and progressively, provided that the arbitrary and exploitative interference of government ceased.

Subsequent writers have assigned Proudhon to syndicalism, a variety of socialisms, and even fascism; but it will suffice here to understand his own identification of himself as an anarchist. Whatever his contracts might have amounted to in practice, he

[7] Woodcock, *Anarchism*, pp. 11–12.
[8] Stewart Edwards, ed., *Selected Writings of Pierre-Joseph Proudhon*, trans. Elizabeth Fraser (Garden City, N.Y., 1969), pp. 88–89.

believed that government and, more generally, "the principle of authority" could be eliminated from social institutions.[9] From this kind of anarchy, or voluntary society, would follow order, expressed in the form of freely initiated social arrangements. Society would not only be orderly; it would also conform to higher laws discovered through natural social processes. (They did not, however, originate in a state of nature.) This sketch of Proudhon's theories suggests another three-part definition of anarchism. In the first place, it seeks the abolition of human government. Second, and on the positive side, it urges the creation of new and uncoercive social arrangements. Third, it looks for justification in a law which is superior to presently established law because it is natural, or naturally evolved, as in the views of Proudhon, or divine.[10]

How does Henry Wright's nonresistance meet this definition of anarchism? Plainly, he did present a version of anarchism. He gave to government the moral status of sin, and the immediatist argument held, of course, that no delay was tolerable in abolishing a sin. His views are as paradoxical as Proudhon's: human attempts to govern result in disorder, while the so-called anarchy of no-human-government is the path to harmony. As for the second point, Wright believed that men, freed of the bonds of government, would discover the initiative to work progressively toward the millennium. At the time of his debate with Scott, nonresistance stressed the negative side of this belief by attacking government and denying the charge of fomenting disorder, but it surely envisioned the approach of a better world. The search for spontaneous modes of activity highlighted the lives of many radical abolitionists. Finally, Wright denounced human government because he knew the force of a higher law: the government of God. Human authority was sinfully presumptuous. It resulted in anarchy and was itself a form of slavery.

[9] *Ibid.,* p. 90.

[10] On defining anarchism, see Leonard I. Krimerman and Lewis Perry, eds., *Patterns of Anarchy: A Collection of Writings on the Anarchist Tradition* (Garden City, N.Y., 1966), pp. 554–557.

ii

Slavery ánd anarchy are antithetical concepts, but this fact means that they may be closely linked: each summons up the other as a view of organized society. From one viewpoint slavery is the only security against anarchy. From another anarchy is the surest antidote to slavery. It is doubtful that there exist many examples of political thought which argue for either slavery or anarchy as an end in itself. On the other hand, slavery and anarchy are highly descriptive terms, while terms such as liberty and stability—the goods which men usually seek—are more abstract and difficult to pin down. For this reason the antithesis between slavery and anarchy often has provided important underpinnings to political thought. The consequence is especially curious if we compare pro-anarchy and proslavery thought, as found in the writings of nineteenth-century European anarchists and antebellum Southerners. Anarchism clarified its versions of liberty and order by distinguishing them from slavery. Proslavery thought attempted to clarify the same terms by distinguishing them from anarchy.

Anarchy is, of course, a highly ambiguous concept. The thought of society without government or authority has ordinarily been frightening; anarchy has come to stand for disorder, violence, war, pandemonium. For most of Christianity, at least, government has seemed necessary to keep mankind under control. Nonetheless, other Christian traditions, intent upon paradise and the millennium, have cherished the thought of society without government or authority. In other words, it is possible to conceive of anarchy as the state in which mankind regains control of itself. In the absence of government there will be no disorder, violence, war, pandemonium. Though few besides Proudhon have been fully aware of the paradox, most anarchists have contended that anarchy, in the good sense of harmonious self-government, is the only escape from anarchy, in the bad sense of lawlessness.

Anarchism has almost everywhere been doomed to misunderstanding. Such is the common fate of paradoxes. It has been vilified as a philosophy of disorder; how could it reveal its concern for order? How could it explain that it was a movement, in one sense, against anarchy? To solve this problem it fixed on the idea of slavery. Slavery was the paradigm of authority between man and man and thus was clearly opposed to anarchy in the good sense of self-government. In addition, slavery was associated with thoughts of violence and licentiousness. Slavery could be considered synonymous with anarchy in its worst sense. In order to clarify itself, therefore, European anarchism explained that it was an antislavery movement.

The book in which Proudhon first called himself an anarchist began with this paragraph:

> If I were asked to answer the following question: *What is slavery?* and I should answer in one word, *It is murder,* my meaning would be understood at once. No extended argument would be required to show that the power to take from a man his thought, his will, his personality, is a power of life and death; and that to enslave a man is to kill him. Why, then, to this other question: *What is property?* may I not likewise answer, *It is robbery,* without the certainty of being misunderstood; the second proposition being no other than a transformation of the first?[11]

Proudhon's equation—property is theft—was widely quoted by friends and enemies of social revolution in the nineteenth century. No one made much of the fact that it was offered as a corollary of antislavery doctrine. Slavery, after all, had long since vanished in most of Europe. But the meaning was plain: enslavement was only the most complete invasion, or theft, of the life of another. And the idiom was familiar; Marx would soon adopt it to tell workers they had nothing to lose but their shackles. History could easily be interpreted to be a progressive, but as yet incomplete, escape from bondage.

After Proudhon, anarchists characteristically justified their vi-

[11] Proudhon, *What Is Property? An Inquiry into the Principle of Right and of Government,* trans. Benjamin R. Tucker (New York, n.d. [1890]), p. 11.

sion of liberty by attacking the slavery which pervaded society. In their writings, moreover, slavery functioned as something more than a reference point in history or a metaphor in exhortations to escape. "Probably no one in the history of political theory," according to Professor Ritter, "has conceived of liberty more broadly than Proudhon, since none has required that men, to count as free, be unhindered by as many restraints." Certainly the conception of liberty in the thought of other anarchists has been at least as broad. What are the restraints which undergo their attack? Many are external; such are the impositions of the wills of other men through violence, government, law, economic privilege, or social pressure. But there are also internal restraints to escape from, such as the force of passion or the compulsion of conscience.[12] Anarchism, in other words, has called for doing what is right because it is right and not because it is required by physical force or moral law. It has been a movement to create a society where "each man could call himself his own master."[13] The phrase, in this instance, is Proudhon's.

Calling for so unbounded an emancipation, anarchism was nearly driven to refer to slavery as something not only in the past but also in the European present. Government, of course, enslaved man; economic injustice merely prolonged ancient systems of class ownership of other classes; legal and penitentiary systems were slave codes; wars revealed man's ultimate lack of possession of his own life; education trained him to accept his bondage; and institutional Christianity, by teaching him that he is irrevocably a sinner, aggravated his slave mentality. Anarchists disagreed sharply over the means of liberation. Some thought the slaves had no recourse except sabotage and revolt. To others—Tolstoy is a good example—violence could not effect liberation but could only alter the forms of slavery. Instead, there must be a revolution in convictions. Men must admit that slavery—and "not in some figurative, metaphorical sense," Tolstoy warned in *The Slavery of*

[12] Ritter, *Political Thought*, pp. 19–21.
[13] Edwards, ed., *Selected Writings*, p. 91.

Our Times—exists all around them. The literature of European anarchism, in all of its various factions and theories, abounds with attacks on "slavery." (Further evidence of the anarchists' dependence on the concept of slavery is presented below in an appendix.)

Proslavery thought in the American South was virtually a mirror image of European anarchist thought, identical in some ways and yet curiously reversed. The ideology of slavery asks us to admit that anarchy, not slavery, is omnipresent and that only slavery can rescue mankind from chaos. If anarchism was doomed to misunderstanding because of its paradoxes, proslavery thought could scarcely escape the contempt of developing liberal and capitalist ideologies. In the effort to clarify and justify itself, the South, like European anarchism, became acquainted with the explanatory value of the antithesis between slavery and anarchy.

Proslavery repeatedly presented itself as anti-anarchy. In this equation the meaning of "anarchy" shifted as the South became more willing to identify slavery as a positive good. There were at least three different definitions of "anarchy": it was seen as a state of mob rule, as the chaotic opposite of rule by force, and as a principle of social and economic organization roughly synonymous with *laissez-faire*. In each case, it was offered by way of contrast to slavery.

The first meaning of "anarchy" is rather imprecise; it often means little more than corruption and mob rule. Thus one Southerner explained: "Anarchy is not so much the absence of government, as the government of the worst—not aristocracy, but kakistocracy."[14] In this instance, the ordinary definition of anarchy is altered, and the proslavery argument consists mainly of an attack on the ruder results of the Jacksonian transformation of American politics; indeed, this is more an antidemocratic than a proslavery argument.

[14] Chancellor Harper, "Slavery in the Light of Social Ethics," in E. N. Elliott, ed., *Cotton Is King and Pro-Slavery Arguments* (Augusta, Ga., 1860), pp. 605, 610.

Similar confusion may be found in the writings of John C. Calhoun, who also lacked a uniquely proslavery argument. Calhoun is famous for the assertion that "there never has yet existed a wealthy and civilized society in which one portion of the community did not, in point of fact, live on the labor of the other."[15] While this might take some of the sting out of criticisms of slavery, there is little effort to show the superiority of slavery to other exploitative arrangements. To be sure, Calhoun pointed out that anarchy is "the greatest of all curses," and he advertised his theory of government as clamping a lid on anarchy while preserving as much liberty as the moral development of a people would allow.[16] But his chief concern seems to have been not anarchy, but the failures of democracy. He presented a highly emotional attack on corrupt politicians, patronage-seekers, spoilsmen, and bosses. Much of his proposed remedy, the well-known theory of concurrent majorities, is so far from uniquely justifying slavery that it is patterned after the English parliamentary system.[17] In short, this kind of proslavery thought, though regularly referring to anarchy, is more concerned with such issues as rabble rule and aristocratic prerogatives; and it falls short of contending that slavery is positively good.

Yet Calhoun does suggest one of the basic lines of argument in proslavery ideology, namely, that all political systems depend on coercion, if not exploitation, and consequently those who attack slavery do so, whether they admit it or not, in the name of anarchy. In a second definition, then, "anarchy" was the opposite of force. J. H. Hammond, in a series of public letters to the English abolitionist Thomas Clarkson, seized on Clarkson's complaint that "our slaves are kept in bondage by the 'law of force.'"

[15] See his Senate speech of Feb. 6, 1837, as reprinted in Eric L. McKitrick, ed., *Slavery Defended: The Views of the Old South* (Englewood Cliffs, N.J., 1963), p. 13.

[16] John C. Calhoun, *A Disquisition on Government; and Selections from the Discourse* (Indianapolis, 1953), p. 42 and *passim*.

[17] William W. Freehling, "Spoilsmen and Interests in the Thought and Career of John C. Calhoun," *Journal of American History*, LII (1965), 26–27.

Hammond asked: "In what country or condition of mankind do you see human affairs regulated merely by the law of love?" Whatever the social system, all rights and powers were always ultimately secured by the availability of force. "Thus, in every turn of your argument against our system of slavery, you advance, whether conscious of it or not, radical and revolutionary doctrines calculated to change the whole face of the world, to overthrow all government, disorganize society, and reduce man to a state of nature—red with blood, and shrouded once more in barbaric ignorance." To attack force in principle, in other words, was really to evoke a state of anarchy where force is arrayed against force and chaos prevails.[18]

In a similar vein George Frederick Holmes reacted against what he saw as a world-wide tendency toward anarchism; he discussed Proudhon in France, Herbert Spencer in England, and Stephen Pearl Andrews in America as precursors of a common movement. Anarchism was spawned by the human tendency to ignore the facts that society is complex and man is imperfect. Holmes saw no shortage of moral axioms which could be twisted into anarchism if relied on exclusively, as was happening to the Golden Rule, natural law, and free market principles. It was necessary to attack perfectionism:

If man were perfect, and not liable to be seduced from the path of right when recognized, or to be betrayed into error by the passions and delusions which beset him on all sides, it might be sufficient to regulate his actions by the compendious maxim of preserving a just compromise between the claims of reciprocal and conflicting rights. But, if such were the condition of human society, government would be nugatory and needless, as these preachers of political individualism perceive and assert, and this particular rule would be as unnecessary as any other rule for the maintenance of harmony in the relations of men.[19]

[18] J. H. Hammond, "Slavery in the Light of Political Science," in Elliott, ed., *Cotton Is King*, pp. 677–678.
[19] Holmes, "Political Individualism," p. 139.

Slavery, with its recognition of human imperfection and inequality, thus stood poised as the alternative to any perfectionist, anarchistic aversion to force. It must be observed, however, that this argument failed to give any specific defense of the South's peculiar institution except that it was one of many manifestations of force in the world.

When slavery was suggested as an ideal social system, there was the strongest affinity between proslavery and anarchistic thought. George Fitzhugh, the greatest proslavery ideologist, expressed respect for Proudhon, though conceding his system was difficult to understand, and for Stephen Pearl Andrews.[20] The proslavery argument, in fact, drew heavy support from the contention of anarchists and other radicals that forms of oppression and injustice amounting to slavery were prevalent in the modern world. The basic theme of the proslavery argument came to be that wage earners in the North and Europe suffered the worst misfortunes of slaves while being blessed with none of the corresponding benefits.[21] At its simplest, this may have been merely a *tu quoque* argument intended to assuage uneasy consciences in the South, but it could also anchor a full-scale ideology for the Southern way of life.[22]

George Fitzhugh synthesized two main themes found in Northern and European protests against emerging capitalism and industrialism. First was the cry that Northern wage slavery exceeded Southern chattel slavery in degradation and cruelty. This

[20] Harvey Wish, ed., *Ante-Bellum: Writings of George Fitzhugh and Hinton Rowan Helper on Slavery* (New York, 1960), pp. 55, 79, 126.

[21] See Wilfred Carsel, "The Slaveholders' Indictment of Northern Wage Slavery," *Journal of Southern History*, VI (1940), 504–520.

[22] That the proslavery argument was addressed to the South to allay strains of antislavery feeling is argued in Ralph E. Morrow, "The Proslavery Argument Revisited," *Mississippi Valley Historical Review*, XLVIII (1961), 79–94. But for an exposition of ways in which the proslavery argument was not merely a gloss over guilt, but a comprehensive ideology for Southern interests, see Genovese, *World Slaveholders Made*, and *The Political Economy of Slavery: Studies in the Economy and Society of the Slave South* (New York, 1965). For important criticisms of Genovese's interpretation, see Frederickson, *Black Image*, esp. ch. II.

argument—to the dismay of abolitionists—was common among labor reformers. Second was the argument, sometimes accompanied by a nostalgic appreciation of feudal servitude, that modern political economy created a world of anarchic irresponsibility. Fitzhugh was most impressed with the writings of Carlyle. Not only was political economy anarchic in permitting those with money to do as they pleased without interference in behalf of the public welfare, but it also fostered, among reformers who were not free of its premises, antiauthoritarianism and even free love. Two great principles, one anarchistic and the other connected with slavery, were vying for the world's allegiance. In Fitzhugh's view the socialist assault on the prevailing system of economy, if it followed its natural logic, might even encompass a movement to re-establish servitude throughout modern society.[23]

Sometimes Southerners were willing, partly ironically, to describe plantations as phalansteries and to advocate slavery over other models of socialism on the grounds that it wiped out labor competition without permitting state despotism. Slavery, it was claimed, combined three advantages: it fostered paternalistic care and loving interdependence; it placed human conduct under adequate governmental controls; and it relied on a highly decentralized version of authority.[24] The alternative was an unjust and anarchic society which would invite an inevitable, tyrannical reaction. Since these were the alternatives, to Fitzhugh it seemed appropriate that antislavery in the North was leading to forms of anarchism. "Abolition ultimates in 'Consent Government'; Consent Government in Anarchy, Free Love, Agrarianism, &c., &c., and 'Self-elected despotism,' winds up the play."[25]

In summary, the South relied on the concept of anarchy in order to argue that slavery was a positive good. Without referring to anarchy, the most the South could claim was that slavery

---

[23] Fitzhugh, "The Counter-Current, or Slavery Principle," *De Bow's Review*, XXL (1856), 90–95.

[24] William Sumner Jenkins, *Pro-Slavery Thought in the Old South* (Chapel Hill, 1935), p. 303; and Wish, ed., *Ante-Bellum*, pp. 41–156.

[25] *Ibid.*, p. 152.

was no worse than the exploitative and hierarchical arrangements of the North. But once the enemy was conceptualized as anarchy in general, proslavery theorists moved directly to the conclusion that slavery was the best possible social system. Slavery was the balanced use of force for control. Northern reformers were already anxious about the breakdown of social control. If they attacked slavery in the name of love, *laissez-faire* individualism, or any other principle, they would hasten the onslaught of anarchy. The abolitionists' assault on the basis of social control, it was claimed, drove them inevitably to anarchism.

This romantic style of thought frequently regarded history as a competition between great principles, in this case between anarchy and slavery. This was generally true of European anarchism, proslavery apologetics, and much of Northern antislavery as well. The anarchists, as we have seen, insisted on extended definitions of slavery in presenting their case. Proslavery theorists made up elaborate definitions not very different from those favored by the most radical Garrisonians. It would be no surprise, for example, to find Henry C. Wright insisting that slavery should be understood as all *"submission or subjection to control by the will of another being."* But this definition was actually written by a Southerner, William Andrew Smith, a Methodist minister and president of Randolph-Macon College. Smith argued that all men are really slaves; even such institutions as the family and democratic government contain elements of slavery.[26] Slavery could thus be identified in principle with good order in society. Like some European anarchists, some abolitionists used the same definition to approach vastly different conclusions, perhaps even that conventional marriage and democratic government would have to be modified or abandoned as history progressed.

It should be noted that proslavery thought, although commonly stressing the law of force rather than the law of love, nevertheless took religion very seriously. Nor is there any reason to

[26] On Smith, see Donald Harvey Meyer, "The American Moralists: Academic Moral Philosophy in the United States, 1835–1880," unpublished Ph.D. dissertation, University of California, Berkeley, 1967, pp. 364–366.

doubt the sincerity of Christianity in Southern thought. "The belief in God and moral accountability," wrote Fitzhugh, ". . . is
necessitous and involuntary. It is part of our consciousness."[27] If
Southern theorists had enjoyed full control over their religious
beliefs, they might well have subjected American Protestantism
to far-reaching changes, for in the notion of "moral accountability" was stored much of the ammunition of the abolitionists.
In proslavery thought, however, the government of God was expressed through human force and men were accountable simply
to serve well in the earthly stations to which they were assigned.
The system of slaves and masters, thus interpreted, realized the
divine government and forestalled anarchy.

To some extent, then, there are links between the concepts of
slavery and anarchy which help to explain the emergence of anarchism in Northern movements to abolish slavery. There was no
necessity, however, for abolitionists to venture into atheism, as
Southerners predicted they would[28] and as many European anarchists subsequently did. Northern Protestantism contained sufficient fuel to supply the fires of anarchism in antislavery.

iii

Although antislavery did produce versions of anarchism, as
Southerners had warned, this result was obviously not due solely
to the connections between the concepts of slavery and anarchy.
The institution of slavery was a major component of social order
in the United States, and to attack slavery was inescapably to
call for extensive social change. Furthermore, we should be familiar enough today with the dynamic in which reformers are
told that the change they demand will jeopardize social order
and they, consequently, move farther in an anti-institutional direction. What is significant is that antislavery radicals seldom
proceeded to demand sweeping economic reforms. Bondage was,
after all, a property relationship, and those who attacked the in-

---

[27] Quoted in Genovese, *World Slaveholders Made*, p. 154.
[28] See Elliott, "Introduction," *Cotton Is King*, esp. pp. x–xi.

stitution were sometimes accused of echoing Proudhon's slogan, property is theft.[29] But abolitionists preferred to regard slavery as a type of government and a violation of divine government. As their radicalism increased, they tended to denounce human government, not property, and to champion the government of God.

To understand this political-theological radicalism we must ask what abolitionists meant by the government of God. Usually it is impossible to locate specific sources or "influences" for their beliefs because they spoke in familiar religious terms and because the problem of the means by which God ruled was discussed almost everywhere in American Protestantism. Indeed the intensity of the abolitionists' search for the law of God places them unmistakably within certain basic traditions of American thought.

Many of the abolitionists who figure in this book were born between 1795 and 1805.[30] This generation, reaching maturity in the 1820s, grew up amid bitter controversies over the role of the church in the new republic. The church was segmented into denominations and was shorn of state support. Did not God command unity in His governance of the world, had the church no role to play in social control? Unitarians challenged New Englanders to place greater faith in the reasonableness of man; revivalists, especially in New York, insisted on the legitimacy of

[29] See Jenkins, *Pro-Slavery Thought*, pp. 300–301.

[30] Relevant birthdates include: William Goodell 1782; Birney 1792; Sarah Grimké 1792; Nathaniel Rogers 1794; Beriah Green 1795; Samuel May 1797; Wright 1797; Gerrit Smith 1797; Bronson Alcott 1799; Scott 1800; Weld 1803; Ballou 1803; Garrison 1805; Angelina Grimké 1805; Maria W. Chapman 1806; Lysander Spooner 1808; Edmund Quincy 1808; Parker Pillsbury 1809; Stephen S. Foster 1809; Abigail Kelly 1810; Wendell Phillips 1811; Stephen Pearl Andrews 1812. Of those born after 1805, Quincy and Chapman were nonresistants; Pillsbury, Foster, Kelly, and Phillips were Garrisonians but tended to be more political than the nonresistants; and Spooner and Andrews were eccentric Liberty Party men who later turned to anarchism. For some observations on the importance of the ages of reformers, see Lois W. Banner, "Religion and Reform in the Early Republic: The Role of Youth," *American Quarterly*, XXIII (1971), 677–695.

new measures to arouse religious emotions. What was the nature
of man, what role was assigned to him in the improvement, possibly even the redemption, of the world? The issues of the sovereignty of God and the moral responsibility of man engaged not
only theologians; they assumed local importance wherever denominations competed for members, state support was lost, new
congregations seceded from old ones, or touring revivalists out-
shone hometown ministers. Few reformers could have escaped
the impact of religious controversy. The sovereign power of God,
on which a great deal of religious debate was centered, should
have provided some certainty in the midst of change. But the
idea of God's sovereignty had already proved itself susceptible
to a variety of interpretations in American history. At least three
of these interpretations—the sovereignty of God, the millennial
kingdom of God, and the moral government of God—had a bearing on nonresistance and abolition.

The religion of the seventeenth-century colonies was deeply
influenced by the insistence of the Reformation on a present sovereign God. This influence did not weaken the day-to-day prac-
ticality of colonial leaders; they made whatever human decisions
seemed necessary to secure peace and stable government. When
they failed, it was a sign of the earthly disorder which a sovereign God despised. In spite of all the rebellion that flourished on
earth it was the mission of Christians to obey God's eternally
established laws. As H. Richard Niebuhr has pointed out, the
God of the Puritans was "not the First Cause of a later Deism,
but neither was he the meddling deity of eighteenth century su-
pernaturalism." He was a present sovereign; He appeared in nature; He loomed in the ordinary events of history. Miracles were
unnecessary: God's law was apparent "in the actual pattern of
reality to which revelation had given the key and which reason,
following upon revelation, could discern."[31] Certainly man must
go about the business of placing a new world in order, but the

[31] H. Richard Niebuhr, *The Kingdom of God in America* (New York,
1959), p. 55.

meaning of his actions was constantly to be found in the judgment of God.

The sovereignty of God, although it underwrote efforts to secure order, could also threaten social authority. Niebuhr has explained:

The converse of dependence on God is independence of everything less than God. On this principle also the early American Protestants were agreed, despite the differences which were to be found among them. Since the relation of man to God is immediate, or mediated only by Jesus Christ, the pretensions of princes and bishops, of state or churchly institutions, to represent divine sovereignty needed to be rejected.[32]

The ways in which Puritans contained this possibility of doctrinal subversion should not detain us here.[33] The "means" and ordinances of earthly institutions—and acceptance of theories which connected them to God—secured social control. Yet for all of God's hatred of disorder, a chief threat to those institutions lurked in the idea of His sovereignty. The threat could arise, in other words, from the attitudes which Perry Miller called "the pure Puritanism of New England. In this tradition, all intermediaries between God and man are resolutely taken away; there is no relaxing of the quest, no indulgence and no confessional."[34]

This is the grim tradition which has won for seventeenth-century Calvinism the most unsympathetic modern judgments, the tradition insisting on the utter puniness of man in the sight of the Almighty. So unworthy is man that no institution nor any pretense to moral uprightness can rescue him from wrath. It was possible to derive from this tradition a radical outlook which, emphasizing

[32] *Ibid.*, p. 69.

[33] They have been examined in many splendid studies, especially by Perry Miller. See his "The Marrow of Puritan Divinity," in *Errand into the Wilderness* (New York, 1964), pp. 48–98; *Orthodoxy in Massachusetts, 1630–1650* (Gloucester, Mass., 1965); *The New England Mind: The Seventeenth Century* (Boston, 1961).

[34] *Jonathan Edwards* (Cleveland and New York, 1959), p. 302. Cf. *ibid.*, p. 31; and *Errand into the Wilderness*, p. 185.

the sovereignty of God and worthlessness of intermediary institutions, raised the specter of anarchy. We may see in this outlook vague foreshadowings of "immediatism." The name the Puritans gave this outlook was "antinomianism," a term whose significance was somewhat similar to the anarchistic views of abolitionists two hundred years later.

The connotations of antinomianism included anti-institutionalism, sedition, and anarchy. The root meaning of the term is opposition to the law, especially the moral law of the Old Testament. Christians, it could be argued, after the coming of Christ, were obliged to depend directly on the mercy of God and not on obsolescent agencies of control. None of this was an illogical deduction from the Protestant substitution of faith for works in God's supervision of the cosmos. Yet persons who insisted on immediate obedience to God, rather than working through the "means" which He was said to sanction, seemed to raise the threat of anarchy. Therefore, as Anne Hutchinson learned in the 1630s, they must be banished.[35]

In point of fact Mrs. Hutchinson did not attack moral law. She merely wanted more emphasis in sermons on the unencumbered sovereignty of God and less attention to the forms of the church and systems of "preparation" for grace. She spoke from a fundamental Protestant impulse to which Jonathan Edwards, a century later, gave succinct expression: "Absolute sovereignty is what I love to ascribe to God."[36] One dilemma of Protestantism was to reconcile this impulse with the necessity for social control. Mrs. Hutchinson did not attack political institutions; she was not a social reformer. Since Puritans, for the most part, did not think of the sovereignty of God as analogous to earthly government—it was an external judgment over sinful human behavior—the anti-

[35] David D. Hall, ed., *The Antinomian Controversy, 1636–1638: A Documentary History* (Middletown, Conn., 1968), esp. p. 3; and Emery Battis, *Saints and Sectaries: Anne Hutchinson and the Antinomian Controversy in Massachusetts Bay Colony* (Chapel Hill, 1962), esp. pp. 40–42.
[36] Clarence H. Faust and Thomas H. Johnson, eds., *Jonathan Edwards: Representative Selections* (New York, 1962), p. 59.

nomianism they feared was a threat more to church than to state. But there was elasticity in the threat. Should the idea of the reign of God approach closer to earth, there was no reason why the "pure Puritan" elimination of intermediaries might not reach human government. There were European precedents. The Garrisonians, in a sense, realized that possibility in America.

A second interpretation of divine sovereignty was the millennial kingdom on earth. Scripture could be read so as to extend the promise that God, at the end of history, will rule directly on earth for a thousand years. To some extent this promise quickened the Puritan hope that the perfection of their institutions might, by force of example, aid in the redemption of the world. Millennialism thereafter has recurred so continuously that we are now quite familiar with the idea of America as a "redeemer nation," although much of the specific religious content of the idea has eroded.[37] Use of the term requires many distinctions, most of which concern the means and timing of the millennium. Will it come through the work of many men, or under the leadership of a single messianic figure, or only after God's own intervention in history? Will it come gradually or like lightning? Will its approach be detectable? Should it inspire believers to resign from earthly turmoil or to redouble their efforts to solve the problems of society? It could be argued plausibly that the period before the millennium must be characterized by a great rise in piety and moral conduct and that perhaps in such a period America might be assigned a special destiny in the progress of civilization.

Belief in the millennium could incite radical re-examination of existing institutions. Millennialists sometimes alternated quickly from exalted visions of imminent perfection to black moods of depression over approaching calamity. Because of the excitement and despair that it inspired, it could unsettle the social order, and therefore champions of reason and calm have often tried to

[37] Cf. Ernest Lee Tuveson, *Redeemer Nation: The Idea of America's Millennial Role* (Chicago, 1968); and David E. Smith, "Millennial Scholarship in America," *American Quarterly*, XVII (1965), 535–549.

suppress it. The millennium, they have said, is God's business; for the historical church to identify itself with the millennium would be presumptuous. The redoubtable Charles Chauncy, during the conflict and excitement of the Great Awakening of the 1740s, opposed the specific timetables of millenarianism. The evidence behind them was flimsy, he wrote, and no good end was served by working on popular expectations. Further, many of the worst scenes of arrogance and delusion in history followed from misguided predictions of the millennium. To say the very least, it was a subject on which "good Men may differ." Chauncy noted that Jonathan Edwards had written that the millennium might soon commence in America and was saying privately "that he doubted not, the *Millennium* began when there was such an Awakening at NORTH-HAMPTON 8 years past." On the other hand, not long before, Increase Mather had written that he was sure that the "blessed Day" was "not far off," but that when it arrived "AMERICA will be HELL" and New England the most sorrowful part of America! Both men were plainly taking their ministries too seriously.[38] But the fact that both Edwards and the Mathers conjectured about the millennium shows the irrepressibility of the idea in American thought. The millennialism of Edwards and the Mathers inspired two different approaches to social reform in America, for unless it expects history to end abruptly in a clap of destruction, millennialism brings the kingdom of God to earth and introduces visions of social perfection.

In the first place, why would America be Hell? The Mathers saw the world around them in a state of dangerous moral declension; whatever the moral condition of New England actually may have been, their horror was a source of energy and commitment.[39] The function of social reform, in this view, is control

[38] Chauncy, *Seasonable Thoughts on the State of Religion in New-England* (1743), as excerpted in Alan Heimert and Perry Miller, eds., *The Great Awakening: Documents Illustrating the Crisis and Its Consequences* (Indianapolis and New York, 1967), pp. 302–303.

[39] See Robert G. Pope, "New England versus the New England Mind: The Myth of Declension," *Journal of Social History*, III (1969), 95–108.

over man. The impulse was not new with the Mathers. Puritans had long been told that the true convert to God is a tireless warrior against sin. According to one minister: "What ever sins come within his reach, he labors the removal of them, out of the familyes where he dwells, out of the plantations where he lives, out of the companies and occasions, with whom he hath occasion to meet and meddle at any time."[40] And there was no shortage of opportunities to meet and meddle.

This impulse found new expressions by the turn of the century. As the kingdom of God descended closer to earth, sin became more closely equivalent to social disorder. The Mathers, in the new design, saw need for a new engine of morality, a combination of "REFORMING SOCIETIES, or *Societies for the Suppression of Disorders,*" organized outside the church and yet closely allied to its work. These societies would exert social, political, and economic pressure. What they could not do themselves they would get new laws and more trustworthy public officials to do. They would attack those who profited from vice, shame those who were lured into it, and aid those who were its victims. Existing schools would be supervised and new *"charity-schools"* founded. Poor people would be discovered and given relief. Cotton Mather unfolded this program in 1710 with the publication of *Bonifacius, An Essay Upon the Good,* reprinted numerous times well into the nineteenth century. Its program of suppression of vice, extension of moral education, and relief of poverty remained appropriate to problems of social control in the republic. Moreover, Mather's anticipation of the wide distribution of edifying tracts came to provide a moral use for improvements in printing and marketing in the nineteenth century. Mather was also shrewd enough to see that benevolent societies could join together Protestants of different "persuasions," thereby countering the fragmentation of the church in America. The entire plan, finally, promised to hasten the millennium. The pattern

[40] Thomas Hooker, as quoted in Edmund S. Morgan, *The Puritan Family: Religion & Domestic Relations in Seventeenth-Century New England* (New York, 1966), p. 6.

of similar societies in England was spreading through Europe; and "men of wisdom . . . have made their joyful remark upon them, *that they cause unspeakable good, and annunciate a more illustrious state of the church of God, which is to be expected in the conversion of the Jews and gentiles. America,* too, begins to be irradiated with them."[41]

This approach to social reform remained an influential interpretation of the meaning of the kingdom of God long after the Mathers' hope that the glorious hour was not far off had proved too optimistic. Moral societies to look after public decorum appeared in many New England towns in the 1790s.[42] The dispersed, mobile population and the weakness of restraining institutions continued to provoke fear of anarchy in nineteenth-century America. Yet social order had to be sought in voluntary ways: America, proudly, did not resemble authoritarian Europe. There was no silencing the sounds of freedom in the rhetoric of the Revolution and the strains of self-liberation celebrated in much of Protestantism. The problem, then, was to reconcile voluntarism and social control. One solution was found in the "evangelical united front," a network of national benevolent societies which distributed tracts and Bibles; promoted improvements in existing schools and created new ones, including colleges; sent missionaries abroad and to native American Indians; fought against intemperance and other vices; made tentative efforts to deal with the urban poor, the so-called "dangerous classes"; and sought to remove free Negroes to Liberia. The key support for these societies came from ministers and laymen of the evangelical denominations, especially Presbyterians and Congregationalists. Their goal was social order, and their rationale was the long understood duty of true converts to meddle and control. Managers of

[41] *Bonifacius, An Essay upon the Good,* ed. David Levin (Cambridge, Mass., 1966), esp. pp. 132–137. See also Perry Miller, *The New England Mind: From Colony to Province* (Boston, 1961), pp. 395–416.

[42] Richard D. Birdsall, "The Second Great Awakening and the New England Social Order," *Church History,* XXXIX (1970), 360.

the societies explained that, without the machinery of evangelical Protestantism, a republic could not work.[43]

The united front offered practical advantages to the churches. For one thing, it forestalled the constant danger of the innovation of new sects, especially adventist ones, out of the millennial excitement of the periodic revivals.[44] More generally, it harnessed millennial energies to the tasks of civic morality and progress. In the light of Henry Wright's later views, it is interesting to observe that in 1834 even he regarded the cooperation of benevolent societies as the means to convert the world. Though his mind was set on the redemption of mankind, most of the societies he praised were concerned with the moral improvement of Americans. The most important, he thought, was the American Sunday-School Union; following in order were the Education and Home Missionary Societies, the Board of Commissioners for Foreign Missions, and the Bible, Tract, and Seamen's Friend Societies.[45] One might be tempted to remark that this rings less of the conversion of the world than it does of Rush Welter's description of the early American ideal: "anarchy with a schoolmaster."[46]

Nevertheless, the ideology of benevolence assumed that the millennium was rapidly approaching and the reform societies were God's instruments for the task. The most elaborate expression of this position was William Cogswell's *The Harbinger of the Millennium*, which celebrated the same societies that excited

[43] Clifford S. Griffin, "Religious Benevolence as Social Control, 1815–1860," *Mississippi Valley Historical Review*, XLIV (1957), 423–444; Griffin, *Their Brothers' Keepers: Moral Stewardship in the United States, 1800–1865* (New Brunswick, N.J., 1960); Charles I. Foster, *An Errand of Mercy: The Evangelical United Front, 1790–1837* (Chapel Hill, 1960).

[44] Louis Billington, "The Millerite Adventists in Great Britain, 1840–1850," *Journal of American Studies*, I (1967), 192–193.

[45] Wright, Journal and Commonplace Book, 1832–1842 (Harvard College Library), V, 305, May 24, 1834. Hereafter cited as Wright Journal (HCL). Additional volumes in the Boston Public Library will be cited as Wright Journal (BPL).

[46] Rush Welter, *Popular Education and Democratic Thought in America* (New York and London, 1962), pp. 59, 61.

Wright. In this view of millennialism antislavery was subsidiary.
Cogswell warned that slavery could only be ended gradually.[47]
The guiding purpose was social control, not emancipation. Although antislavery men and women did come out of these societies, the hope that the benevolent machinery might assist the
forces of abolition was never realized.[48]

The model of reform in Edwards' millennialism is harder to
delineate. The alternative it posed to social control might be described as spontaneity. That is, rather than concentrating on the
moral control of disorderly impulses, it suggested that a spontaneous kind of self-control might spring from individual religious
experience. The emphasis is positive: the experience of conversion, as defined in the Great Awakening, promised to rid man of
selfishness and to release powers of loving sympathy. The immediate result might be disruptive to old institutions. Sometimes, Edwards admitted, "God is pleased to convince the consciences of
persons, so that they cannot avoid great outward manifestations,
even to interrupting and breaking off those public means they
were attending, [but] I do not think this is confusion, or an un-
happy interruption, any more than if a company should meet on
the field to pray for rain, and should be broken off from their
exercise by a plentiful shower."[49] The long-run effect would be
a world renewed in harmonious piety and love. There was no
need to imagine that America would be Hell. America would
draw near to the kingdom of God communally, optimistically,
without cataclysm.[50]

In this approach to reform there was originally no desire to set
up societies outside the churches. The kingdom of God was not

[47] William Cogswell, *The Harbinger of the Millennium* (Boston, 1833),
pp. iii–iv, 175–187, and *passim*. Cf. Perry Miller, *The Life of the Mind in
America: From the Revolution to the Civil War* (New York, 1965), pp.
79–81.

[48] Wyatt-Brown, *Lewis Tappan*, pp. 115, 313–315.

[49] Heimert and Miller, eds., *Great Awakening*, p. 209.

[50] See Alan Heimert, *Religion and the American Mind: From the Great
Awakening to the Revolution* (Cambridge, Mass., 1966), esp. ch. II, "The
Work of Redemption."

the work of religion against the secular world; it was the extension of the church throughout that world. A certain amount of disrespect for secular authority might be inevitable; and misguided, antinomian deviations from moral law might be a short-run liability. But though it was anti-institutional and antihierarchical, the tradition sought a new kind of order, based in religious experience, which secular machinery could not effect. God's kingdom was to spread as He gave "further light" on earth and secular controls became outmoded.[51]

This tradition did not, of course, dominate the reform societies, and it was subdued as the denominations, however cautiously, embraced revivalism. But millenarian piety and spontaneity found expression in the antislavery movement. Churches were again disrupted. Anti-institutional and antihierarchical impulses were let loose. The excitement of an immediate relationship to God became explosive. Immediate abolitionists were inclined to think of their societies, not as adjuncts to religion, but as a kind of "surrogate religion" of which the Garrisonians might be called "a schismatic sect."[52] The kingdom of God, with its wonderful new harmony, could supplant both church and state. Man, in a word, could be emancipated.

The sovereignty of God and the millennial reign of God were familiar notions with long histories. Of more recent origin was the idea of the moral government of God. In the 1780s and 1790s Calvinists had faced renewed criticism of the doctrines of original sin and human inability to influence salvation, doctrines which had previously been at the heart of the Calvinist conception of the majesty of God. Now it was asked whether the crucifixion of Christ had not rescued man from hopelessness, whether

[51] Most of these themes are evident in William G. McLoughlin's excellent *Isaac Backus and the American Pietistic Tradition* (Boston, 1967), pp. 74–77, 92–100, and *passim*.

[52] Cf. David Brion Davis, "The Emergence of Immediatism in British and American Antislavery Thought," *Mississippi Valley Historical Review*, XLIX (1962), 229; Anne C. Loveland, "Evangelicalism and 'Immediate Emancipation' in American Antislavery Thought," *Journal of Southern History*, XXXII (1966), 179–180; and Thomas, *The Liberator*, p. 5.

all men might not be saved in the love of Jesus. An important
Calvinist response was what has been called the governmental
theory of atonement. Christ had not paid a ransom or offered an
expiatory sacrifice to an arbitrary sovereign; the atonement, instead, upheld the honor of divine laws. An awesome God was
transformed into a benevolent moral governor, setting laws, requiring obedience, and providing the ability to obey through the
great love manifested in Jesus. In effect, reasoned appreciation
of the moral law was substituted for dread and mystery in Protestant attitudes toward God. All men should, therefore, strive for
both rectitude and holiness.[53]

The governmental theory became orthodoxy in the nineteenth
century. Though it might originally have had the gloomy consequence of imposing the moral law with new severity, God's government turned out to have a liberalizing influence. Emphasis
increasingly fell on human ability to obey the law and attain
holiness. In general American clergymen and theologians were
able to overcome or absorb the worst threats of the enlightenment and enthusiastic revivalism, but at the price of virtually
abandoning the old Calvinist understanding of the relationship
beween man and God.[54] More and more, religious thought was
devoted to questions of ethics. The conclusion seemed irresistible
in the new republic: if God was lawgiver, then He must have
implanted both knowledge of the law and the capacity to fulfill
it in the constitution of man.

From the concept of divine sovereignty was deduced that of
human responsibility. God became the moral superviser of "accountable" human actions, and His punishments were just responses to the transgressions of men. As a recent study states:
"Lacking the means of social leverage through which social con-

[53] Joseph Haroutunian, *Piety versus Moralism: The Passing of the New
England Theology* (New York, 1970), pp. 166–176; Frank Hugh Foster,
A Genetic History of the New England Theology (New York, 1963), pp.
191–213.
[54] See William G. McLoughlin, "Introduction," *The American Evangelicals, 1800–1900* (New York, 1968), pp. 2–14.

trol might have been possible, the conservative moralist turned to instruments of persuasion and the theory of individual accountability." The government of God, as depicted in the influential theological writings of Yale's Nathaniel William Taylor or in the practical and extraordinarily successful revivalism of Charles Grandison Finney, stressed the divine source of law and individual responsibility for sin.[55]

This development is often called a "breakdown" of Calvinism, but it did not necessarily relax the demands made on man; rather, man could be exhorted to aspire to perfect holiness since there was no impairment in his ability and no qualification to his accountability. In the aspiration for perfection, furthermore, the millennial kingdom and the moral government of God could fuse. Although the origins of these two terms, and also of the sovereignty of God, may be discussed separately, all three terms were current in the period of the development of abolitionist immediatism. The "breakdown" of Calvinism was not experienced gently and happily. One set of purposes may have been served for conservative moralists. The abolitionists, on the other hand, were spokesmen of a Jacksonian America to whom perfection was a serious obligation, the millennial kingdom was a burning hope, and the sovereignty of God might yet be vindicated in all its awesomeness.

The idea of the government of God was central to the immediatism of the 1830s. The implication of God's government which received most frequent emphasis was individual accountability: slavery was a sin from which individuals had to disconnect themselves immediately. If divine government meant for some men a dilution of Calvinism, it could spur others, including the abolitionists, to the task of restoring sovereignty to God. Earthly interlopers ought to be abolished and God's rule begun. The alternative was cataclysmic millennialism—that is, civil war. With their

[55] Meyer, "American Moralists," pp. 80–101, 241–263. See also Sidney Earl Mead, *Nathaniel William Taylor, 1786–1858: A Connecticut Liberal* (Chicago, 1942), and William G. McLoughlin's "Introduction" to Finney, *Lectures on Revivals of Religion* (Cambridge, Mass., 1960).

minds set on the government of God it was possible for abolitionists to seek an end to slavery, to call for governments of perfect moral purity or to say, with Henry Wright, that human government was no more necessary than sin.

iv

Some abolitionists retained their connections with the evangelical united front and tried to keep antislavery merely a reform
among other reforms. The Church at Lahaina in the Sandwich
Islands, therefore, was able to offer one hundred dollars to the
American and Foreign Anti-Slavery Society as a prize for the
best essay on the theme, "American Slavery: A Formidable Obstacle to the Conversion of the World." Of six essays submitted,
the winner was by William Goodell, long-time opponent of the
Garrisonians and champion of political action. His opinions may
be read as acceptable to orthodox, conservative abolitionism.

The purpose of Christianity, in Goodell's opinion, was the millennial mission to convert the world to Christ. Such was the object for which Christ had suffered on earth and for which the
church was instituted. It was not a nominal change in faith that
was sought; it was a new birth, a change of heart, expressed in
a general renunciation of sin. The mission was communal and
revolutionary:

The conversion of the world must be nothing less than the conversion
of the masses of its inhabitants, and this would involve the moral
renovation of SOCIETY, as well as of the *individuals* of whom society
is composed. The conversion of the world will be its conversion from
sin, its conversion to God, its conversion to Christ. When the world is
converted to Christ, it will be governed by the principles of Christ,
the precepts, the example, the spirit of Christ—the spirit of benevolence, equity, mercy, brotherly kindness, and truth. The character
of Christ will become, in some good measure, the character of individuals, of communities, of states, and of nations. . . . All injustice,
oppression, and violence, will then cease, or be generally suppressed.

It is important that Goodell stressed the example of Christ, for
it is sometimes said that the government of God merely gave new

sanction to Old Testament law. Those who yearned for the conversion of the world believed in the possibility of a general "conversion from sin" as well as in the control of specific sins. Only Goodell's last phrase—"or be generally suppressed"—harked back to older notions of social control. In the law of Christ he looked forward most of all to an end of violence and the ordinary work of human government. He tried to imagine "a state of society completely the opposite of all this" and concluded that such a state was slavery. Under slavery man was a thing rather than a moral agent. The conflict between slavery and antislavery involved the highest principles; at stake was the millennium.[56]

Goodell was no theological liberal. His intellect was sharpened in a long unsuccessful struggle to preserve Calvinism. On the eve of the Civil War he still insisted that the theology drawing "the darkest picture of human corruption" had need to demand the most uncompromised reform. Conversely, the less corrupt man seems to be, the more likely is reform to be regarded as fanatical. Indeed, the long stubborn opposition to antislavery was fresh evidence of human depravity. Goodell presented the principle of radicalism—immediate, uncompromising repentance—as an application of the governmental view of God. The basis of compromise and gradualism was any theology which removed morality from the control of "the Moral Governor of the Universe," thereby hindering strict constructions of sin, guilt, and just punishment. Because of their failure to insist on moral law, he labeled gradualist theologies as "antinomian" (one wonders how much fright value the word still contained). Slavery was absolute authority, and true Calvinism, with its knowledge of divine sovereignty and human depravity, should have been able to see that absolute human authority was totally sinful. The slaveholder was playing God.[57]

[56] Goodell, *American Slavery: A Formidable Obstacle to the Conversion of the World* (New York, 1854), pp. 3–6. Haroutunian maintains that the governmental theory stressed the old moral law and weakened the idea of a new birth in Christ; see *Piety versus Moralism*, pp. 175–176.

[57] Goodell, "The Theologies and the Reforms," *Principia*, Nov. 19, 1859, p. 1; Nov. 26, 1859, p. 1; Dec. 10, 1859, pp. 25–26.

Goodell's theology stressed the basic doctrines of antislavery: divine sovereignty and individual accountability. These doctrines existed not only on the eve of the Civil War, when they had become largely irrelevant; they appeared also in the early writings of the two most outstanding immediatists, Garrison and Weld. These doctrines worked almost invariably toward anarchism, or toward antinomianism, despite Goodell's endeavor to pin the label on conservative opponents. Goodell was no nonresistant, but his views attacked human authority and envisioned a world where God was the sole governor.

Why was slavery a sin? William Lloyd Garrison and Theodore Dwight Weld—and the great majority of abolitionists were inspired by one or both of these leaders—arrived at essentially the same answer. Slavery, as sin, was rebellion against God. It interfered with man's role as "an accountable moral agent." The imagery is legal: all men would stand before the bar of God and account would then be taken of their lives. For this reason, of course, slaveholders should be fearful and repentant. The same reasoning indicated the particular quality of their sin. When a man presumed to claim that he owned another man, he competed with God for control and government over mankind. He tried to make his slave accountable to him instead of to God. This original sin of presumption—like Adam, the slaveowner reversed the order of creation—necessarily engendered further sins. Bondage in the South inevitably manifested itself in sexual laxity, violence, ignorance of the Bible, profanity, and the countless other horrors on which antislavery writings dwelt.

This understanding of the sin of slavery underlies Garrison's 1832 tract, *Thoughts on African Colonization,* which, in its assault on the American Colonization Society, elucidated the meaning of immediatism. Garrison showed great concern about the accountability before God, not only of slaves and masters, but of himself. Though he expected attack, possibly even martyrdom, this "lively sense of accountability to God" forbade him to be silent in denouncing sin. In Garrison's view, the notion of accountability strengthened conscience and reason. When man's awareness of the inevitability of judgment was deadened, he fell back into his brutal nature and neglected the higher plane of conduct expected of him. In short, the duty of Christians, keenly aware of their eternal responsibility, was to rebuke others and destroy the worldly rationalizations by which hypocrites postponed thoughts of their accountability. Garrison performed this duty in the *Thoughts*.[58]

In meeting his Christian duty to denounce slaveholding, Garrison turned to the accountability of Negro slaves:

Man is created a rational being; and therefore he is a subject of moral government, and accountable. Being rational and accountable, he is bound to improve his mind and intellect. . . .

The slaves are men; they were born, then as free as their masters; they cannot be property; and he who denies them an opportunity to improve their faculties, comes into collision with Jehovah, and incurs a fearful responsibility. But we know that they are not treated like rational beings, and that oppression almost entirely obliterates their sense of moral obligation to God or man.[59]

Garrison's greatest wrath was reserved for colonizationists rather than slaveholders. Though colonizationists sponsored token educational programs in Liberia, Garrison argued that they were as adamant against religious and intellectual instruction for free blacks in America as masters were for their slaves. When respectable leaders of church and state allied themselves with sin, the nation had reached a dark hour.

Colonizationists argued that education was wasted on Negroes in America because the races could not live amicably together. To Garrison this was a rationalization of sin. It contradicted the Christian vision that all men must stand equally before the bar of God and that He does not respect earthly distinctions. Although colonizationists professed support for Christian missionary endeavors, their attitude toward the religious education of American blacks pointed to a sinful belief that there was no power

[58] Garrison, *Thoughts on African Colonization* (reprint ed., New York, 1968), pp. 3, 6–7, 66, and *passim*.
[59] *Ibid.*, p. 71.

in Christ to reunite mankind. The only response to human antagonisms would then be to erect walls of separation. Colonizationists, in other words, denied the Christian mission to convert and reconcile the world; they denied that widening recognition of man's common accountability to his Creator was the pathway to the millennium.[60] Colonization was odious in two ways: it tolerated slavery, competition with God; and it tolerated anarchy, the divisions among men which follow from sin.

Thoughts on African Colonization is prophetic, millennial. But millennialism does not always imply abstract visions of future utopias. In Garrison's case it was a tendency to judge present behavior against standards necessary to usher in the millennium. Slaveholders insisted they were not "accountable" for slavery in a legal sense; the present generation had not started the institution. But history is filled with sin, and sin is always accompanied by pharisaical rationalizations. According to Garrison, it was a curious Christianity which justified sin by its prior existence and present durability. The accountability that concerned him was not defined by human legal systems but rather by the government of God.[61] The notion of accountability, then, indicated the sinfulness of slavery and of its hypocritical apologists and mandated denunciatory reform.

In setting the higher law of divine accountability over ordinary legal accountability and in directing human energies toward the millennium rather than accepting the secular endurance of sin, Garrison was undermining traditional props of government. Here are sources of anarchism. But the *Thoughts* are explicitly republican, by which Garrison simply meant a governmental form which, unlike slavery, did not presumptuously invade God's authority over man. Soon, however, the anarchistic implications of the government of God would become more apparent.

Theodore Weld's view of the sin of slavery differed little from Garrison's. In January 1833 he wrote to Garrison and revealed his theory of immediatism:

[60] *Ibid.*, esp. pp. 13, 36, 130, 141–143.
[61] See quotations in *ibid.*, pp. 62–63, also p. 90, and *passim*.

That no condition of birth, no shade of color, no mere misfortune of circumstances, can annul that birth-right charter, which God has bequeathed to every being upon whom he has stamped his own image, by making him a *free moral agent*, and that he who robs his fellow man of this tramples upon right, subverts justice, outrages humanity, unsettles the foundations of human safety, and sacrilegiously assumes the prerogative of God.

Anyone willing to inherit the status of master became "joint partner in the original sin."[62] Whether or not Weld intended a double meaning, slavery did in his thought resemble Adam's sin: the order of creation was reversed, man put above God. As in Garrison's thought, it was the moral accountability of man within the government of God that made the authority of slavery sinful. Accountability also gave impetus to reform: "As long as I am a moral agent," Weld wrote one week later, "I am fully prepared to *act out* my belief." What should be the message of antislavery reformers? Weld taught them not to waste much time on the physical cruelty of masters, but to stress "the inflictions of slavery on mind . . . its reduction of accountability to a chattel."[63]

In 1836 Weld supervised the training of a host of agents for the American Anti-Slavery Society. One of them was Henry Wright, who took careful notes. The first business of the training sessions was to define slavery, since the emphasis of the agents was to be on its categorical sinfulness. There was some disagreement, particularly between Weld and his dearest friend, Charles Stuart, whose background lay in British reform rather than American evangelicalism. Stuart held out for a simple economic definition: slavery was involuntary labor without compensation. But this made the state of mind of the slave a relevant consideration. Even if the slave was willing, Weld argued, slavery was sinful because of what it did to a moral agent. The proper definition of slavery was: *"Holding & treating persons as things."* Wright

[62] Gilbert H. Barnes and Dwight L. Dumond, eds., *Letters of Theodore Dwight Weld, Angelina Grimké Weld, and Sarah Grimké, 1822–1844*, 2 vols. (Gloucester, Mass., 1965), I, 98. Hereafter cited as *Weld-Grimké Letters.*

[63] *Ibid.*, I, 99, 296.

noted: "In this Weld maintains consists the essential sin of slavery. It takes man out of the sphere in which God placed him &
puts him in a sphere designed to be occupied by others," such
as horses and other animals.[64]

Theodore Weld later opposed the ventures of antislavery into
anarchism, and he strongly disliked Wright. But his definitions
could be turned against other social institutions as well as chattel
slavery. Even during the agents' training sessions Wright recorded
these thoughts in his journal:

God has a Government & Man has a government. These two are at
perpetual *War*. . . . Man is trying to subject his fellow man to himself. . . . God gave to man dominion over all beasts & fowls & fish.
But this does not *satisfy*. Man is not content to rule over the animal
creation. He would get dominion over man. He tries all arts to obtain
this end. *I regard all Human Governments as usurpations of God's
power over Man.* [65]

By 1840 the nonresistance movement had come together, and
it was useful for Wright to write to Weld and remind him of his
definition of slavery as "MAN sunk to a *thing*." In Wright's view,
the use of force by governments and armies similarly violated
personal accountability and reduced man to a thing, often a
corpse. The "principle of abolition," consequently, would eradicate not only slavery, but also warfare and armed resistance.
After all that Weld had written "about the distinction between
men and things—which you say 'is the crowning distinction of the
universe' "—could he continue to support human governments?

That this distinction is, as you say—"the centre and circumference of
God's moral government"—I have not a doubt. That it is as sacred as
that between the GREAT I AM and a *thing*, I doubt not, and I have
no doubt that the spirit of armed resistance, which, in an individual
or a government, would, in self-defense, sink Man to a thing—would
extinguish all LIFE and consign the universe to the dominion of
DEATH.[66]

[64] Wright Journal (HCL) XXXII, 189–215, Nov. 1836.
[65] *Ibid.*, XXXII, 302, Nov. 24, 1836.
[66] *Liberator*, Aug. 28, 1840, p. 4.

Weld refused to join the movement. It is significant, nonetheless, that Wright needed few categories other than those taught by Weld to explain nonresistance. Extreme radicalism could easily be derived from the idea of the government of God as filtered through antislavery.

In his correspondence with Weld, Wright's thought is paradoxical. He stated that man cannot any more escape from regulation and order than can the solar system. God insisted on government, but He despised men's efforts to pre-empt the governance of others for themselves. God required that each man judge for himself the will of God and govern himself by that private understanding: "Thus each human being, man and *woman*, is invested with sovereignty over himself—and no one over another. . . . Thus over our physical and spiritual natures God wields the sceptre of absolute dominion."[67] Nor was this view of individual accountability peculiar to Wright. Many abolitionists had a hard time justifying any authority between man's private judgment and the ultimate judgment of God. The struggle against slavery could resemble a private exercise in self-mastery.

Self-control, under the government of God, might be regarded as the true source of public order. The paradox was everywhere; movements which we would call anarchistic hated anarchy, in the sense of strife and disorder. The principal newspaper of nonresistance described its own appearance as incongruous "in this seditious, warring, anarchical age."[68] Garrison put the paradox beautifully at an 1855 convention: "Non-resistance makes men self-governed. The kingdom of God is within them. Some speak of anarchy in connection with non-resistance. But this principle teaches those who receive it to be just, and upright, and kind, and true, in all the relations of life. It is the men of violence who furnish anarchists." The men of violence included governments and slaveholders.[69] Sin and anarchy existed in America be-

[67] *Ibid.*, Sept. 4, 1840, p. 4.
[68] *Non-Resistant*, Jan. 1839, p. 3.
[69] *Practical Christian*, Apr. 7, 1855, p. 2; Apr. 21, 1855, p. 2.

cause virtue had been entrusted to coercion rather than peaceful conversion.

The Garrisonians, then, voiced the paradox of all anarchism— that slavery causes anarchy. The only escape from slavery and the only reliable source of public safety was individual sovereignty. This viewpoint could be expressed completely within terms that had become familiar in the history of American evangelicalism. The government of God could make abolitionists wary of all the restraints in their own lives. Self-mastery was escape from bondage. The duty of abolitionists could become liberation from bondage, not only in the South, but also at home.

III

Nonresistant Anarchism
and Antislavery

The founding of the New England Non-Resistance Society in September 1838 provided the most famous instance of the emergence of anarchistic ideas in antislavery. American conservatives saw in nonresistance the ultimate expression of the seditious nature of abolitionism—abolition turned into anarchism. According to Calvin Colton, whose *Abolition a Sedition* was an astute, sustained attack on the antislavery movement, renunciation of government was the logical outcome of immediatism. He urged reformers to pay greater heed to the institutional consequences of their demands; too frequently, he thought, American Protestantism had stressed the possibility of individual sinlessness, and too seldom it had taught the importance of social order.[1]

In some ways it was unfair to tar all of antislavery with the brush of nonresistance. Nonresistance leadership was always confined to a small area of New England, though adherents were scattered throughout the North. While for a time it gained the attention or support of many prominent and gifted persons, it was not as large or as durable a movement as antislavery.[2] Many

---

[1] Colton, *Abolition a Sedition. By a Northern Man* (Philadelphia, 1839), esp. pp. 61, 71–78, 115. On Colton, see Alfred A. Cave, *An American Conservative in the Age of Jackson: The Political and Social Thought of Calvin Colton* (Fort Worth, 1969).

[2] For an extensive discussion of nonresistance, see Peter Brock, *Pacifism in the United States: From the Colonial Era to the First World War* (Princeton, 1968), chs. 12–14.

abolitionists refused to subscribe to nonresistance, some because they shared the conservatives' horror at its anarchistic tendency, others because they did not wish the cause of the slave to be burdened with additional unpopular issues. Furthermore, there were important differences in emphasis and opinion even among those abolitionists who did become nonresistants.

On the other hand, nonresistance was an extension of several ideas that were central to immediate abolitionism: Colton identified perfectionism and we might add the government of God. Many abolitionists who shunned the new movement held beliefs that were largely compatible with nonresistance, and it was not the only anarchistic development in the history of abolitionism. Although the Non-Resistance Society was kept separate from the American Anti-Slavery Society, the connections between nonresistance and abolition were strong enough to foil efforts to purge nonresistants from the older society.[3] In addition, for those abolitionists who set up the Non-Resistance Society there was, as Tolstoy later understood, a doctrinal interrelationship between antislavery and nonresistance. If nonresistance was really anarchistic, then conservative critics were right: radical abolitionism could lead to anarchism.

This chapter examines the New England Non-Resistance Society as an expression of abolitionism. It will be helpful at the outset to define nonresistance historically; it must be distinguished from the ideas of passive obedience and passive resistance. The term "nonresistance" is derived from Christ's injunction to individuals not to resist evil. But there is nothing inherently radical, let alone anarchistic, in the term. In British political theory it referred to those who held it to be a Christian duty not to oppose even a tyrannical ruler, a submissive doctrine which had been spurned in the ideology of the American Revolution.[4] The abolitionists of 1838 decidedly did not have in mind

---

[3] On the separateness of nonresistance and on efforts to purge, see Kraditor, *Means and Ends,* pp. 82–83, 87, 96–102, and *passim.*

[4] Thus the full title of Jonathan Mayhew's famous 1750 sermon is "A Discourse Concerning Unlimited Submission and Non-Resistance to the

this absolutist meaning of nonresistance; they were not sworn to passive obedience. Even discarding this meaning, however, does not remove all confusion. The term nonresistance draws attention to the commitment of the abolitionists to personal non-violence. We might, therefore, be reminded of the modern technique of passive resistance and its apostles, Gandhi and Martin Luther King. But the commitments of the Garrisonians went beyond pacifistic methods of social change, and nonviolence was certainly not the basic issue in the disputes among abolitionists. Opponents of Garrisonian nonresistance—religious abolitionists such as Orange Scott, Theodore Weld, and William Goodell—also preached personal nonviolence, turning the other cheek when under attack. This was "old-fashioned" nonresistance.[5] They wished to coin a new term for what they deplored among the Garrisonians: "no-governmentism." Some abolitionists had come to believe that the Biblical injunctions against violence meant that Christians had to renounce all manifestations of force, including human government; this is the belief we call nonresistance.

Actually, the Garrisonian nonresistants resented and disclaimed the name of no-governmentism. They insisted that they were striving for, and placing themselves under, the only true and effective government, the government of God. They maintained that they opposed not government, but human pretensions to govern. There was seldom much discernible irony in this insistence. Henry Wright, for example, was deadly serious when he complained that the audiences he met as agent of the Non-Resistance Society

seemed to think . . . that all who refuse "to acknowledge allegiance to human governments," but feel it a duty "to obey God rather than

---

Higher Powers." See Bernard Bailyn, ed., *Pamphlets of the American Revolution, 1750–1776* (Cambridge, Mass., 1965), I, 203–247.

[5] Donald G. Mathews, *Slavery and Methodism: A Chapter in American Morality, 1780–1845* (Princeton, 1965), p. 161; Benjamin P. Thomas, *Theodore Weld: Crusader for Freedom* (New Brunswick, N.J., 1950), p. 146; *Liberator*, June 12, 1840, p. 2; June 26, 1840, p. 4.

man," are "no government men" and "jacobins["]:—to be under the
government of Christ—of *moral principle*—was, as has been taught by
the religious and political newspapers of the land, and by the American
Peace Society, to be under "no government"—to be in a state of
anarchy.[6]

In Wright's view, simply to state this charge was to refute it.

Opponents of nonresistance described it as antinomianism. If
this word is divested of its disparaging overtones, it might describe the beliefs behind nonresistance. Nonresistants were Christians who were concerned for the coming of the millennium,
which they understood to be the government of God. Any intermediaries between the individual and God were rivals to God's
sovereignty and impeded the coming of the millennium. The
term antinomian may be more useful than the term anarchist to
understand this view. As their resentment at being called no-
governmentists suggests, the Garrisonian nonresistants opposed
anarchy and yearned for government. If there is a paradox here, it
is at the heart of their faith. They were anarchists—or, more properly, we would call them anarchists—because they detested anarchy. In their categories, human government was synonymous
with anarchy and antithetical to the rule of Christ and moral
principle.

Slavery, government, and violence were considered identical
in principle. All were sinful invasions of God's prerogatives; all
tried to set one man between another man and his rightful ruler.
Slavery served as a paradigm of all human authority, the condition in which one man takes possession of another and removes
him from God's sovereignty. Nor was all this a question of abstract theology. The Garrisonians were intent on the problem of
order and security, as their obsession with the most violent and
immoral aspects of slavery indicates. In their view, the fact that
men tried to rule one another explained the prevalence of violence and bloodshed on earth. Their logic unfolded categorically:
to end slavery was to end all coercion; to end all coercion was to

[6] *Non-Resistant*, March 2, 1839, p. 2.

release the millennial power of God; to end coercion, again, was to secure peace and order on earth; and to secure peace was, of course, to realize the millennium. Schematically, slavery, government, or coercion was the intermediate state between self-government and divine government. Self-government and divine government reinforced one another, but the intermediate stage was "anarchy" or pandemonium in which men were not under moral law. All that was needed to usher in peace was to expel the intermediaries who pretended to keep the peace.

In short, the nonresistants took Christ's opposition to violence, even in response to injury, and extended it to oppose all institutions based on force. Armies were one such system and so were slavery and human government. Many difficulties lay ahead for this viewpoint. There were difficulties concerning the apparent justifications of violence in the Old Testament, which kept some abolitionists from joining the new movement.[7] There were difficulties concerning the limits of nonresistance. Did the elements of coercion in nongovernmental institutions—churches, communities, reform societies—mean that participation in organizations was generally forbidden to Christians? There were grave difficulties concerning the obligations of nonresistants toward the slave. However clear the categories of nonresistance seemed in 1838, there would be times when the temptation to condone violence would be strong. But these difficulties lay in the future. The founding of the New England Non-Resistance Society was accompanied by the simple, exuberant feeling that the meaning of a Christian life had become clear. All Christians could and should forswear involvement in every form of coercion.

ii

In tracing the origins of the New England Non-Resistance Society, we must turn briefly from abolitionism to another conflict-ridden reform movement, the American Peace Society.[8] Founded

[7] A good example is Sarah Grimké. See *Weld-Grimké Letters*, II, 705–706.

[8] The following account depends on Brock, *Pacifism*, ch. 11; and Merle

in 1828, it had taken its stand within the evangelical united front and concentrated on the evils of international war. It avoided such troublesome issues as personal nonviolence and the right of governments to use coercion to punish and rule. In its opposition to war it stressed the evils of aggression and left open the possibility that nations might justly defend themselves. But the society always contained some absolute pacifists who thought that all violence was unchristian. As debate centered increasingly around the issue of defensive wars, the pacifist wing insisted that the society must oppose all warmaking because even the worst aggressors customarily justified themselves in terms of some offense.

Henry Wright served as an agent of the American Peace Society for a few months in 1836. The association was not a happy one, for Wright followed principles of reform quite different from those held by the officers of the society. The differences emerge clearly in a letter to Wright from William Ladd, the highly respected secretary of the society. Ladd agreed with Wright's absolute pacifism, but advised that other men could be brought to the same position only *"gradually."* Neither of them, he wrote, had come to pacifism all at once, and audiences simply would not listen if that was where the agent began. The potential convert should be allowed to reach pacifism as his *"own* conclusion." In other words, Wright should generally oppose war in his speeches, but should evade such specific instances of force as defensive war, capital punishment, or even slavery. He could plant arguments, but should not be so "final" that people are offended. "You go," wrote Ladd, "like John the Baptist, to *prepare* the way of the Lord." Later it might be possible to take higher ground, "but it is not politic to begin so."[9]

Wright could not follow this advice. How, he asked, could he honestly answer questions and objections unless he felt free to state his beliefs fully? He dissented from the policy of the be-

---

Eugene Curti, *The American Peace Crusade, 1815–1860* (Durham, N.C., 1929), esp. pp. 68–84. See also Curti's "Non-Resistance in New England," *New England Quarterly*, I (1929), 34–57.

[9] Ladd to Wright, July 23, 1836, Garrison Papers, Boston Public Library.

nevolent societies "that we must get people to go one step & then get them another." He did not like the role of John the Baptist. "I would declare the whole truth at once just as Christ did & say to men—cease from all *sin* at once & I would tell them at once what is *sin*."[10] The issue between Ladd and Wright was one of gradualism versus immediatism; it closely resembled the issue between colonization and abolition. More was at stake than mere tactics. The two men were divided over the timing of the world's reception of the word of Christ. Wright wished to preach it now, while Ladd thought the world must wait.

As early as January and February 1836, Wright and other pacifists from the Boston area held a series of meetings to discuss setting up a new and more radical peace organization, but nothing came of these discussions. Indeed, the American Peace Society itself began to make some concessions to the pacifists; in 1837 it passed resolutions seeming to condemn all wars. In order to placate conservative supporters, however, an attempt was made in May 1838 to nullify the new position. At this point the idea of launching a new organization appeared more urgent to the radicals. A committee was formed to plan for a September convention to consider the subject of peace in all its bearings on individuals and nations. Ladd and another officer of the American Peace Society were asked to sit on the committee, but both declined on the grounds that the society should not appear responsible for the discussions. The committee planning the convention, therefore, consisted entirely of abolitionists. These discussions led to the founding of the New England Non-Resistance Society.[11]

It is important that, although dissent in the American Peace Society was not restricted to antislavery people, those who formed

[10] Wright Journal (HCL), XXX, 66–68, Aug. 2, 1836.

[11] Wright Journal (BPL), XXVII, 105, Feb. 15, 1836; and an incomplete MS. account of the origins of the New England Non-Resistance Society in Wright, Fragments of Diaries Written in 1832, '35, '45, '47, '48 and Miscellaneous Papers, Harvard College Library. See also Brock, *Pacifism*, pp. 520–521.

the new Non-Resistance Society were mainly abolitionists.[12] Debate over nonresistance soon shifted from the peace movement
to the antislavery movement. While other abolitionists—especially
Wright, Adin Ballou, Edmund Quincy, and Maria Weston Chapman—gave more time to the new venture, Garrison was its cyno-
sure; we may speak of Garrisonian nonresistance. As Peter Brock
has written, Garrison "contributed little to the formulation of the
ideology of nonresistance, yet he gave it its shape and its drive,
and his energy made of it for a brief while a force that attracted
many of the best minds and finest spirits in the New England
of that day."[13] Garrison played, by his own account, a much
stronger role than he intended at the organizing convention. He
composed the Declaration of Sentiments, described by him as the
"'disorganizing' instrument" which contained "all the fanaticism
of my head and heart." He expressed amazement that it was
adopted "by a vote of more than 5 to 1" of the one hundred and
fifty persons present. All who voted for it, he exulted, were abolitionists.[14]

The immediatist argument, as applied to peace in the Non-
Resistance Society, was, then, especially attractive to abolitionists. Nonresistance was for persons who wanted whole principles,
as the saying went, not halfway measures. This kind of thinking
made nonresistance appealing, for example, to the New York
abolitionist, Gerrit Smith, although he was later deterred by
Theodore Weld from joining the movement. As a temperance

---

[12] For example, the Greenfield, Massachusetts, *Gazette,* in reviewing the
formation of the Non-Resistance Society, assumed that it was an abolitionist enterprise: "Thus, in their zeal to break the material fetters of the
southern slave, they have slipped on a mental yoke, which almost inca-
pacitates them from calm and candid judgment. . . . While we are
decided abolitionists . . . we are not, and hope we never may be, such
abolitionists as to destroy all the old landmarks, uproot all government,
make men and women of babies, and fools of grown people." See the
excerpt in *Non-Resistant,* Jan. 9, 1839, p. 4.

[13] Brock, *Pacifism,* p. 527.

[14] Garrison to Helen Garrison, Sept. 21, 1838, and to Mary Benson, Sept.
22, 1838, Garrison Papers, Boston Public Library. John Thomas, *The
Liberator,* p. 259, claims that Garrison's figures were terribly inaccurate.

man, Smith had tried to give up distilled liquors and not fermented ones; it was his sad experience "that it is nothing short of the adoption of *a whole principle,* which can secure a reasonable expectation of persevering obedience to any of its requirements."[15] By the same logic the peace movement would learn to oppose all varieties of force. The logic of reform seemed to move in a radical direction, from partial to total abstinence, from colonization to abolition, from peace to nonresistance. Nonresistance was a key instance in an eruption of romantic radicalism which was visible in nearly every reform movement.[16] And yet nonresistance was not based, at first, on a principle of individualism. It appealed to the sovereignty of God—God has forbidden injurious force; He supervises the consequences of human action.

A major influence on the origins of nonresistance was religious perfectionism. The quest for perfect holiness and the idea that such perfection might be immediately possible have been identified as "one of the nineteenth century's most persistent and socially significant religious themes."[17] Perfectionist ideas permeated the major denominations and inspired a variety of shockingly radical splinter movements. It was possible for those who deemed their personal sanctification to be perfect to attack the practices of institutional churches and hold themselves to new standards of morality. Rumors of sexual promiscuity particularly haunted the career of perfectionism in upstate New York. John Humphrey Noyes proceeded from the development of perfectionist religious theories to preach common marriage among the saints, a belief which, as practiced by Noyes and his followers at the Oneida

[15] *Non-Resistant,* May 4, 1839, p. 2. The New Haven *Record* (quoted in *ibid.,* Aug. 17, 1839) noticed these remarks and singled out Smith's concern for whole principles as a characteristic defect of reformers. Reformers disregard "tendencies and circumstances, upon which in reality the moral nature of an action entirely depends." On Smith and nonresistance, see Ch. VI below, n. 49.

[16] This tendency is well described in John L. Thomas, "Romantic Reform in America, 1815–1865," *American Quarterly,* XVII (1965), 656–681.

[17] Timothy L. Smith, *Revivalism and Social Reform: American Protestantism on the Eve of the Civil War* (New York, 1965), p. 103 and *passim.*

Community, was popularly referred to as free love.[18] Though free love and the disruption of churches were of course widely condemned, it was difficult for the evangelical orthodoxy to distinguish its basic perfectionist beliefs from those of scandalous radicals.

Abolitionists could be attracted to perfectionism without intending to tamper with the conventional morality of sex and marriage. What was attractive was the immediatist message that a Christian must eschew sin at once. This message depended on a distinction between human government and divine sovereignty, which was popular with orthodox as well as radical perfectionists. The drift of perfectionist beliefs among the orthodox may be observed in Caroline Fry's *Christ Our Example*, to which Sarah Grimké referred several times. Fry wrote:

The world, as distinguished from the people of God, is called in Scripture, "A kingdom, the kingdom of this world," as distinguished from "The kingdom of God." Now, a kingdom has not only a separate king; it has laws, administrations, and sanctions, distinctively its own. Its judicature takes no cognizance of the transgression of the laws of other nations. . . . How true is this of the kingdom of this world, as alienated from the government of God.[19]

Christ Our Example was scarcely interested in the reforms; nonetheless, in its concern for perfect holiness it emphasized distinctions which could be brought to the defense of immediate abolitionism or nonresistance. Christians were to be loyal to God, not to the laws of man.

Perfectionism among abolitionists was not restricted to the nonresistants. Antislavery opponents of Garrisonian nonresistance —for instance, Theodore Weld and William Goodell—were influenced by the radical perfectionists of upstate New York. It was

[18] Whitney R. Cross, *The Burned-Over District: The Social and Intellectual History of Enthusiastic Religion in Western New York, 1800–1850*, (New York, 1965), pp. 189–197, 238–251.

[19] Caroline Fry, *Christ Our Example* (2d ed., New York, 1834), pp. 59–60. On Sarah Grimké's interest in this book, see *Weld-Grimké Letters*, II, 706, 922.

only necessary to be an immediatist to feel this influence.[20] But perfectionism did play a special role in the evolution of non-resistance. In the crucial year 1837, Henry Wright referred to heady conversations on the subject, and Garrison was especially receptive. In November 1837, for example, he read to close associates a letter from the New York radical, James Boyle. The letter argued "that all Institutions, that stood in the way of Christ's Kingdom, must be done away. He regards the Sabbath, Governments, &c. as opposed to the spiritual Kingdom of our Lord."[21] In 1838 and 1839, Boyle became quite close to Garrison, served as an antislavery agent in Ohio, and published long letters on perfectionism in the *Liberator* and in the *Non-Resistant,* the journal of the new society.[22] When he was suggested as an agent for the society, however, there was too much opposition.[23] Boyle may nevertheless have been an important figure in the formulation of nonresistance.

The most notorious perfectionist was John Humphrey Noyes. Noyes had been brought up as an orthodox New Englander and educated in the "New Divinity" at Yale. In this view of theology, Calvinist doctrines had been attenuated in ways that secured the justice of God and the efficacy of revivalism: God, as a governor, gave man the ability to step forward and obey divine law. From this background Noyes proceeded to the extreme conclusion that Christians could clear themselves altogether of sinfulness and stand outside the ordinary inhibitions and restraints of society. Those who wished to draw a line between the moderate

[20] Cross, *Burned-Over District,* pp. 279–283.

[21] Wright Journal (BPL), XXXVI, 56, Nov. 8, 1837. See also Wright Journal (HCL), XXXIII, 102, 111, Feb. 14, 1837, and Apr. 9, 1837. Besides Boyle, other famous New York perfectionists were Charles Weld, brother of the abolitionist, and Luther Myrick. Wright did not meet either until after the start of the Non-Resistance Society. There is no reason to believe that the influence of either on nonresistance was significant. See Wright Journal (HCL), XL, 88, Apr. 8, 1839, and XLIII, 42, Apr. 20, 1840.

[22] Garrisons, *Garrison,* II, 286–287.

[23] See Edmund Quincy to Caroline Weston, Aug. 14, 1842, Weston Papers, Boston Public Library.

perfectionism of contemporary revivalism and the immoderate conclusions reached by Noyes accused him of advocating an "antinomian perfectionism,"[24] but they did not dissuade him from his loyalty to the sovereignty of God as he understood it. Although Noyes went on to practice his own version of sexual liberation at the Oneida Community, he was distressed by the extravagance and eccentricity of other perfectionists, particularly those in upstate New York. In 1837 he was attempting to gain converts to his understanding of perfectionism from among men who were in the mainstream of American moral reform.[25] Therefore, in the spring of that year, he ventured into the antislavery office in Boston to observe a heated debate over politics. Afterward he introduced himself to Garrison. According to Noyes, Garrison "said his mind was heaving on the subject of Holiness and the Kingdom of Heaven, and he would devote himself to them as soon as he could get anti-slavery off his hands." Noyes addressed him "especially on the subject of government, and found him, as I expected, ripe for the loyalty of heaven."[26]

Nonresistance was an old Christian doctrine, which, as the example of the Quakers indicates, could be stopped short of anarchism. Noyes showed little personal interest in nonresistance, but he provided an antigovernmental program which led it in exciting new directions. Garrison did not follow Noyes when he took the path leading to the Non-Resistance Society. Yet it is plain that perfectionism was very attractive to him. When Edward Beecher in 1841 lumped nonresistants together with perfectionists, deists, atheists, and pantheists as agents of darkness, Garrison disavowed the last three partners but was cagier about perfectionism. He pretended not to have conversed with believers in that doctrine and said that if reports of their marital practices were true they had "turned the grace of God into licentiousness." Perhaps they were only slandered, as nonresistants were and even Christ in the modern world would be. At any rate, what the

[24] McLoughlin, "Introduction" to Finney, *Lectures,* pp. xlvi–xlvii.
[25] Cross, *Burned-Over District,* pp. 245–246.
[26] Garrisons, *Garrison,* II, 145.

churches really hated in perfectionism, he said, was its demand for "total abstinence from sin, and immediate emancipation from the chains of the devil." A doctrine that fit so closely the terminology of temperance and abolitionism was surely reasonable: "He is a rebel against the government of God who advocates an opposite doctrine."[27] Noyes had shown Garrison how to convert the negative duty of nonresistance into an assertion of grace.

Most of Noyes's influence probably came from a long letter which Garrison's sons said made a "profound impression" on their father.[28] The perfectionist announced that he had retracted his allegiance to the United States government and now championed the claim of Jesus Christ to the throne of the world. He depicted the government as a fat libertine flogging Negroes and torturing Indians. A Christian could not befriend such a blackguard, and yet he could not easily flee the association because "every other country is under the same reprobate authority." Noyes had found just the mixture of categorical logic and gaudy characterization to seize Garrison's attention.

Short of leaving the world, how could one cease to partake in the sins of government? According to Noyes:

I grant that "the powers that be are ordained of God," and this is not less true of individual than of national slaveholders. I am hereby justified in remaining a slave—but not in remaining a slaveholder. Every person who is, in the usual sense of the expression, a citizen of the United States . . . is at once a slave and a slaveholder—in other words, a subject and a ruler in a slaveholding government. God will justify me in the one character, but not in the other. I must therefore separate them and renounce the last.

Government thus had the moral status of enslavement. A Christian subject may obey his ruler, but he may not get involved in the earthly, guilty process of ruling.

Noyes quickly pointed out that even obedience had its limits.

[27] *Non-Resistant*, Nov. 24, 1841, pp. 2–3.

[28] For the text of the letter, from which the following quotations are taken, see Garrisons, *Garrison*, II, 145–153.

It was not enough to cease doing evil. A Christian must "commence war" on government by means of a personal "declaration of independence." Noyes probably used the example of slavery because of its rhetorical effect on the man he wished to convert. But how was he to justify all-out insubordination, which his argument up to this point tended to reject? His concern was not to reform the nation but to end it. He now argued that the government occupied territory promised to Christ, that its constitutional claim of perpetuity mocked God's plan of redemption, and that it stood "in the way of God's kingdom, just as Colonization once stood in the way of Abolition." The central theme of Noyes's letter was millennial: the United States was to be the spot where Christ's onslaught on government would commence. Whereas conservative benevolence societies, such as those led by Lyman Beecher, hoped to suppress disorder and elevate piety in order to realize utopia under the American form of government, Noyes had a different conception of the millennial process.[29] "*My hope of the millennium,*" he wrote, "*begins where Dr. Beecher's expires—VIZ., AT THE OVERTHROW OF THIS NATION.*" He warned Garrison that abolitionism, despite the role it had played in preparing for the millennium, would soon fall beneath the shadow already covering colonization unless it was made subservient to "UNIVERSAL EMANCIPATION FROM SIN." Because Garrisonian abolitionism was a "city" on a "high hill," Garrison could bring many others with him to the cause of holiness. Others would abandon him, "but you will be deserted as Jonah was by the whale—the world, in vomiting you up, will heave you upon the dry land."

This remarkable letter contained premonitions of almost every theme in New England's experiment with nonresistance. Abolitionists were captivated by the notions that governments com-

[29] On different types of millennialism, cf. Tuveson, *Redeemer Nation;* David E. Smith, "Millennial Scholarship in America," *American Quarterly,* XVII (1965), 535–549; and George Shepperson, "The Comparative Study of Millenarian Movements," *Millennial Dreams in Action,* ed. Sylvia L. Thrupp (The Hague, 1962), pp. 44–52.

peted with God for allegiance and that the sole escape from slaveowning was forfeiture of the privileges of democracy. It is impossible to establish the extent of Noyes's direct influence, but his letter illuminates some important perfectionist themes which were repeated in the nonresistance movement. When abolitionists subscribed to the Declaration of Sentiments of the New England Non-Resistance Society, they were merging the absolute pacifist commitment to return good for evil with the millenarian intention to wage war on evil.

Noyes had not sought the leadership of this kind of organization. He had tried to lower the importance of abolitionism in Garrison's mind, and he had failed. Neither the Non-Resistance Society nor the American Anti-Slavery Society restricted its membership to those who were perfectly sanctified; both, in Noyes's view, were broad enough to include infidels. In 1843, therefore, he urged "all believers who are mingling themselves with abolitionists, non-resistants, &c., *As you love the Bible and Bible doctrine and practice,*—COME OUT FROM AMONG THEM, AND BE YE SEPARATE."[30] The come-outer, perfectionist argument, as Garrison employed it, meant that abolitionists should sever connections with churches and governments which associated themselves with slavery. Noyes felt that Garrison similarly refused to go far enough toward perfection and turned the same argument on him.

Three years before Noyes's call for perfectionists to desert Garrison, a woman from Pawtucket had withdrawn from the New England Non-Resistance Society, although her faith in the power of love remained steadfast. She had decided that only a Christian ("I mean one who has found peace through the blood of the Lamb") could be a nonresistant at heart, but the organization failed to seek a purified Christian membership. The editors of the *Non-Resistant* noted that others resigned because antiproperty, antimoney, or special religious views were not prerequisites to membership.[31] But they did not comment acrimoniously. Seceders

[30] *Liberator,* Dec. 15, 1843, p. 1.
[31] *Non-Resistant,* Aug. 12, 1840, p. 3.

themselves from other organizations, they knew the difficulty of agreement about who were the elect. Nonresistance followed the Garrisonian organizational strategy of keeping the reforms separate while searching for universally applicable principles. In other words, nonresistance, despite its borrowings from perfectionism, stayed within the bounds of secular reform. Nonresistance was the distinctive movement of abolitionists who had withdrawn from the American Peace Society. In their synthesis of the needs of earthly reform and the rules of divine sovereignty may be discovered the sources of future variation and discord. The organization they created, as we shall see, would never be free of ambiguities and contradictions. Was it a sect preparing for a new moral world? Was it only one of many benevolent societies promoting short-run improvements in the world of the present?

iii

At first glance, nonresistance, as a plan to secure an orderly society without resorting to force, possessed an almost tautological clarity. That is, it insisted that to end fighting meant to give up fighting. There is no doubting the sincerity and excitement brought to this insistence. Even in its origins, however, the movement was threatened by contradictions: it tried to fuse the quietistic attitude of nonviolence with the revolutionary purpose of millennial perfectionism. The early years of nonresistance witnessed considerable confusion and many changes in individual positions, and the nonresistants repeatedly seemed ambivalent on the means and ends of social change.

Some problems are apparent in Garrison's Declaration of Sentiments, the document most fundamental to the new society. The Declaration, as Garrison exulted, was very radical; there is a strongly anarchistic cast to its opposition to government. On the other hand, it had to be revised to gain a wider range of support.[32] The document follows two quite different lines of argument. First, and most simply, came the syllogism: the New Testa-

---

[32] Garrison to Samuel Joseph May, Sept. 24, 1838, Garrison Papers, Boston Public Library.

ment forbids the use of force; government is upheld by force; therefore a Christian must abstain from government. This line of argument depended on the sovereignty of God, the "one KING and LAWGIVER, one JUDGE and RULER of mankind." The second line of argument depended more strictly on human needs and motivations. It pointed out that physical coercion could not change human hearts and was therefore inappropriate to the task of moral regeneration. Here the appeal was made not to Scripture or divine law but to "evidences" from the "history of mankind." Garrison stressed the "great security" in meekness, which apparently promised both immediate safety and future salvation; an appeal to self-interest could be derived from either authority, the evidence of human nature or the laws of God. Stylistically the Declaration of Sentiments favors great conglomerate sentences, such as one which urges nonresistance on grounds "of sound policy,—of safety to property, life, and liberty,—of public quietude and private enjoyment,—as well as on the grounds of allegiance to HIM who is KING OF KINGS and LORD OF LORDS."[33] The arguments seem jumbled together.

Admittedly, it is not unusual to find a doctrine defended along varying lines of argument. Garrison may have felt heartened by the convergence of Scriptural authority and empirical fact to uphold his stand. Indeed, in the kind of simplified perfectionism which characterized much of nonresistance, it was to be expected that whatever God commanded would have a humanly reasonable quality. To the extent that Garrison recognized any difference between divine law and lessons from historical experience, at this time the perfectionist in him probably preferred the former source of truth. His leading theme was: "We are bound by the laws of a kingdom which is not of this world." But some speakers at the founding convention were less otherworldly: one emphasized that killing was "repugnant to reason and to the common sympathies

[33] The most complete version of the Declaration appears in *Principles of the Non-Resistance Society* (Boston, 1839) and in *Non-Resistant*, Jan. 1839, p. 1. An abbreviated version is reprinted in Henry Steele Commager, ed., *The Era of Reform, 1830–1860* (Princeton, 1960), pp. 172–174.

and principles of human nature and destructive to the peace and good order of society." His resolution, which concluded that killing was "detrimental to the best interests of individuals and nations," was not passed.[34] This type of highly secularized reasoning was not specifically disavowed, but the delegates may have originally been more interested in the sovereignty of God.

Was there really any conflict between these lines of argument? That the divine command to eschew violence ought to preclude earthly reckonings of expediency and social ethics was made plain at once in influential articles by the perfectionist James Boyle. Since God is "the only independent sovereign in the universe," he explained, man is forbidden to set rules "either for his own government or for the government of others." For this reason, America's "*experiment,* designed to prove the sufficiency of man to govern himself," would fail "as has every similar one to invent a self-moving machine, or to detect a universal specific among medicines."[35] Boyle proved too much and became nearly incomprehensible. Seemingly, only a state with no human volition whatsoever would satisfy God. Yet for several years Henry C. Wright echoed much of this argument; and so to a lesser extent did Edmund Quincy, Garrison, and others. Divine government was said to preclude human government.

In order to reconcile God's sovereignty and man's will, it was necessary to keep track of a complex and shifting theory of the historical process. The Declaration of Sentiments, for example, was ambiguous concerning time, social change, and the present rule of God. It began with the straightforward view that the "old covenant" of retaliation had been abrogated by Christ in favor of a "new covenant" of love. Besides referring to the New Testament, it looked forward to the millennium, for nonresistants dedicated themselves to efforts to "hasten the time, when the kingdoms of this world will become the kingdoms of our LORD and of his CHRIST, and he shall reign forever." Furthermore, in fol-

[34] *Non-Resistant,* Jan. 1839, p. 1.
[35] *Ibid.,* p. 2. The articles are anonymous, but Boyle is identified as the author in Garrisons, *Garrison,* II, 286.

lowing the new covenant and pursuing the millennium, nonresistants accepted as "a self-evident truth" the idea that "whatever the gospel is designed to destroy at any period of the world, being contrary to it, ought now to be abandoned."[36] No credit is given to the old Christian assumption that man must be controlled by governments until sin is ended and the reign of Christ begins. On the contrary, it seems to be assumed that divine sovereignty exerts itself through human actions and decisions.

Samuel E. Coues, a veteran of the controversies in the American Peace Society, sketched out the nonresistants' understanding of the millennium in a response to the objection that nonresistance was not meant to be practiced before the second coming of Christ. Coues insisted that the world had not been "created as a mere three-score-and-ten of anarchy and confusion, as a dreary prison house to hold the captives until ready for trial." Man has reason to expect a genuinely divine revelation to provide "an element of social order" and promote happiness on earth. Such in fact is the effect of the revolutionary meekness taught by Christ. If the Bible were to demand no change in human nature, it could not come from God, for it is typically human to "form half-way expedients." Human nature is not fixed and unchanging, and reliance on the government of God should not be construed as inexpedient or self-sacrificial.[37] In other words, it could be argued that God worked through man in history toward the millennium and that some aspects of the millennium, therefore, need not be deferred. A committee of the first nonresistance convention similarly employed the idea of the millennium to show the consistency between human nature and divine law. To say that it was not yet safe to practice the law of love was "like placing a ball in the centre of gravity, so that the coming of the millennium must remain in an eternal quietus, at least as far as human agency is concerned. For wars and fighting, and all the black catalogue of kindred and connected evils, will

[36] See note 33, above.
[37] Samuel E. Coues, "Is Christianity, the Religion of Peace, Adapted to the World?" in *Liberty Chimes* (Providence, 1845), pp. 55–63.

of· course perpetuate themselves, unless we cease to fight, or the
world should be regenerated without human agency."[38] In both
these instances, millennialism was employed to justify personal
pacifism rather than antigovernmental views. There was even a
kind of gradualism implicit in the argument that the millennium
would be introduced by human means. (We shall see that this
gradualism was made explicit in the views of Adin Ballou.) So
long as nonresistants wished to contend for immediate emancipation from government, they might have trouble in keeping together the sovereignty of God, human agency, and the millennium. In the early writings of nonresistance it is hard to find
much consideration of the problem of historical change, even
though one almost had to think of oneself as an historical agent
in order to become a nonresistant. There may be some significance, then, in the fact that one member of the original executive
committee of the Non-Resistance Sociey—Joshua Himes—by 1840
was converted to a radically different view of the millennium.
He became editor of the *Signs of the Times* and publicized the
view, known as Millerism, that history would abruptly end with
the second coming of Christ in 1843.[39]

Further ambiguity surrounded the personal safety of being a
nonresistant. If the doctrine had simply followed from the sovereignty of God, this question would have been irrelevant. It
might have been argued that the demands of obedience to God's
law and the glory of playing a part in the approach of the millennium more than compensated for any penalty or pain, including martyrdom. Some historians have been impressed by a strain
of martyr psychology in the abolitionist mind.[40] Occasionally
nonresistants did visualize the possibility of losing their lives
rather than resisting evil. Thus Henry Wright wrote: "Let the

[38] Charles Simmons, E. W. Robinson, and Thomas Haskell, *Report on the
Tendency and Effects of the Pacific Principle* (Boston, 1838), pp. 17–18.

[39] *Practical Christian,* July 1, 1840, p. 2. See Alice Felt Tyler, *Freedom's
Ferment: Phases of American Social History from the Colonial Period to
the Outbreak of the Civil War* (New York, 1962), pp. 72–78.

[40] See Hazel Catherine Wolf, *On Freedom's Altar: The Martyr Complex
in the Abolition Movement* (Madison, Wis., 1952).

injured party suffer and die, and leave the whole business of punishing evil-doers to Him who alone knows how to do this strange work—to adjust penalties to crimes and execute them." To do so was *"a duty and a privilege in all cases"* for all persons who "prefer the moral beauty, and grandeur, and bloodless honor of the no-fighting, no man-killing kingdom of God."[41] But such statements were unusual, even for Wright, however logically a willingness to die might be associated with loyalty to a higher kingdom.

Instead of stressing martyrdom the Garrisonians frequently argued that their faith afforded immediate protection. At this point the side of nonresistance which favored evidence from human nature and human history was important; hundreds of anecdotes from history and folklore were gathered to show that gentleness and nonviolence turned aside rough treatment.[42] Garrison insisted on the safety of nonresistance when he commented on the murder of Elijah Lovejoy, an antislavery editor, by an Illinois mob. It was only after repeated attacks on a succession of printing presses that Lovejoy had armed himself to protect his fourth press rather than flee the area. He was then shot. Garrison was straining historical accuracy when he wrote:

For a time, indeed, Lovejoy acted the part of a non-resistant, in the most perilous emergencies; and during all that time . . . [when] his soul was sustained by a high and sublime trust in God, not a hair of his head was injured, the mouths of the hungry lions tha[t] sought to devour him were stopped, and he triumphed over the powers of darkness. It was not till he forsook this course, and resorted to carnal weapons in defence of his rights and the laws of the State, that he became a victim to his mistaken sense of duty.[43]

The nonresistants were not wrong to insist on the pacifying qualities of meekness and nonviolence, but they were curiously un-

[41] *Non-Resistant,* Feb. 16, 1839, p. 2.

[42] For the most compendious treatment, see Adin Ballou, *Christian Non-Resistance, in All Its Important Bearings, Illustrated and Defended* (Philadelphia, 1846).

[43] *Non-Resistant,* Nov. 24, 1841, p. 3.

willing to admit that a political commitment to nonviolence might not always prevent martyrdom. And they virtually ignored the possibility that a religious commitment to nonviolence might even be advanced through martyrdom.

Nonresistance, if one believed empirical evidence offered by the movement, worked well; it had a high pragmatic cash value. It kept a man safe, and it might even make him wealthy. An Indiana nonresistant and a Vermont storekeeper provided anecdotes to the effect that a man could more easily collect his debts when everyone knew he would not resort to law. It was also boasted that Samuel Coues and his brother ran a business of several thousand dollars around the world while spending less than eight dollars annually on legal costs.[44] This kind of optimism, with its advertisements for the safety and prosperity to be gained from nonresistance, may have had important consequences. It hindered the movement from finding in the coming of the millennium any role for the slave, who might have to endure harsh treatment but who could not count on increasing prosperity. It left the movement ill equipped to understand future setbacks and tragedies, such as fugitive slave cases in the 1850s.

There is an additional area of ambiguity in the doctrines of nonresistance; not even the rejection of government was free of problems. The theoretical consequences of the government of God were clear enough, but the practical applications were problematical. The main contention was, of course, that the government of God and human efforts at government were mutually exclusive; accordingly, those who placed themselves under the rule of God could take no part in and admit no need for human government. This contention sufficed for the rhetoric of the meetings and periodicals of nonresistance, but difficulties arose when men sought to conform their lives to their principles. For example, a Philadelphia man hailed nonresistance as part of "the cause of emancipation from all slavery, physical or mental, political or ecclesiastical, individual or national"—he had caught on to the

[44] *Ibid.*, July 6, 1839, p. 3; Feb. 9, 1842, p. 2; Nov. 2, 1839, p. 2.

extended definitions of slavery of which abolitionists were fond. But he had a very practical question. Was it right to pay taxes which perpetuated government? The editors of the *Non-Resistant* told him it was innocent to pay taxes (to do so was not to join in government, but only to submit nonresistantly to its demands); but he was dissatisfied with this answer. For both antislavery and antigovernment movements he advocated strategic boycotting: "If there be no consumption, nor demand for slave *produce;* there will be no consumption, nor demand for slave *labor.* Is it not so with government? Taxes purchase its protection; and if there be no demand for its protection; no purchasers for its commodity, there will be none manufactured."[45] The apparent assumptions are that government is an easily isolated institution, that its only function is protection, and that individuals can readily separate themselves from it.

To other nonresistants, like Edmund Quincy, the complexity of government was troubling. Although he went on to become an uncompromising nonresistant and editor of the society's paper, he was at first exceedingly reluctant to sign the Declaration of Sentiments because some of the administrative and regulatory functions of government seemed to be harmless. Were nonresistants opposed to the use of the coinage or of banks and insurance companies chartered by government? So uncertain was Quincy's view of the limits of nonresistance that it was a full year before he resigned a commission he held as justice of the peace for the state of Massachusetts.[46]

Probably most Garrisonians agreed that nonresistants should not be officers in any branch of government, but the problems did not end there. No clear answer was given to the question whether a nonresistant could testify in court.[47] A few felt they could not sign petitions addressed to the government, but most of the leaders disagreed with this position.[48] And it may be sur-

[45] *Ibid.,* Feb. 16, 1839, p. 3; March 16, 1839, p. 2.
[46] Garrisons, *Garrison,* II, 234–237, 328.
[47] *Liberator,* July 31, 1846, p. 4.
[48] For a tortured letter on the petition question by one of Wright's

prising to discover that Garrison did not believe that nonresistants had to engage in civil disobedience when called to militia duty. He advised a young man named Charles Stearns (who later played an important role in the movement) to pay a fine which relieved him of military duty rather than go to jail. Payment of a fine was no worse than tax-paying.[49] On the whole, the problem of conscientious objection to military service took up little of the movement's time, perhaps because few of these reformers were young. A committee of the founding convention in 1838 considered the problem, but its report did not go much beyond appealing for exemptions for peace men from militia laws.[50] The committee evidently did not ask whether such a favored position might compromise the radicalism of nonresistance, which, after all, supposedly renounced allegiance to human government. Nonresistance, quite simply, did not offer a comprehensive practical understanding of the evils of government, of anarchistic alternatives to the existing arrangements, or of the duties of nonresistants in the present dispensation. What really mattered to the movement was the declaration that the only proper government was divine.

Nonresistants were not supposed to vote, but there was some indecisiveness even on this point. "*Vox populi, vox diaboli,*" wrote Bronson Alcott. Yet nonresistants were seldom indifferent to the results of elections, as might have been expected of a movement which held even republican government to be a usurpation of God's throne. For example, a single column of Garrison's *Libera-*

---

friends, see *Non-Resistant,* Feb. 2, 1839, p. 2. The question was raised especially by nonresistants who later formed the Hopedale Community; see *ibid.,* Apr. 6, 1839, p. 3; and *Liberator,* Aug. 2, 1839, p. 4. Quincy recognized that there was much doubt on the subject and argued that petitioning was, first, a matter for individual consciences and, second, a prayer to a *de facto* power, whereas voting was a confirmation of power. See the *Non-Resistant,* June 15, 1839, p. 3.

[49] *Liberator,* Feb. 14, 1840, p. 4; Sept. 17, 1841, p. 3.

[50] Edmund Quincy, *Report on the Injustice and Inequality of the Militia Law of Massachusetts, with Regard to the Rights of Conscience* (Boston, 1838), pp. 3–12.

tor, at the height of nonresistance, urged antislavery men to vote against proslavery congressmen and simultaneously ridiculed a vote for either presidential candidate.[51] The problem was largely due to the uncertainty of the Garrisonians as to whether nonresistance was merely one among other secular reforms or the most fundamental and divine of all reforms.

A good illustration of their uncertainty—perhaps we should say their defensiveness—is a speech given by Garrison at the first anniversary meeting of the society. He wished to show that nonresistance was "abolition in the broadest and best sense of the term," inasmuch as the renunciation of dominion over man involved, among other things, the impossibility of further slaveholding. In reality, nonresistants were giving "an everlasting suffrage against *all* violence," and they could not be accused of forgetting the slave. But he was unable to detach himself completely from politics:

And how will our course affect political action? Will there be many votes lost? No. Just in proportion as we stay away, the indifferent will be roused up to go. Since we organized, the clergy have found out that *they* can vote. The effect of non-resistance begins to be felt powerfully at the polls. Thousands who are not prepared to come into the fulness of our principles, have been aroused by the light they cast upon the corruption of governments to labor to purify them. . . . These are the men whom I expect to go on, and to become finally, non-resistants, in all the aggressive extent of that misunderstood name, thus awakening others to follow in their turn. No votes will be taken from the slave.[52]

This is the general argument that greater radicalism, whatever its proper merits, serves to embolden and empower lesser radicalism and thus to move history in a progressive direction. It would not seem, however, to be appropriate to a movement dedicated specifically to the reign of God. As Garrison now phrased the argument, nonresistance sounded more like an instrument of po-

[51] Odell Shepard, ed., *The Journals of Bronson Alcott* (Boston, 1838), p. 136; *Liberator*, Nov. 6, 1840, p. 3, col. 3.

[52] *Non-Resistant*, Dec. 7, 1839, p. 2.

litical influence than a declaration of independence from government.

One point, however, was perfectly clear: one obligation of nonresistants was not to vote. All civil government was at variance with the government of God; all civil governments assumed the right to harm anyone who resisted legal processes, although this assumption was so well understood that it seldom came out in the open. Human government without at least the threat of force and violence was unthinkable. As Edmund Quincy explained, in the United States the people were sovereign and, by voting, pretended to have the right to confer powers of coercion and life taking on their representatives. Nonresistants could not join in this blasphemy. To be sure, opponents of nonresistance denied that government always rested on force, and they conjured up images of governments based on the principle of peace among men. In Quincy's view, nonresistants could also imagine "an organization of society uniting all the advantages with none of the vices of the existing arrangements—and such a government we are ready to support." But since the United States was not organized so innocently, to vote here was to make oneself accountable for violence which was constitutionally employed.[53] The legal aphorism was that, *qui facit per alium, facit per se.* In the short run, therefore, the duty not to vote was clear; in the longer run, attention might have to be paid to finding innocent alternatives to government.

There was, in sum, significant ambiguity and confusion in the early years of the New England Non-Resistance Society. There was theoretical confusion over whether authority for the doctrine came from the edicts of God or from the verdicts of historical experience. And there was practical confusion concerning the applications of nonresistance. These points need emphasis because they indicate directions in which change might take place in the attitudes of some of these reformers. Even though there was ambiguity and indecisiveness, timidity and caution were not mixed

[53] *Liberator,* Oct. 30, 1840, p. 4.

with nonresistance. It was a brave movement intended to signify loyalty to God's government and independence from the temporary, arbitrary laws of men.

iv

One of the clearest-thinking nonresistants was Bronson Alcott, who is usually thought of in other connections, such as in his role as a controversial educational reformer or as a transcendentalist consociate of Emerson and Thoreau.[54] Alcott was an active Garrisonian reformer, having been one of his earliest converts to abolitionism. In November 1830 he and Garrison, with four others, formed what he later called the "preliminary Anti-Slavery Society."[55] His acquaintance with greater writers did not diminish even the literary dimensions of his respect for Garrison; thus he once wrote his brother-in-law, Samuel Joseph May, that he had been moved to weeping while reading five of Garrison's sonnets.[56] As a reformer Alcott was especially inspired by the nonresistance movement, and he participated vigorously in virtually every convention. Close examination of Alcott's point of view clarifies further the origins and the theoretical problems of nonresistance.

In the first place, Alcott was a transcendentalist. In tracing the origins of the New England Non-Resistance Society, we have discussed developments in the benevolence societies and in evangelical Protestantism. It might be asked whether transcendentalism has been overlooked. In fact Alcott was the only well-known transcendentalist to join the new movement. Nonresistance flourished in Boston and elsewhere in New England, but not in Concord. Although Emerson took note of the Garrisonians in lectures and essays, neither he nor Thoreau was prompted by theory or

[54] There is no fully adequate study of Alcott. Odell Shepard's *Pedlar's Progress: The Life of Bronson Alcott* (Boston, 1937) was meant to be supplemented with Shepard, ed., *Journals.* Also helpful is F. B. Sanborn and William T. Harris, *A Bronson Alcott: His Life and Philosophy,* 2 vols. (New York, 1965; 1st pub. 1893).

[55] Shepard, ed., *Journals,* p. 26.

[56] Garrisons, *Garrison,* II, 99.

temperament to join a reform association. Not even antislavery gained much of Emerson's attention; the idea of the government of God was associated with a fatalistic attitude in Emersonism as surely as with militancy in Garrisonism. Emerson confessed in his journal that sometimes he berated himself for not giving greater support to abolitionism: "But then, in hours of sanity, I recover myself, and say, 'God must govern his own world, and knows his way out of this pit, without my desertion of my post, which has none to guard it but me. I have quite other slaves to free than those negroes, to wit, imprisoned spirits, imprisoned thoughts, far back in the brain of man.'" Nor do the nonresistants appear to have been influenced by Emerson. Nonresistance was not justified, as it might have been, in terms of such Emersonian notions as the sacredness of the private man or the permanency of laws reflected in human consciousness. Nonresistance stayed close to the sovereignty of God, and to Emerson the Garrisonians were simply "the continuation of Puritanism."[57]

Alcott, though a transcendentalist, was an important figure in the Non-Resistance Society and helped in such tasks as the revision of the Declaration of Sentiments and the planning of conventions.[58] His excitement concerning the new movement was virtually unrestrained. "I regard Non-Resistance as the germ of the New Church," he wrote in his diary. "This doctrine is destined to work deeper than any other now proposed to the consideration of the people." On one hand, nonresistance reasserted "the primitive doctrine of the Cross"; on the other, it heralded new types of organization, both secular and religious, which would not trample on the human soul. "It is an Assertion of the right of Selfgovernment, and of private judgement, in which both Church

[57] Quoted in Stephen E. Whicher, ed., *Selections from Ralph Waldo Emerson* (Boston, 1957), pp. 355, 186. On Emerson and reform, see Whicher, *Freedom and Fate: An Inner Life of Ralph Waldo Emerson* (New York, 1961); and Maurice Gonnaud, *Individu et société dans l'oeuvre de Ralph Waldo Emerson. Essai de biographie spirituelle* (Paris, 1964).

[58] See Garrison to Samuel Joseph May, Sept. 24, 1838, Garrison Papers, Boston Public Library; Edmund Quincy to Alcott, Jan. 4, 1842, Alcott Papers, Harvard College Library.

and State take root."[59] His enthusiasm was most clearly revealed in a letter written to his brother after attending the 1841 nonresistance convention. He prophesied that "all things are doomed." The world of sin and error was about to be cleansed, and reformers were gathering who would "restore the worship of the True and loving God in the Hearts of men." He chose to join in the work.[60]

In Alcott's case, transcendentalist beliefs were not irrelevant to nonresistance. When other nonresistants spoke of the inconsistency between divine and human government, they tended to depict God as a distant, supernatural sovereign. Alcott identified the operation of divine government more nearly with unwritten laws of conscience knowable to the private man. From this point of view he called the democratic theory of government diabolical because it valued the decisions of masses of men over the will of God which may be discovered in "the seclusion of a single soul." "Beelzebub rules the masses," he wrote, "God individuals. The Kingdom of Truth is within, not out there in Church or State."[61]

Alcott had mastered the paradoxes of nonresistance in which divine government, self-government, and self-control became interchangeable. If he revealed a distinctive, transcendentalist understanding of the natural conscience, he also obeyed his heavenly sovereign. At one time, for example, he grew impatient with the nonresistants' discussion of whether force was sinful in circumstances of great danger. "Whoever, says Christ, is not ready to give up father and mother, wife and children, brothers and sisters, *yea, even his own life,* cannot be my disciple. Yet we make it a question!" This concern to be uncompromisingly submissive to the Almighty, however, implied an antinomian freedom on earth. Alcott went on: "I look upon the Non-Resistance Society as an assertion of the right of self-government. Why

[59] Alcott, Diary, XIII, 180, Aug. 28, 1839, Alcott Papers, Harvard College Library.

[60] Richard L. Herrnstadt, ed., *The Letters of A. Bronson Alcott* (Ames, Ia., 1969), p. 57.

[61] Shepard, ed., *Journals*, p. 136.

should I employ a church to write my creed or a state to govern me? Why not write my own creed? Why not govern myself?" Then follows the paradox: the nonresistant who should enjoy such freedom is the man "who has overcome himself."[62]

One of the most enthusiastic and talkative participants in the new movement, Alcott was also very critical of his fellow non-resistants. To some extent his criticisms were derived from his transcendentalist emphasis on the private man; nevertheless, they may help to clarify the ambiguities in the movement. In brief, he found the nonresistants too combative, too political, and too narrow in their conception of their goals.

As early as September 1839, Alcott began to show misgivings about the combativeness of the movement. He recorded in his diary doubts that the people at the nonresistance meetings could be the source of better institutions because they lacked "faith in meekness: they assume a warlike manner."[63] At the 1841 meetings he warned nonresistants against "vocabulary . . . taken from the camp." How seriously others took this warning may be guessed from the fact that, a few minutes later, Garrison was saying: "I believe in 'fighting the good fight of faith'; and I like the expression well." Alcott was arguing for a philosophy of reform in which the general behavior of reformers was their most important means of converting others, while Garrison spoke simply to the point that "the philosophy of all reform is commotion—agitation."[64] In time Alcott arrived at a perceptive, though rather bitter, analysis of Garrison's fighting spirit:

It is much to have a platform as free as the minds of the freest of the time; and this service Garrison has done for us moderns. But Garrison himself, I now discern, is far from catholicism and the comprehension of the whole truth. He does not see it. The most intolerant of men, as trenchant as an Ajax, he has not yet won those self-victories which lead to the discovery of the unconquered territory of the enemy, and

[62] *Non-Resistant*, Oct. 19, 1839, p. 4.
[63] Alcott, Diary, XIII, 262, Sept. 27, 1839, Alcott Papers, Harvard College Library.
[64] *Non-Resistant*, Nov. 19, 1841, p. 4.

so of the superior powers of those who have won themselves and are the willing subjects of self-rule.

He snuffs the prey like a vulture, nor will he rest till his beak and talons are fast in the eagle's breast and the lion has seen him torn in pieces. He has perfect skill in the use of his own weapons, nor has he ever lost a battle. He cannot give quarter even, and is as unrelenting to friends as enemies. Mercy is no attribute of his justice. He knows all the manners of the snake, and, were he self-freed, might crush his head; but, as it is, will only scotch the hydra and play with his tail.[65]

Besides finding nonresistance too combative, Alcott criticized its concern with politics. He told the first anniversary convention that he wished "governments occupied less of our thoughts." Something was amiss, he felt, in the constant debates about the evils of governments. They would be ended "whether we make it an object or not," and did not deserve much attention: "Our only reliance is in the Theocracy in the human soul. We take too much notice of states and masses, if we think them more mighty than individuals." Even the manner of the nonresistants betrayed touches of politics, that is, they declaimed at one another rather than conversing freely and spontaneously.[66]

Nonresistance appeared too political in the way in which it thought of *"influence."* In Alcott's view, the movement did not need to be concerned with the number of its adherents or their position in society. Men are most deeply impressed, he said, not by those with power, prestige, or followers, but instead by those who, like Jesus, "speak and act most simply and heartily." Reform ought to be conducted as the revival of true, simple ideas: "I believe we might get statements so clear and true, that there would no argument be needed about them." Reform, in other words, was a matter of appealing properly to the conscience, of reawakening moral sentiments. It was not a matter of mass action or political power. "Speak to the feelings and instincts," he said,

[65] Shepard, ed., *Journals,* p. 191, by permission of Little, Brown and Co. Copyright 1938, by Odell Shepard. Copyright renewed © 1966 by Odell Shepard. The entry is for Feb. 1847.

[66] *Non-Resistant,* Nov. 19, 1841, p. 4.

"and that will be sufficient."[67] He thus urged the simplification of their methods.

Alcott's third general criticism was that their goals were too narrowly conceived. For one thing, the society's name, with its stress on nonviolence, limited its scope. There was a broad movement in the land against the authority of church and state, and it should have been allowed time to clarify itself before being confined by a name. What was sought was not nonviolence, but "an entire revision of Society."[68] Moreover, the concerns of nonresistance should have extended beyond church and state; a principal concern should have been the family. "The family is the church—the family is the state—is the school." Nonresistants should attempt to govern all of their own domestic relationships with love and meekness and then try to extend the same spirit throughout society.[69] To put it another way, he thought the society should be directed toward sentimental rather than political reform.

Alcott was best known as an educational reformer. While he felt nonresistance was too narrowly conceived, an interest in education was actually a repeated theme among nonresistants.[70] Fur-

[67] *Ibid.*, Nov. 16, 1839, p. 3.

[68] Alcott, Diary, XIII, 263, Sept. 27, 1839, Alcott Papers, Harvard College Library.

[69] *Liberator*, Nov. 19, 1841, p. 4.

[70] A Michigan delegate to the 1841 convention described a school of sixty or seventy pupils in a newly settled area run on nonresistance principles (*Liberator*, Nov. 19, 1841, p. 4). Rowland Robinson, a prominent nonresistant whose son later achieved fame as a Vermont writer, began a similar venture. Oliver Johnson described Robinson's school after Alcott had explained that children's instincts are less perverted than those of adults (*Non-Resistant*, Nov. 16, 1839, p. 3). Maria Weston Chapman illustrated the truth of nonresistance from her long experience as a teacher: "The school that is managed by coercion—by force—is, in the most important respects, ungoverned" (*ibid.*, Sept. 21, 1839, p. 3). The founding convention (*ibid.*, Jan. 1839, p. 3) criticized the warlike toys and books given to children as "among the most effectual means of laying the foundation of slavery, anarchy, bloodshed and ruin." No nonresistant was more interested in education than Henry Wright, who called his two years of service as a children's minister the happiest and most useful in his lifetime (see Mary Howitt, "Memoir of Henry Clarke Wright," *Howitt's Journal*, II [1847], 133).

thermore, Alcott's belief in vicarious punishment, in which the teacher insisted that he be punished for a pupil's misbehavior, bore some resemblance to nonresistance, or the refusal to inflict punishment.[71]

Behind all of Alcott's criticisms was his desire for comprehensive, universal reform. Garrisonian nonresistance was a secular reform to be fought for with military zeal and with tactics that might be termed political. The Garrisonians often spoke of nonresistance as the fundamental principal of all reform, but they kept it as a separate reform and usually advocated a piecemeal approach to the renovation of social relations. None of this satisfied Alcott. If Alcott was clearer and more consistent than some other nonresistants and if his criticisms were frequently on target, it was in part because his interest in secular reforms, such as the abolition of slavery, took second place to his aspiration for a complete overhaul of society. His search for a broader approach to reform led him to believe that opposition to property was more important than either antislavery or nonresistance and that Garrison's cause would for a time be "lost" behind that of the transcendentalist labor reformer, Orestes Brownson (who soon became a leading convert to Roman Catholicism).[72] Alcott's search took him briefly in 1843 to a utopian attempt to found the community known as Fruitlands. He moved away from the Garrisonians, though there is no reason to believe he was ever anything but a nonresistant. As such, he was capable of clear gestures. In 1843 he refused to pay taxes to the government and finally went to jail. One of his associates explained to the *Liberator* that, while everyone agreed it was wrong to establish a religion by force, no one previously had dared to act on the principle that it was wrong to compel support of a government. The communication

---

[71] Edmund Quincy distinguished nonresistance from armed resistance: both fight evil, but "the one believes that the evil which is in the world, is to be overcome by the infliction of suffering or death upon the evil-doer; the other, by the voluntary endurance of suffering or death themselves in his stead" (*Non-Resistant*, Nov. 16, 1839, p. 3).

[72] Herrnstadt, ed., *Letters*, p. 53.

was aptly captioned, "State Slavery."[73] Henry David Thoreau, who was not a nonresistant, was nonetheless familiar with this precedent when he spent his celebrated night in jail.[74]

v

Much of the ambiguity which characterized nonresistance was due to problems in a truly antinomian understanding of the universe. On the one hand, there was no doubting the unchallengeable sovereignty of God. On the other, each individual was completely accountable for his own beliefs and behavior. From either assumption an argument could be devised against any institution which sought to coerce, govern, or enslave man. But after all intermediary authorities were rejected there still remained two potentially conflicting sovereigns—God and man. The antinomian reformers saw themselves as God's slaves and their own masters; it is hardly surprising that they took inconsistent approaches to the tasks of justifying and applying the new doctrine. In any event, nonresistance sometimes appeared to be an expression of fealty to the divine ruler and at other times to be only one movement among many involved in the piecemeal process of earthly reform.

Most of the nonresistants were abolitionists, and we must consider how they reconciled one commitment with the other. In two moods found prominently in nonresistance—quietistic endurance of the world as oppression and millenarian anticipation of a transformation of all earthly relationships—slavery had mainly a metaphorical significance. It was a sort of personal condition to be transcended in a mystery of surrender or a prototype of all the shackles that would be broken in the better time to come. Nonetheless, most of the nonresistants also desired the abolition of America's peculiar institution. How was nonresistance related to that objective?

[73] *Liberator,* Jan. 27, 1843, p. 4.
[74] See John C. Broderick, "Thoreau, Alcott, and the Poll Tax," *Studies in Philology,* LIII (1956), 612–626.

Organizationally, as Aileen Kraditor has shown, the Garrisonians tried to maintain a wall of separation between abolition and other radical reforms, particularly nonresistance.[75] It has sometimes been charged that the nonresistants aimed to foist their doctrine on the American Anti-Slavery Society. But if nonresistance was directly relevant to the schism in abolitionism around 1840, it was because Garrisonians resisted efforts to get the Anti-Slavery Society to declare it the duty of every abolitionist to vote. Even Henry Wright valued the wall of separation. He wrote that the question of voting, like that of religious beliefs, should be left "to every man's private judgment." All the constitution of the American Anti-Slavery Society required, or should require, was that every person pursue whichever course he chose as a devoted abolitionist. Nonresistants were a "mere handful" anyway, "and we should be glad if the Society would keep in its *appropriate* sphere and let us alone."[76] For all of their uncompromising perfectionism in regard to other reform movements, the nonresistants upheld a doctrine of toleration when it came to the original antislavery society. In a few years, however, they would prove bitterly antagonistic to new-style political abolitionism.

Nonresistance met with heated opposition from political and conservative abolitionists. It was accused of dereliction to the cause of the slave, and a defensive note may be detected in answers to this charge. We have previously noted Garrison's claim that the participation of prominent abolitionists in a movement asserting that to vote was to sin would not take any ballots away from antislavery forces. Perhaps defensiveness reached its limit when Henry Wright, in an article in the *Liberator,* asked himself whether he would vote if his single ballot could abolish slavery. After a tortuous explanation, he replied in the negative: even in this hypothetical situation, to vote meant to ensure the prolongation of man's bondage to man.[77] When due allowance is made for

[75] See note 3, above.
[76] *Non-Resistant,* June 15, 1839, p. 2.
[77] *Ibid.,* March 23, 1842, p. 2.

the defensive stance of nonresistance, we may still see that, in its early years, the movement was expected to contribute to the cause of abolition.

The first anniversary convention of the New England Non-Resistance Society unanimously adopted the resolution that "the abolition of slavery is involved in the doctrines of non-resistance, as the unit is included within the aggregate: for if a slaveholder become a non-resistant, he never again could . . . resort to that law of violence in which the relation of master and slave originated, and by which it must be continually sustained."[78] This almost sounds like a response to Alcott's call for statements of uncontestable verity: obviously, a nonresistant could not hold slaves. This statement does not indicate how existing slaveholders might be converted into nonresistants, and yet this was how the relevance of nonresistance to the plight of the slave was most frequently conceived. There was one curious oversight: no role was assigned to the slave, as a potential nonresistant, in winning his own liberation. But it must also be observed that nonresistance was an evangelical movement which proceeded with sublime confidence in the government of God. The slavemaster would be converted as surely as the world would be brought to recognize Christ, and the slave would be set free. This kind of "immediatism" might take a long time, but it was as reliable as the will of the Almighty.

What must be understood, finally, is the "aggregate" of which antislavery was merely a part. To Henry Wright, it was *the redemption of man from the dominion of man.*" He explained: "This is abolition. It looks to nothing less than an entire deliverance of Humanity from the thraldom of man & we would put it under the control of Him whose sole right it is to rule."[79] Similarly, Garrison, in the prospectus for the *Liberator* in December 1837, dedicated himself to the cause of "UNIVERSAL EMANCIPATION." He defined this objective as "the emancipation of our whole race

[78] *Ibid.,* Dec. 7, 1839, p. 2.
[79] Wright to Maria Weston Chapman, May 2, 1839, Weston Papers, Boston Public Library.

from the dominion of man, from the thraldom of self, from the government of brute force, from the bondage of sin—and bringing them under the dominion of God, the control of an inward spirit, the government of the law of love, and into the obedience and liberty of Christ."[80] In some ways nonresistance might have implied dereliction to the cause of the Southern slave, for it suggested that his oppression was only one among many instances of the sinfulness of force in human society. It also represented a radical quest for universal abolitionism.

But the movement revealed from the start considerable confusion and ambivalence which needed resolution before this radicalism could go through further theoretical or practical development. Such resolution was not forthcoming for most abolitionists. Although Garrisonians continued to regard human government negatively and to express their fidelity to God's higher law, few of them managed a full, consistent elaboration of these attitudes. The viewpoint of the Garrisonians remained antipolitical, but following the schisms in the antislavery movement, the nonresistance movement began a slow, steady decline.

[80] Garrisons, *Garrison*, II, 200.

IV

Coming out of Bondage

One of the most important manifestations of anarchism in ante-bellum reform was come-outerism, a type of religious hostility to the organized churches. The term "come-outerism" was slightly ambiguous because it was in general use throughout evangelical Protestantism and because it referred both to social movements outside of antislavery and to radical religious tendencies among the abolitionists themselves. It also became identified with groups of abolitionists, especially in rural New Hampshire and the factory town of Lynn, who felt that even the Garrisonians were too authoritarian and who found organized antislavery as deadening as the church. According to come-outers, any institution which frustrated human aspirations for spontaneity and impeded the governance of God over man was neither more nor less than slavery.

The term "come-outer" was part of the vernacular of revivals, where it meant a "new light," one who was converted to a public profession of faith and entered into a new relationship with the sinful world. It could be given a variety of extended meanings. It could refer, for example, to those who migrated westward, and the connection between faith and mobility was sometimes unmistakable. As one historian puts it, "come-outers in America have always been go-outers."[1] The term could even refer to the unruly volunteers who wandered to Mexico to join General Taylor and

[1] McLoughlin, *Isaac Backus*, p. 101.

fight for national glory.[2] But there were usually more radical connotations. It had Biblical roots in favorite apocalyptic texts, such
as the angel's prophecy of Babylon's fall: "Come out of her, my
people, that ye be not partakers of her sins, and that ye receive
not of her plagues" (Rev. 18:4). As derived from the revivals,
come-outerism insisted on a millennial duty to secede from sinful
institutions.

In an early study of what the revivals contributed to abolition,
Gilbert Hobbs Barnes stressed the Christian obligation to rebuke
sin: "Denunciation of the evil came first; reform of the evil was
incidental to that primary obligation."[3] But come-outerism may
suggest another evangelical contribution: it was the duty of
Christians not only to criticize evil but to sever all institutional
connections with it. To reform was to come out and, perhaps, to
create anew.

Come-outerism may be regarded as a latter-day instance in a
long tradition of *"Chrétiens sans Église,"* that is the tradition defined by a recent scholar as including "religious ideas which . . .
posit that there exists a constant antagonism between the fundamental values of Christianity and ecclesiastical institutions . . .
[and] which, for that reason, consider the totality of the religious
life organized around no matter what confessional formula and
set of rituals and sacraments as taking part in the corrupt world
of nature." Separatist, individualistic beliefs of this sort not only
incited recurrent conflicts with the Catholic hierarchy; they also
were evident throughout the "Second Reformation" of the seventeenth century in which radical protests were leveled against the
churches of the Protestant states.[4] In America the New England
Puritans detested such tendencies as "enthusiasm," or emphasis

[2] Bernard De Voto, *The Year of Decision: 1846* (Boston, 1961 [1st pub.,
1943]), p. 206. "In this decadent age," wrote De Voto, "it may be proper
to remind the reader that this is a revival phrase."

[3] Barnes, *The Antislavery Impulse, 1830–1844* (New York, 1964 [1st
pub., 1933]), p. 25.

[4] Leszek Kolakowski, *Chrétiens sans Église. La Conscience religieuse et
le lien confessionnel au XVIIe siècle,* trans. into French by Anna Posner
(Paris, 1969), pp. 9–10.

on the indwelling of the Holy Spirit in the soul of the individual Christian, "sectarianism," or the cutting up of Christ's church into small, separate sects, and "antinomianism." But Puritan beliefs allowed some room for the development of separatist and individualistic beliefs.[5] Moreover, some religious groups migrating to America—such as the Quakers, the Pilgrims, and others from continental Europe—had participated in the "Second Reformation," although they were generally caught in what Leszek Kolakowski calls "the paradox of religious individualism." "Arising . . . in opposition to the apparatus of the church, this individualism was only capable of attacking it to the degree that it was itself a collective movement; therefore it could not realize itself except by negating itself."[6] In America organized heresies could become regional orthodoxies.

Periodically, local sectarian and individualistic movements had emerged and identified themselves with either the pure spirit of the primitive Christians or the free way of life of the approaching millennium. This process was most familiar in the Great Awakening of the 1740s and the brushfire revivalism of the early nineteenth century. Sometimes these movements disintegrated swiftly; sometimes, as in the case of numerous kinds of Baptists, they achieved organizational permanence. Ultimately "sectarianism" itself became the American orthodoxy; religion in the United States, where no church was established, became a system of sects competing among themselves for the voluntary allegiance of churchgoers. Come-outerism, accordingly, had to attack not the worldliness of a single state church but the "sectarianism" of the many churches which corrupted Christian life by stressing the importance of particular, competitive rituals and doctrines. Come-outers saw themselves as advocates of unity in freedom and the myriad of denominations as the slavery from which it was necessary to separate.

[5] Edmund S. Morgan, *Visible Saints: The History of a Puritan Idea* (Ithaca, 1965); Ellwood Johnson, "Individualism and the Puritan Imagination," *American Quarterly*, XXII (1970), 230–237.
[6] Kolakowski, *Chrétiens sans Église*, p. 60.

As it affected antebellum reform, come-outerism represented the convergence of two different versions of sectarian thought, one from outside and one from within antislavery. In the first place was the old belief that true Christians ought to be religious individuals without organized churches. Eruptions of this belief tended to coincide with the growth of antislavery, and its spokesmen were regular participants at reform conventions. Second was increasing disenchantment with the churches on the part of abolitionists who scarcely doubted the necessity of sectarian institutions. The denominations sometimes argued that antislavery, organized outside the churches, was a sectarian religious enterprise. Abolitionists could agree that "the church *ought* to be an anti slavery Society (for certainly its charter [the Bible] is both an Anti Slavery Constitution and Declaration of Sentiments), and if it were there would be no need of other organizations for the same object."[7] But a dead church, in effect, made antislavery societies legitimate. Why not go a step farther and consider antislavery itself as a new nonsectarian religion restoring ancient Christian beliefs? Perhaps no abolitionist approached come-outerism in quite so orderly a fashion. But even one of the oldest writings on immediatism in America, George Bourne's *The Book and Slavery Irreconcilable* (1816), may be interpreted as being "far more interested in the purification of religion than in slavery as an institution."[8] And in the 1840s, when antislavery drew some support from free spirits who sought to rid religion of institutional impurities and when abolitionists, at the same time, were pulled farther away from churches which failed to preach the gospel of freedom, the prospects of antislavery as a religious movement could appear very exciting.

Each of these converging forces—revivalistic come-outerism and antiecclesiastical abolitionism—must be discussed separately. Out of their convergence arose some confusing questions, related to the paradox of religious individualism. Was come-outerism the

[7] See the troubled letter on the churches by J. A. Thome in *Weld-Grimké Letters*, II, 750–751.

[8] Davis, "Emergence of Immediatism," p. 224.

renunciation of all sects? Or was it the replacement of old pro-slavery institutions with new, hopefully freer ones?

ii

Trying to recapture the quality of antebellum reform for his readers at the end of the century, Thomas Wentworth Higginson had to explain that the "refined votaries" of transcendentalism were generally not social radicals. Antislavery, in particular, re-lied on "a less educated contingent—known popularly as 'Come-Outers,'—a name then as familiar as is that of the Salvation Army today." The factories, especially at Lynn, were radical, and even uneducated shoe workers plunged into Second Adventism. Come-outers were likewise plentiful on Cape Cod, "and the 'Cape Cod-ders' were a recognized subdivision at reform meetings." Their parliamentary disorderliness was a constant problem; they enthusi-astically harrassed clergymen. Their protest, Higginson remem-bered, was not against religion "but against its perversions alone."[9]

Higginson was describing not the abolitionists who parted with proslavery denominations but the less well known, enthusiastic movements which often supported abolitionism. These move-ments have never been carefully studied, and information about them is scarce. They were probably short-lived and illiterate, per-haps in some cases clandestine. They seized a good deal of public attention, however, and some account may be pieced together from second-hand reports.

There is a vivid portrait of a come-outer sect which began in Lower Canada in the 1820s when some people "began to talk about the deadness and unworthiness of all churches, as bodies; and they were anxious to separate from them, in order to com-pound a more perfect society." After selling their belongings and starting a journey toward the Southwest, they gathered about fifty converts in Vermont and New York. An attempt was made at cooperation with the Shakers, but the Shakers were too neat in

[9] Higginson, *Cheerful Yesterdays*, pp. 115–117. This would, of course, play hob with the theory that abolitionism depended on displaced social elites.

the eyes of these "Pilgrims," as they called themselves. These come-outers apparently believed in wearing clothes on the body without changing—"and the more patched and particoloured the better." They also acquired a leader, called "the Prophet," who led them near New Madrid in the lower Mississippi Valley. They marched in single file, chanting "Praise God! Praise God!" The tribe was soon killed off by a swamp pestilence, partly because of their leader's revelations that they should not bury their dead and partly because they refused to settle in a safe, well-drained spot. They claimed, instead, that they were past the calculating wisdom of this world and furthermore that suffering was consistent with their mission. Another source of hardship was that frontier boatmen joined their numbers, took them at "their profession of having no regard for the world, or the things of it, and robbed them of all their money."[10]

No account of come-outers is exactly typical of others, and this one plainly has an air of folklore about it. Without taking the details too literally, we may notice two themes which run through much of come-outerism and, for that matter, through much of the Christian adventist tradition: first, social discontent and the search for a better life, and second, hostility to the things of this world, from conventions of dress to money. In the 1830s and 1840s antislavery provided a means of bringing these themes together in a general repudiation of "slavery"; it was then less necessary to be a go-outer as well as a come-outer. But the same themes persist, as the example of the Hutchinson Family Singers may indicate. The Hutchinsons were a large family of come-outers and abolitionists, who were gifted with beautiful voices and gave extremely successful concerts throughout the North. Although prosperity allowed them to underwrite a reform community in the West, their money was deeply troublesome to them. Judson Hutchinson, the brother who was most anxious to escape the formalities of the world—he later killed himself—disrupted at least one concert

[10] Timothy Flint, *Recollections of the Last Ten Years, Passed in Occasional Residences and Journeyings in the Valley of the Mississippi* (New York 1968 [1st pub., 1826]), pp. 275–280. See Richard H. Thornton, *An American Glossary* (reprint ed., New York, 1962), *s.v.* "Come-outers."

by throwing into the audience all his silver money and then the receipts the singers had collected.[11]

As come-outerism came closer to the secular reform movements, including abolitionism, it may have inspired forms of working-class organization. In a novel published much later, Moncure D. Conway, who had been deeply involved in antebellum religious controversies, portrayed the "Out-and-Outers" as a secret, anti-capitalist, violent society of textile workers.[12] It is not certain in this case who mingled religious release with labor reform—Conway, employers, or the workmen. Conway was most likely taking a novelist's liberty with the facts that come-outerism and other kinds of adventism flourished in some factory towns and that come-outerism signified a greater disaffection with changing contemporary society than was evident in other modes of reform.

In general come-outerism was a social movement, or a series of local movements, showing both revivalistic exaltation and discontent with things of the world. There were reports of fence walking and animal imitation in the spirit of frontier camp meetings. Some come-outers were said to renounce property and money and to go naked in the summer. Their intention was to escape from church, state, and every form of "social bondage."[13] An important conviction of come-outers was that men and women are equal in religion and all other things, not subordinated one to the other.[14] Predictably, rumors circulated that they were against marriage as well as against church and government.[15]

[11] Higginson, *Contemporaries*, pp. 335–336; Carol Ryrie Brink, *Harps in the Wind: The Story of the Singing Hutchinsons* (New York, 1947).

[12] Moncure D. Conway, *Pine and Palm* (New York, 1887), pp. 42–46.

[13] Henry C. Kittredge, *Cape Cod: Its People and Their History* (Boston and New York, 1930), pp. 257–260, 288–291; Thomas Low Nichols, *Forty Years of American Life* (London, 1864), II, 45–46; P. Douglass Gorrie, *The Churches and Sects of the United States* (New York, 1850), pp. 224 ff.; John Hayward, *The Book of Religions; Comprising the Views, Creeds, Sentiments, or Opinions, of All the Principal Religious Sects in the World* . . . (Concord, N.H., 1845), pp. 177–181.

[14] William Hepworth Dixon, *New America* (Philadelphia, 1867), pp. 449–457. To Dixon come-outerism seemed the "final fruit" of a "seceding spirit" and "excess of freedom" found throughout American life in the years before the Civil War.

[15] Clipping in Autobiographical Collections, 1840, Alcott Papers, Harvard

The "Cape Codders" were the most notorious exemplars of come-outerism, and fortunately there exists a fairly good account, based on first-hand reports, of their religious beliefs and practices. They numbered two or three hundred persons who had seceded from their churches for various causes—sometimes because of disbelief in a doctrine, but "chiefly that they might enjoy 'the largest liberty of the sons of God.' " They had neither organization nor church building. They passed money and goods easily among themselves. And they applied to religion the disjunction between divine government and earthly government which also existed in nonresistance.

Their common bond seems to be a desire "to establish the kingdom of Heaven," or produce in their own neighborhoods such a state of things that each man shall live a divine life,—but in his own way, fettered by no church, creed, or minister. They distrust "organizations," but place their faith in "the church of the Holy Spirit which is in the heavens." Each good man, say they, is "the only true church on the earth."

Two men were indeed called "ministers," but only in a sense thought to originate in the primitive church. That is, anyone could speak in their meetings, and anyone could perform a baptism, but ministers were recognized leaders who spoke more or less regularly. No distinction was made between church officers and laity. The Cape Codders asserted: *"There is no profane or secular calling to a Christian."* Similarly, they believed that all meals were the Lord's Supper if one's heart was Christian, though occasionally they celebrated an informal communion. They met on Sunday "for convenience and utility," but also met on other days and insisted that life and work were more important than meetings. Among the books they praised were the writings of the early mystic Jacob Boehme and the great seventeenth-century Quaker leader George Fox (Fox's journal, said one woman, contained "almost everything"). They used the Bible constantly but

College Library. Alcott gave the clipping the heading, "Groton Convention," It is unsigned, and I have been unable to identify the author.

were concerned not to worship it: *"It is the Scripture of the Word, not the Word itself."*[16] Lacking creeds, church governance, and membership requirements, the Cape Codders represented to some reformers of the period a model of harmonious self-government, founded in piety. They were in the long tradition of religious individualism and mysticism; in their own time, they held an attitude toward religion much like that of the nonresistants toward politics. They believed in the superintendence of God, without need of intermediaries, and they felt their lives were adequately regulated in this belief.

The Cape Codders were not primarily reformers, but they took an active interest in reforms, particularly in abolitionism and in reform conventions on religious subjects. Sometimes, as Higginson noted, their participation was disruptive. Reform conventions must frequently have resembled solemn church meetings, and all come-outers had a reputation for returning to disrupt churches from which they had withdrawn. On the other hand, it is important to observe that they did feel called to reform meetings and attended them sometimes in spite of considerable obstacles. There is a description, for example, of a "white bearded queer chap"— one of "the original Cape Cod Come-outers"—who walked from the Cape and slept overnight in a hayloft in order to attend an 1848 convention held in Boston to discuss the standing in Christianity of the Sabbath. He was disruptive, but not because he disapproved of the proceedings. As the speakers, mainly abolitionists, explained that all days were equally holy in Christ or that the special significance of the Sabbath was an invention of priestcraft, he would cry out, " 'Amen, Truth—Praise the Lord— Go it brother' & the like."[17] How much of the notorious disruptiveness of the Cape Codders was the result of revivalistic exuberance rather than explicit protest against organizational forms is impossible to determine.

Extensive descriptions of come-outerism may be found in

[16] *Ibid.*
[17] Wright Journal (BPL), XXXVIIb, 1–3, March 24, 1848.

Parker Pillsbury's *Acts of the Anti-Slavery Apostles,* an exciting volume of reminiscences published in 1884.[18] Pillsbury had been one of the most anticlerical of abolitionists, one who blamed the churches for the perseverance of slavery; much of his agitation had taken place in rural New England.[19] Probably his account exaggerates the antislavery content of come-outerism in general, although it does include long excerpts from contemporary documents. Many other come-outers were closer to the antislavery impulse than were the Cape Codders. Come-outers often left the churches in protest against two kinds of slavery: denominational tolerance of slavery in the South and the cold formality of doctrine and ritual that frustrated individual spontaneity in the North. As on the Cape, loosely organized substitutes for conventional religious practices were developed. Even Pillsbury's examples, however, seem more like latter-day versions of the tradition of *"Chrétiens sans Église"* than expressions of the outrage of modern secular reform societies against the churches. But it is also significant that come-outerism and reform were converging.

The Cape Codders stressed a sort of voluntary self-discipline akin to the principles of nonresistance. It is not surprising, therefore, that some come-outers were drawn to meetings of the New England Non-Resistance Society. In 1839 and 1840, Michigan and Indiana come-outers sent delegates to the nonresistance meetings to report on their experiments in setting up congregations each of which acted "as a Church and State unto itself." They criticized the authoritarianism of ordinary political and ecclesiastical arrangements; their goal was a society of unwritten law where sanctions and incentives flowed only from the moral approval of the group. They thought they anticipated the type of noncoercive government which would be known in the millennium. Although they favored family property and condemned community property as "anti-republican and anti-reformation," they gave new meaning to the confluence of come-outerism and

18 Pillsbury, *Acts of the Anti-Slavery Apostles* (Boston, 1884).
19 See Louis Filler, "Parker Pillsbury: An Anti-Slavery Apostle," *New England Quarterly,* XIX (1946), 315–337.

reform; quite plainly, they gave evidence of a communitarian impulse.[20] But like other manifestations of rural come-outerism, after a flurry of reform activity they left little record of their efforts.

There was one further dimension of religious come-outerism. For the most part the movement seems to have been fairly illiterate and to have arisen from the evangelical churches; however, the revolt of the highly literate transcendentalists within Unitarianism was related to come-outerism. Transcendentalists renounced the institutional coldness of the religion advocated by their fathers. They denied that religious wisdom was the preserve of the clergy as opposed to more common people, and they believed, in the words George Ripley used in resigning from his Boston pastorate, that religion consisted "not in any speculative doctrine, but in a divine life." (Ripley went on to guide the communitarians at Brook Farm.) As others resigned or were driven from their pastorates, the term "come-outerism" was extended to apply to a number of "Jerusalem wildcat" churches following the example of Theodore Parker's society in Boston. No claim was made of institutional sanctity; what was sought was the willingness of a free congregation to listen to a minister who held no denominational commission, simply because inspiration was found there.[21] These free churches, of course, were not guilty of tolerating Southern slavery.

An important distinction must be made, however, between this kind of come-outerism and the more rural and enthusiastic kinds which we have been discussing. The spontaneity of the Cape would very likely be taken as disruptiveness in Parker's meetings at the Melodeon. A sermon, even when given in lecture form and outside denominational auspices, would still be a sermon to the ears of anyone who wanted all Christians to be liberated from

[20] *Non-Resistant*, July 6, 1839, pp. 1, 3; Aug. 12, 1840, p. 1.
[21] William R. Hutchison, *The Transcendentalist Ministers: Church Reform in the New England Renaissance* (New Haven, 1959); Perry Miller, ed., *The Transcendentalists* (Cambridge, Mass., 1966), p. 252; Higginson, *Cheerful Yesterdays*, pp. 113–114, 130.

the institutional formality of the church. There was a range of possible attitudes toward religion between these two extreme cases of come-outerism—between, say, the large audience listening to an address by Parker, Higginson, or some other favorite minister and the small gathering of enthusiasts acting out their belief that all should be free to speak and reciting "Go it, brother," when they liked what they heard. The point is that come-outers confronted, in various ways, the paradox of institutionalizing their escape from religious institutions. And their meetings, as we might expect, could give birth to considerable antagonism.

Sometimes disagreements simply concerned the procedures to be followed at meetings of come-outers, for there were attempts to unify the movement. One of the most articulate come-outers expressed his anger at the procedures of an 1845 meeting in New York in these words:

One reform Christian Convention I was at, I rode forty-three miles in the rain to attend; and when there, a committee of talented men were chosen to tell us what we were to talk about; and these men were identified with the very errors that wanted to be opposed. . . . All that is wanted in a Convention is, to have liberty for all to speak, one at a time.[22]

There were underlying issues which were not simply procedural, issues concerning the extent to which the duty of coming-out entailed the duty to build new institutions and concerning the possibility of any contemporary institutions sharing in the government of God. These issues distressed the most famous attempt to unite the come-outers, the 1840 Groton Convention on Christian Union, in which the nonresistant Edmund Quincy was an elected officer, Bronson Alcott one of the most vigorous participants, and Theodore Parker an interested observer; among the roughly 275 other New Yorkers and New Englanders who attended were a goodly complement of Cape Codders. According to a neutral report:

[22] Alfred Wells of Colosse, N.Y., in *Liberator*, Jan. 10, 1845, p. 4. For Wells's praise of another convention, see *ibid.*, Nov. 7, 1845, p. 4.

The house seemed to divide into two general parties—the one maintaining that local Churches were a sort of divine organization, with
peculiar authority and prerogatives—and the other that they were a
purely human organization, or voluntary association, which could not
in the nature of things assume any authority or prerogatives not possessed by the individuals of which they were composed.[23]

Both parties rejected notions of outside authority, but within de-
centralist doctrines there was still plenty of leeway for antagonism. Local ties and awe of God were stronger than the sense of
a growing national movement.

iii

The varieties of come-outerism considered thus far arose, in
the main, outside antislavery circles. They made a sensation in
rumor and report. They also inspired abolitionists who grew dis-
enchanted with the refusal of the churches to condemn slaveholding and expel slavemasters. The view developed that there
was a community of purpose between abolitionism and come-
outerism, that the latter was simply antislavery in religion. This
view seems oversimplified, whether meant to attack or support
either movement. But the two movements did give voice to similar antiauthoritarian sentiments: no man, no slaveholder, no
priest could stand sinlessly between another man and God. Both
movements shared in the spirit of what Ernst Cassirer called
"the actual central principle of Protestantism":

the affirmation that "no one can believe for another"; that not only in
religion, but in the whole circle of life as well, "everyone must stand
on his own and dare to wager his entire self"; that there exists "no kind
of inspiration outside the sphere of personal experience," that "the
deepest, indeed the only form of self-experience was the experience
of conscience."[24]

For a time at least antislavery and come-outerism, sharing simi-

[23] *Practical Christian*, Sept. 1, 1840, p. 2.
[24] Quoted and paraphrased in Staughton Lynd, *Intellectual Origins of
American Radicalism* (New York, 1969), p. 34.

larly in this spirit, promised to converge; and our discussion must turn from developments starting outside antislavery to antiecclesiastical tendencies among the antislavery reformers themselves.

Such tendencies were by no means restricted to the Garrisonians. Abolitionists generally felt a libertarian impulse in religion; moreover, they had to face disappointment with churches showing no zeal for reform. The conservative abolitionist William Jay described a pattern which became familiar:

It often happens when an abolitionist abandons an alleged pro-slavery church he finds no other that suits him. Hence the public worship of God and the sacraments are neglected. Gradually he and his family learn to live without God in the world, and finally enter upon that broad road which leads to destruction.

And yet, as Louis Filler has pointed out, even Jay could not avoid criticizing a church which "has been with few exceptions cold, secular and devoted to the sum of all villainies."[25] In these words of Jay, both the proslavery stance and formal coldness of the church are criticized. The distinction was unlikely to be meaningful to abolitionists whose commitment to the cause of temporal freedom for the slaves was linked to personal searches for liberation from sin. A good example would be the case of Sarah and Angelina Grimké, who, in departing from "the spiritual bondage" which they had found in the Society of Friends, were looking for a wider field of self-expression than either denominational or reform organizations would allow.[26] For a time they were very close to the nonresistants of New England, but that supposedly liberated circle proved as constraining as the Quakers. "They wanted us," wrote Sarah, "to live out William Lloyd Garrison, not the convictions of our own souls; entirely unaware that they were exhibiting . . . the genuine spirit of slaveholding, by wishing to curtail the sacred privilege of conscience."[27] They found their

[25] Filler, *The Crusade against Slavery, 1830–1860* (New York, 1960), p. 116; cf. Wyatt-Brown, *Lewis Tappan,* p. 311.

[26] See *Weld-Grimké Letters,* I, 373, 402, and *passim.*

[27] Quoted in Higginson, *Contemporaries,* pp. 250–251.

soulmate in Theodore Weld, whom Angelina married in 1838, and developed a sort of domestic circle of uninhibited religious worship. Two important features of their famous wedding were that they "could not conscientiously consent to be married by a clergyman" and that they refused to "bind themselves to any pre-conceived form of words." The nearest thing to an act of authority among the friends who gathered to marry them was that Garrison read a certificate. The Weld-Grimké wedding was one of the most beautiful moments in the romantic come-outer movement among reformers.[28]

The quest for personal liberation from repressive institutions was not always so pronounced, and come-outerism led to the establishment of hundreds of new local churches, regional associations, even denominations. In most cases the problem was mainly the refusal of an old body to adopt an antislavery position; the remedy was therefore not to escape from all churches but to start fresh ones which took the desired position.[29] Confused with these secessions was the idea promoted by New York abolitionists, especially Gerrit Smith, that there could be only one church in any locality and that higher bodies might rightfully be organized along geographical lines, but never doctrinal ones. This form of antisectarianism was closely allied with the Liberty Party (it will demand further attention in a subsequent analysis of political antislavery).

Although come-outerism undeniably transcended party lines in the schisms within abolitionism, it was probably strongest among the followers of Garrison. It may also have been more anarchistic, for they were generally less interested in creating new churches and denominations. Their estrangement from the old-line churches was so severe, and they associated true religion with freedom so insistently, that come-outerism took a variety of forms in their lives.

[28] Weld-Grimké Letters, II, 678–679.

[29] William Goodell, Slavery and Anti-Slavery; A History of the Great Struggle in Both Hemispheres; With a View of the Slavery Question in the United States (New York, 1855), p. 544; cf. Douglas C. Stange, Radicalism for Humanity: A Study of Lutheran Abolitionism (St. Louis, 1970).

Prominent Garrisonians proudly called themselves come-outers. Garrison had admitted as early as 1836 that religious scruples barred him from being a partisan of human creeds and ceremonies, and by 1844 he described himself as a come-outer.[30] The escaped slave Frederick Douglass was a come-outer who preached on the theme that he remained a fugitive because American religion doomed him to continuing bondage. Douglass played heavily on the metaphorical meanings of slavery, and he was a source of encouragement to those who escaped from churches which failed to deny fellowship to slaveholders and which insisted on formal doctrines. In Lynn he preached on the utility of prayer to the slave preparing to run away. Parker Pillsbury wrote: "And Douglass might have added, perhaps he did add, you *'Come-outers' are but fugitive slaves escaped from your spiritual and ecclesiastical plantations.*"[31] Douglass transmitted a similar message to a listener in Millville, Massachusetts, where he was denied use of the meetinghouse. "Frederick the fugitive" lacked the formal credentials required by the church; but like all those striving to overthrow "*all* slavery" he would accept credentials only "from Him 'who came to preach deliverance to the captive.' "[32] In some ways come-outerism was not separate from antislavery reform; it represented instead the belief that there were forms of slavery from which the abolitionist must escape.

For the Garrisonians, nonresistance and come-outerism were closely related movements. In nonresistance there were repeated signs of an attempt to regain an ideal church in which the voluntary laying on of hands was not formalized and corrupted by secular force. Edmund Quincy found models for reform organizations in the disciples of Jesus and the seventeenth-century followers of George Fox. Maria Weston Chapman explained that the "church originally" and "voluntary associations" of her day were essentially the same.[33] The New England Non-Resistance

[30] Garrisons, *Garrison*, II, 112; *Liberator*, Jan. 12, 1844, p. 4.
[31] *Herald of Freedom*, Feb. 16, 1844, p. 2; Pillsbury, *Acts*, pp. 482–484, 322–323.
[32] *Practical Christian*, June 11, 1843, p. 3.
[33] *Liberator*, July 2, 1841, p. 2; May 14, 1841, p. 3.

Society was a simple, peaceful, voluntary sect. Its executive committee gave full freedom of speech to its traveling agent, Henry Wright. They would not presume to tell him what to say because effective arguments could emerge only from the individual heart. They would send him suggestions occasionally, but never instructions, for they felt that a man "who yields his own judgment . . . in obedience to the will of any executive committee, is not fit for the office of a teacher of divine truth."[34] Here was the kind of clergy a purified church required!

The best-known form of come-outerism was carried out by Stephen S. Foster, the man historians usually have in mind when they mention the Garrisonians and come-outerism. Foster perfected the tactic of rising in the middle of church services to speak in behalf of Negroes in bondage. He used the disruptions he caused and the beatings and imprisonments he suffered as a set of devices to focus attention on slavery. There are problems, however, in linking Foster to come-outerism. Except that he specialized in disrupting churches, it is difficult to connect him to the come-outers' religious commitments. He seems not to have been concerned with the ecstasy of secession from the churches, nor does he seem to have experimented with liberated forms of religious practice. Rather, he entered all sorts of churches to correct their position on the particular issue of slavery. To be sure, he was uplifted by "conquering my own servile slavish fear of man"[35]—there were slaveries from which all abolitionists had to be fugitives. But he developed a philosophy of free speech rather than a vision of the true church.

One of Foster's allies, Thomas Parnell Beach, breathed the come-outer spirit more deeply. After his conversion to the antislavery cause, Beach told the New Hampshire congregation to which he was minister that an individual alone could judge whether he had faith. He released them from their contract and nullified a promissory note as well. Rejecting any denomination but a religious life, he stepped down from the pulpit, explained

[34] *Non-Resistant*, Feb. 2, 1839, p. 3.
[35] Pillsbury, *Acts*, p. 266. There is not as yet an adequate study of Foster.

that the congregation should be as free to speak as their minister, and finally attacked the mummery of sermon writing. Thereafter he joined Foster in interrupting services and was jailed for three months on a charge brought by the Quaker assembly of Newburyport, which was not moved by his claim to be following the practice of George Fox and Edward Burroughs.[36]

Beach then published a newspaper, *A Voice from Jail,* in which he stressed the right of unlimited speech as crucial to regeneration. One correspondent in a conceit of federal theology congratulated him on his powerful position: "*You* are not only in slavery, but universal humanity is enslaved in your person." It was a vantage point for demolishing the church and through it the public will that fostered slavery.[37] Beach enjoyed the paradox of coming out: he gained liberation by giving himself up. Although this kind of coming out was not designed simply as an antislavery tactic, as was Foster's version, it stood very close to antislavery.

Since the Society of Friends supposedly was based on traditions of nonresistance, free meeting, and the priesthood of all believers, come-outerism appealed markedly to those who found the Society disloyal to its past.[38] William Bassett, a leading abolitionist, nonresistant, and come-outer, had been virtually driven out from the company of Friends. He had exasperated them by a published indictment of their prejudice and silence on the slavery question. Worse still, he charged that they were imitating other sects in forcing obedience to *"the church"* and suppressing private judgment. They were forsaking George Fox's doctrine of the "new covenant—that Christ will teach His people himself." But perhaps the root of Bassett's disaffection lies in this description of the Society, abstract from slavery or doctrine: "The light of its ancient testimonies has become dim, and instead of their life-giving power, we find little but a cold and heartless formality."[39]

[36] *Ibid.,* pp. 94–95, 302–323.

[37] *Herald of Freedom,* Dec. 16, 1842, p. 3; Dec. 30, 1842, p. 3.

[38] For resentment of Quaker apostasy, see *Liberator,* Dec. 30, 1839, p. 4; March 20, 1840, p. 2; March 27, 1840, p. 2; May 8, 1840, p. 1. For a narrative of tensions leading to Quaker come-outerism, see Elizabeth Buffum Chace, *Anti-Slavery Reminiscences* (Central Falls, R.I., 1891).

[39] The text of this indictment is in [William Bassett, ed.], *Proceedings*

It would be hard to locate a better brief statement of the discontent of the come-outers.

Like some other abolitionists whose commitments to social reform were related to desires for personal liberation, William Bassett seemed to be seeking something for which he lacked words. He brought to his search two ideas we have met previously. He told the Friends that God's power precluded human assessments of the results of following divine commands. Second, he believed every man had access to all truth.[40] Evidently in his longing for freedom and vitality he could not endure the ambiguity in these two beliefs. In the spring of 1845 other come-outers were saddened to learn that he had become a "Rechabite." The rituals of this temperance organization appalled them: "It was painful to see so many men who are wise in other things, performing, at the dictation of organization, such tomfoolery,—and instead of being men and putting away childish things, decking themselves out with scarves, badges, tassels, &c., and going through with such solemn mummery." It was, to the eyes of a come-outer, a new sect, based on the Old Testament. What about Bassett? "I had known him as a stiff Quaker, almost a Pharisee, in his sec-

---

of the *Society of Friends in the Case of William Bassett* (Worcester, 1840), pp. 13–15. One passage in Bassett's account of his expulsion (p. 17) is especially interesting. When the overseers were explaining to him the duty to obey the decisions of the Society, "in order to enforce this Papish doctrine, one of the overseers . . . brought with him 'Barclay's Anarchy of the Ranters,' which he wanted me to read." Bassett expressed admiration for the book and immediately read "some extracts showing that by 'the church' whose decisions Barclay considered infallible, he did not mean any outward body of men, as such, but 'all those that truly and really have received and hold the truth as it is in Jesus;' and that we are to bring their conclusions to 'the test or examination of the spirit of God in ourselves.' . . . On my reading these extracts, the individual who brought the book observed that, *that* was not the part which he wished me to read!" Bassett explained to the *Non-Resistant* (June 15, 1839, p. 2) that the great principles of the Friends could be advanced only outside the denomination.

[40] Bassett, *Letter to a Member of the Society of Friends, in Reply to Objections against Joining Anti-Slavery Societies* (Boston, 1837), pp. 38–39; *Liberator*, Jan. 15, 1841, p. 1. Bassett was editor of the *Reformer* (Worcester) and Essex County *Washingtonian* (Lynn).

tarian exclusiveness,—more alarmed at an extra roll in a member's coat-collar, than an *extra roll* in the man. . . . I had seen him . . . come out of that sectarian enclosure, and stand free in God's great temple." Now "he had got back again into bondage."[41] Bassett was not the only case of recoil from the undefined freedom sought by come-outerism. Though he sadly disappointed some come-outers, he remained an ardent abolitionist. Come-outerism could provoke intemperate and sometimes unfair criticism among reformers.

The Garrisonians exhibited a double-edged sort of religious individualism; they could, at one and the same time, pay respect to the absolute sovereignty of God and yet come strikingly close to skepticism. In a world without ecclesiastical authority or established creeds, what was to indicate truth except individual, private judgment? There even arose among come-outers, as previously among the Unitarians, a dispute over the authenticity of miracles and the plenary inspiration of Scripture. While come-outerism ordinarily seems completely God-oriented and holds the churches to judgment by a higher law, it was obliged to allow so much room to human intelligence that it could sometimes plausibly be accused of "*Deism.*" Having abandoned their churches on the grounds that Biblical Christianity had been forsaken, come-outers were apt to argue subsequently that even the Bible must be judged by "the *amount of truth*" it contained.[42] This was potentially true of all come-outerism—and it was true with a vengeance of the Garrisonians.

On the one hand, the Garrisonians honored the ideal of a fully religious life, eschewed institutional connections with sin, and prophesied the impending judgment of an awesome God. These attitudes could be combined in chilling forecasts of conflict.[43] More frequently, they were expressed in milder forms, such as the proposition that every aspect of daily living should be carried

[41] *The Pioneer*, March 26, 1845, p. 2.

[42] See the discussion of Hayward's *Book of Religions* in *Practical Christian*, Sept. 3, 1842, pp. 2, 4; Oct. 29, 1842, pp. 1–2.

[43] A good example is Pillsbury's editorial, "The Warfare," in *Herald of Freedom*, Sept. 8, 1840, p. 2.

out in a holy way and that institutional churches, with their special days and rites, minimized the importance of religion by giving legitimacy to the separation of the secular and divine. On the other hand, the drift of their thought ultimately placed limits on the power of God. In curious ways the Garrisonians tended to secularize their own religious impulses. They chose, for example, to make the case that every day and all aspects of life should be regarded as holy by means of an "Anti-Sabbath" movement. This was to pursue the goal of true religion with tactics borrowed from secular reform, and rather negative ones at that. All that was needed for reform was to remove certain institutional errors; the proper assault on error was to call conventions to discuss the matter. Increasingly, Garrison and his followers emphasized "enlightened reason" and freedom of speech; they spoke of absolute moral truths which neither the Bible nor even God had any right to ignore. There were tendencies in the direction of a religion of humanity: nothing could be truly religious which did not serve mankind. This side of Garrisonian come-outerism may be explained in two ways. First, it was obviously concerned with the tactics of agitation and reform and grew out of arguments with conservative churchmen.[44] Second, it may have had sources in the logic of religious individualism. Belief in divine sovereignty, without earthly intermediaries, always had a tendency to throw man back on his own self-government.

Although there had been promising signs of convergence between types of come-outerism arising outside antislavery and the growing religious radicalism of the abolitionists, the promise was not fulfilled. In the end we miss among the abolitionists the feeling of escape and unrestraint that is evident among the more rural or working-class come-outers. The expectations of the Garrisonians, for the most part, were held in check by the purposes of secular reform societies; in this sense they were really institutional reformers who harnessed the vision of anarchy to the

---

[44] See Kraditor, *Means and Ends,* ch. 4, "Religion and the Good Society."

ends of antislavery. If one were looking for unhampered anarchistic ideas in antebellum America, however, this convergence
between come-outerism and antislavery would still be the proper
place to look. Out of this convergence appeared new radical figures and movements—as anarchistic as anything in their time.
One consequence was a great deal of conflict, sometimes playful,
but finally tragic, between radical come-outers and Garrison.

iv

If come-outerism frequently became identified with reform activities, it could also work at cross-purposes with them. For one
thing, there could be a curious selfishness in the loss of self which
religious perfectionists sought. According to one come-outer peri-
odical, giving was more blessed than receiving, and thus the
abolitionist might have more to gain than the slave. Guiding him
past sect and wealth, the antislavery spirit drew him "to Christ
the AUTHOR of Anti-Slavery—and so in making others free he
shall himself be made FREE INDEED."[45] In addition, the objective of religious purification, however vaguely defined, could
be given a higher priority in the thinking of come-outers than
any particular social reform. The link between come-outerism
and antislavery could easily be broken. One man reluctantly
canceled his subscription to the *Liberator* because God had indicated that "it is not my duty to meddle with any society, that is
set up to exclusively put down any particular sin, but simply to
stick close to the power of God in my soul, that opposes every
sin." He was at rest among the invisible company of saints,
moved, like "so many little wheels," by the inspiration of Christ.[46]
The task of harnessing together the goals of internal purity and
influence on society was not easy. Those free spirits who resigned
from organized reform, however, did not cause serious problems
for those who remained committed to hastening social change.

The Garrisonians were greatly troubled, on the other hand, in
dealing with come-outers who wished to reform the reform socie-

45 *The Disciple,* reprinted in *Herald of Freedom,* Sept. 30, 1842, p. 1.
46 Alfred Wells in *Liberator,* Apr. 17, 1846, p. 1.

ties and convert them into models of the purest sort of free meetings or spontaneous religious activity. Garrison found opponents of this temper especially in the factory town of Lynn, Massachusetts and rural New Hampshire. Both places produced articulate spokesmen; therefore we can examine their versions of come-outerism in some detail.

At Lynn come-outerism was frequently called no-organizationism, and as such was amplified into a general philosophy. Less emphasis was placed on the duty of escaping from the churches than on the evils of any organization. No-organizationists pursued the logic of nonresistance to its farthest reaches: all coercion is sinful.

No-organizationism differed from come-outerism in its diminished attention to the awesome power of God and its increased appreciation of the sentiments of man. But this is to draw distinctions more narrowly than they really existed. No-organizationism began with hostility to the church, and it echoed familiar strains of protest against the materialism of the world. One no-organizationist decided it was a sin to earn a living except by tilling the soil. The movement was distinctive, however, in the special animus it developed against the ways in which reform societies resembled the churches. The same no-organizationist who castigated all vocations except farming also condemned organized antislavery as "the greatest hindrance to the anti-slavery enterprise, because of its sectarianism"; he urged abolitionists to comply with their own advice "when they called upon others to leave church organizations." Garrison, aware of this threat, tried without success to get the New England Anti-Slavery conventions to censure the idea of no-organization. In his view, no-organization, although its attacks came from a different direction, was like the "*new* organization" of conservative abolitionists who had left the American Anti-Slavery Society. Both stood "in diametrical opposition to the genius of the anti-slavery enterprise."[47]

The chief representative of no-organizationism in Lynn was Henry Clapp, Jr., a very articulate editor for whom the Garri-

[47] Garrisons, *Garrison*, III, 23–25.

sonians had little use. "I know of no more strenuous advocates of 'law and order,'" he wrote, "than that class of persons called 'no-organizationists.'"

It is *because* they love law and hate anarchy, that they resist the un-reasonable edicts of self-constituted authority, and deny infallibility to that God of organization, *the popular voice.* They see nothing of the beauty of order in a gathering of men and women, each of whom is bitted, and bridled, and kept in check, by an officious chairman. But they do see the beauty of order, in its highest development, where the same people, attracted together by a common thought, exhibit that true "peace," whose only "bond" is unity of spirit.[48]

This statement reveals that there was considerable affinity be-tween nonresistance and no-organizationism in spite of the an-tagonism between Clapp and Garrison. Both movements para-doxically insisted that they were not anarchistic, no-government movements, that in rejecting conventional means of securing or-der they were simply looking for a higher principle of perfect harmony. No-organizationism differed from nonresistance in its open recognition of the paradoxes of anarchy and order, in its attention to the problem of how people should associate with one another after liberation, and in its assault on the reform societies as well as on governments and churches. More than anything else, no-organizationists disliked the paraphernalia of officers, committees, agendas, and orations at reform conventions.

No-organizationism also showed considerable affinity with the Quaker ideal of free meeting, as did so much else in come-outer-ism. This religious concern for the quality of their meetings blended with the nonresistants' repudiation of earthly politics.

---

[48] Henry Clapp, Jr., *The Pioneer: Or Leaves from an Editor's Portfolio* (Lynn, 1846), p. 152. Clapp was editor of the Lynn *Pioneer,* formerly the Essex County *Washingtonian.* The editor before him was the come-outer William Bassett; after him was the antislavery legislator George Bradburn. The owner of the paper was Christopher Robinson, a non-resistant with the latitude to care more about the talents than the tenets of his editors. See the series on "Come-Outers of Lynn" by "Noggs" in *Herald of Freedom,* n.s., Oct. 17, 1845, p. 1; Oct. 31, 1845, p. 2; Nov. 28, 1845, p. 1; March 6, 1846, p. 2.

After one satisfactory reform gathering, Clapp spoke of the thrill of being "loosed for a while from this great cage which we call *Government*." The meeting was not disorderly though it was free: "It was truly inspiring to see how a new thought . . . would fly around the magic circle like electricity." When such a meeting weighed the usefulness of politics to antislavery, the consensus was inevitable. They concluded that their sole demand of government was for it "in the high name of Humanity instantly to disband."[49]

Similarly, Clapp came to nonresistance meetings to explain that right is without "a shadow of turning" and thus could not vary with majorities. It followed that the doctrine of majority rule, "or, in equivalent words, that 'might is right,' is the corner stone of all slavery." Thus he agreed with many other New England abolitionists that antislavery was by definition precluded from association with politics.[50] But by the same definition he would have ended much of the familiar business of antislavery organizations. His attacks, even though his tone was often light, were intolerable to abolitionists who imposed limits on their own comeouterism. Part of the significance of no-organizationism and of related tendencies in New Hampshire is that they reveal a sense of limits and balance with which the Garrisonians are not often credited.

Clapp, who later became a prominent New York editor, was so eloquent and persuasive that one speech of his was remembered by Thomas Wentworth Higginson as doing "more than anything else to make me at least a halfway socialist for life."[51] Clapp's form of socialism depended on the sentiments uniting emancipated individuals rather than state controls. As leader of the anarchic come-outers of Lynn, he pointed out directions other abolitionists would subsequently travel: toward a religion based on the sovereignty of God but increasingly defended "in the high name of Humanity"; and perhaps, in his emphasis on

[49] Clapp, *Pioneer*, pp. 117–119.
[50] *Liberator*, Nov. 8, 1844, p. 4.
[51] Higginson, *Cheerful Yesterdays*, p. 85.

the electricity of the sentiments, toward spiritualism and free
love.

V

Although Lynn nurtured some of the most anarchic elements
of nonresistance and come-outerism, it was a minor theater of
conflict with the Boston Garrisonians compared to New Hampshire. There antislavery and no-organizationism were synonymous, and Nathaniel P. Rogers, at the forefront of this anarchistic movement, rhapsodized on free meeting.[52] Rogers was a widely
respected reformer. Descended from the Smithfield martyr John
Rogers and from American Puritan divines, he was the "pet and
darling" of abolitionism, at one time editor of the *National Anti-
Slavery Standard* and a delegate to the world convention in London in 1840 when he was in his forty-sixth year.[53] According to
the political abolitionist William Goodell, Rogers was second
only to Garrison, and perhaps surpassed him, in energy and tal-
ent. Together they might easily have dominated the antislavery
societies if Rogers' nonresistance had not been total.[54] From opponents of nonresistance came further testimony: Higginson, who

[52] "We have never attended a meeting of any character so splendidly
sustained and so orderly, voluntarily and beautifully conducted," he wrote
of the Stafford County Anti-Slavery Society's annual meeting in 1842. "It
was a self-governing meeting. Our nominal president declined *keeping
order;* and when, once or twice, some, who came in to dispute, called for
order and bred some little disorder, he threw the meeting on its *self-government,* and all was quietness" (quoted in Pillsbury, *Acts,* p. 222).
[53] Garrisons, *Garrison,* III, p. 123; the phrase was Quincy's. Useful
sketches of Rogers' life are David W. Bartlett, *Modern Agitators: or Pen
Portraits of Living American Reformers* (New York and Auburn, 1856),
pp. 225–239; Robert Adams, "Nathaniel Peabody Rogers: 1794–1846,"
New England Quarterly, XX (1947), 365–376; and John Pierpont's "Introduction" to *A Collection from the Miscellaneous Writings of Nathaniel
Peabody Rogers* (Manchester, N.H., and Boston, 1849), hereafter cited as
Rogers, *Miscellaneous Writings.* Rogers' likeness to his martyred ancestor
was much discussed; see Orson S. Fowler, "Hereditary Descent," *Works of
Phrenology, Physiology, and Kindred Subjects* (Manchester, Eng., n.d.),
[I], 57–58.
[54] Goodell, *Slavery and Anti-Slavery,* pp. 529–531.

knew about such things, recalled that Rogers' journalism had "a spice and zest which would now command a market on merely professional grounds." But he was a "Non-resistant of non-resistants" and "out-Garrisoned Garrison."[55]

As editor of the *Herald of Freedom*, Rogers came close to making no-organizationism a coherent theory touching on every aspect of culture and society. Though his style had zest, this American romantic nonetheless did not believe in formalities of style. Nature and speech were key words he used. He was led to distinctions resembling those favored by Alcott: "*Argument*," he said, meant less for reform than "STATEMENT"; or action is necessary only for unjust causes which will not bear earnest speech.[56] Probably no other reformer has placed a higher value on free speech. Rogers literally expected to talk slavery out of existence.

Although Rogers started out with faith in speech, his destination was always the end of slavery. His earliest rejection of the ballot was based exclusively on the proslavery character of the available parties.[57] In April 1839, Orange Scott still thought that Rogers might be enlisted in opposition to Garrison's nonresistance, but Rogers explained that he respected both Scott and Garrison and did not worry about the extraneous opinions of dedicated abolitionists. As a budding no-organizationist, he denied that any leader spoke for him.[58] As he became increasingly committed to nonresistance, he confessed that his mind had

[55] Higginson, *Contemporaries*, p. 333.

[56] He also criticized "the cultivation of mere letters" in the *Boston Miscellany* and praised the "almighty power" of human speech, "unalloyed by learning." For these and other comments on language and style, see Rogers, *Miscellaneous Writings*, pp. 248, 227, 321, 357–359.

[57] *Herald of Freedom*, March 30, 1839, p. 2.

[58] *Ibid.*, Apr. 13, 1839, p. 2. Already he dismissed fears of Garrison's leadership: "We should say rather it would not be safe to *have a leader*. We are a band of volunteers and the principle of our embodying is that men can properly *have no earthly leaders*." Probably Garrison converted Rogers to nonresistance, as is implied by Pierpont (in Rogers, *Miscellaneous Writings*, p. xiii).

changed. He was now "convinced that all legislation was force, and that as anti-slavery, in our opinion, was a strictly moral and religious movement, a work of repentance and reformation, we could not resort to physical force."[59] The basis of his radical career, then, was evangelicalism.

Ten months after writing Scott that nonresistance was a matter for private judgment, of little concern to antislavery, Rogers was prepared to argue that legislation could create only "free niggers," that laws could never eradicate prejudice and racial domination.[60] Thereafter his antislavery position was fixed: emancipation was as wrong as legislated abolition was futile, for it presumed an "act of *mastery*" to give up slaves, and masters must, in justice, disappear along with slaves.[61] The real problem was to transform a national character in which men were willing to hold slaves and think of themselves as masters. That problem seemed obviously religious.

There was great excitement in Rogers' successive conversions. His ecstasy for come-outerism went to the limit of calling the "leap" of Thomas Parnell Beach from being a minister to joining his laymen "one of the most decisive steps, that has been taken— and one involving a good deal more of consequences, than any thing ever done by Martin Luther." The comparison was prolonged in Beach's favor by reference to Luther's use of "the military government."[62] While Rogers had once hoped the churches would rally to the antislavery cause, his hatred of them now carried him to exaggerate their power over communicants; inevitably, he said, they enslaved the men and women of the North.[63]

[59] Pillsbury, *Acts,* p. 248.
[60] Rogers, *Miscellaneous Writings,* p. 90.
[61] *Herald of Freedom,* Sept. 27, 1844, p. 2.
[62] *Ibid.,* March 15, 1844, p. 1. A few months earlier, a writer in the *Liberator* (Dec. 22, 1843, pp. 2–3) predicted that the come-outers were bringing on the "SECOND REFORMATION." Rogers reprinted this view in his *Herald of Freedom,* Dec. 29, 1843, p. 4.
[63] See the violent statements in *ibid.,* March 12, 1842, p. 3: "Under a cunning priest they [the churches] are worse than the Inquisition. . . . A woman is a perfect slave in them, as much as she is in a Turkish Harem.

In fact the "priests" deepened his suspicion of politics because of their apparent preference for political action so long as the issue of slavery had to be confronted at all. They knew that politics "generates a superficial and fictitious animation, like the stimulus of alcohol—but torpor and lethargy follow, and become the permanent condition of community." At the same time they preferred pestilence "(among the laity)" and famine "(not extending to the parsonage)" to the threat of moral agitation in the community. An attack on the church, he insisted, was the only method "to annoy slavery out of the community."[64]

Sweet-tempered on most subjects, Rogers became nasty at the thought of the clergy, whom he characterized as "Popery, only Protestantized."[65] As he relinquished the hope of obtaining denominational aid for abolitionism, he provided an interesting case study in the ways in which the religious principles of abolitionists could undergo fundamental change. It would provide no satisfaction if Northern churches occasionally refused fellowship to slaveowners. He actually opposed schisms in the churches on the grounds that they were caused by pressures of antislavery agitation and not by differences in religious outlook; what was needed was the disintegration of formal religious institutions.[66] It was no longer a matter of opposing the churches for dereliction to their duty of whipping up antislavery opinion. There was a larger battle between the principle of authority and the principle of liberty, and the churches ought to be on the wrong side.

This shift in viewpoint had far-reaching implications. As Rogers switched from attacking the extended metaphor of slavery,

---

. . . A christian cannot live in one of them, any more than a freeman can live under an overseer's whip on a plantation." Therefore whatever "exposes their anti-christian character advances anti-slavery." For Rogers' own account of his earlier views, see *ibid.*, July 22, 1842, p. 3.

[64] *Ibid.*, Apr. 8, 1842, p. 2.

[65] He was aware of his inconsistency: "I am for treating everybody kindly, and in a way to make them feel the happier, and be the better. But when a man puts on the Priest, he not only forfeits all right and title to *human* courtesy, but it would be wrong to extend it to him." See *ibid.*, May 17, 1844, p. 2.

[66] *Ibid.*, n.s., May 30, 1845, p. 2.

as all abolitionists did, to attacking the principle of authority, as any abolitionists might have, he became a thoroughgoing revolutionary, quite different from the stereotype of the antebellum reformer expecting by the removal of one evil institution to set the social machine on an easy course to the millennium. Authority was everywhere. For example, Rogers' attention was directed toward the white slaves of the North. If the Northern conscience tolerated institutions by which "Capital" buys labor "at auction," as he thought it did, then it could hardly be effective against Southern slavery.[67]

The idea of property certainly seemed to need revision; everyone ought to have as a birthright the means of living.[68] While Rogers was vague about the remedy, he felt certain that the factory system was so evil that it could scarcely be reformed: "It is vain to go over a dunghill and crop or pull up weeds. . . . The heap must be demolished." After visiting the Northampton Community for a week he concluded that, despite the admirable piety and fraternity there, it would not suffice to "retreat" into such a venture. "I think it is my duty rather to stay amid the great community, destitute of *communion* as it is, and go for *communityzing* the whole."[69]

His assault on authority undermined his respect for church, state, and capitalism and resulted in a confrontation with the greatest autocrat of all—that same God in whose service Rogers had begun his errand. It was implicit in his come-outerism that clergymen falsely claimed to speak in God's name; on the contrary, true Christian ministers should be "unpretending *men* and *women*, claiming to speak as *human beings*, merely, and asking to be heard and regarded *for the truths they tell*, and not from any authority."[70] He denied that the Bible commanded obedience, "however Anti-Slavery and however true and glorious its contents may be." It was "useful" only insofar as it appealed to

[67] Rogers, *Miscellaneous Writings*, p. 308.
[68] *Ibid.*, pp. 285–288.
[69] *Herald of Freedom*, Jan. 26, 1844, p. 1; *Liberator*, Sept. 8, 1843, p. 4.
[70] *Herald of Freedom*, May 17, 1844, p. 3.

"human understanding." The great question of the age, in the opinion of this foe of all authority, was "how man discovers what is right." It was a contradiction to call for the freedom of the slave on grounds of Scriptural authority.[71]

John Pierpont, his friend and eulogist, thought Rogers relied on a revelation older than the Bible to learn—"for he was a lover of music—that slavery was a discord, that could never be brought into union with the harmonies of the universe." We might better say that Rogers' antislavery played hob with the autocratic government of God and helped to produce an antiauthoritarian religion of humanity. In any case, Pierpont gave the example of a debate in which Rogers was told that Christ had never preached abolitionism. He said he had two answers: first, the charge was false, for application of the Golden Rule alone would end slavery in twenty-four hours; and second, "admitting—what I deny—that Jesus Christ did not preach the abolition of slavery, then I say, *he didn't do his duty.*"[72] Another associate remembered a peace gathering where it was generally agreed that human life could be taken by divine command. The presiding officer marshaled evidence for this position. Rogers finally asked:

"Does our brother yonder say that if God commanded him, he would take a sword and use it in slaying human beings, and innocent, helpless human beings?["] [It was a problem, of course, that the government of God could readily inspire a John Brown as well as a nonresistant.] "Yes, if God commanded," was the answer. "Well, I wouldn't," responded Rogers.[73]

Eventually Rogers admitted that he worried very little about God. Before vexing himself with duties in the realm of the supernatural, man should perform every natural duty toward his fellows. Probably the duties were identical, but in any case Rogers scorned those with no time for humanity because of their fixation on God.[74]

[71] Rogers, *Miscellaneous Writings,* pp. 280–284, 311–313.
[72] *Ibid.,* p. xxi.
[73] Pillsbury, *Acts,* p. 45.
[74] *Herald of Freedom,* n.s., Jan. 9, 1846, pp. 2–3.

He had come far from the otherworldly attitudes of much of come-outerism. He was well on his way to a situational ethics: a good position, as distinct from a political position, was of the moment and defied definition, yet it would compel opponents to define themselves.[75] Perhaps only such a theory could reconcile his use of moral suasion to abolish slavery with his insistence that any kind of threatening, such as was evident in religious schisms and political disunionism, clashed with the principles of anti-slavery.[76] Slavery was "a vicious *habit*," nothing more, to be elim-inated by persistent statements of truth, not by resolutions or laws or coercion.[77] Whatever the merits of his theory, it is plain that Rogers felt less changeable in following his own understand-ing to undefined positions than he would have in serving the codes of law of any authority. He consistently appealed to "uni-versal human convictions." One could not say, for instance, that capital punishment was wrong because it was a sin, for that was to invoke the threat of capital punishment by God. Better simply to say that everyone understands it is wrong.[78] By the same token, antislavery should not address man as a slave of God.

vi

Rogers is an abolitionist remembered by historians neither for his unusually thorough radicalism nor for his alienation from di-vine authority. Instead he is portrayed as a kind of left-wing deviationist who was badly treated. He may not really hold the sympathy of historians, but he is a useful foil for attacks on Garrison.

It is hard to uncover what really happened in the dispute among abolitionists. For several years Rogers, with a touch of local chauvinism not uncommon among abolitionists, praised re-form activities in New Hampshire to the detriment of those in Massachusetts.[79] New Hampshire symbolized the freedom of

[75] *Ibid.*, Aug. 30, 1844, p. 3. This attitude of Rogers forces us to look to many sources to define his "position."

[76] *Ibid.*, n.s., May 30, 1845, p. 2; *Liberator*, June 6, 1845, p. 3.

[77] *Herald of Freedom*, March 8, 1844, p. 3.

[78] *Ibid.*, Jan. 26, 1844, pp. 2–3.

[79] See, for example, *Liberator*, Feb. 7, 1840, p. 3.

speech and impulse that abolitionists must accord each other if their pleading for the slave was to have the ring of conviction. In 1844 the New Hampshire Anti-Slavery Society voted that the *Herald of Freedom* would no longer be their official organ. Rogers wanted it that way. No one had actually interfered with his editorial decisions, but he wanted the paper separate from the society because editing, like speech, ought to be "unshackled."[80] In a subsequent disagreement over the finances and ownership of the paper, a committee of Boston abolitionists intervened and determined that it really belonged to the New Hampshire society and should be supervised by a special board. His worst fears thus materialized, Rogers refused further editorship.

In a "new series" of the *Herald of Freedom* and in the Lynn *Pioneer*, Rogers traced the causes of his bitterness. He said that so few persons had ever bothered to vote in New Hampshire meetings that the Boston committee could not have generalized about majority sentiment. Also, three of the new supervisory board were not even members of the society, and one was a schismatic political abolitionist.[81] But if a sense of the vulnerability of free meeting against outside attack colored his animosity, he was more directly enraged at the insistence of the Bostonians that they were concerned only with tidying up an organizational dispute and were in no way punishing him for his theories of no-organizationism.

Before the fracas Rogers had appealed for funds to build a house for Parker Pillsbury (who ironically succeeded him as editor of the *Herald of Freedom*). In the course of this appeal, he declared his belief in subscriptions only for specific individuals. The national antislavery societies, he claimed, had previously wasted money on political action; there was an implication that

[80] *Ibid.*, July 5, 1844, p. 2.

[81] *Herald of Freedom*, Oct. 18, 1844, p. 3; Nov. 8, 1844, p. 2. Earlier (*ibid.*, July 5, 1844, p. 3) Rogers had ridiculed those few who did vote at their conventions. After the third-party abolitionist, J. H. Ela, became "publishing agent" of the *Herald*, there began to appear reprints from such non-Garrisonian periodicals as the *Christian Politician* and the *True Wesleyan*. See *ibid.*, Apr. 18, 1845, p. 1; May 16, 1845, p. 1.

organizations were likely to spend money irresponsibly. At this point Edmund Quincy had privately warned Rogers not to impugn the financial reliability of all reform organizations. He called Rogers "a little intolerant and bigotted on your NO ORGANIZATION theory." Probably the issue could not be dodged much longer, for Quincy had threatened that if Rogers continued to undermine the antislavery effort, "I WILL PITCH INTO YOU WITH ALL MY MIGHT." And there were hints of situations which might in turn undermine Rogers' position of strength in New Hampshire.[82] It was understandably galling to be told that Quincy and the Massachusetts visitors were disinterested neutrals.

However, John Pierpont, a dear friend who was not a Garrisonian, refused to take sides in his introduction to a collection of Rogers' writings published in the heat of the dispute. He knew his friends in Massachusetts had also meant well.[83] Probably no one had suspected how deep a hatred could be generated in Rogers by his yearning for freedom. There is no reason to ignore Quincy's claim that abolitionists had always handled Rogers "like a cracked tea-cup" on account of his inability to argue with friends. "His *No-Organizationism*," Quincy admitted ironically, "was the original cause of all this trouble, but originating from himself and not us." Unable to bear Garrison's taunts about the oddity of a no-organizationist serving as editor of the organ of a society, he tried to appropriate what was not his. Then the train of hostility could not be stopped.[84] Before the bitterness had any chance to subside, in 1846 Rogers died in Lynn, with Judson Hutchinson of the Hutchinson Family Singers by his side.[85]

[82] Rogers reprinted his editorial and Quincy's letter in *Herald of Freedom*, n.s., July 25, 1845, pp. 3–4.

[83] Rogers, *Miscellaneous Writings*, p. xv. Pierpont also (p. xvi) thought it unrealistic to attribute Rogers' early death to a broken heart, as some did, because Rogers had been afflicted with illnesses all his life. Moreover, when Quincy objected to certain passages in the introduction, Pierpont agreed to withdraw them from future editions. See *Liberator*, Dec. 17, 1847, p. 2; Dec. 31, 1847, p. 2.

[84] Garrisons, *Garrison*, III, 123–127.

[85] Rogers, *Miscellaneous Writings*, p. xviii.

One may question whether Massachusetts would have interfered in the slightest had all the consequences been foreseeable.
Rogers' own paranoiac rejoinders to the *Liberator* were surely
embarrassing to abolitionism. To the modern reader, moreover,
they are very tiresome. With an increasing tendency to attack
Garrison with the same millenarian invective he had once aimed
at the corporate church, Rogers lost his earlier ability to concentrate on remediable inconsistencies in nonresistant abolitionism.[86]
As a result, one check on the inclination of nonresistants to con-
fuse the message of moral suasion with the hope of political
gains was lost in the mid-1840s.

It would be a mistake to use the unfortunate case of Rogers
to show that the Garrisonians had been impressionable or even
insincere in adopting anarchistic ideas. Rogers was for a time a
trenchant critic of hazy attitudes toward divine authority, political expediency, and organizational restraints; to some extent
he anticipated the critique of the ambiguities in nonresistance
presented earlier in this book. Nevertheless, Rogers spoke from
within the same complex of convictions that were associated with
Garrison, Quincy, or Wright. In their own ways they all employed the logic of separatism, moral suasion, and free meeting
to forecast the liberation of mankind from coercion. If Rogers
rebelled against the restrictions of even God's government, other
Garrisonians were to follow the same path. When he noted that
he had joined Clapp in the "Refuge of Oppression," the *Liberator*
column reserved for proslavery voices, Rogers had reason to wonder whether at some point Garrison might not have to place himself there.[87]

It remains puzzling to watch the growth of hostility between

[86] Pierpont and Richard Hildreth more gently explained that broken-
heartedness sapped his talents (*ibid.*, p. xv). For one indication of the
regret of Rogers' antagonists, observe that in Pillsbury's treatment (in
Acts, passim) of Rogers, himself, and other New Hampshire abolitionists,
no mention is made of the dispute.

[87] *Pioneer*, July 9, 1846, p. 3. For the presentations of both sides in the
case of Clapp, see *ibid.*, July 24, 1846, p. 2. Garrison had waited until
Clapp was abroad to launch an attack insinuating immorality.

Garrisonians and no-organizationists in spite of their common affection for nonresistance and coming-out. Regional differences
at times seem weightier than ideological ones. The hub city was
estranged from some currents of feeling in the hinterlands. Perhaps in Boston it was difficult to question the apparent purpose
in delivering addresses, publishing tracts, passing resolutions. In
the come-outer regions of Cape Cod, New Hampshire, and the
factory towns, the outlook for antislavery was more personal, less
conventional. Rogers thought the deference of his opponents to
"aristocracy" was their undoing.[88] His was a Jacksonian viewpoint that emphasized a rural-versus-urban conflict of values.
And there had developed conflicting visions of voluntary societies. Certainly in Boston the idea of a voluntary society remained
harnessed to the hope of secular reform, while in the outlying
areas this idea suggested the style of a new life.

There is no doubt that Garrison himself was badly stung by
this affair. His affection for Rogers had been unusually strong,
even if it was a trifle patronizing. "As Jonathan loved David," he
wrote to a mutual friend before the clash, "so do I feel my attach-
ment drawn out toward N.P.R." He delighted in the rapid and
"wonderful transformation" in Rogers' views toward greater and
greater radicalism. But after the disputes began, no love was possible, and he was more aware of Rogers' "strong tendency of
mind toward speculative atheism." Rogers, in his changing view,
had grown foolish on the subject of freedom and had fallen in
with others whose opinions were like those described by Milton:
"License they mean, when they cry liberty." The break was both
personal and theological. Garrison complained that "his malignity
will surpass his former friendship," and at the same time compared his fall to Lucifer's—he would never rise to goodness again.
Garrison avoided reading Rogers' writings in the last year of his
former friend's life.[89] After this bitter tragedy we may be sure

[88] *Herald of Freedom*, n.s., Aug. 15, 1845, pp. 2–3.
[89] Garrison to Maria W. Chapman, Sept. 9, 1843, Weston Papers, Boston
Public Library; Garrison to R. D. Webb, March 1, 1845; to George Ben-

that the remaining Garrisonians were concerned to avoid atheism and license, however deep may have been their thirst for liberation.

The Rogers affair impresses us with the complexity of the motives and goals in Garrisonian reform. In his excellent biography of Garrison, John L. Thomas has revealed the influence on him of the theocratic benevolence organizations through which ministers like Lyman Beecher, disturbed by the separation of church and state, tried to improvise controls over the people at large.[90] What had been an engine of the saints to control the unregenerate was transformed by the Garrisonians' discovery of immediatism: the goal was no longer to check vice but to end it, and the society became a sort of replacement for the church. From our survey of come-outerism, however, it is evident that there was another source for the aspirations of reform societies. Besides the model of theocratic control, Garrison had the model of lower-class come-outerism and, behind it, a long history of religious individualism. This second model denied the possibility of order through control. Indeed, it celebrated the enthusiasm of the churchless. Garrison and his colleagues mixed the two models of a reform society, but Rogers was purely a come-outer. The clash between Rogers and the Garrisonians revealed unavoidable frustrations in the attempt to organize men and women to seek individual spontaneity. It also demonstrated that Garrison and Quincy would not permit the quest for self-liberation to discredit or detract from the movement on behalf of the slave.

---

son, May 19, 1845; to J. M. McKim, July 19, 1845, Garrison Papers, Boston Public Library.

[90] Thomas, *The Liberator*, p. 70.

V

From Nonresistance
to Community

Nonresistance sorely needed theoretical clarification. To a large extent this need was met by Tolstoy's forgotten American, Adin Ballou, but Ballou's understanding of nonresistance led him toward a type of communitarian experiment which most other Garrisonians were unprepared to imitate. It led away from hopes for a swift end to slavery.

When Ballou joined the nonresistants, they stood accused of encouraging the most chaotic sort of anarchy. To those who distrusted Garrison's leadership of abolitionism, it seemed obvious that nonresistance was being stretched beyond the simple Christian injunction to turn the other cheek. The Garrisonians seemed to be denying that man had social obligations. James G. Birney, for example, thought they struck at "the root of the social structure" and threatened "to renew, under the sanction of religion, scenes of anarchy and license that have generally heretofore been the offspring of the rankest infidelity and irreligion." Birney knew church history well enough to see that some of the precedents did not belong to the history of infidelity: "The 'No-Government' theory is but a new growth of one of the *fungi* which sprung up in the early period of the Reformation, when the minds of men were heated by the new ideas presented to them. It soon led to the most horrible excesses." The editors of the *Non-Resistant* reprinted Birney's charges next to the chapter of William Robertson's history of the Reformation on "The Anabaptists of Münster."

They thought it ludicrous to compare modern pacifists with Christians who fought government with the sword.[1]

In addition to accusations from outsiders that they were fomenting anarchy, the nonresistants experienced a good deal of internal confusion. In fact, they faced something of a theological quandary. They firmly believed in the sovereignty of God. Yet questions were being raised concerning the consistency of nonresistance with the Old Testament, which gave divine sanction to the warfare and governmental system of the Jews. There was also the problem that Jesus instructed his followers to obey Caesar and the powers that be. Both external accusations and internal confusion required nonresistants to clear up the relationship between converted reformers and the unconverted world of sinful force. Perhaps the only man capable of a systematic, theological defense of nonresistance was Adin Ballou.

At the 1839 meetings of the New England Non-Resistance Society, Ballou made his first public appearance as a Christian nonresistant. He was immediately asked to write out his impromptu remarks, and they were published in the *Non-Resistant* and Garrison's *Liberator* as well as in pamphlet form. Ballou, who was not yet a member of the society nor even a subscriber to its press, had provided, in Edmund Quincy's words, "the best explanation of the true nature of non-resistance principles, and the most effectual reply to the most common objections, that we have yet seen."[2] Ballou had thought carefully about the theological underpinnings of abolitionism; his address merits careful scrutiny.[3]

---

[1] *Non-Resistant*, June 1, 1839, p. 1. A modern account of Münster, within the setting of centuries of anarchic Christian outbursts, is Norman Cohn, *The Pursuit of the Millennium: Revolutionary Messianism in Medieval and Reformation Europe and Its Bearing on Modern Totalitarian Movements* (2d ed., New York, 1961).

[2] *Non-Resistant*, Dec. 7, 1839, p. 3.

[3] For the text, from which the following quotations are taken, see Adin Ballou, *Non-Resistance in Relation to Human Governments* (Boston, 1839); *Liberator*, Dec. 6, 1839, p. 4; and *Non-Resistant*, Nov. 16, 1839, pp. 1–2. A portion is reprinted in Krimerman and Perry, eds., *Patterns of Anarchy*, pp. 140–149.

Ballou spoke in favor of a resolution that the purpose of all true nonresistants is "neither to purify nor to subvert human governments, but to advance in the earth that kingdom of peace and righteousness, which supersedes all such governments." Human government he defined as any condition in which the will of one man holds authority over another; whether democratic or tyrannical in its superficial form, this condition means man is "the slave of man." Divine government was the condition in which the will of God claims the "primary, undivided allegiance" of a man as his "sole King, Lawgiver, and Judge." It followed from these definitions that "in no case" could human government be harmonious with its divine superior. A Christian's obligations remained the same whether human law contravened, ignored, or reiterated God's law. At best human law was superfluous.

To this point his scheme applied only to Christians or nonresistants. Next he confronted the question, "What is the object of non-resistants with respect to human government?" Here his concentration on sin allowed him a conservatism not found in most abolitionist thought. If slavery was nothing more than a sign of prolonged sinning, as other abolitionists argued, then perhaps slavery was necessary so long as sin persisted. Ballou was aware of this. The simple antinomian disjunction—either God's law or man's law, with nothing in between—falsely ruled out all government on grounds that were valid only for the regenerate who required no government.

On the contrary, we believe it to be among the irrevocable ordinations of God, that all who will not be governed by *him* shall be governed by one another—shall be tyrannized over by one another; that so long as men will indulge the lust of dominion, they shall be filled with the fruits of slavery; that they who will not be obedient to the law of love, shall bow down under the law of physical force; that "they who take the sword shall perish with the sword;" and that while so many as twenty ambitious, proud, selfish, revengeful, sinful, men remain in any corner of the world, they shall be subject to a government of physical force among themselves. . . . So if men will not be governed by God, it is their doom to be enslaved by one another.

In this way Ballou clarified the abolitionist argument that violence, war, government, and slavery were equivalent penalties of sinful alienation from the rule of God. But he also brought out an unwanted implication: at least in the short run these forms of coercion were "a *necessary* evil to those who will not be in willing subjection to the *divine*."

This doubtless gave some ground to the proslavery argument, but Ballou had kept the regenerate free from the necessities of government. And he was able to distinguish his view from that which held it to be the doom of all mankind to be enslaved by one another until the millennium. "And as to the millennium," he asked, "what is it?" It would take place in history:

Alas! how many are expecting the millennium to come "with observation"—just as the Jews of old were expecting the kingdom of God; not knowing that the millennium and kingdom, must be *within* men, before it can ever be *around* them. Let us have the spirit of the millennium, and do the works of the millennium. Then will the millennium have already come.

Ballou's version of antislavery would always be bound up in his understanding of the dynamics of the millennium. But in order for there to be any dynamics at all, he had to reject the notion that there could be no serviceable intermediaries between an Almighty God and a sovereign individual. Of course there was no questioning God's might, but there were great differences in the sovereignty of individuals. Most men were enslaved and governed. For the regenerate, however, coercion was superfluous. The millennium would come—government would be outmoded, slavery abolished—as the regenerate guided increasing numbers of men and women outside the control of sin. The mark of regeneration was nonresistance, which we must understand as not merely a tactical nonviolence but a general freedom from coercion.

Although the regenerate and reformed were free of government, Ballou did not isolate a relationship between man and God without any social obligations. If nonresistants became a majority anywhere, he said, they would be extremely efficient in such community problems as food supply, education, and relief of distress for they would be anxious to learn their duty and would perform it voluntarily. In this way "finally may all human governments be *superseded* by the divine *government.*" Ballou did not spell out this hope; perhaps he did not know where it was leading him. But he soon devoted most of his energies to the Hopedale Community, and the route from antislavery to communitarianism was already marked in his theology. There had to be some place to lead fugitives from the necessary evil of slavery, some outward manifestation of the kingdom that is within.

Before the communitarian venture got under way, however, the conservative basis of Ballou's theology was underscored by an exchange in the letters column of the *Liberator.* His address to the nonresistants encountered the objection that to deny the authority of a government, however peacefully, was really resistance to that government and therefore a violation of the Scriptural command to obey the powers that be. Ballou in reply attacked the significance which "political Christians" assigned to the thirteenth chapter of Romans. There was no order to influence, join with, or control the powers that be, nor to resist such powers when they are deemed tyrannical. Always tyrannical, the authorities can still deter sin among the unconverted. For individual Christians to judge the legitimacy of particular governments, to enter into the politics of states, or to rule in God's name was to invite the grimmest consequences of fifth monarchy, anabaptism, and papistry. A Christian's role was that of a subject, not a citizen; in that role he might look for means of demonstrating a more excellent way of life to the unconverted.[4]

Ballou had, in effect, turned back on political abolitionists like Birney the charge of evoking the most horrible scenes in Christian history. But in doing so he was obliged to confront some of the more pessisimistic implications of the antislavery argument. His beliefs might even have fostered a kind of defeatism: after all, Southerners defended slavery on the grounds that in the state

[4] *Liberator,* Jan. 3, 1840, p. 3; Feb. 7, 1840, p. 4; Feb. 28, 1840, p. 4; March 13, 1840, p. 4.

of man since Adam's fall it was essential to social order that some
men control others. But Ballou became one of the most faithful
nonresistants and abolitionists. Under his leadership, the Hopedale Community was designed as a mediating agency between
the present world of sinful coercion and the peaceful future of
the millennium. The Hopedale Community, in other words, was
a response to the obligation of abolitionists to create new institutions which stayed clear of complicity with sin, did not condone the endurance of slavery, and did not negate the sovereignty of God.

ii

As Ballou refined and elaborated on religious beliefs held by
many abolitionists, he showed a special sensitivity to the endurance of sin. His early life had given him extensive training in
theological argument concerning the role of sin in human society.
He had been brought up in rural Rhode Island. With his family,
he had enlisted in the "Christian Connexion," one of countless
small, regional sects arising from waves of religious enthusiasm.
Although this sect preceded come-outerism, it revealed a similar
spirit. It had no creed; and it taught Ballou, as a young zealot
called to preach, to rely on "inspiration, as thoughts and words
should be given me at the moment." Furthermore, he learned to
think of his ministerial calling as "self-renunciative"; all his life
he trusted in God's provisions for him and accepted only "free-
will offerings" for his services.[5]

But he grew dissatisfied with the Connexion's attitude toward
unrepentant sinners; he could no longer agree that their souls
were annihilated after the death of their bodies. His own reading
of the Bible persuaded him that not even the wickedest sinner

---

[5] Ballou, *Autobiography of Adin Ballou,* ed. William S. Heywood
(Lowell, 1896), pp. 45, 67, 212, and *passim.* For a lucid presentation of
some of Ballou's views, see William O. Reichert, "The Philosophical
Anarchism of Adin Ballou," *Huntington Library Quarterly,* XXVII (1964),
357–374. See also Barbara Louise Faulkner, "Adin Ballou and the Hopedale Community," unpublished Ph.D. dissertation, Boston University, 1965.

would suffer annihilation, and he had rejected the idea of infinite torture. To his family's chagrin, Ballou joined the Universalists, a denomination built on the premise that a loving God promised salvation to all of His children.

There were important links between Universalism and antebellum reform. At one time 303 Universalist ministers—roughly half the denomination—protested against slavery because its failure to distinguish man from property violated universal brotherhood.[6] The reform activities of Universalists ranged from night classes to improve the minds of Lowell factory girls to clairvoyant visions of a new society, from the exertions of Charles Spear in behalf of the imprisoned to the campaign of Theophilus Fisk to win workingmen over to Jackson's Democracy.[7] Of course, there were also Universalists who opposed reform and many who balked at any such ultraism as nonresistance. Moreover, reformers were frequently opposed to Universalism.[8] It should be clear enough that religious and reform movements elude simple equations. On the other hand, although Ballou was not yet a reformer when he joined Universalism, this youthful religious choice gives clues to his subsequent career.

Two articles of Universalist faith could easily coincide with a

[6] *Liberator*, Apr. 24, 1846, p. 2; May 8, 1846, p. 2.

[7] Emerson Hugh Lalone, *And Thy Neighbor as Thyself: A Story of Universalist Social Action* (Boston, 1959), pp. 27–45; E. Douglas Branch, *The Sentimental Years, 1836–1860* (New York, 1965), pp. 333, 368–369; Tyler, *Freedom's Ferment*, pp. 64, 84, 86, 121, 148; Arthur Schlesinger, Jr., *The Age of Jackson* (Boston, 1945), p. 250.

[8] Sylvanus Cobb was a Universalist minister and prominent abolitionist who feuded with the Garrisonians on the Sabbath issue, with Universalist headquarters on the priority of reform, and with come-outers on the utility of denominations. Alanson St. Clair, one of Cobb's students, nearly joined the nonresistants, then became a vehement opponent of the doctrine. See the *Autobiography of the First Forty-One Years of Sylvanus Cobb, D.D.* (Boston, 1867), pp. 273, 330–331, 417–418; Richard Eddy, *Universalism in America*, II (Boston, 1886), 256; *Liberator*, Sept. 11, 1842, p. 4; March 10, 1848, p. 2. Oliver Johnson was editor of an anti-Universalist paper before becoming a Garrisonian abolitionist. See Russel B. Nye, *William Lloyd Garrison and the Humanitarian Reformers* (Boston, 1955), p. 77.

staunch commitment to antislavery, nonresistance, and communitarianism. First, there was the Universalists' distinctive belief that
all souls were destined to be saved by God. It was sometimes
argued that fear was an improper incentive for doing good; therefore, it would have been a moral count against God if punishment had been required to effect His purposes. Similar analyses
of the relationship between fear and the divine law recur
throughout the literature of nonresistance.[9]

Second, eternal punishment was held to be inconsistent with
the role of God as father. From the paternity of God followed
the brotherhood of man. When Ballou embraced abolitionism and
nonresistance, he was not reacting to any shocking event; instead,
he acted on the reflection that slavery and war violated the po-
tentiality of human brotherhood. He hardly needed to identify
the sources of the language he later used to describe his grandest
undertaking: "The Hopedale Community was a systematic attempt to establish an order of Human Society based on the sublime ideas of the Fatherhood of God and the Brotherhood of
Man, as taught and illustrated in the Gospel of Jesus Christ."[10]
Then as now, "brotherhood" had a variety of vague, maudlin
usages, but at that time it could also signify a specific theological
viewpoint on the relationship between God and society. In a
sense slavery, war, and government erred by allowing the brother
to play the father.

Belief in universal salvation, however, might easily have fed
complacency regarding human efforts for improvement, and we
have already seen that Ballou made sharp distinctions among his
brethren when it came to the utility of government. It is therefore not surprising to find that he left the Universalist church before becoming a reformer. He favored the doctrine that, while
all persons are eventually saved, some must experience temporary

    [9] See *Herald of Freedom*, n.s., July 11, 1845, p. 4, for an example of the
same logic being turned against Universalist sermons.
    [10] Ballou, *Autobiography*, pp. 280, 308; Ballou, *History of the Hopedale
Community, from Its Inception to Its Virtual Submergence in the Hopedale
Parish*, ed. William S. Heywood (Lowell, 1897), p. 1.

punishment after death in compensation for their sinfulness. This doctrine was called restorationism because it held the souls of sinners to be *restored* rather than saved at once if they had not experienced conversion. Controversy over this doctrine created a schism within Universalism in the late 1820s.[11]

In casting his lot with the restorationist faction, Ballou did not contemplate a new venture in religion; rather, it seemed vastly important that they were preserving "the old ground" of the earliest Universalists against "new-fledged speculatists, iconoclasts, and superficial radicals." Yet he spoke of his colleagues in the movement as "Separatists."[12] In antebellum reform there were familiar analogues to this strategy of restoring the purity of the faith by acts of secession.

To one outside observer, it seemed that the restorationists stressed the materiality of the soul, which was to remain dead until the general restoration of mankind. Furthermore, they believed in "conversion, or change of heart, in order to [achieve] holiness here and happiness hereafter, and they insist more strenuously than do their brethren of the Universalist denomination upon a life of faith and good works."[13] On the one hand, then, the restorationists operated within a sense of restricted time to be interrupted by God while the Universalists envisioned a steady progress of souls into heaven. On the other hand, the restorationists were perfectionists: that is, in their view the millennial character of man was immediately available to individuals. It would be a mistake to think belief in uniform progress more con-

---

[11] Restorationism is discussed recurrently in Ballou's *Autobiography;* see also Eddy, *Universalism*, II, 260–342; and Eddy's more hostile account in Joseph Henry Allen and Richard Eddy, *A History of the Unitarians and Universalists in the United States*, Vol. X of the *American Church History Series* (New York, 1894), 454, 456, 458–459.

[12] Ballou, *Autobiography*, pp. 175, 182, 197.

[13] Gorrie, *Churches and Sects*, pp. 221–223. For a presentation by a restorationist (and congressman), see Charles Hudson, "Restorationists," in I. Daniel Rupp, ed., *An Original History of the Religious Denominations at Present Existing in the United States* (Philadelphia, 1844), pp. 637–655.

ducive to reform. In restorationist time, the significance of an
immediate gesture could be mighty; one could act in the belief
that the millennium would occur through a complicated sequence
of events, with present-day gestures being fulfilled in a later
phase of history. Here, then, was the distinction, which Ballou
explained to the nonresistants, between those persons who were
bound to be punished for the duration of this life and those who
could effect their metaphorical escape from slavery and begin to
realize the millennium. From restorationism Ballou carried beliefs
in the intrusion of God into history and the ultimate grace of
all men as he fashioned a communitarian plan to restore the
world to freedom and holiness.

Caution is necessary lest we simplify restorationism into a reform movement. By Ballou's estimate, half of his associates in the
movement were politically conservative.[14] Not everyone with their
religious opinions seceded from Universalism.[15] Others who did
secede followed routes to reform quite different from Ballou's.[16]
What determined Ballou's successive changes in his denominational allegiances were attitudes toward the place of sin in human
history; and one by one he also convinced himself of the sinfulness of drink, tobacco, slavery, and fighting. He became a reformer concerned with the assault on specific sins. And he began
to acquire followers.

Restorationism was split apart in 1838 when Ballou and six
others proposed a long code of conduct and a scheme of disen-
gagement from government, concluding that "we acknowledge
ourselves bound by the most sublime, solemn, and indispensable
obligations to be perfect as our Father in heaven is perfect, in
all possible respects." They renounced all forms of coercion, including vigorous proselytism and physical punishment of chil-

[14] Ballou, *History of Hopedale*, pp. 2–3.
[15] Eddy, *Universalism*, II, 334–335.
[16] Orestes Brownson, for example, took part in the Massachusetts Restorationist Association's convention of 1835 (Ballou, *Autobiography*, p. 262).
Two others to gain fame were Alanson St. Clair, a bitter foe of nonresistance, and George Bradburn, the antislavery legislator (Eddy, *Universalism*, II, 334).

dren. Much as this disturbed the brotherhood of restorationists, it delighted other parties: it was front-page news in the *Non-Resistant.*[17] By 1841 restorationism was dead, but its saving remnant was prepared for a new venture: "We were 'a peculiar people' in the professing Christian world. . . . We had gathered a new species of grape from the primitive Christian vintage, and had extracted therefrom a sample of the 'new wine' of the Kingdom of God. But where were the bottles to hold and preserve it?"[18] The Hopedale Community was launched in 1841. It was the culmination of Ballou's inquiries into the persistence of sin and enslavement in the history of his time and into the role of reform in the coming of the millennium.

iii

The Hopedale Community was founded as an exaltation of Christianity, a place where Christians could behave on a plane unfamiliar to governmental civilization. A network of such places —an expanding area of regeneration—was contemplated, but in the end there was only the Hopedale Community in Milford, Massachusetts. Some estimates of membership may be useful in discussing the community. In April 1842 the community numbered 28 settlers. In 1853 there were 229 residents (76 members, 22 probationers, 79 family dependents, and 52 others). In 1856, when the community was at its peak of success, there were about 300 residents, of whom 110 were members. At one time or another, about 196 persons enjoyed membership in the community. In 1876, 14 of these persons were still in residence.

The early 1840s, of course, saw many other communities, and Hopedale was careful in defining its relationship to them. The people of Hopedale were Christian nonresistants. Since they wished to "know whether there is any such thing as man's being and doing right from the law of God written on his heart, without the aid of external bonds and restraints," and since they be-

[17] *Non-Resistant,* July 20, 1839, p. 1; Ballou, *History of Hopedale,* pp. 3–8; Eddy, *Universalism,* II, 292–293, 313.
[18] Ballou, *Autobiography,* pp. 9–10.

lieved "that it is every man's privilege, by the grace of God, to attain such a state," they had little use for "the governmental machinery employed" in some other communitarian movements, such as the Shakers.[19] But it was the movement called Owenism that they really despised. John A. Collins was a former Garrisonian who had gone to England and been convinced by Robert Owen that personal behavior was molded by environmental circumstances. Collins' community in Skaneateles, New York, advertised its "disbelief in any special revelation of God to man, touching his will and thereby binding upon man as authority in any arbitrary sense." Here was a form of freedom for which Hopedale had no use. Its folly seemed confirmed when Skaneateles applied for a state charter in order to check the lawlessness of some members. Collins' abrupt personal reversion to the Whig Party and orthodox religion reminded them of the instability in the careers of other contemporary reformers, most notably Orestes Brownson.[20] Hopedale might be defined, then, as an effort to avoid both the regimen of the Shakers and the license of Skaneateles. The community felt that exclusive attention to either the regimen of God or the problems of man could lead to unpredictable reversals of direction.

Toward other communities the attitude of Hopedale was less severe. There was even some thought of merging the resources of Brook Farm and Hopedale. The former had wealth and refinement; the latter, righteousness and familiarity with hard work. But Brook Farm could not be persuaded to adopt the practical Christian standard of conduct, on which membership in Hopedale was based. The questions of individualism and divine law separated the communities. When the Brook Farm transcendentalists charged Hopedale with sectarianism, Ballou thought this was nonsense:

[19] *Practical Christian*, Sept. 15, 1840, as quoted in Ballou, *History of Hopedale*, p. 17. This is from the preliminary plan for a community.

[20] Collins is quoted in J. Humphrey Noyes, *History of American Socialisms* (Philadelphia, 1870), pp. 164–168; the document was soon repudiated for being too much like a creed. See also *Practical Christian*, May 17, 1845, p. 3; Sept. 19, 1846, p. 3.

We confess ourselves a good deal puzzled to understand what is meant by "*sect*," "*sectarian*," and "*sectarianism*," as the terms are getting to be used latterly. It would appear that devotion to distinctive Christianity on the most *enlarged* grounds is "*sectarianism*," as contradistinguished to believing in abstract universal religion and morality or *humanity*. To define and insist on any great virtue as a ground of fellowship, (for instance, total abstinence from the infliction of injuries even on enemies, from slavery, from war, licentiousness and intoxicating beverages) has got to be "*sectarian*," almost as much as to contend for transubstantiation, particular election, the Trinity, &c., as articles of faith essential to salvation. . . . Is a man *sectarian* because he is a Christian?[21]

The transcendentalists' *Dial* commended Hopedale's plans, but insisted that the test for membership made "their community a church only, and not *the* church of Christ's idea, world embracing." That church could be based "on nothing short of faith in the universal man, as he comes out of the hands of the Creator, with no law over his liberty, but the eternal ideas that lie at the foundation of his being." At this juncture the dispute mirrored the one which occurred between the come-outers and the churches, with Brook Farm espousing a religion of humanity and Hopedale championing the saving importance of institutions. Hopedale, founded in secession, soon divorced itself from "non-organizationists" and "*stay-outers*."[22]

At every point in Hopedale's relationships with other communities we are reminded of the implicit conservatism of Ballou's theological views. He had told the nonresistants that it was possible to begin to realize the freedom of the millennium while recognizing the necessity of control in the modern world where sin and slavery prevailed. Hopedale was neither an engine of social control nor a celebration of individual emancipation; it

[21] Ballou, *History of Hopedale*, pp. 24–26; *Practical Christian*, Jan. 22, 1842, p. 2.

[22] *Dial* is quoted in *ibid.*, Nov. 27, 1841, p. 2. A more condescending Brook Farmer thought Hopedale lacked "the aesthetic features which a just state of society must wear." See *ibid.*, Sept. 3, 1842, p. 3; Oct. 27, 1849, p. 3.

was a congregation leading itself into conformity with the dispensations of God.

In histories of the antebellum years, communitarianism is usually singled out as one reform and abolitionism as another. Moreover, some historians have seen in communities like Hopedale a modern reform with its basis in economic and social theories rather than the religious evangelicalism which influenced antislavery.[23] Both these views may be questioned. In the case of Hopedale, at least, the importance of a proper solution to the problem of human government under the sovereignty of God outweighed whatever economic or social wisdom might have been learned from other communities. And although the members of Hopedale eventually came to differ from abolitionists who supported war and politics, for a long time they were able to identify their venture with abolitionism. As the controversy with the Brook Farmers revealed, Hopedale was greatly concerned with the institutional promotion of reforming moral principles. It should not be surprising, then, to discover that Hopedale was peculiarly close to antislavery.

The *Liberator* in the early 1840s was filled with letters from abolitionists longing for communities where Christianity would be more important than economic details or organization charts.[24] Garrison joined Ballou in defending membership tests when other communities ridiculed them, and in 1844 he praised Hopedale as the only community based on nonresistance.[25] Few famous abolitionists, however, were willing to separate themselves from society by signing on at Hopedale. One object of those who did

[23] See Thomas, *The Liberator*, pp. 312–313, and Bernard Weisberger, *They Gathered at the River: The Story of the Great Revivalists and Their Impact upon Religion in America* (Boston, 1958), pp. 156–157.

[24] Besides Hopedale documents in *Liberator*, Dec. 25, 1840, p. 4, and Feb. 26, 1841, pp. 1–2, see especially the letters by "Humanitas," Dec. 25, 1840, p. 3; by Abby Folsom, Jan. 8, 1840, p. 2; by N. H. Whiting, March 5, 1841, p. 2; and by eight Ohioans, March 5, 1841, p. 3. There was another surge of interest in communities in the autumn of 1843. The *Liberator* (Jan. 5, 1844, p. 3), like Ballou, criticized the Owenite subversion of individual moral accountability in the Skaneateles community.

[25] *Practical Christian*, Sept. 28, 1844, p. 3; *Liberator*, Nov. 8, 1844, p. 4.

come was to concentrate forces of moral reform on which the countryside could draw: visitors from Hopedale spoke and swelled the audiences at antislavery rallies in dozens of small towns. Ballou himself was twice sent by the American Anti-Slavery Society to lecture in Pennsylvania and New York (these trips gave him opportunities also to solicit contributions for his community).[26] Meanwhile the celebrities of reform arrived regularly to speak at Hopedale, especially for the First of August commemorations of emancipation in the West Indies. One resident thought he remembered hearing Anna Dickinson, the enchanting young girl who helped bring the political message of abolitionism to Northern crowds during the Civil War, make her first speech.[27]

It is not quite accurate to say that no celebrated abolitionists were moved to live at Hopedale. Henry C. Wright made the community his headquarters as "the voluntary, unhired agent" of the New England Non-Resistance Society.[28] Surprisingly enough, urbane and aristocratic Edmund Quincy asked permission to join the quarterly meetings of those who initially planned the community.[29] Oliver Johnson actually joined the "Practical Christian Ministry" of the community and edited the *Practical Christian,* the community's paper, before going to manage the *Anti-Slavery Bugle* of Salem, Ohio.[30] Nevertheless, most abolitionists found ways of acknowledging the significance of Hopedale without giving themselves over to the venture.

Frederick Douglass visited in 1842, when the venture was scarcely under way. Three years later he left in the keeping of Hopedale Rosetta Hall, an escaped slave whom he had known

[26] Ballou, *Autobiography,* pp. 356, 370. See also Ballou to J. Miller McKim, March 25, 1845, McKim Papers, Cornell University.

[27] William F. Draper, *Recollections of a Varied Career* (Boston, 1908), p. 25.

[28] Ballou, *Autobiography,* pp. 380–381; *Practical Christian,* Jan. 8, 1848, p. 3. At this time the *Non-Resistant* was briefly merged with the Hopedale paper in an attempted revival.

[29] *Practical Christian,* May 15, 1840, p. 2.

[30] *Ibid.,* Sept. 30, 1848, p. 2; Feb. 3, 1849, p. 2; July 21, 1849, p. 3; Ballou, *Autobiography,* pp. 381–382.

in bondage. Among other famous fugitives who found sanctuary there were the Crafts and the slave rescuer known as the Man with the Branded Hand.[31] Many books were sent to the Hopedale Library by Senator Charles Sumner, although as nonresistants these constituents were "of no political account."[32] Out of Hopedale came the standard collection of antislavery hymns.[33] On a visit from England, the abolitionist George Thompson made a special trip to Hopedale; in England, the abolitionist Elizabeth Pease published Ballou's address on nonresistance in relation to human governments.[34] When a new church building was dedicated in 1860, Samuel Joseph May, who had once been a regular contributor to the *Practical Christian* though never a member of the community, reported the event for the *National Anti-Slavery Standard.* He noticed how unusual it was for a church-raising to be of much interest to antislavery people.[35]

Hopedale's school was run by Ballou's daughter and Morgan Bloom from the Five Points Mission. May sent his son to the school, as did a well-known abolitionist merchant from Boston, Charles F. Hovey. Of more interest, William Lloyd Garrison sent one of his sons.[36] These young men identified themselves strongly with the community. George Thompson Garrison and Edward

[31] Ballou, *History of Hopedale*, pp. 77, 143; Anna Thwing Field, "Anti-Slavery, and Other Visitors, to the Community," and Nellie T. Gifford, "Childhood Days in the Hopedale Community and Other Recollections," both in *Hopedale Reminiscences: Papers Read before the Hopedale Ladies' Sewing Society and Branch Alliance* (Hopedale, 1910), pp. 24, 52.

[32] *Practical Christian*, Apr. 2, 1839, p. 2.

[33] George W. Stacy, *Anti-Slavery Hymns, Designed to Aid the Cause of Human Rights* (Hopedale, 1844). There was also Ballou's *The Hopedale Collection of Hymns and Songs, for the use of Practical Christians* (Hopedale, 1850), with heavy emphasis on antislavery and reform.

[34] *Practical Christian*, Feb. 15, 1851, p. 3; *Liberator*, Dec. 4, 1840, p. 3.

[35] Ballou, *History of Hopedale*, pp. 327–330. May's name was listed with regular contributors to the *Practical Christian* on July 15, 1840, and for a while thereafter.

[36] Gifford, "Childhood Days in Hopedale," Sarah E. Bradbury, "Community Life as Seen by One of the Young People," and Ellen M. Patrick, "Our Community School and Its Teacher," *Hopedale Reminiscences*, pp. 54, 14, 41. On Hovey, see Garrisons, *Garrison*, III, 220–221n.

May were two of the three editors of the *Diamond,* a paper in which the young people of Hopedale condemned slavery in the world outside and praised their home as "an exemplification of a *true* government—a Christian state, in which violence and oppression and vengeance have no place . . . in fact, a true local church of the Lord Jesus Christ."[37]

The point made by this kind of evidence is that Hopedale was closely connected to the antislavery movement, but this did not make it simply an abolitionist organization. Its larger purpose was to pose an alternative to enslaved worldly morals. The children of abolitionists were freer to join in that pursuit than their fathers who simultaneously sought immediate piecemeal reforms. Furthermore, some of Ballou's chief associates left Hopedale in dissatisfaction, and near the surface of each dispute was the community's inattention to specific causes which they deemed all-important. These disputes help to clarify both the goals of Hopedale and the theoretical tensions of antislavery.

George W. Stacy had been a representative to the Massachusetts legislature before landing in Hopedale. As a young abolitionist, he had watched Garrison being mobbed; unlike other members of the community, he considered the cause of the slave to be *"paramount."* In 1845 he withdrew from the community with the vague complaint that the deference shown to Ballou, however admirable his sense of religious duty, bordered on despotism. Stacy still yearned for "a *social reform,*" by which the law of love might come to unite mankind, but he was presently more anxious for the reconstruction of the South than for the success of communities. Before long he was again active in political prohibitionism as well as abolitionism and, late in life, he was sent again to the legislature. He also strengthened his conviction that communities were themselves a form of "bondage," an impediment to the work of antislavery. Each person must retain responsibility for the "individuality" implanted by God "in the nature of our being."[38] Stacy's was a kind of individualism,

---

[37] *The Diamond,* Nov. 15, 1851, p. 66.
[38] Adin Ballou, *History of the Town of Milford, Worcester County,*

set on immediate goals, which had no patience for the progressive millennial renovation of society and very little tolerance of disagreement concerning the means of reform.

A major issue over which contention arose at Hopedale was whether there should be private property. Once more it is instructive to trace individual careers. Clother Gifford, the most stubborn advocate of a community of goods, had been a member of the Society of Friends in Fairhaven, Massachusetts, until the elders advised him to be silent in meetings "and not avail myself of the common privilege of the saints, as described by the apostle when he says, 'Ye may all prophesy one by one, that all may be comforted.'" Gifford had become a nonresistant and a comeouter. After Henry C. Wright visited Fairhaven, Gifford expressed a longing to become a professional in the cause of reform. All he needed was support for a small family; all he asked was to share "in the work (not the reward) of RENOVATING the world." Two years later he was inspired by widespread interest in communities, for he thought that the Holy Ghost freed man from the desire for private property. A few more months found him in more material pursuits: "CLOTHER GIFFORD, PRACTICAL PHRENOLOGIST, and Teacher of Natural, Mental, Moral and Physiological Science" read a large advertisement in the *Liberator*. Another year and he was with the founders of Hopedale and writing didactic verse.[39]

Gifford was spokesman for a group which early quit Hopedale because it was not based on common property. As Ballou told the story, Gifford moved rather slyly from discussions of "dietetic, physiological, and economic" themes to accusations that too much "aristocracy" prevailed in the community.[40] Probably

Massachusetts, from Its First Settlement to 1881 (Boston, 1882), pp. 1025–1026; *Practical Christian*, Dec. 27, 1845, pp. 2–3; Aug. 21, 1841, p. 4; Feb. 1, 1841, p. 4; *Liberator*, Oct. 9, 1846, p. 4; Nov. 27, 1846, p. 4; Nov. 9, 1855, p. 3; June 1, 1848, p. 4.

[39] *Liberator*, Aug. 2, 1839, p. 4; Nov. 13, 1840, p. 4; Jan. 8, 1841, p. 3; March 5, 1841, p. 4; *Practical Christian*, June 11, 1842, pp. 3, 4; June 25, 1842, p. 4.

[40] Ballou, *History of Hopedale*, pp. 87–90.

he was more an enthusiast than a conspirator. When he first saw the light of nonresistance, he had attacked those who questioned the practical effects of the doctrine. "I thought that it had become the creed of abolitionists that supposed consequences were not the rule of action; but that the commands of God were to be obeyed, and consequences left to him who gave the commands."[41]

Gifford is a perfect illustration of the vagaries of antinomianism. He ascribed absolute authority to God and thus established the inflexibility of the great principles of reform. This inflexibility led to fickleness of another sort, for he was left as his own interpreter of those great principles. Otherwise he would have had to let intervening authorities diminish the supremacy of God. Much as the individualistic Stacy and the communistic Gifford disagreed in temperament and viewpoint, they both understood slavery to be a sign of all the coercions and restrictions of earthly life, but they had no program to abolish that kind of slavery. Therefore they operated on a level where specific tasks, such as the prohibition of drinking, the promulgation of phrenology, or the liberation of the slaves (even of a particular slave) characterized the millennium.

Often the tension between the exalted spirit and the limited objective became so disturbing that it was impossible to stick to any organization. A possible side effect was recoil into authoritarian methods incongruously used to seek out freedom. For example, one of Ballou's dearest associates, David R. Lamson, rebelled against individualism and private property at Hopedale and briefly joined the Shakers.[42] Another friend, Daniel S. Whitney, floated into political prohibitionism and later was a delegate to the state constitutional convention.[43]

[41] *Liberator*, July 5, 1839, p. 4. Compare Stacy's conversion in *Non-Resistant*, Feb. 16, 1839, p. 3.

[42] Ballou, *History of Hopedale*, pp. 101–102; *Practical Christian*, June 10, 1848, p. 3; David R. Lamson, *Two Years Experience among the Shakers* (West Boylston, 1848), esp. pp. 18–27.

[43] Ballou, *Autobiography*, p. 366.

While there were defections on the part of members with inflexible understandings of reform, Hopedale sustained a dialec-
tical freedom. It was not committed to a specific blueprint. In
fact, the community went through numerous constitutional revisions as they tried, in Ballou's words, "to escape the Scylla of
threatening Communism" and "the Charybdis of selfish, unscru-
pulous Individualism."[44] This freedom to innovate and to change
course was certainly related to Ballou's understanding that the
millennium would follow the dynamic interaction of individuals
bound to different planes of morality. But a community based on
Ballou's theological views was bound to irritate persons who were
committed to specific political or economic reforms.

Hopedale did not depend on any economic dogma. It mixed
private and common property in its arrangements and changed
the mix from time to time. People who stayed at Hopedale
shared a vague economic criticism of the outside world; they
thought there was too much selfishness, as was to be expected
because most of the world was still enslaved to sin. "Property
must be Christianized" lest it "Mammonize and Atheize nominal
Christendom" was their opinion; yet they all agreed that property was obviously good. The trick was to subject it to the Christian law of love, to make it serve peace and righteousness instead
of selfishness and antagonism. How was this possible? "By making divine moral principle supreme in the minds of as many individuals as possible, and then associating those individuals in
Practical Christian Communities under obligations, pledges and
arrangements, the natural working of which shall be to abridge
individual selfishness, to secure for every one all needful advantages of employment, education, religion, government and whole-
some order."[45]

Land reform, for instance, seemed silly, however commendable
were the intentions of Gerrit Smith and its other advocates. Why

[44] *History of Hopedale*, pp. 95–97. These changes are summarized
handily in Thomas, "Antislavery and Utopia," in Duberman, ed., *Antislavery Vanguard*, pp. 249–254.
[45] *Practical Christian*, May 12, 1849, p. 3.

was ownership of land worse than ownership of money? Were the tenants of a prosperous employer worse off than they would be owning their land but dependent on him for capital? Again, if present-day land speculators were forbidden to own land but retained "the same lack of high moral principle, the same capital, and the same skill which have heretofore rendered them scourges to the poor," might they not "go into the breadstuff speculation, or any other of the thousand and one monopolies of this commercial age," and be more oppressive than ever?[46] These questions were typical of the community's outlook. Their economics was fundamentally concerned with sinful relationships among persons rather than the evils of particular institutions.

Ballou remained true to the convictions expressed in his first speech to nonresistants: he sought institutions that served the regenerate and were free of coercion. His community was intended to guide individuals under God's law and then to construct Christian institutions. Outside of Christ, even haphazard and undemocratic controls were necessary evils; indeed, part of Ballou's indictment of the church was that it neglected its pastoral duties for the sake of worthless ceremonies. For those in Christ's care, the story is plain to any reader of Ballou's history of the community. Constitutions and economic arrangements were of secondary importance; they were at the level of "polity" where expediency was a legitimate consideration. Much more crucial were the responsibilities of teaching the young, of raising adults from probationary membership to true religion, of encouraging hymns and festivals to assure the good character of the community. Ballou easily acquired the phrase, "Christian nurture," to describe his chief concerns.[47] Hopedale was not a machine of social control, but neither was it antinomian. It was not opposed to intermediaries between God and man.

---

[46] *Ibid.*, Nov. 25, 1848, p. 2.

[47] Ballou, *History of Hopedale*, pp. 154, 195; Ballou, *Human Progress in Respect to Religion* . . . (Hopedale, 1867). See also the essay by William H. Fish in *Practical Christian*, Feb. 14, 1852, p. 2.

iv

Several studies of American anarchism have pointed to Hopedale as an important nineteenth-century expression of anarchist ideas,[48] and this is certainly justified by Ballou's equation of government with slavery and sin. On the other hand, Ballou recognized the necessity of government for those who remained enslaved to sin. Hopedale made no pretense of being "a renewed garden of Eden," and those who came looking for easy, uncontrolled bliss were disappointed. The community sought a "middle passage" between arrangements and spontaneity.[49] Even on free meeting in religion they hedged: in theory they opposed this ideal of come-outerism, but when their theory was attacked, their services were revealed to be in keeping with the ideal.[50] We cannot help noticing curfews, taxes, moral police, and the work force called the Hopedale Industrial Army.[51] It was a strange anarchism which maintained that "everyone may enjoy as much freedom and individuality as is conducive to the *general good,* including of course his own good," but that everyone must sacrifice some liberty until the community is perfected.[52]

On the other hand, force was never used or contemplated. So successfully did the community rely on persuasion that the worst charge made by disgruntled individualists was that too much deference was paid to some residents. If there had been more stubborn resistance to authority, it might have tested and thereby enriched Ballou's conception of government under nonresistance.

---

[48] Eunice Minette Schuster, *Native American Anarchism: A Study of Left-Wing American Individualism* (reprint ed., New York, 1970), p. 80; Corinne Jacker, *The Black Flag of Anarchy: Antistatism in the United States* (New York, 1968), pp. 80–81.

[49] Ballou, *History of Hopedale,* p. 169; Ballou, *Autobiography,* p. 358.

[50] *Practical Christian,* Sept. 19, 1846, p. 3; Oct. 3, 1846, p. 3.

[51] Ballou, *History of Hopedale,* pp. 190–193, 202.

[52] *Practical Christian,* Oct. 31, 1846, p. 3. It would be unfair not to notice that William H. Fish wrote the last statement during the period when Stacy's recent defection was intriguing the abolition press. Nothing quite like it can be found in Ballou's writings.

Simple as that conception may have been, it was based on a complex theology, and twenty years at Hopedale did not shake it.

The purpose of government, according to Ballou, was "true moral order," which had to be contrasted, in good nonresistant fashion, with arbitrary human attempts at order. The only possible "supreme moral authority, or government," was divine. Everything else was expediency: "There is, strictly speaking, no such thing as human government." Indeed, those who upheld some human right to govern were *"would-be deicides"* and *"genuine no-governmentists."* Nonetheless, divine government had to be "clothed in *human forms* and administered by *human organizations,"* with the element of coercion removed. If two-thirds of the professing Christians were won to nonresistance, government everywhere might operate without force as it did at Hopedale. In the process of conversion, Ballou assumed, many persons would have "reconstructed neighborhood society by voluntary associations" so as to eliminate nearly all "intemperance, idleness, debauchery, miseducation, poverty and brutality." Everywhere would prevail both "self-improvement" and "strong moral guardianship." One way or another, most of the tasks now delegated to governments would be taken up voluntarily; what was left for government could be done cheaply and simply.[53]

Stated in this way, Ballou's projection of government may appear simple-minded. He boasted that Hopedale was composed of America's middle class and thus included more ministers, farmers, and craftsmen than vain fanatics.[54] Possibly his sketch of the future was circumscribed by the middle-class norms of his day. And surely the obscurity of his community and his social dreams is due to their sobriety: they were neither weird enough to be a side-show attraction in popular narratives nor militant enough to be serviceable in left-wing chronicles. The boldness of Hopedale, however, can be surveyed only in its theology. When pressed to

53 Ballou, *Christian Non-Resistance, in All Its Important Bearings, Illustrated and Defended* (Philadelphia, 1846), pp. 84–85, 214, 229–233.
54 Ballou, *History of Hopedale*, pp. 339–340.

depict the future, as he seldom let himself be, Ballou could scarcely rise above his rural and middle-class surroundings. But he had the nerve to commit his entire life to a venture for which he knew no precedent, without any certainty that the direction of history was really comprehensible.

Ballou was determined to resurrect the original precepts and practices of Christianity, a determination leading to both nonresistance and community.[55] His theology, therefore, started from a way of reading the Bible. In an "Exposition of Faith" for the founders of Hopedale, Ballou maintained that the Bible included "a complete revelation of the divine perfections, of human duty, and of the future state." It was "an infallible directory of religious faith and practice." But in consulting this directory, he pointed out, great caution is needed. Stanza divisions are usually misleading; Jesus and the apostles spoke with changing degrees of inspiration; translation magnifies the difficulties; and sometimes it is absolutely impossible to establish whether a passage is reliably given. Moreover, much of the language of the Bible, indeed of all language, is *"figurative"* and demands prayerful rumination before its *"internal purport"* becomes visible. In fact, the Bible must always be construed "according to the evident *spirit* of its text, rather than the mere *letter*." Concentration on the language, which is merely human, gives birth to sectarian creeds.[56]

The difference between letter and spirit, between the expression and the inspiration, in a larger sense defines the relationship of the Old Testament to the New:

There is the difference of anticipation and reality—of type and antitype—of sign and thing signified—of shadow and substance. This is a great difference; but yet it is one of *agreement,* not *contradiction.* . . . A whole system of types and shadows, branching out into hundreds of particular external observances, was instituted for the purpose of attaching the Israelites to the true God, and preparing the way for the

[55] Finally Ballou wrote a three-volume *Primitive Christianity and Its Corruptions* (Boston, 1870; Lowell, 1899, 1900), which revealed his diligent search for the practices and doctrines of those closest in time to Christ.
[56] *Practical Christian,* May 15, 1840, pp. 1–2; June 1, 1840, pp. 1–2.

coming of the just One. . . . In due time the promise was fulfilled, the expected Messiah made his appearance, his spiritual religion was established, the anticipation gave place to reality, the type to the anti- type, the sign to the thing signified, the shadow to the substance. Consequently, all doctrines and duties peculiar to the typical dispen- sation expired with it.

Jesus and the apostles distilled the spirit beyond the mere letter of the old laws. "Thou shalt not kill," for example, was transfig- ured into "Resist not evil."[57]

In short, Ballou, while seeking to live a Biblical Christianity, confessed that in many ways the Bible was barely intelligible. To use the proper term, he was a typologist: he stressed the dis- continuity between the two bodies of Scripture and explained the relationship between the two dispensations of God by means of theories of figurative language. Typology had been familiar to the Puritan founders of New England as a method of Biblical exegesis by which the secrets of the stages of history and of the timing of the millennium might be glimpsed; with the related notion of "further light," or evidence that men were approaching a new break in time, it reappeared frequently in separatist reli- gious movements.[58] Typology served two purposes in Ballou's thought. First, it obviously eliminated the objection to nonresis- tance that it was inconsistent with the divine sanction of war and government in the Old Testament. Christian reformers were sup- posed to teach the law of love as found in the New Testament. Second, typology enabled Ballou to relate the fortunes of his community to the second coming of Christ and the millennium.

Ballou admitted that John Humphrey Noyes's writings had changed his mind about the second coming. Previously, even dur- ing the restorationist controversy, he had assumed that Christ's return lay in the future and therefore that the millennium was unthinkably far off. Now he understood that the second coming

[57] *Ibid.*, July 15, 1840, pp. 1–2; Ballou, *Christian Non-Resistance, in All Its Important Bearings*, pp. 66–80.

[58] This background is traced more extensively in my "Adin Ballou's Hopedale Community and the Theology of Antislavery," *Church History*, XXXIX (1970), 385–387.

had already occurred and, for all his dislike of Noyes, he was better able to read the Bible.[59] For example, with this understanding it was possible for him to urge men to act out the spirit of the millennium. But had he taken something else from Noyes? In his remarkable letter to Garrison, which played a role in the formulation of nonresistance, Noyes had explained: "I regard the existing governments as bearing the same relation to a dispensation that is to come, as that which the Jewish dispensation bore to the Christian—that is, they are preparatory forms of discipline, fitted to the childhood of the race—'shadows of good things to come,' which are to be taken away when the substance appears."[60] Ballou conceived of Hopedale in a similar scheme of history. By keeping in mind the distance between types and antitypes, he adjusted himself to the ambiguity between piecemeal reforms and an enlarged hope of liberation—an ambiguity which baffled some other abolitionists.

The community carried out the promise of his earliest remarks as a reformer. It was a break with complacent Christians who "looked for the kingdom of God to come on earth in the old miraculous way and traditional millennial form" and who accordingly denied the possibility of anything more than "gradual improvement" so long as human nature is defective.

Is not the kingdom of heaven "within" and "among" men, and thence, like leaven hid in three measures of meal, destined to ferment and rectify the whole mass? Ought not each true Christian's heart to be a germ of the millennium, and each Christian community a proximate miniature of it?[61]

From the perspective of typology, Hopedale could be thought of

[59] *Practical Christian*, Apr. 15, 1843, p. 3. For Noyes's version, see Robert Allerton Parker, *A Yankee Saint: John Humphrey Noyes and the Oneida Community* (New York, 1935), pp. 112–113.

[60] Garrisons, *Garrison*, II, 147. I would not suggest that Ballou got his typology from Noyes, only some of its implications. He was well-read in ecclesiastical history and greatly admired Origen as a kind of proto-Universalist.

[61] Ballou, *Autobiography*, p. 336; Ballou, *Christian Non-Resistance, in All Its Important Bearings*, pp. 178–179.

as a sign—neither the first nor the last—prefiguring the approach of the millennial government of God. Thus Ballou could compare the withdrawal of reformers to Hopedale with the journey of the Jews from bondage and even with Jesus' being called out of Egypt. They were not of the world, but their pilgrimage would play a role in the world's redemption from bondage. The original members of the community, in their first advertisement, spoke of their "faith in such small things" as their present endeavor and expressed their hope that it might point to the day when "the kingdoms of this world should be absorbed in the glorious kingdom of our Lord Jesus Christ."[62] We may observe that an intense awareness of types and figures in the recorded past could inspire a great deal of labor on enterprises which were small in their immediate prospects.

As a tool of literary criticism to relate Old and New Testaments—to find correlations between types and antitypes, shadows and substances—typology enjoys the advantage that both levels of discourse are recorded in the Bible. But in turning typology into a principle of social action and interpreting the present period of history as a stage of apprenticeship prior to a stage of fulfilled perfection, Ballou lacked that advantage. His community was a hopeful venture into the unknown. There is no reliable chain of present causes and future effects. It is absurd for anyone but God to infer the antitype from the type; only God knows the future as history. Knowledge of the dispensation yet to come is shadowy; but it is at least that, and man must steer as well as he can by the flickering outlines. It might be possible to find the passage between Scylla and Charybdis which Ballou continually sought. Within the limitations of uncertain knowledge, therefore, Hopedale was expected to provide a model of the eventual church of God. Ballou was reconciled to being "a sort of modern John the Baptist" getting things ready for the divine kingdom.[63]

Hopedale was not expected to restore Paradise on earth; all that

[62] Ballou, *History of Hopedale*, pp. 65, 67–68. The advertisement is reprinted on pp. 20–21.
[63] Ballou, *Autobiography*, p. 406.

was claimed for it was that it was a "presage" of "a world ultimately regenerated and Edenized."[64] This limited expectation
undoubtedly contributed to its ability to survive two decades with
many changes but without disbanding. The same outlook, however, made it possible suddenly to give up present hopes and live
on in stubborn otherworldliness: "So shall the Hopedale Community have a glorious resurrection,—an apotheosis, of which its
earlier manifestation was but the harbinger and prototype." This
distant resurrection was imagined as taking place on "virgin
soil."[65] Ballou's long *History of the Hopedale Community* proceeds on two levels: it records information to benefit future plan-
ners of communities, and it explains why human deficiencies presently prevent their success. It is, in short, an old testament of
Christian socialism.

John Humphrey Noyes greatly admired one of Ballou's books,
Practical Christian Socialism; its lack of fame he attributed to
American bewitchment by French and British schemers. But he
dismissed Ballou's account of the devolution of Hopedale as "the
old story of general depravity."[66] Ballou passed over all the immediate causes of Hopedale's decline. The heart of the matter,
in his account, was that the church was bound to the plane of the
world and could not supply "Christlike" material for an elevated
experiment. Only with difficulty could he distinguish his viewpoint
from the skepticism of those who were "forever postponing the
advent of a truly Christian dispensation."[67] His perfectionism

[64] "The Hopedale Community," a tract reprinted in *Liberator,* Dec. 12,
1851, p. 4.

[65] Ballou, *History of Hopedale,* p. 293. The same sort of typology may
be found on pp. 291, 298–300.

[66] Noyes, *American Socialisms,* pp. 127–129, 131; Ballou, *Practical
Christian Socialism: A Conversational Exposition of the True System of
Human Society* (Hopedale and New York, 1854).

[67] Ballou, *History of Hopedale,* pp. 359, 21–22, and *passim.* Ballou was
extremely taken with a letter received from William Ellery Channing at
the outset of the community experiment. Channing expressed his own
dream of community and warned that the greatest perils lurked in personal
and selfish sources of discord: "The Catholics have provided against these

proved to be much more modest than Noyes's. Ballou's techniques of reading Scripture and his understanding of God's historical designs—his typology—obliged him to claim for his community only a limited achievement, confined by its historical moment.

Hopedale was, in summary, a sustained response to the reformer's obligation to assist others in their escape from slavery and to foreshadow the coming of the kingdom of God. Ballou was a devoted abolitionist; the community was connected in many ways to organized antislavery efforts; and the theological beliefs behind the community presented solutions to some of the theoretical problems vexing Garrisonian nonresistance. And yet, in spite of the closeness of Ballou and Hopedale to antislavery, he emphasized a pessimistic view of human nature that was usually dismissed or kept silent in antislavery thought. His awareness of the persistence of sin in history required him to limit his expectations of success for all reform endeavors, even his own community. Ballou was one of the most stalwart nonresistants, and his community lasted longer than most. His life showed remarkable success and consistency. But his pessimistic views and his commitment to the cause of a single community increasingly isolated him from other abolitionists, who were understandably impatient for the freedom of the slaves. The anarchistic implications in much of antislavery thought were, in his case, held in check by a complex, typological approach to the government of God. He was never ready to swerve over into adventures in war and politics—and much of the future of antislavery lay in that direction.

---

evils in their religious communities by establishing absolute power, and teaching the members that the first duty is obedience. Whether sufficient unity can be preserved in a free institution built on the foundation of brotherhood and equality remains to be proved." Ballou reprinted this letter (*ibid.*, pp. 42–45) and used it as a running theme throughout his history.

VI

The Politics of Anarchy

After the schism of the American Anti-Slavery Society in 1840, antagonism was fairly constant between the Garrisonians and other abolitionists who founded an independent, radical political party—the Liberty Party. Historians have tended to sort abolitionists into two categories: those who were anarchists and those who were politically oriented. But the divisions were not so simple. On the one hand, Garrisonian anarchism was rather easily diverted into a quest for political influence. On the other, Garrison's antagonists, usually described as political abolitionists, shared some of his most anarchistic assumptions and, in practice, shunned the pressures for compromise and expediency typically associated with politics. Both the Garrisonians and their opponents displayed ambivalent attitudes toward politics and anarchy. There was great complexity in the relationship between radical abolitionism and politics.

The term "political abolitionism" is used here to refer to that part of immediate abolitionism which ventured into independent political action while the Garrisonians were moving toward nonresistant anarchism. There was a "schism" of two groups which originally had been joined in the American Anti-Slavery Society. The politicians discussed here are those of the Liberty Party, not other political organizations which may have included in their platforms the restriction of slavery from the territories. Failure to make this distinction has sometimes handicapped modern writers, but it was once clear even to those who lived in the glory of the Republican North.

Political parties commonly originate in the union of self-interest with some political theory, and this was true of the Republican party; but the Liberty party was founded wholly on principle,—the principle that every man has a right to the fruit of his labor; and this served to give it an energizing element and a moral impetus not unlike that of the crusades.[1]

This quotation does more than elaborate on the distinction between the Liberty and Republican parties. In comparing political abolitionism to the crusades, it may lead us to wonder whether the schism within abolitionism had more to do with the ecstasies of religion than the exigencies of reform.

ii

Some of the ambiguities of politics for abolitionists may be seen in the decline of nonresistance and the rise of disunionism. The life of the New England Non-Resistance Society was remarkably brief. Henry Wright, who had tirelessly kept the doctrine of nonresistance at the forefront of antislavery discussions, spent the mid-1840s in Europe convalescing from consumption. Maria Weston Chapman also spent a good deal of time abroad. Edmund Quincy lost interest in the movement; in September 1841 he confessed he found nonresistance a "dead bore" and almost wished it would fail. Though still claiming to be a nonresistant by conviction, he became quite cynical in his attitude toward the organized movement. He opposed periodic attempts to revive the *Non-Resistant* and absolutely refused to be editor. He stayed away from meetings so as to rid himself of the presidency of the Society and privately rejoiced when the 1843 meetings elected his successor, "Adin I, the first of the name & founder of the Ballouean dynasty."[2] Ballou, who was regularly re-elected

[1] Frank Preston Stearns, *The Life and Public Services of George Luther Stearns* (Philadelphia, 1907), pp. 59–60.

[2] Quincy to Maria Weston Chapman, Sept. 1, 1841; to Caroline Weston, Aug. 14, 1842; to [Caroline?] Weston, Nov. 10, 1843, Weston Papers, Boston Public Library.

president thereafter, was too busy steering Hopedale between Scylla and Charybdis to give much time to nonresistance.

William Lloyd Garrison was from the start apologetic about his lack of time to promote this new reform enterprise, even though he sometimes said it was more important than antislavery. As he left for an antislavery convention in London in 1840, he wrote Maria Weston Chapman that the liberation of the slave was only preliminary to "the reconciliation of the world to God"; he longed for a world convention to establish Jesus as the only ruler of the earth. Mrs. Chapman had the letter printed in the *Non-Resistant* as evidence that, although abolitionism kept him from writing for the paper, his spirit was enlarged.[3] By 1843 Garrison was writing Henry Wright that "the Executive Committee of our little Non-Resistance Society are so occupied with their anti-slavery labors and responsibilities, that they have neither the time nor the means to put any efficient machinery into motion." Yet Garrison persuaded himself that the doctrine of nonresistance was advancing and gaining adherents as a consequence of "the radical character of the anti-slavery movement" and that the organization would snap back to life as soon as Wright returned to America.[4] The Garrisonians had tried to think of nonresistance both as a separate reform, parallel to antislavery, and as a comprehensive religious doctrine of which antislavery was one small part. Now they were either ignoring or postponing the importance of nonresistance.

At some meetings of the Non-Resistance Society no antislavery celebrities appeared; almost no one outside of Hopedale could be depended on. The meetings in December 1848 were held in Boston, so that once again members of the *Liberator* clique attended. But snow kept Hopedale people away (and debate centered uneasily around the question: does the Old Testament God support war?).[5] After 1849 there were no regular conventions, although occasionally meetings were called to rescue the grand

[3] *Non-Resistant,* Aug. 12, 1840, p. 3.
[4] Garrison to Wright, Dec. 16, 1843; Oct. 1, 1844, Garrison Papers, Boston Public Library.
[5] *Liberator,* Jan. 5, 1849, p. 3. For one list of delegates with almost none of the great antislavery names, see *ibid.,* July 9, 1847, p. 4.

doctrine in times of trouble. It is important to note, however, that in this decade of organizational decline there were no dramatic retractions. Nonresistance presumably remained an article of faith among followers of Garrison, but there was less need for conventions. Nonresistance as a separate reform had lost its sense of urgency.

Furthermore, nonresistance was replaced on the abolitionist agenda by disunionism, an antigovernmental movement which was more clearly related to antislavery. On May 13, 1842, the *Liberator* first sported the epigram: "A repeal of the Union between northern liberty and southern slavery is essential to the abolition of the one, and the preservation of the other." In May 1844 the American Anti-Slavery Society adopted the resolution that "secession from the present United States government is the duty of every abolitionist; since no one can take office, or throw a vote for another to hold office, under the United States Constitution, without violating his anti-slavery principles, and rendering himself an abettor of the slaveholder in his sin."[6] This theme dominated Garrisonian abolitionism thereafter. It was an effective substitute for nonresistance.

Disunionism, however, was not a happy application of nonresistance principles, for instead of viewing slavery as but one horrible instance of the ubiquitous sinful habit of governing and coercing, it made slavery a sectional issue and identified Northern governments with liberty. Garrison seemed to sense the difficulty when he proposed an awkward resolution to the last annual meeting of the New England Non-Resistance Society. Somehow disunionism and nonresistance had to be reconciled. It was as necessary for "friends of peace," he contended, to use the motto, "No union with warriors or war-makers," since the United States Constitution sanctioned war, as it was for friends of the slave to withdraw from a constitutional government which protected slavery.[7] Leaving aside the perilous fascination with slogans, we

[6] Quoted in Wendell Phillips, *Can Abolitionists Vote or Take Office under the United States Constitution?* (New York, 1845), p. 3.

[7] *Practical Christian*, Dec. 8, 1849, p. 1. In another resolution, perhaps significantly, Garrison was back contending against defensive war.

may observe that he was narrowing the grounds on which non-resistance opposed government and implying that antislavery and nonresistance were totally separate reforms. In a way, it was disunionism that forced the separation.

It was perfectly in keeping with nonresistance to call for individual secession and the dissolution of the government. But disunionism always had sectional implications. As early as 1842 Henry C. Wright expected the North to secede unless slavery were abolished.[8] Eventually he advocated the formation of a Northern republic. A bewildered Ohioan wrote that he too would be pleased to see "the masses" in the North pull out of their compact with the South "even for the comparatively unworthy object of establishing another arbitrary government in its stead," but it was nothing that a nonresistant should work for. It was time people learned that, slavery or no slavery, voting is wrong and "genuine government does not come from ballot-boxes." A few other obscure correspondents made the same point, showing, if nothing else, that nonresistance was not just a hobby of the leaders of abolitionism. Garrison defended Wright by saying that he was still free to criticize institutions in a Northern republic but that the moral division of the country followed geographical lines so clearly that the separation of the North would truly be a glorious day of liberation.[9]

The only prominent nonresistant to reject disunionism was Nathaniel P. Rogers. First he urged upon the New England Anti-Slavery Society the motto, " 'No union' *in Slaveholding,*" instead of "*No Union with Slaveholders.*" Reasoning and moral influence, in his view, were incompatible with threats of any kind.[10] Then he explained in two editorials that he did not care about the political union; what protected slavery was "the moral union." His target was the "agreement in the hearts of the whole people that the colored man shall not have liberty among us." The Constitution was irrelevant. Disunionism would mean war and unfavor-

---

[8] *Liberator,* Apr. 29, 1842, p. 3.
[9] *Ibid.,* Nov. 2, 1855, p. 4; Nov. 7, 1856, p. 2; March 13, 1857, pp. 2, 4.
[10] *Ibid.,* June 6, 1845, p. 3.

able conditions for ending slavery. (He still looked forward to the day when the union would disintegrate because people no longer believed in governmental coercion—a hope once shared by the Garrisonian nonresistants.) Rogers found his enemies "political" in three ways: they organized a meeting to vote on mottos; they could not keep their minds off the Constitution; and their remedy for slavery was disunionism beginning with ballots and ending inevitably with bullets.[11]

In this case Rogers' analysis certainly was right. Disunionism was political because it insisted that *"slavery exists only by virtue of the Union."*[12] Law, rather than prejudice or immorality, became the issue. Adin Ballou, for example, drew up for the Massachusetts Anti-Slavery Society resolutions protesting against the "violation of sacred constitutional pledges" that their state had suffered in Southern ports and urging their representatives to regard South Carolina and Louisiana as foreign nations and to institute "non-intercourse" with them.[13] And Ballou was the ablest spokesman for nonresistance.

It should be emphasized that only in the minds of political abolitionists and other critics of Garrisonism were disunionism and nonresistance thought of as synonymous. To the Garrisonians they were quite separate; indeed, one of the tactical advantages of disunionism was that it could be supported by those who thought nonresistance too extreme a doctrine. Wendell Phillips ridiculed the logic by which opponents of disunionism argued that dislike of the present federal government was equivalent to dislike of all government. It was "arrogance" to assume the Constitution so perfect "that one who dislikes it could never be satis-

[11] *Herald of Freedom,* June 14, 1844, p. 2; July 12, 1844, p. 2.

[12] Charles E. Hodges, *Disunion Our Wisdom and Our Duty* (New York, n.d. [1854]), p. 7.

[13] *Liberator,* Jan. 31, 1845, p. 3. Charleston had treated outrageously an emissary sent by Massachusetts to discuss the jailing of some Negro seamen. C. K. Whipple, one of the most clear-minded nonresistants, suggested that petitions be circulated asking the Massachusetts legislature to convoke all the free states to discuss the dissolution of the union. Garrison added his hope that such petitions would be circulated at once (*ibid.,* Jan. 3, 1845, p. 3).

fied with any form of government whatsoever." He compared his own attitude to that of Daniel O'Connell and other Catholics who boycotted Parliament rather than forswear the Pope and to that of the nonjuring bishops who turned down political power rather than deny the Stuarts. "It were a rare compliment indeed to the nonresistants, if every exhibition of rigid principle on the part of an individual is to make the world suspect him of leaning towards their faith."[14]

Because Phillips was the leading advocate of disunionism, his relationship to nonresistance is worth examining more closely. He had been on the negative side of several debates at the inaugural meeting of the New England Non-Resistance Society and disavowed the sentiments that it arrived at. Afterward he became expert at defending the principle of nonresistance against unfriendly criticism without making any commitment of his own.[15] The nonresistants were, of course, his dearest associates, and the profit he gained from association with even the most anarchistic of them can be assessed in his view of government:

Government is precisely like any other voluntary association of individuals—a temperance or anti-slavery society, a bank or railroad corporation. I join it, or not, as duty dictates. . . . From the necessity of the case, and that constitution of things which God has ordained, it follows that in any specified district, the majority must rule—hence results the duty of the minority to submit. But we must carefully preserve the distinction between *submission* and *obedience*—between *submission* and *support*. If the majority set up an immoral Government, I obey those laws which seem to me good, because they are good—and I submit to all the penalities which my disobedience of the rest brings on me.[16]

The distinction between submission and obedience also exists in the writings of Ballou, but not the conception of government to which it is applied. Rather than a necessary evil, government appears to be a highly flexible institution. In principle, Phillips

[14] Phillips, *Can Abolitionists Vote,* pp. 3–4.
[15] *Non-Resistant,* Jan. 1839, p. 1; *Herald of Freedom,* Oct. 15, 1840, p. 1.
[16] Phillips, *Can Abolitionists Vote,* p. 26.

might have joined a majority setting up a government of moral control.

Although it sounds anarchistic to call government a "voluntary association," we must remember that there were various competing models of voluntarism. Nathaniel Rogers hated Phillips as an aristocratic spokesman of social control. Certainly Phillips thought of himself as a political agent, and his tone could be aristocratic. Once he quoted the *Edinburgh Review* to the effect that the sacrifice and duty of governmental service demanded infinitely high motives, then added: "In the place of 'Government,' put 'Reform,' and the sentiment is still more applicable to a cause like ours."[17] Phillips also tried to distinguish "influence" from "power." The rejection of political methods, in this perspective, might augment the political influence of abolitionists, as a disinterested elite educes more respect than a group of vote-grubbers.[18] In his disunionist approach to political influence, Phillips defined clearly one boundary of the movement of antislavery toward anarchism.

Phillips championed the Garrisonians against those who found slavery unconstitutional and who believed in politics as the key to abolitionism. Goaded by charges that he was afraid to tackle the most famous antislavery analysis of the Constitution—Lysander Spooner's *The Unconstitutionality of Slavery*—Phillips produced a lengthy brief showing that the framers of the Constitution intended it to legalize slavery and that judges like John Marshall and James Kent interpreted it as doing so. Despite these conservative citations, it might appear that Phillips, the disunionist lawyer and disrespecter of the Constitution, was taking the radical side of this dialogue. But no one could reach that conclusion after reading Phillips' argument.

He fastened on Spooner's definition of law as the rule of right arising out of social relations and not a set of arbitrary rules based on "mere will, numbers, or power." Did Spooner only mean, as a disunionist might, that nations ought not to defy the law of God? Phillips understood that he went farther and claimed

---

[17] *Liberty Chimes* (Providence, 1845), p. 21.
[18] Phillips, *Can Abolitionists Vote*, pp. 28–29; *Liberator*, Oct. 20, 1843, p. 3.

that majority rule was not decisive. This understanding drove Phillips to an insight of great importance to our inquiry:

Indeed, Mr. Spooner's idea is practical no-governmentism. It leaves every one to do "what is right in his own eyes." After all, Messrs. Goodell and Spooner, with the few who borrow this idea of them, are the real no-government men; and it is singular, how much more consistent and sound are the notions of Non-resistants on this point,—the men who are generally considered, though erroneously, to be no-government men.[19]

Phillips and Spooner parted ways on the remedy for immoral law. Spooner did not consider an immoral contract binding; a judge was obliged to adhere to natural law in a case where statutes or charters were unjust. In such a case Phillips thought the judge should resign. He valued "uniform and regular government," which only majority rule could provide.

The supreme authority of individual judgment and conscience is sound doctrine in matters of religion: and what is the result? The healthful emulation of a thousand rival sects. Introduce the same principle into government, and instead of one system of laws and one interpretation, we should have, as in the case of the Bible, a thousand; and uniform government would be impossible.

Obviously, nonresistants did not share Phillips' acceptance of sectarianism and his skepticism about a common human conscience. And yet they were increasingly allied with him in disunionism, while nonresistance was more and more neglected. But Phillips himself suggests a new area in which antislavery and anarchy may have been connected as he explains his horror of antislavery constitutionalism: "It is the first step toward anarchy."[20]

iii

Probably no aspect of the history of antislavery has been as misunderstood as the schism which divided the American Anti-

---

[19] Wendell Phillips, *Review of Lysander Spooner's Essay on the Unconstitutionality of Slavery* (Boston, 1847), pp. 9–10.
[20] *Ibid.*, pp. 10–18.

Slavery Society around 1840. In a highly influential study, Gilbert Hobbs Barnes condemned Garrison's personality—his vanity, lack of integrity, impetuosity, vituperativeness—while scrutinizing in detail the religious background rather than the character of his opponents. To Dwight Lowell Dumond, who has shown little of Barnes's fascination with either psychology or religion, was left the task of extended definition of the two factions. He stressed disagreement between anarchism and politics, between the unrealistic East and the practical West. Anarchism and politics became neat, unmixed categories. Garrison opposed political action simply "because he was an anarchist." As for the identity of politics, Dumond described the Liberty Party as "the political party which was to gain control of the government within twenty years." Religious historians have also exploited Barnes's discovery of the schism; they have gone on to argue that the failure of the denominations to support abolitionism as they did less immoderate reforms was mainly due to the recklessness of the Garrisonian schismatics.[21] None of these interpretations is likely to inspire attention to ideas, anarchistic or otherwise, which were shared by the nonresistants and the leaders of the Liberty Party.

Fortunately, some recent scholarship has begun to show that the factions within abolitionism were more diverse and that the relationships among them were more complex than was previously imagined.[22] There is probably little point in trying to assign culpability for causing the schism; a biographer of Garrison found his protagonist guilty of foisting disunionism on the American Anti-Slavery Society, and a student of the Liberty Party found Birney guilty of trying to drive the nonresistants out of the same society in order to construct a political organization.[23]

[21] Barnes, *Antislavery Impulse, passim;* Dumond, *Antislavery,* p. 297; Smith, *Revivalism,* pp. 180–187.

[22] See Kraditor, *Means and Ends;* Wyatt-Brown, *Lewis Tappan;* Mathews, *Slavery and Methodism,* p. 147; and James M. McPherson, *The Struggle for Equality: Abolitionists and the Negro in the Civil War and Reconstruction* (Princeton, 1964), pp. 3–7.

[23] Thomas, *The Liberator,* esp. p. 293; Margaret Louise Plunkett, "A History of the Liberty Party with Emphasis upon Its Activities in the

Nevertheless the Liberty Party people joined the Garrisonians on the issue which first served to sever the society: the rights of women to full participation. And when Henry Wright toured upstate New York in 1839, he found the most stalwart political abolitionists "very strong & decided against a great central power" in New York City.[24]

The career of Theodore Dwight Weld, which in Barnes's treatment brilliantly exemplified the diversity of antislavery leadership, has not fit into interpretations requiring a clean break between anarchism and politics. Weld has usually been cast as the heroic opponent of Garrisonian anarchism, and, true enough, he was strenuously opposed to nonresistance. Yet he also denounced parliamentary tricks that were being used to silence opponents of political action as "the spirit of slaveholders undiluted."[25] He regarded the secession of conservative abolitionists from the original Anti-Slavery Society as harmfully schismatic. He was sternly opposed to third-party political abolitionism and worked in Washington to demonstrate that the regular parties might become responsive to antislavery agitation. With his opposition to nonresistance, third-party activism, and conservative abolitionism, after 1840 it was increasingly hard for him to find any role within the movement. His biographer describes him as "almost a castaway" after the schism; certainly he went into a kind of retreat.[26] The sharpest critic of Garrison's irreverence for institutions has not been able to exonerate Weld, who defined slavery as a sin rather than a social or economic problem and who pursued the government of God.[27] At most Weld provides a central reference point for the immediate abolitionism of the 1830s, from which

Northeastern States," unpublished Ph.D. dissertation, Cornell University, Ithaca, N.Y., 1930, p. 62.

[24] Wright Journal (HCL), XL, 79, Apr. 4, 1839.

[25] Weld is quoted in Mathews, *Slavery and Methodism*, p. 173.

[26] *Weld-Grimké Letters*, II, 812, 881, 1005n.; Thomas, *Theodore Weld*, pp. 189–190.

[27] Stanley Elkins concludes that from Weld's formula to Garrison's it was "the merest step." See his *Slavery: A Problem in American Institutional and Intellectual Life* (New York, 1963), pp. 182–183.

both nonresistants and political abolitionists veered in the 1840s. A less kind opinion would be that he could not keep up with the exigencies of antislavery, as interpreted by either side.

In a marvelously fair account of the division of the movement, William Goodell, a leader of the Liberty Party, started from the assumptions that men will disagree about right principles until the world is actually reformed and that it is no reproach to any reformer to say that he would not gain harmony at the cost of compromising his principles. His analogy was that to repair a machine one must follow requisite principles and not compromise on slipshod expedients. Almost all abolitionists had deviated from the original plans, though they remained in agreement on immediatism, anticolonization, and the importance of racial integration and equal rights. In the 1830s the problem had been simply to spread these basic beliefs. "When a large body of people *were* convinced of the truths abolitionists had taught them," according to Goodell, "the question arose, How shall they best be led to put their principles in practice?" On a question of such extreme importance, demands of conformity and unity would have been vain and sinful.[28] Goodell's interpretation seems preferable to those which assign the blame for the schism on one faction or another. It indicates that an explanation of the rise of political antislavery might depend on religious beliefs every bit as intransigent as those that characterized nonresistance. Antislavery in the 1840s spawned a variety of submovements, all retaining the revivalistic goal of securing the kingdom of God by individual conversions, but differing considerably over the methods by which this anarchistic hope might innocently be sought.

Political abolitionists, no less than the Garrisonians, shared the heady objective of evangelizing the people of the nation and bringing them under the government of God. And we have already seen that a good deal of anarchism lurked in the vocabulary of evangelicalism. Perry Miller begins one chapter of his survey of revivalism in American thought with this quotation from Lyman Beecher's *The Spirit of the Pilgrims:*

[28] Goodell, *Slavery and Anti-Slavery,* pp. 447–456.

The Government of God is the only government which will hold
society, against depravity within and temptation without; and this it
must do by the force of its own law written upon the heart. This is
that unity of the Spirit and that bond of peace which alone can perpetuate national purity and tranquility—that law of universal and impartial love by which alone nations can be kept back from ruin. There
is no safety for republics but in self-government, under the influence
of a holy heart, swayed by the government of God.[29]

The Garrisonian "no-governmentists" maintained that they were
in favor of the only true government—that of God. Furthermore,
as Gilbert Barnes himself demonstrated, political abolitionists
came from ardently revivalistic backgrounds; they were certainly
less cautious than Beecher and his followers and would go at least
as far as Beecher in minimizing the importance of human government. It is not surprising that there were similarities between the
government they sought through politics and the millennial government the Garrisonians sought through nonresistance.

The entire subject of political abolitionism needs closer study.
The remainder of this chapter concentrates on the Liberty Party,
the one political venture indisputably related to the original antislavery impulse. This venture was as antipolitical, as moralistic,
and as individualistic as Garrisonism. Since Garrisonism was open
to the political implications of disunion, it makes little sense to
judge which branch of the antislavery movement was more or less
anarchistic. They were both radical pursuits of the government
of God.

iv

Garrison, in his *Thoughts on African Colonization,* explicitly
believed in an ideal of republican government which was antithetical to slavery, would not tamper with individual moral accountability, recognized the distinction between persons and
lower orders of creation, and in sum was consistent with the sovereignty of God. Nothing in nonresistance contradicted this belief. When such an ideal was described to the "no-government-

[29] Miller, *Life of the Mind,* p. 36.

ists," they answered that they would willingly support it if it existed. In the meantime it was purely imaginary, and a Christian's duty was to oppose the false, coercive governments which presently existed. Except for those who went to Hopedale, they may perhaps be faulted for failing to work toward their positive ideal of government. Political abolitionists, on the other hand, worked to realize a kind of republican government consistent with God's sovereignty.

When political abolitionists referred to *civil* government, they meant what nonresistants called human government, as distinct from *divine* and *self*-government. That their political theory preserved these distinctions in a curiously anarchistic fashion is evident from a passionate speech of Beriah Green to the Buffalo convention of the Liberty Party in 1848. Green had been the first president of the American Anti-Slavery Society and a leading convert to political antislavery. This was his view of government:

Civil Government has intrinsically and necessarily a character of its own. . . . Its origin and authority, all true Thinkers describe as divine. It is as truly and plainly a principle of Philosophy as it is a declaration of the Bible, that *"God is the only potentate."* Civil government must be a reflection of his throne. Whatever is not this is not—can never be Civil Government. Repeat its titles and assert its claims as you will; if it be not true to the principles of the Eternal Throne—if it be not conformed to the arrangements of the Heavenly Kingdom, it may be a cunningly devised, a plausibly defended, a stoutly executed conspiracy. It can in no-wise, for no purpose be a Government.

This is, of course, precisely the viewpoint from which many nonresistants repudiated all human government. Green similarly insisted that Christians must refuse obedience to "conspirators" who named themselves governments.[30]

Green had a harder time explicating the positive political objectives of a Christian. His major theme—*"Put true Rulers at the helm, and all is well"*—had the ring of monarchism.[31] And in cor-

[30] *Model Worker,* July 28, 1848, p. 1.
[31] *Ibid.*

respondence with James G. Birney he made explicit the antidemocratic direction of his thought:

A greater delusion was never hatched from any cockatrice's egg, than
what is commonly boasted of as the *Democratic* principle. . . . We
must insist upon the control of Wisdom. The wisest and strongest we
must seek out and welcome to their proper places. We must put the
sceptre into the hands of Moses whatever Korah and his converts may
say; into the hands of Jesus, whatever the less of two Devils may urge
in the way of objection.

Green was skeptical whether even the Liberty Party was pure
enough to avoid compromised choices between greater and lesser
evils. But he insisted that, in the divine plan, "the wisest, strongest man in any community is its King; and Earth and Hell can by
no means deprive him of the Sceptre."[32]

For all of the monarchist overtones in his thought, Green believed that decentralism or small government most closely suited
the divine scheme. Although other abolitionists said they disliked
taxes simply because the government used them to protect slavery, Green saw a general, instinctive aversion to taxation itself.
True rulers would not present much of a tax bill: "For engrossed
with their *work*, they will not clamor for their *wages*." What little
they required would be cheerfully paid. He was suspicious of
platform provisions for free homesteads and the ten-hour day.
These were not actions of true government but versions of slavery for they assumed that one man could take responsibility for
others. Such laws would in fact constitute a slave code—the antithesis of true civil government reflecting the government of
God.[33]

"Rulers" are men "distinguished for their Godlike qualities"
whose counsel automatically impresses the consciousness of others. "These are Rulers by a 'divine right'—they are Heaven-
anointed. . . . They are just as truly so, against as with, the suf-

---

[32] Dwight Lowell Dumond, ed., *Letters of James Gillespie Birney, 1831–
1857* (Gloucester, Mass., 1966), II, 1067, 1080.

[33] Buffalo convention speech, as cited in note 30.

frages of their fellows." They are a defense against demagoguery because "their character is royal." The majority cannot create and destroy rulers as the folly of the day would have it. The hopes currently placed in democracy are pathetic: character, not votes, can really change things. Green's argument was very abstract; he provided no examples of true or false rulers. But he plainly had little interest in publicity to draw voters to the polls. On the contrary, he believed in a mysterious operation of influence by which men sift themselves, some becoming leaders and some followers, without any trace of coercion.

Like other abolitionists, Green used slavery as a kind of extended metaphor for coercion and sin. As he abhorred slave codes, his vision of politics was really an expression of antislavery immediatism:

We can at once, and where we are, in despite of fraud and force, under any form and in any degree; we can, in God's name, do whatever our improvement and welfare demands. If we will open our eyes, we shall see that the Idea of Government shines like the face of God upon our consciousness—asserting there the authority of Wisdom, Goodness, Power. To this authority we may submit—to this, in the very face of cunning and violence, may swear allegiance. Thus bound, we may maintain our integrity and fidelity with the high result of a character which can no where, and in no way be manifested without presenting to mankind THE MODEL *on which Government is to be constituted and maintained.*

Individuals can pay heed to the laws of this government since they are engraved in human nature. The basic law, which follows from the old antislavery distinction between a man and a thing, is that every piece of creation should be treated "according to its character," a person as a person, a thing as a thing, a ruler as a ruler. The political activity which Green recommended was, then, no more than voluntarily honoring true leaders and commending their leadership to others: "THIS IS THE ONLY WAY IN WHICH IT IS NOT DISGRACEFUL AND INJURIOUS TO ELECTIONEER." While this did not necessarily preclude voting, it had more in common with sectarian competition in reli-

gion. The expansion of true government, like that of the true
church, required no other propaganda than right action.

Such a vision passed easily from civil government to the millennium. By avoiding political intrigues and securing voluntary order, abolitionists would find more than their own "self-posses-
sion and inward harmony," important as these goals obviously
were to Green. They would gather others in preparation for the
"sublime ends" of God's pledge to institute the reign of the "True
King." Like many of the nonresistants whom we have discussed,
Green anticipated that his views would be dismissed as unrealistic, as applicable only to "Utopia." Unlike them, he answered
in highly personal terms. "If it be impracticable to assert the demands and maintain the claims, and secure the influences of what
may deserve the name of Government—if we cannot hope to avail
ourselves *in this world* of the guidance of wisdom and protection
of power, then we are either orphans or outcasts; either God is a
mere figure of speech, or he has thrown us upon the 'tender mer-
cies' of the devil!"[34] There is an almost frenzied passion in much
of Green's writing about government. He plainly had no use for
the Jacksonian system of popular politics.

Prolonged attention to Green's address has seemed necessary
to establish the fact that a leader in making abolitionism political
justified his course on grounds that we would call antipolitical.
In the first place, he repudiated the strategy of political compromise in order to attain power and thus, eventually, to free
the slaves. In addition, he embraced a definition of government
excluding the coercion of majority rule and relying on free-will
adherence to right principles. We cannot generalize about all political antislavery on the basis of the views of one leader, but
Green's views signify unexpected tendencies in the politics of
liberation.

It might be objected that Green was speaking in 1848 when
antislavery politics was being dragged the way of John P. Hale,
Martin Van Buren, and, perhaps one might add, Abraham Lin-

[34] *Ibid.*

coln. To admit that he could not tolerate seeing his party move in the direction of opportunism, however, does not mean that he said things he did not believe. If we think of politics as being associated with opportunism, realism, compromise, and limited objectives, then Beriah Green was antipolitical. Furthermore, some of the recurrent contentions of other political abolitionists acquire new meanings in the light of Green's political, antipolitical theory. Let us examine two of these contentions.

First, the quest for true rulers as an alternative to coercive politics was pursued by abolitionists often regarded as the conservatives of the movement. Edward Beecher, for instance, in a famous report on the murder of Elijah Lovejoy, returned monotonously to the same symptom of the unsoundness of the body politic: since good men failed to exert their influence in the community the mob followed "the demon of anarchy." Despite his forthright attacks on nonresistance, Beecher did not call for legislative and military enforcement of moral law. He actually shared the nonresistants' convictions that politics could not transcend the moral level of the electorate and that the only safe basis for morals lay in the human heart. Where he differed from them was in placing guilt more on the community than the individual. The nature of that guilt was that good men withheld their counsel.[35]

In this context we can best understand the fact that James G. Birney, though a bitter foe of the Garrisonians, furnished much of the evidence for blaming the churches of America for the prolongation of slavery. He had hoped to discover a clerisy or moral elite by whose example slavery would be abolished without governmental action. All he asked was for the ministers and elders of one denomination to free their slaves: "Small as is your number, you will have crucified the giant-sin of our land." But these religious leaders would not use their power to end slavery "*tomorrow*," and Birney turned to immediatist politics and to writing harsh indictments of proslavery churches. Birney was, of

[35] Edward Beecher, *Narrative of Riots at Alton*, ed. Robert Merideth (New York, 1965; 1st pub., 1837).

course, the man of inherent virtue whom abolitionists like Green preferred over opportunist politicians as their candidate.[36]

Secondly, Beriah Green was not the only one of these peculiar politicians to denounce majority rule and to value a ballot primarily as a record of individual moral character. William Goodell described his associates as devoted to *"the moral obligation of a practical conformity to all ascertained truth,* believing that the God of truth can control 'consequences' and bring to pass results which no human sagacity could calculate or foresee beforehand." But they had discovered that this "moral principle, in voting, . . . could not be acted upon, in the existing state of the country without a new political party."[37] H. P. Crozier, of Gerrit Smith's home town, derived antislavery politics from every individual's "God-given *manhood*—his personality, forever and eternally distinguishing him from property." God himself, "in the administration of his government," was obliged "to treat man according to his actual and appropriate character." The application, as with the Garrisonians, was typically negative: reformers were determined *"not* to vote" for men who dishonored these principles.

Would they keep us eternally in political boyhood and swaddling bands? Would they have us forever content with patch-work? Forever seeking, and never securing a just government? Do they think such a government can be secured upon any cheaper conditions than those we are fulfilling, viz. sternly demanding its existence, and earnestly working, sacrificing and voting for it? . . . To give up our characteristic principles, is to give up our political selves, and annihilate our moral senses!

---

[36] *Mr. Birney's Second Letter to the Ministers and Elders of the Presbyterian Church in Kentucky* (n.p., Sept. 2, 1834), p. 16.

[37] Their view, said Goodell, was opposed to that of Yale's Nathaniel Taylor, who said that an enlightened Christian would vote for the least bad of two devils, if one or the other were certain of victory, rather than throw away his vote. See Goodell, *Slavery and Anti-Slavery,* pp. 470, 472–473, 484. Beriah Green in 1844 had concentrated on the vote as evidence of an individual's moral record, not as a strategy of collective action. In his view, the Liberty Party had nothing to do with "the expedients of a carnal wisdom." See his *Belief without Confession* (Utica, 1844), p. 15.

Crozier, like Green, denied that adherence to principle was less expedient than compromise. Furthermore, his emphasis was quite similar to that of the Garrisonians. That is, he valued individual moral character as the means of reaching the millennial maturity of mankind.[38] Of all the phrases which historians have coined to describe the Liberty Party, perhaps the most accurate is "the new religion of political affiliation."[39]

It is important to understand that the *Model Worker*, which spoke for radical political abolitionists, was sincere in its declaration that if antislavery politics truly required the compromises that some were asking of it, then Garrison's disunionism made sense.[40] Less extreme, but in the same vein, were the graceful essays of James Russell Lowell. Although Lowell did not condemn government but instead followed antislavery into politics, he thought enthusiasm for votes incompatible with a moral cause.[41] Even the Liberty Party's campaign literature strangely qualified the importance of the ballot: "We do not pretend that in the very instant that we vote, the shackles will fall—but we do mean that if we refuse to vote against Slavery, we can not do any good by *talking*, writing or praying against it."[42] We are left to wonder what millennial expectations required this disclaimer. Were there some partisans who actually believed that, the moment their suffrage was cast, slavery was finished? Certainly to vote against slavery was one way to free oneself from slavery immediately; the Liberty Party provided something for immediatists to do besides talking. And even as it campaigned, the party

[38] *Model Worker*, Aug. 11, 1848, p. 1.
[39] Howard H. Bell, "National Negro Conventions of the Middle 1840s: Moral Suasion vs. Political Action," *Journal of Negro History*, XLII (1957), 249.
[40] *Model Worker*, July 21, 1848, p. 1. The philosophy of this paper was expounded on July 14, 1848, p. 2, written probably by Beriah Green or his son who edited it. It attacked "the dogma of Availability" and expediency and promised to "expose" and break up conspiracies which pretended to be governments.
[41] *The Anti-Slavery Papers of James Russell Lowell* (Boston and New York, 1902), esp. I, 8–15.
[42] *Liberty Almanac*, No. 2 (1845), p. 8.

wanted none of the political excitement that dampened religious ardor.

v

Political antislavery frequently went hand in hand with come-outerism. This is apparent in a letter which James Caleb Jackson wrote to Gerrit Smith in 1838 when New Yorkers were beginning to contemplate third-party abolitionism: "I am in favor of a distinct political organization—for these reasons: . . . Respect for our principles demand[s] it. . . . Respect for ourselves requires it . . . 'Come out from among them and *be ye separate* and touch not the unclean thing and I will receive you.' *Jesus Christ*—[.]"[43] The silliest charge which New Englanders leveled at the Liberty Party was that, although as politicians they were "'COME OUTERS' of the most radical stamp," in religion they were still able to have fellowship with slaveholders.[44] On the contrary, in both religion and politics they wanted organizational proof of their disconnection from evil. Understanding the ardent come-outerism of men like Gerrit Smith and William Goodell will clarify the ideal of community autonomy implicit in political abolitionism.

It was obvious from the outset that the reasons for "*political* secession" might also demand "*ecclesiastical* secession," especially since the church was expected to be purer than the state. At the Albany convention in 1839, where the idea of the Liberty Party took shape, church members gathered before breakfast for daily prayer and consultation. They decided to try once more to abolitionize the churches and, if that proved impossible, to withdraw from them. Christian antislavery conventions followed the Liberty Party throughout New York, and resulted in the creation of "local independent churches."[45]

[43] Quoted in Gerald Sorin, *The New York Abolitionists: A Case Study of Political Radicalism* (Westport, Conn., 1971), p. 96.
[44] Noah Jackman in *Herald of Freedom,* Apr. 14, 1843, p. 4.
[45] Goodell, *Slavery and Anti-Slavery,* pp. 487–489.

Gerrit Smith condemned his denomination for failing to denounce slavery in 1839. He ceased taking communion at his local Presbyterian church in 1843; its affiliation with the sinning denomination was evidence of its inability to be "such a company of reformers,—such a 'city set on a hill,' as a true Church of Christ must necessarily be." In December of that year he joined others in establishing "The Church of Peterboro" to be part of no association and to be guided by a teacher who was not guaranteed a salary. This church condemned slavery as well as individual votes for slavery.[46] There was nothing temperate about Smith's outlook. The clergy was "the most guilty and corrupting body of men in the land"; their failure to befriend the slave made them the enemies of God. They were imposters slyly supporting proslavery politicians in order to prevent the moral revolution which would expose them.[47]

Smith developed an ecclesiastical theory to go with his hatred of the proslavery clergy. His basic distinction was: "A sectarian or man-selected church . . . is, as a general fact, made up, in part, of the regenerate, and, in part, of the unregenerate persons of the place, where it exists. But . . . a local church is, in the eye of God and the Bible, made up of all the regenerate persons in the given locality and no others." By means of a somewhat circular argument, he avoided the traditional problems of identifying the saints. To be sure, only faithful Christians deserved membership, and flagrant sinners ought to be disfellowshiped. Rather than voting on membership, however, a true local church would automatically display so much moral excellence that no slaveholder or tippler would choose to enter. Under no condition was belief in a creed or ritual to be substituted by man for this self-regulating principle.[48]

[46] Octavius Brooks Frothingham, *Gerrit Smith* (New York and London, 1909), pp. 51–62.

[47] *Herald of Freedom*, Apr. 4, 1843, p. 1; Ralph Volney Harlow, "Gerrit Smith and the Free Church Movement," *New York History*, XVIII (1937), 275.

[48] Gerrit Smith, *Abstract of the Argument, in the Public Discussion of*

Sectarianism was evil because it, like slavery, broke up the "endearing" and "tender" relations of the world-wide mystical union of Christians—of those who were under the divine government. The regenerate corresponded to one another like parts of the body, and making war among them was unnatural. By the same logic, "national prejudices" violated the body of the church. So important were these thoughts that, to the dismay of his friends, Smith nearly joined the nonresistants and never could understand why he should not![49] Furthermore, like many of the Garrisonians, as he moved farther from the Christian denominations Smith became increasingly unorthodox in his religious beliefs. He began to question the authority of the Bible and approached a religion of science and humanity.[50]

The most intelligent presentation of come-outerism was made by William Goodell, whose beliefs were rigidly orthodox. To secede from corrupt churches was a duty taught both by the Bible, in the same texts which the New England come-outers favored, and by the history of Protestantism. It was a corollary of the duty

the Question: *"Are the Christians of a Given Community the Church of Such Community?"* (Albany, 1847), *passim.*

[49] *Ibid.*, pp. 6, 21–22. Smith sent $100 to support the *Non-Resistant* and left the Declaration of Sentiments hanging on one of his walls for years. Henry Wright labored hard to convert him in 1839 and thought both Smith and his wife agreed that the "spirit of slaveholding must be entirely crucified in man, before he can become a non-resistant." He came close to joining and admitted to Wright that he was having trouble conceiving of any justification for human government. Leaders of the venture into politics, especially Henry Stanton and Elizur Wright, were worried that Smith would join the nonresistants unless a pure party could be quickly shown to him. Long talks with Theodore Weld may have saved him. Like Weld, he began to criticize the Garrisonians for "saddling" the antislavery cause with nonresistance; he also insisted that the political organizations must be kept apart from the antislavery societies. He never was "at rest" on nonresistance, as he wrote Whittier in 1844 and told a visitor from Hopedale in 1855. See *Non-Resistant*, Apr. 6, 1839, p. 3; May 4, 1839, p. 2; Garrisons, *Garrison*, II, 317n.; Thomas, *Theodore Weld*, p. 184; *Liberator*, Apr. 24, 1840, p. 1; Dec. 13, 1839, p. 2; *Gerrit Smith's Constitutional Argument* (n.p., 1844), p. 1; *Practical Christian*, June 30, 1855, p. 2.

[50] Harlow, "Gerrit Smith," pp. 280–287.

of securing "gospel doctrine" in a true church. All men were accountable to God for living out their private judgments: "IT WAS AS COMPETENT IN LUTHER TO EXCOMMUNICATE THE POPE AND THE ROMISH CHURCH, AS IT WAS IN THE POPE AND THE ROMISH CHURCH TO EXCOMMUNICATE LUTHER." And come-outerism was the doctrine of the Puritan fathers. (Though Goodell mistook their plans for gathering churches out of churches to fill a western void for a scheme of purification of their own churches, he certainly shared their concern for separating saints from unregenerate.) The corruption of present-day churches, furthermore, was exactly that of the old Roman church, for sale of indulgences and toleration of slaveholding were alike trafficking in men's souls. The American Anti-Slavery Society, recognizing the value of Goodell's exposition, reprinted it with a foreword by Wendell Phillips. They claimed to agree with him in every particular. But they could not refrain from footnotes disavowing the analogy between come-outerism and the Liberty Party and denying that abolitionism included the duty of establishing pure new churches.[51] Thus Goodell had plausible grounds for contending that Garrisonian abolitionism was neither as thoroughgoing nor as constructive as its political rival.

Goodell disagreed with Beriah Green and others who thought that the Liberty Party should not advance positions on issues other than slavery. But though he favored a diversified platform, he too thought that government ought to be small and decentralized. As he explained in *The Democracy of Christianity*, one of the most ambitious discussions of political theory by an abolitionist, no man should dare to claim superiority over his fellow men for fear of violating the sovereignty of God. Government was ordained to be the opposite of violence and coercion, which were the products of human sin and presumption. The Christian way was for all officers to be elected and all powers to be severely

---

[51] Goodell, *Come-Outerism: The Duty of Secession from a Corrupt Church* (New York, 1845). Hodges, *Disunion Our Wisdom*, p. 4, also states that for the clergy not to call slavery a sin is a Protestant indulgence.

limited; the emphasis must be on the consent of the community.
When government passed beyond narrow restrictions, "it trenches
more or less seriously upon that individualization of man, which
forms so marked a feature of the Christian religion." Goodell
continued: "It steps in between a man and his conscience—between a man and his God. It assumes individual responsibilities.
It forgets that 'the Government' cannot stand for the individual,
at the bar of the final judgment."[52] Goodell could not have sympathized with Green's yearning for true rulers. At the heart of
his politics was a passionate anti-authoritarianism; the ideal he
upheld was that of a fully democratized, local community.

Goodell was horrified at Stephen S. Foster's practice of interrupting church services to press the cause of the slave. Any voluntary group possessed the right to set its own procedures; any
individual had the right to shun their company. He believed that
the original church elected its teachers and allowed time for any
member to speak, and he wished to promote a return to "the
primitive standard." But he could not "force free principles" on
the churches or assert his rights "by invading theirs." Goodell's
remarks provoked an exchange with Nathaniel P. Rogers, who
saw in Foster's tactics "a sort of incipient *insurrectionary* assertion" of the right of free expression against the "*Genius of corporation.*" Rogers thought this kind of self-assertion was crucial to
antislavery. Because the question of free speech had been dodged,
all previous reforms, "even the great Reform of Christianity itself," had degenerated.

In reply, Goodell attacked the "feudal" doctrine that an individual surrenders rights by entering society. Man's nature is social
and his rights must be social. Foster's example threatened freedom of expression and religion. For Goodell, then, come-outerism
and antislavery led to the discovery of true social units, not to the
removal of all social inhibitions.[53] As his position was clarified

[52] Goodell, *The Democracy of Christianity; or, An Analysis of the Bible
and Its Doctrines, in Their Relations to the Principle of Democracy,* 2 vols.
(New York, 1849, 1852), II, 69, and *passim.*
[53] *Herald of Freedom,* June 24, 1842, pp. 2–3; July 8, 1842, pp. 2–3.

by this exchange, it was perhaps less individualistic than no-organizationism, but it was entirely consistent with voluntary principles. This high estimation of free local institutions gave political antislavery the color of community anarchism.

The combination of separation from evil and local constructiveness is well illustrated by a group of Philadelphia Friends who published the *Non-Slaveholder*. They commended Ballou's writings but disliked his contention that Christians cannot try to elect Christian officials. But they expended little time on such an issue. Politics was of trivial importance. Instead they advocated, as the remedy for slavery, a consistent life: "Let the principle of non-participancy be adopted and carried out by a body of people, not numerically greater than the Religious Society of Friends, and it would make the BELSHAZZAR of slavery tremble on his throne, for he would see written on the wall of his palace, 'THY KINGDOM IS DIVIDED.' " Mostly this meant abstinence from the products of slave labor, a plan which they carried to the extent of maintaining a "free labor factory" for cotton in Philadelphia.[54]

But the best illustration of the political innocence of the ballot was provided in the home state of Nathaniel Rogers. In Milford, New Hampshire, abolitionists wanted the union repealed and their votes to that effect counted. When they learned that ballots with the word "Repeal" written across them would not be counted, they invented for each office a name like John C. Repeal or Martin Van Repeal and had these names printed on their ballots. In that way they could vote against everybody.[55]

vi

We may conclude that the antislavery impulse was so anarchistic that even when it ventured into politics it was unlikely

---

[54] For their general philosophy, see the prospectus in the *Non-Slaveholder*, First Month, 1846, p. 1, and "Disconnection from Evil a Gospel Duty," Ninth Month, 1846, p. 144; on Ballou, Eighth Month, 1846, p. 123; and on the factory, Second Month, 1854, p. 15.

[55] *Herald of Freedom*, March 8, 1844, p. 3.

to favor compromise or coercion. This conclusion should be modified in several respects. Our emphasis has repeatedly been on leaders of the Liberty Party and, for the most part, on those who refused to accept the tactics of the Free Soil and Republican parties. Many of the men whom Smith, Goodell, and Green criticized also belonged to the antislavery movement in a general sense, though probably not to a continuous movement flowing from the original American Anti-Slavery Society. Whether they were influenced by anarchistic ideas is, unfortunately, impossible to answer. They did not write as Christian politicians, come-outers, or nonresistants. Not enough is known about political antislavery to justify further generalization or inference.

A second important modification is that these anarchist-sounding strains could take on stridently governmental overtones. We have seen something of this in regard to Beriah Green. There may well have been problems in identifying government with divine right. For example, Nathaniel Colver, who was vehemently against nonresistance, mystified Henry C. Wright when he "assumed as his theory, that men were to be put to death, *only* for such crimes as God has designated. . . . He professed to abhor the doctrine that *men* have the right to *define crimes* and affix penalties in kind and degree—even to death." It was almost impossible for Wright to arrive at a difference in principle between himself and his adversaries.[56] But he detected a difference in emphasis and shuddered at what it meant to be governed by God and still covet civil authority. It was possible at any time that a John Brown, filled with a conviction that he was God's viceroy, might head South on a course of guiltless slaughter.

Even with these modifications, the schism of the antislavery movement was not simply between politicians and anarchists. Disunionism, coming out of nonresistance and hatred of the Constitution, theoretically favored government, whereas the Liberty

[56] *Non-Resistant,* Oct. 19, 1839, p. 2. For Wright's similar frustration with Goodell, see *Non-Resistant,* Apr. 20, 1839, p. 2; with Luther Lee, *ibid.,* Sept. 21, 1839, p. 1; and with Alanson St. Clair, *Herald of Freedom,* Feb. 25, 1842, p. 1.

Party was often against human authority and virtually anarchistic. This observation forces us to heed the comment of a Syracuse come-outer to a Hopedale member: "Most Abolitionism when it passes from your state to ours becomes, or is very prone to become, Liberty Party." It still had the strengths and shortcomings of moral reform in Massachusetts.[57] Rather than a clear-cut difference between politics and anarchy, then, perhaps there were two groups with similar structures, with moral-political majorities and anarchistic minorities.

Even to reconstruct our understanding of the movement in this way will not resolve all the paradoxes. It is perhaps easy to understand why the Garrisonians preferred political parties which made no pretense of having the moral earnestness of abolitionism and why the Liberty Party hated these others. But there was also steady, respectful contact between the extreme libertarians among the politicians and the extreme Garrisonians, the come-outers and no-organizationists. Goodell and Rogers may have disagreed about the inviolability of the local church, but they paid compliments to each other of a kind seldom found in the arguments of either with Garrison. The *Liberator* attacked Henry Clapp, the prince of no-organizationists, for his heresy in advising anyone who believed in politics to vote for the Liberty Party.[58] Lysander Spooner, champion of the Constitution, savored all of Rogers' idiosyncrasies and none of Garrison's.[59] George Bradburn, the legislator who became editor of the Lynn *Pioneer,* was admired by Rogers because he was staunchly antislavery in politics as well as because he was badly treated by "the Regency at Boston." Parker Pillsbury was finally able to reconcile himself to Rogers' enmity by noticing that he had become "the fawned over, and petted friend of the New Organization, Third Party, and other bitter foes of the cause of Freedom and Humanity."[60]

[57] *Practical Christian*, Aug. 2, 1851, p. 3.

[58] See the report of the controversy in Lynn *Pioneer*, June 24, 1846, p. 2.

[59] Spooner to George Bradburn, Oct. 27, 1846, Dec. 7, 1846, Lysander Spooner Papers, New York Historical Society (hereafter cited as Spooner Papers, NYHS).

[60] *Herald of Freedom*, Apr. 1, 1842, p. 2; May 23, 1845, p. 2; Rogers,

Among the advocates of political abolitionism who were closest
to no-organizationism were John Pierpont and the famous historian and utilitarian philosopher Richard Hildreth. Both were
rationalists who had left most of Christianity behind. Appalled
at some of the tactics which disunionists used to gag their opponents in the abolitionist movement, Hildreth worked out a perceptive explanation:

Unfortunately, this anti-slavery movement had its birth in the bosom
of the church. . . . They denounce slavery not as a wrong, a crime,
a delusion, a blunder, a folly,—but as a sin against God, to be immediately repented of and abandoned. Thus they set themselves up not as
expositors of mere human science, not as teachers of morals, and politics, and political economy, but as expositors of the will of God; and
according to the usual course of things, from being expositors, they
have proceeded to act as God's vicegerents, judges and executors. . . .
Hence it is easy to understand and explain the fierce spirit of unex-
tinguishable hatred, never forgetting and never forgiving, with which
they pursue all those with whom they differ. . . . Those persons call
themselves *come-outers*. They have come out from the church; but
they have brought with them the very things in the church, to which
I make the greatest objections, to wit: the claim of infallibility, and
the domineering, denouncing, excommunicating spirit which apper-
tains to all priesthoods. They are just as much friends of impartial
liberty, as our puritan fathers were, who *came out* of the English
church, and then commenced at once to drive other people out of
theirs.

Their slanders and haughtiness would prevent them from ever
being "pure moral suasionists," Hildreth concluded. He was ready
to lend his hand to Rogers' newspaper. In Rogers' opinion, he
was also ready to take a short step from the politics of moral
suasion to no-organizationism.[61]

Rogers' own flight from every variety of coercion made him
hospitable to the rationalism of Hildreth and Pierpont. But Hildreth's observations do more than explain why utilitarians and

Miscellaneous Writings, pp. 332–333; Frances H. Bradburn, *A Memorial of
George Bradburn by His Wife* (Boston, 1883), p. 163.
   [61] *Herald of Freedom*, n.s., June 13, 1845, pp. 1, 3.

no-organizationists could form an alliance; they lead to an understanding of the hostility between Garrisonians and the Liberty Party. It was worse, said Goodell in his theory of come-outerism, to be false to a true creed than to be true to a false one.[62] How strange that Goodell, who preferred no-organizationists to disunionists, could not comprehend Garrison's preference of the Free Soilers to the Liberty Party!

Political abolitionism may be interpreted as an attempt to give the regenerate an opportunity to set their moral record straight and, perhaps, to have a salutary influence on the community. Its hatred of Garrison, therefore, contained a kind of compliment: he ought to have known better than to oppose them. The Garrisonians also exhorted individuals to be faithful to their highest conception of truth, and from this viewpoint they berated the Liberty Party. Both parties shared the strengths and weaknesses of the anarchistic impulse in antislavery.

[62] Goodell, *Come-Outerism*, pp. 8–9.

VII

Law and Love: The Problem of Authority

Radical abolitionism had split into two parties, each a puzzling mixture of political and antipolitical sentiments, each in search of personal liberation from the rule of sin as well as the abolition of chattel slavery. Some abolitionists, like Samuel Joseph May, cooperated with both sides and saw them as complementary. May thought he could observe signs of antislavery reunification in the early 1850s, as political abolitionism grew disillusioned with the compromises and opportunism that politics seemed to entail.[1] Few of these signs, however, are a matter of historical record. Instead, a disunited and confused antislavery movement reacted inconsistently to the turmoil and violence of that decade. Antislavery radicals conducted a prolonged, confusing debate over the nature of the United States Constitution. In their desire to emancipate all individuals from sinful human authority, some radicals began to turn to spiritualism and marital reform for the secrets of earthly order.

Interpretation of the role of slavery in the Constitution was critical to the strategies of abolitionists. Not only did the Garrisonians and political abolitionists disagree with one another about the Constitution, but there were inconsistencies and variations in the constitutional attitudes of each party. The political crises of the 1850s regularly brought the Constitution into public controversy. Both disunionists and those who thought slavery

---

[1] *Liberator,* May 23, 1851, p. 1; May 16, 1856, p. 2.

was unconstitutional found it possible to base campaigns of propaganda and agitation on their views of the Constitution.[2] But the abolitionists were not merely responding to a course of events outside their movement; they were reformulating their views of the governments of God and man. Much of the difficulty in understanding their constitutional controversy is due to their attempt to fuse political theories which we customarily regard as historically antithetical. Generally speaking, abolitionists took seriously the claim that representative government depended on the immediate consent of individuals. They also believed that such consent was immoral unless the resulting government merited a claim to divine right. Was the Constitution a moral covenant to be won back from the hands of political hypocrites or was it contractual evidence of human depravity? When Garrison burned the Constitution at a public meeting in 1854, it was because in his opinion it transgressed against divine law; other abolitionists, however, believed that in a libertarian Constitution human and divine law might be joined. But in spite of the concern for divine law which promoted the controversy, the extensive, legalistic attention which abolitionists gave to the American Constitution may have tended to secularize their concerns, if not their beliefs.

The start of the debate was innocent enough. All assailants of slavery had met the charge of meddling with an institution which was constitutionally shielded against interference so long as it served the interests of states where it prevailed. Samuel Joseph May in 1837 sketched out a reply: "It seems to us that the framers of our Constitution[,] finding they had not the power to abolish slavery, were determined to do the next best thing—*not commit the national government to its support.*" For example, they refrained from using words like "slaves" or "chattels personal." The subject was designated for legitimate agitation by generations coming after them.[3] May's argument was clear and

---

[2] Less familar than disunionism, the view that slavery was unconstitutional is traced in William M. Wiecek, *The Guarantee Clause of the U. S. Constitution* (Ithaca, 1972), esp. pp. 154–165.

[3] "Slavery and the Constitution," *Quarterly Anti-Slavery Magazine,* II

temperate, did not contradict the notion that slavery was immune from federal legislation, and was free of polemics against anti-slavery heresy.

Soon the debate became more twisted. To enter American politics at all, most Liberty Party men felt obliged to find that the Constitution was not tainted by slavery. But the strange turns the debate took among the Garrisonians left William Goodell almost tongue-tied: "Some changed their views of the Constitution in the opposite direction—perhaps changed twice;—repudiating, in the first place, 'the compromises,' and holding the Constitution (as did N. P. Rogers) to be thoroughly anti-slavery—and then (assenting to the pro-slavery construction) denouncing it, very consistently, as a 'covenant with death, and an agreement with hell.'"[4] In 1837 Rogers had followed May in exposing the anti-slavery possibilities of the Constitution. He had used all his ingenuity as a lawyer to dispense with its proslavery articles. An "insurrection," for example, was not technically a rising against oppression; if Negroes revolted it would be "justifiable self-defense." Again, slavery was not established by positive law in any state even where it was regulated as an existing institution. Thus there was no constitutional reason to return a fugitive from unlawful slavery.[5] When Lysander Spooner expressed identical views in the 1840s, Rogers denied that slavery was against the law of the land and prophesied that this view of law would "exclude not only Slavery, but citizenship and subject."[6] In Spooner he repudiated his old self and recognized his new one.

Men could also change in the direction opposite to Rogers. Addison Davis was a come-outer who had been fired from his

---

(1837), 73–90, 226–238. For the chronology of discussions of the Constitution, see Goodell, *Slavery and Anti-Slavery*, pp. 476–477; and Plunkett, "History of the Liberty Party," ch. 5, n. 40. On the omission of words for slavery in the Constitution, see Staughton Lynd, *Class Conflict, Slavery, and the United States Constitution* (Indianapolis, 1967), pp. 159–160.

[4] Goodell, *Slavery and Anti-Slavery*, p. 454.

[5] "The Constitution," *Quarterly Anti-Slavery Magazine*, II (1837), 145–153. See also the 1838 article reprinted in Rogers, *Miscellaneous Writings*, pp. 15–21.

[6] Rogers, *Miscellaneous Writings*, pp. 332–336.

post as a public school teacher in Lynn for doubting the infallibility of the Bible and had been ostracized by other come-outers
for scorning " 'Free Meeting' cant."[7] He showed the same wandering independence on the constitutional question. Reviewing
Spooner, he warned against mistaking what should be for what
is: "The abolition of slavery must be brought about as a means
of creating such a government as that of which Mr. Spooner talks;
not the government established as a means of abolishing slavery."
But eventually he earned the contempt of the *Liberator* by his
own "repetition of the old and oft-refuted argument, that the
United States Constitution contains no compromises with, or
guarantees to, slavery."[8]

It is easy to understand how some disunionists, conscious of
the religious and Revolutionary backgrounds of abolitionism,
could believe that the Constitution outlawed slavery. George W.
F. Mellen had an *a priori* conviction that the kind of men who
fled Archbishop Laud's persecution and struggled to overcome
imperial domination must have opted for freedom over slavery.
In part he was inspired by George Bancroft's historical drama-
tization of conflict between these irreconcilable principles. He
also knew that his grandfather, a member of Congress in 1778–
1779, had manumitted his slaves upon the adoption of the Massachusetts constitution, under no compulsion but his own understanding of the Revolution. These biases did not deter Mellen
from thorough study of the state and national constitutional conventions, in which he found abundant evidence of doubt and
guilt on the subject of continuing slavery. Mellen might favor
secession from a covenant soiled by Southern dishonor, but he
proposed a simple test for those who disparaged the handiwork
of the fathers: "I will ask Mr. Phillips, as a lawyer, . . . on what
principle, in the constitution he would rely, provided some person came and stole him, to make him a slave, to regain his freedom, as an American citizen?"[9]

[7] Lynn *Pioneer*, March 12, 1845, p. 3; Aug. 20, 1846, p. 2; Oct. 8, 1846,
pp. 2–3.

[8] *Liberator*, Oct. 24, 1845, p. 3; Feb. 7, 1851, p. 4.

[9] Mellen, *An Argument on the Unconstitutionality of Slavery, Embracing*

The positions taken in the controversy are often bewildering. Consider the curt exchanges in 1854 between Francis Barry of Erie County, Ohio, and William S. Flanders of Cornville, Maine. Barry found the Constitution to outlaw slavery, but called the issue unimportant because popular government was an illusion. He added that there was no God—only immutably operating laws. Flanders rejoined that the Constitution was proslavery and that popular government was a reality. "But that no such government is right, is proved from the fact, that the idea of popular sovereignty, as supreme law, is diametrically opposite to self-evident truth, consequently in direct opposition to the government of God."[10] Both men belonged to the Garrisonian resistance to the Liberty Party.

Nor was there unanimity among political abolitionists. Some admitted that they cared about neither the intentions of the framers nor the preservation of the union. One of them thought George Washington was a hypocrite. Since the framers had concealed their meanness, however, the Constitution happened to be useful for abolitionism; every vagueness should be exploited.[11] On the other hand, Gerrit Smith's fancy was that the framers deliberately promoted an end to slavery: the three-fifths clause, in particular, put a bounty on freedom.[12] Alvan Stewart, passionate in his defense of the Constitution against "piratical legislation," denied that a man could ever be legally enslaved without his mature consent.[13] William Goodell thought that since his own

---

an *Abstract of the Proceedings of the National and State Conventions on This Subject* (Boston, 1841); *Liberator*, June 21, 1844, p. 3.

[10] *Ibid.*, Oct. 27, 1854, p. 3.

[11] *Ibid.*, Feb. 27, 1857, p. 3; March 27, 1857, p. 4.

[12] *Gerrit Smith's Constitutional Argument, passim.* Frothingham (in *Gerrit Smith*, pp. 173–175) perceptively noted that Smith dealt with the Constitution as he had with the Bible: it simply had to be an antislavery document.

[13] Luther Rawson Marsh, ed., *Writings and Speeches of Alvan Stewart on Slavery* (New York, 1860), esp. pp. 257–258; Alvan Stewart, *A Legal Argument before the Supreme Court of the State of New Jersey, at the May Term, 1845, at Trenton, for the Deliverance of Four Thousand Persons from Bondage* (New York, 1845).

views were "formed more in the light of what I call *first prin-*
ciples than of *legal technicalities*," he differed from Spooner as
New York did from New England.[14] It would be hard to demonstrate that either party of abolitionists was principally concerned
with a scholarly reconstruction of the content of the Constitution.

From this confusion there did emerge one faint sign of antislavery reunification: disunionists began to abate their anticon-
stitutional fervor. With a new tone of relativism on the means of
abolitionism, Garrison offered a kind of faint praise for antislavery politics. A man's sincerity on the slavery issue mattered
more than his position on the nature of the Constitution: "If he
understood it to be a pro-slavery instrument, then he virtually
becomes a slaveholder by giving it his support; but if he inter-
prets it as an anti-slavery instrument, as his friend Gerrit Smith
does, (however preposterous such an interpretation may be,) he
could not charge him logically with being pro-slavery."[15]

To be sure, Garrison continued to prefer disunionism. In attacks on the Constitution he honored the idea of a religion of
individualism which would tolerate no compromise with slavery.
Sometimes disunion meant something more to him than the secession of the free states; he knew that such secession would not
even separate antislavery from proslavery sentiment. He harked
back to a point close to no human government: "And do you ask
where you should draw the line? . . . I would say to you, 'draw
it around yourselves.' The world is greatly in need of *men* and
women, such as will not worship at the shrine of the 'Union' and
slavery, but have rather true reverence for God and humanity."
In his new latitudinarianism he was capable of contradictory
arguments. As an example of the effectiveness of the no-union
theory, he pointed out that in the areas where it prevailed there
was a big vote for the Republican John C. Frémont.[16]

If not reunification, this was a cessation of hostilities. By 1861
even Adin Ballou was prepared to argue that if the Constitution

[14] Goodell to Spooner, Dec. 3, 1855, Spooner Papers, NYHS.
[15] *Practical Christian*, Apr. 7, 1855, p. 2.
[16] *Liberator*, Feb. 27, 1857, p. 3.

had not been "violated against the liberty and human rights it so solemnly guarantees, the convulsions now rending our Republic would never have happened." Though defective when compared to the Sermon on the Mount, the Constitution was still a better document than those who claimed to venerate it had made of it. The Constitution's protections of slavery had been extended, its guarantees of liberty stifled, and its tacit understanding that the evil of slavery should not spread forgotten.[17] By that time, however, John Brown's "Provisional Constitution" had already been seized at Harper's Ferry. And Garrison, the nonresistant, was beginning to visualize the utility of the war power as a constitutional weapon against slavery.

ii

Lysander Spooner was the leading authority for the view that slavery was illegal under the Constitution,[18] and he was greatly respected by other abolitionists. He was a maverick abolitionist who belonged to none of the familiar factions in the movement. He must be considered separately because his cast of mind was distinctively legal or political rather than religious. While most of the anarchism found in abolitionism was based on views of the true church and the government of God, Spooner's concentrated on the courts and placed its authority in natural law. Nonetheless, his version of anarchism, like that of other abolitionists, was presented as the antithesis of slavery.

[17] Ballou, *Violations of the Consitution in the "Irrepressible Conflict" between the Pro-Slavery and Anti-Slavery Sentiments of the American People* (Hopedale, 1861), pp. 4–5.

[18] This is the judgment of Plunkett, "History of the Liberty Party," ch. 5, n. 40. Gerrit Smith took Spooner as chief authority on the Constitution and got the Liberty Party to commend his works as "perfectly conclusive" (Frothingham, *Gerrit Smith*, pp. 190, 350). For Goodell's reliance on Spooner, see his *Slavery and Anti-Slavery*, pp. 22, 25, 78. Accounts of his life and thought may be found in Rudolf Rocker, *Pioneers of American Freedom: Origin of Liberal and Radical Thought in America* (Los Angeles, 1949), pp. 86–96; Schuster, *Native American Anarchism*, pp. 143–152; and James J. Martin, *Men against the State: The Expositors of Individualist Anarchism in America, 1827–1908* (DeKalb, Ill., 1953), pp. 168–201.

Spooner was a deist. His first book attacked revealed religion, and he doubted that miracles were anything more than the products of diseased imaginations. He wrote Gerrit Smith that he was "a Deist pure and simple" who believed "that the order of nature was rightly established in the first place"; it was man's proper goal to understand the laws of nature instead of chasing after supernatural substitutes. He was pleased that Smith, with his religion of humanity, was approaching the same view.[19] Spooner's deism, moreover, was evident at the start of his influential essay on *The Unconstitutionality of Slavery*. In defining law as "an intelligible principle of right, necessarily resulting from the nature of man; and not an arbitrary rule, that can be established by mere will, numbers or power," he underscored the close analogy with laws in physics and biology. The laws he was interested in were "*natural*, unalterable, impartial and inflexible."[20]

The idea of law, according to Spooner, depended on the universality of the rights of men. Contracts in violation of these rights were always declared null and void—and government was legally nothing more than a contract. (The only alternative, he said, was the divine right of kings.) It followed that judges, like any other individuals, owed nothing but resistance to an illegal, immoral law. Admittedly, "self-styled governments" asserted the right to declare law arbitrarily because they possessed power, and, sadly, people tended to condone this nonsensical presumption. But then law meant only force. If that were true, then law was extinct or suspended whenever factions contended for power.[21] Spooner resembled other abolitionists, both nonresistants and Liberty Party men, in his rejection of coercion and arbitrary law.

He might have concluded that no statute or constitution could legalize an unnatural institution. In finding slavery unconstitu-

[19] A. John Alexander, "The Ideas of Lysander Spooner," *New England Quarterly*, XXIII (1950), 203; Spooner to Smith, Sept. 30, 1860, Spooner Papers, NYHS.

[20] Spooner, *The Unconstitutionality of Slavery* (Boston, 1860), pp. 5–6 (originally published in two parts in 1845 and 1846).

[21] *Ibid.*, pp. 5–15.

tional he insisted only that whenever law is ambiguous the most
innocent meaning must be accepted. In order for law to contra-
vene natural justice, it must be unambiguously, positively declared.[22] His first key argument was based on the recognition in
all colonial charters that common-law rights were extended from
the homeland to the settlements. In 1772 Lord Mansfield, as
Chief Justice in the Somerset case, had decided that slavery was
so repugnant to English liberty that to bring a slave into England
was in effect to free him. Consequently slavery was unlawful in
America before the Revolution, however much it was tolerated.
Lord Mansfield had honored the principle that it would take
positive law establishing the privilege of enslavement to make
the custom legal.[23]

Secondly, Spooner noted the assertion of the Declaration of
Independence that life, liberty, and the pursuit of happiness are
self-evidently natural rights. On this assertion the legality of independence was based, so that even if slavery had been legal up
to that time it could not have been thereafter. Self-evident truths,
particularly when they have been explicitly adopted, can never
be rescinded. "To deny, in any case, that 'self-evident truths' are
a part of the law, is equivalent to asserting that 'self-evident
falsehood' is law." Nothing in the Articles of Confederation or the
state constitutions raised slavery above "a mere abuse sustained
by the common consent of the strongest party, in defiance of the
avowed constitutional principles of their governments." Thus,
unless the Constitution had formally established the institution
of slavery, as no one claimed, and designated those persons to
be enslaved, it could not have succeeded in any supposed intention to permit its continuation.[24]

It only remained to dismiss the notion that the Constitution
"intended" to establish slavery, as can be shown from extraneous
historical information. A legal document was not a person with

[22] *Ibid.*, pp. 15–19, 61–67.
[23] *Ibid.*, pp. 21–36.
[24] *Ibid.*, pp. 36–39, 54–55.

passions and motives: "Its 'intentions' are nothing more nor less than the legal meaning of its words." As a new critic who turned his back on historical contexts Spooner went on: "And this is the true test for determining whether the constitution does, or does not, sanction slavery, viz. whether a court of law, strangers to the prior existence of slavery or not assuming its prior existence to be legal—looking only at the naked instrument—could, consistently with legal rules, judicially determine that it sanctioned slavery." Yet slavery was not even mentioned. In short, the framers, whose intentions were worth no more than those of any other equal number of persons, did not sanction slavery because, "after all their debates, they agreed upon an instrument that did not sanction it."[25]

It was this plausible sketch of the constitutional foundations of the United States that attracted other abolitionists to Spooner's writings. But Spooner could not overlook Wendell Phillips' charge that this theory of natural justice would render law uncertain and government impossible. In the second part of *The Unconstitutionality of Slavery*, he indicated that the imperfections of language would make law truly uncertain without a definite rule of interpretation, namely that ambiguities should always be resolved in favor of natural justice. In practice, a great deal of law already was natural law, since judges acted where no statutes existed and the common law of different countries was remarkably identical. Spooner distinguished three kinds of statutes: "useless repetitions" of natural law; "positive violations" of it; and arrangements not infringing on it and expedient for specific social purposes. (In a lengthy note, he related the "science" of natural law to "an almost intuitive perception" of basic principles underlying ever-varying circumstances, but he was not much concerned with the psychological dimensions of the problem.)[26]

Moreover, if the definition of natural law really made government impossible, "would that be any argument against the definition? or only against government?" Spooner did not share the

[25] *Ibid.*, pp. 56–60, 116.
[26] *Ibid.*, pp. 137–142.

view he now imputed to Phillips that government was naturally unjust. But he was suspicious of constitutions and statutes because, in his opinion, the power of the state could hardly reflect the consent of the governed. The electorate was restricted; only a fraction of it voted; only a majority of representatives was requisite; and elections hinged on few of the issues that actually arose. There was no reason to trust written law more than natural law interpreted by a judge. George Bradburn called Spooner's *Unconstitutionality of Slavery* "so great a work" that he never dared review it. "It is a work, as N. P. Rogers said, to make one's 'head ache' in the reading, if one will so read it as to understand its meaning, which, so far as we know, no one has yet done"[27] The solution to the riddle, however, probably lay in the fact that this work which expounded the fundamental document of American law and government, in the name of antislavery, actually repudiated much of politics and government. Implicit in it was a natural-rights anarchism.

Spooner's suspicion of government was further disclosed in a tract contending that fugitive slave laws were unconstitutional. To rescue a person deprived of his liberty without proper legal authority was presented as a moral and legal obligation. The protection of the right to bear arms in the Bill of Rights implied the right to use them. Indeed this was a cornerstone of the Constitution: unless the people could protest with force against any abrogation of power, no check on any government was meaningful. If Spooner's dislike of the rule of force reached this limit—and at this point he diverged from the nonresistants—his reasoning was nonetheless a version of antislavery. Without the right to take up weapons, the people would be *slaves*. With that right, they were not rebels but executors of the Constitution which they supposedly instituted.[28]

A judge might be no less reliable than a government, but Spooner was not content with relative security for freedom. In

---

[27] *Ibid.*, pp. 141–146, 153–154; Bradburn, *Memorial*, pp. 156–157.
[28] Spooner, *A Defence for Fugitive Slaves, Against the Acts of Congress of February 12, 1793, and September 18, 1850* (Boston, 1850) pp. 27–30.

An Essay on the Trial by Jury, he went back to Magna Carta to demonstrate that a jury, chosen by lot to represent all the diversities of the land, must have every kind of discretion with regard to evidence, guilt, and the justice of the law itself in order for the people to have liberty:

If a jury have not the right to judge between the government and those who disobey its laws, and resist its oppressions, the government is absolute, and the people, *legally speaking,* are slaves. Like many other slaves they may have sufficient courage and strength to keep their masters somewhat in check; but they are nevertheless *known to the law* only as slaves.[29]

Any tyranny could tolerate a jury which it selected and instructed. And like so many men in Jacksonian America, including other abolitionists, Spooner feared the tyranny of the majority. "The will, or the pretended will, of the majority," he warned, "is the last lurking place of tyranny at the present day." All the protections needed under the divine right of kings were still needed. The two most important protections were trial by jury and no taxation without consent. It should come as no surprise that, after the Civil War, Spooner became an inspiration to a forthrightly anarchistic movement. Already, to escape from the legal category of slavery, he conceived of government as nothing more than a "voluntary association."[30]

Actually Spooner's latent anarchism sometimes put him in bad faith in his dealings with other abolitionists. James Haughton, a Dublin correspondent of many of the nonresistants, discerned that Spooner's beliefs, put into practice, would be the same as theirs.[31] Spooner hinted to his best friend, George Bradburn, that he probably could not vote for any antislavery party, but it was pointless to make "noise" about his "theory of voting." Bradburn was almost ashamed to let anyone know "that such notions are

[29] Spooner, *An Essay on the Trial by Jury* (Boston, 1852), pp. 5–11, 17. Perry Miller places the essay in the context of resistance to equity law in American legal thought in *Life of the Mind,* p. 179.

[30] Spooner, *Trial by Jury,* pp. 206, 222–224, 132.

[31] George Bradburn to Spooner, Feb. 26, 1846, Spooner Papers, NYHS.

held by him, who wrote the 'Unconstitutionality of Slavery.'"
What these notions were may be inferred from Bradburn's advice
that in politics one idea can be put across "only at the expense
of sacrificing or postponing other ideas."[32] To Spooner, even trial
by jury would not be "theoretically accurate" if America really
became a voluntary association, "for theoretical accuracy would
require that every man, who was a party to the government,
should individually give his consent to the enforcement of every
law in every separate case." The closest practical approximation—
in law—was to select twelve men at random and act only on
unanimous sentiment.[33] In politics Spooner presumably would
accept no approximations.

It annoyed Bradburn that Spooner could request him to peddle
a constitutional theory to the Liberty Party and still privately
disclaim any interest of his own in politics. Spooner replied that
he would use any forum to "advocate natural law, and constitutional law, (where it was consistent with natural), . . . because
all men, in office, and out of office, are bound by them, without
regard to minorities or majorities among the people." But he
shunned politics as categorically as did the nonresistants:

I do not rely upon "political machinery" (although it may, or may not,
do good, according as its objects are, or are not, legal and constitutional) . . . because the principle of it is wrong; for it admits . . .
that under a constitution, the *law* depends on the will of majorities,
for the time being, as indicated by the acts of the legislature.

He could not be much impressed by the resentment of several
abolitionists, including Salmon P. Chase, that he did not belong
to *"The* Liberty Party." They would probably never ascend to
his principles concerning the foundation of government on natural law. "So long as the Liberty Party set up men, who, believing
the constitution supports slavery, will yet swear to support the
constitution, they are an essentially pro-slavery party—and an

[32] Spooner to Bradburn, Dec. 26, 1845; Bradburn to Spooner, Jan. 1,
1846 [wrongly dated 1845], *ibid.*
[33] Spooner, *Trial by Jury*, p. 132.

anti-slavery man might, with substantially the same consistency, vote for Calhoun."[34] Garrison could scarcely have been more of a separatist!

Since these opinions were unpublished, Spooner was generally assumed to be a good political abolitionist. We have already seen that other abolitionists agreed with Spooner in opposing the Free Soil Party; in its opportunism and prejudice, it failed to represent a unique principle that could abolish slavery.[35] In 1856 Gerrit Smith, Lewis Tappan, William Goodell, Frederick Douglass, and others hoped that "thorough abolition candidates" might once again be presented for election. They expected Spooner to join them; after all, he had loudly condemned the Free Soil Party and its anxiety not to jeopardize the union.[36] When they asked him to sign a call for a convention, however, he was at last prepared to make noise about his theories.

"If I were going to vote for any candidates," he told them, "I should certainly wish them to be 'thorough abolition candidates.'" But since no one agreed with him about the true principles of government he could not "consistently aid in nominating any candidates whatever." It was time to explain why he had never supported the Liberty Party:

A system of government must be honest throughout, (and not merely on a few, or even on many, points) to be entitled to the support of honest men. I think our constitution is a thousand times better—not only in its relations to slavery, but in relation to *most* other things— than it is generally understood to be. But I do not think it perfect—or such as honest men who know its true character can consistently support.

[34] Spooner to Bradburn, Aug. 25, Dec. 5, 1847, Spooner Papers, NYHS.
[35] For Spooner's analysis of the Buffalo convention, see his letter to Bradburn, Nov. 8, 1847 [probably 1848], *ibid.*
[36] In a letter to the *Commonwealth* (reprinted in Garrisons, *Garrison*, III, 406; and with great approval in *Liberator*, Feb. 24, 1854, p. 3) he attacked the "contradictory motto, *'Freedom National, Slavery Sectional.'*" He recognized no "compacts with slavery" and even hoped the Nebraska Bill would pass if that would bring slavery face to face with freedom "with no question between them except which shall conquer and which shall die."

In particular, "no robbery is more flagrant or palpable—nor hardly any more unjustifiable—than taxing men for the support of government, without their *personal* consent." This robbery promoted all other kinds of tyranny. Thus he was compelled to stand outside the Constitution and, "*on those points wherein it is right,*" to ask those professing to follow it "to act up to their own standard." He was able to make such an appeal "on the same principle that, standing outside the Mohammedan religion, I should feel at liberty to interpret the Koran, and appeal to believers to act up to their own creed, *wherein* it was right." Gerrit Smith kept this letter from the attention of the others. He did not want it printed, for criticism from the leading authority on the Consitution would hurt the cause. "I am very radical in my notions of Civil Gov[ernmen]t—but you are more so."[37]

In spite of his private reservations, Spooner pushed his view of the unconstitutionality of slavery with a somewhat disagreeable tenacity. In part, he desired to be better known and to make money out of his writings.[38] He also believed that antislavery deserved the widest possible audience. But neither of these motives completely accounts for his peculiar insistence that slavery was unconstitutional.

[37] Spooner to Gerrit Smith, Lewis Tappan, William Goodell, and others [unspecified], March 12, 1856; Smith to Spooner, March 16, 1856; and a printed letter requesting signatures, Spooner Papers, NYHS.

[38] Lack of funds is the constant theme of his letters. He had "given the Abolitionists nearly every valuable idea they have had for years," he claimed; yet he was "literally a beggar" (Spooner to Bradburn, March 9, 1849, Spooner Papers, NYHS). He wrote angry letters charging Gerrit Smith and William Goodell with having purloined his ideas about the Constitution and violated his copyright (Spooner to Goodell, Dec. 27, 1853; Goodell to Spooner, Jan. 3, 1854, Jan. 9, 1854; Spooner to Smith, Apr. 23, 1850, *ibid.*). For a while Spooner sent very insulting letters to Smith and billed him for ideas in their correspondence. Smith withdrew financial support from Spooner's books, and the hatred grew deeper. On the other hand, Smith was awed by Spooner's intellect. The upshot was that he got him a legal role in the libel trial concerning Smith's involvement in the John Brown episode. As part of the settlement, Spooner received $2000 (Smith to Spooner, July 18, 1856; Spooner to Bradburn, Nov. 8, 1849; Spooner to Smith, July 17, 1849; Smith to Spooner, Apr. 2, 1850; Oct. 25, 1860; Apr. 1, 1861; and the folders marked "Smith, Gerrit, Jan–Jun 1860" and "July–Aug 1860," *ibid.*).

A closer look at his schemes reveals that he worked from two different attitudes toward the social basis of reform. In neither case was he laying a legal basis for coercive legislation. First, there were schemes to publicize the principle that slavery violated the Constitution. Not only did he hope the Liberty Party would provide publicity; he often tried to persuade his friends Richard Hildreth, George Bradburn, and Samuel E. Sewall to start a paper called the *Constitutionalist*.[39] He did sometimes care about public opinion, for all his disparagement of majorities, and he was sure men could be enlightened to his viewpoint. "Many a one, indeed almost every one, who feels no particular sympathy for the black, will yet admit it to be wrong to make him a slave, and I think would give his vote for his freedom, if he could see that he had a right to vote thus, and that his vote would be effectual."[40] Liking for justice was a trait of human nature, not in some perfected or converted state, but as it already existed.

Here he clearly disagreed with both political and nonpolitical abolitionism. "You and I judge very differently of mankind," he wrote Bradburn. "You divide them all into two classes—angels and devils. I am a Sadducee—(is it not the Sadducees?)—and believe neither in angels nor devils—but that the best and worst are but *humans*—not very wide of each other either, in their intrinsic characters."[41] While a perfectionist or millenarian might be constrained to postpone reform until the mass is converted, a skeptic like Spooner might trust a state of affairs in which the general public frustrates tyrants—in this case, the government and the slaveholders. To put the distinction another way, Spooner

[39] See Spooner to Bradburn, Nov. 23, 1845, Apr. 13, 1851, Apr. 19, 1854, *ibid.* Also contemplated in this scheme were Nathaniel Rogers' old partner, John French, John Pierpont, and even John Greenleaf Whittier. Spooner, Bradburn, Hildreth, Sewall, and Pierpont comprised another circle of abolitionists overlooked in the common emphasis on Garrison and Weld. If the Spooner-Bradburn correspondence is any indication, this group was both more scintillating and scandalous than any of the evangelicals.

[40] Spooner to Bradburn, Nov. 8, 1847; to Smith, July 3, 1848, *ibid.*

[41] Spooner to Bradburn, March 15, 1850, *ibid.* This draft may not have been sent.

was less concerned with individual will than with general freedom.

Second, there were endless schemes to put *The Unconstitutionality of Slavery* in the hands of various elites. The American Abolition Society, though founded by the men whom Spooner refused to join in politics, eventually sent his essay to every congressman.[42] But that had not been Spooner's plan: he wanted it sent to the nation's thirty thousand lawyers.[43] It is probably accurate to compare Spooner's expectations of lawyers to those which Birney and Garrison once held of ministers. They were men of key influence and without military power. Because of their special calling they would recognize the moral law and without violence rectify social wrongs. In any event, Spooner doubted that the public would change the law by revolution; the task as revealed in these schemes was to change the law by the enlightenment of the elites. One consequence would be that nonslaveholders in the South, learning that slavery was unconstitutional, would agitate the subject. And slavery could not endure internal opposition.[44]

Spooner's Southern strategy gains additional interest because it implicated him in the plotting of John Brown, who carried a "Provisional Constitution" with him to Harper's Ferry. Since Spooner and all other parties censored or burned incriminating papers, we cannot fill in all the details, but we can see the outlines of his involvement. A man named Richard J. Hinton, who described himself as under orders to Captain Brown, wrote

[42] Lewis Tappan to Spooner, Nov. 3, 1855, Nov. 15, 1855, Nov. 21, 1855; Goodell to Spooner, Jan. 5, 1855; Smith to Spooner, March 1, 1856, *ibid.* Tappan was anxious to direct some profit toward Spooner, perhaps at Smith's urging.

[43] Tappan was willing to send to every lawyer whatever Spooner could compress onto three foolscap pages, but apparently Spooner did nothing about the offer. It may have led to the more limited distribution of the book to congressmen. Smith was about to send the book to every lawyer in his county when he was deterred by Spooner's animosity toward him (Lewis Tappan to Spooner, Aug. 22, 1853; Bela Marsh to Spooner, Oct. 11, 1849, *ibid.*).

[44] Spooner to Smith, March 14, 1847, *ibid.*

Spooner of a plan to send "some of your documents" to Missouri, following Brown's raiding activities in Kansas. Wendell Phillips, whose relationship with Spooner was cordial despite their disagreements over the Constitution, had agreed to pay for the printing of five hundred copies of these documents, and Hinton had the means of getting them to Brown.[45]

Late in 1858 Spooner drafted a circular, "To the Non-Slaveholders of the South," and wrote a number of abolitionists about his plans for distributing it. He wished to incite nonslaveholding whites to form vigilance committees to replace their governments and to make war on slaveholders with the cooperation of the blacks. Spooner believed that the slaves had a right to take their liberty and that it was the duty of others to aid them; but he also devised an economic incentive for whites to give their aid. The slaves, he argued, had a right to compensation. They could pay their liberators out of spoils taken from their former masters, just as nations paid their soldiers out of the spoils of the enemy. Together, slaves and nonslaveholders could revolutionize Southern society. The responses indicated the variations in antislavery beliefs in the 1850s. Lewis Tappan abjured "all resort to deadly weapons" as inconsistent with "the overruling Providence of God." Hinton Rowan Helper, a Southern abolitionist, feared that it would actually strengthen proslavery attitudes in the South. Francis Jackson applauded Spooner's motives, but said he was still a nonresistant. Wendell Phillips, Thomas Wentworth Higginson, and Theodore Parker approved the spirit of the proposal, but felt it was impractical. Stephen S. Foster was enthusiastic about the notion of "small associations for the purpose of attacking individual slaveclaimants" and promised some aid, although he was now more interested in developing a radical abolition party to compete with the Republicans. Favorable responses came from less well-known abolitionists.[46]

---

[45] Hinton to Spooner, n.d., n.p. [Boston]; Phillips to Spooner, rec'd Feb. 6, 1855, Spooner Papers, Boston Public Library; hereafter cited as Spooner Papers, BPL.

[46] "To the Non-Slaveholders of the South" (plus several drafts); Tappan

In January 1859 Spooner was informed of John Brown's plot. He immediately wrote Gerrit Smith that it lacked the men or resources to succeed. Slaves were too fearful and untrained to help very much. It was important to train some slaves; it was even more important to gain the support of nonslaveholders; this could be done by circularizing them on the natural and constitutional rights of the slaves to freedom and on the possibility of compensation for their aid. Then there would be incessant, bold assaults on the slaveholders and their property; they would be forced to free their slaves to avoid being "stripped of everything." Probably an actual invasion could be avoided. Spooner mentioned that Wendell Phillips had already contributed to print the circular. He had sent a copy of it to Captain Brown in the hopes that he would modify his plans.[47]

Somehow the anonymous circular was released, and it caused considerable furor in Boston and the South. After Harper's Ferry the papers linked it to Brown. Spooner, signing as "The Author of the Circular," wrote a somber letter to Governor Henry Wise of Virginia in an effort to clear Brown of responsibility for the hated circular. He wrote that after he had begun to circulate it "two men" had come to him and asked that he desist; they feared that it would put the South on guard against Brown, whose plot he had not previously known about. Then he had conferred with "others." Finally he had met with Brown on the subject. It was his opinion that propaganda and education should precede any raids such as Brown's, for whites were more likely to rise up than slaves. When enough opposition to slavery was mobilized, slaveholders would surrender without a fight in order to protect their other property. But he had desisted, partly because he was persuaded that the Brown project would have at

---

to Spooner, Oct. 7, 1858; Helper to Spooner, Dec. 18, 1858; Jackson to Spooner, Dec. 3, 1858; Higginson to Spooner, Nov. 30, 1858; Parker to Spooner, Nov. 30, 1858; Foster to Spooner, Jan. 8, 1859; Daniel Mann to Spooner, Jan. 16, 1859, Spooner Papers, BPL.

[47] Spooner to Smith, Jan. 31, 1859, Spooner Papers, NYHS.

least a little success. Consequently Brown should not be blamed for the circular.[48]

After Brown was sentenced, Spooner turned his imagination to a series of plans for rescuing him. Most of them were rejected by Higginson on the basis that they depended on hiring criminals and mercenaries who could make more money by betraying them. But plans were made to kidnap Governor Wise and offer him as a hostage for the life of the invader. When this project fell through, attention was shifted to sending a band of German 1848ers on a direct assault on the prison where Brown was held captive. Lack of money impeded both ventures, but they are evidence of the seriousness with which Spooner held the idea that citizens had the right to take the law in their own hands when self-styled governments violated natural law.[49]

The kidnapping plot apparently was a deviation from Spooner's normal course. He theoretically preferred the dissemination of legal principles to acts of symbolic violence. Indeed, he had envisioned the reunification of antislavery around his interpretation of the Constitution. William Lloyd Garrison, the nonresistant, and Christopher Robinson, the come-outer publisher, would be recruited to the beauties of his idea of law; the political abolitionists had less far to go. Soon there might be "Anti-Slavery Constitutional Leagues" in every American town, all distributing his writings to lawyers.[50] But the 1850s failed to permit

[48] Hinton Rowan Helper to Spooner, Jan. 31, Nov. 4, 1859; and clippings from Boston *Atlas, Courier,* and *Post;* [Spooner] to Wise, Nov. 2, 1859, Spooner Papers, BPL. Spooner, typically, could not resist instructing Wise in the law: "There is no crime where there is no criminal intent." How could Wise consent to Brown's death? Details concerning the circular are also cleared up in Spooner to O. B. Frothingham, Feb. 26, 1878, *ibid.*

[49] Anon. [Spooner] to Higginson, Nov. 20, 1859; Higginson to Spooner, Nov. 28, 1859; J. W. LeBarnes to Higginson, Nov. 15, Nov. 22, Nov. 27, Nov. 28, 1859, Jan. 11, Feb. 11, Feb. 27, 1860; John Brown Papers, Boston Public Library. Cf. Oswald Garrison Villard, *John Brown, 1800–1859: A Biography Fifty Years Later* (Boston and New York, 1910), pp. 514–516; Tilden G. Edelstein, *Strange Enthusiasm: A Life of Thomas Wentworth Higginson* (New York, 1970), pp. 214–216, 229–231.

[50] Spooner to George Bradburn, Sept. 10, 1845, Jan. 4, 1848, May 19,

such a simplification of antislavery methods and purposes.

Of course, symbolic violence eventually provided the key to the Constitution which could reunite wartime abolitionists. There was a foreshadowing of such an occurrence in 1856 when Gerrit Smith sent *The Unconstitutionality of Slavery* to David Wilmot. Smith expressed pleasure that this famous legislator was serious about the question of the legal basis of slavery. The Constitution was "full of power to abolish slavery."

What is slavery? It is the highest crime against man. It is a blasphemous attempt to unman man. It is the great pirate of the earth—the great enemy of man. What if the murderers of all nations should collect & take possession of an island of the sea? Might not any nation feel at liberty to break up that nest of murderers? Clearly. Just so—on the very same principle—any Nation, or State or people have the right to break up our Southern nest of pirates.[51]

It was superfluous to enclose the legal reasoning of Spooner's essay. The old antislavery distinction between a man and a thing under the government of God would now sanction unremitting violence.

By the time this constitutional theory came to life, Spooner had gone back to the Declaration of Independence to prove the Consitution null and void. But it was not just political abolitionism, disillusioned in its search for an honorable, noncoercive form of politics, that surrendered to the mysteries of power. Nonresistant anarchism eventually found new categories with which to approve some acts of violence. The 1850s was a decade of confusion for antislavery. Long before Harper's Ferry, controversies over spiritualism and free love had shown how ambiguous the quest for a metaphorical escape from slavery could become.

iii

The community at Modern Times, Long Island, which had between fifty and one hundred members in the early 1850s, pro-

May 27, 1851; to Stephen Pearl Andrews, March 31, 1847, Spooner Papers, NYHS.

[51] Smith to Wilmot [copy in Spooner's hand], March 20, 1856, *ibid.*

vides a convenient backdrop for the vagaries of antislavery. Unlike Skaneateles and Hopedale, it was not founded by abolitionists. Rather, it was an experiment in the philosophy of Josiah
Warren, who from his participation in the Owenite failures at
New Harmony, Indiana, had developed an economic system of anarchism. To avoid the flaw of authoritarianism that he believed
corrupted New Harmony, Warren proposed to unify men's affections by loosening their economic bonds. The task was to perfect
the exchange of labor for labor so that no man could impose an
unearned obligation on another. But Warren's theories soon took
second place at Modern Times. The authority of the institution
of marriage was called into question; then, as though to renew
order after chaos, residents were attracted to fantastic nomen-
clature and the novel authority of social science. John Humphrey
Noyes conceived of it all as the wandering of an Old Testament
tribe: "Owen begat New Harmony; New Harmony (by reaction)
begat Individual Sovereignty; Individual Sovereignty begat Modern Times; Modern Times was the mother of Free Love, the
Grand Pantarchy, and the American branch of French Positiv-
ism.."[52]

Warren refused to join the abolition movement because he
believed chattel slavery to be only a special instance of the general problem of economic oppression. He even took the side of
South Carolina in the tariff controversy: any taxation of other
people's labor was a potential cause of civil war.[53] This does not
mean, however, that he failed to exploit the concept of slavery.
"You never will find any satisfactory solution of the great problem now up between *labor* and *capital*, or *slavery* and *liberty*,
until you understand what justice is, and what a circulating
medium, or money, ought to be," he told Americans.[54] If money
represented labor performed by the bearer, individuals would
own their own time—and hence themselves. Warren's thought

[52] Noyes, *American Socialisms*, p. 94.
[53] Martin, *Men against the State*, pp. 39–40, 80.
[54] Quoted in Yehoshua Arieli, *Individualism and Nationalism in American Ideology* (Cambridge, Mass., 1964), p. 292.

bridges two preoccupations of American reform, money supply and wage slavery.

Stephen Pearl Andrews, who became Warren's foremost advocate, was an abolitionist, a defender of the Constitution, and an associate of Spooner's.[55] From a distinguished family of Massachusetts Baptists—his father was a leader in the struggle against the established church and one of his nephews became a famous president of Brown University—Andrews went South to make his fortune. As the first attorney (the litigation continued for decades) in the weird New Orleans real estate case of Myra Clark Gaines, he was experienced in the perplexities of private property in an expanding nation. Moving to Texas from Louisiana, he was mobbed for being an abolitionist. In 1843 he traveled to England with Lewis Tappan with the idea that, if Texas could be kept out of the clutches of the United States, freedom might be secured within the territory.[56]

In London Andrews learned of Isaac Pitman's system of shorthand. When he got back to Boston he tried to publicize it as a device for educating the illiterate slaves.[57] To be sure, New Englanders placed a high value on literacy, and Andrews had more firsthand knowledge of slavery than most New Englanders. But Andrews was also experienced in the chaos of the frontier. He began to pursue social order in Swedenborgianism and spiritual-

[55] Andrews joined Pierpont, Mellen, Hildreth, Walter Channing, and others in defending the Constitution at the 1844 meetings of the New England Anti-Slavery Society (*Liberator*, Nov. 22, 1844, p. 2). His view of the Constitution appears in his "Abolition Reasons against Disunion," *Young American's Magazine*, May 1847, pp. 159–166. He was associated with Spooner in both abolitionism and postal reform (see note 50 above, and Andrews to Spooner, Dec. 13, Dec. 28, 1850, Spooner Papers, NYHS).

[56] For this stage in Andrews' career, see Madeleine B. Stern, "Stephen Pearl Andrews, Abolitionist, and the Annexation of Texas," *Southwestern Historical Quarterly*, LXVII (1964), 491–523; and Charles Shively, "An Option for Freedom in Texas, 1840–1844," *Journal of Negro History*, L (1965), 77–96.

[57] Madeleine B. Stern, "Stephen Pearl Andrews and Modern Times, Long Island," *Journal of Long Island History*, IV (1964), 1. The *Liberator* (July 11, 1845, p. 1) was enthusiastic about the shorthand idea.

ism, Fourierism and socialism.[58] When he met Josiah Warren, he was ready to learn that only individual sovereignty could establish order and abolish slavery. He published this solution to the problem of authority:

Individuality is the essential law of order. This is true throughout the universe. When every individual particle of matter obeys the law of its own attraction, and comes into that precise position, and moves in that precise direction which its own inherent individualities demand, the harmony of the spheres is evolved. By that means only natural classification, natural order, natural organization, natural harmony and agreement are attained. Every scheme or arrangement which is based upon the principle of thwarting the inherent affinities of the individual monads which compose any system or organism is essentially vicious, and the organization is false—a mere bundle of revolutionary and antagonistic atoms.

Like Spooner, Andrews sought a "true constitution," but he did not look backward to English common law. He turned, instead, to science, as developed by history. The Reformation had ended man's subordination to the church; the American Revolution had freed man from subjection to the state; and French socialism was subverting the subtlest form of domination, that of society. One might feel certain that history tended toward the sovereignty of every individual.[59]

Andrews remained an abolitionist, although he warned the American Anti-Slavery Society that its failure to justify human freedom scientifically robbed its appeals of conviction.[60] The lack of a "scientific definition" of slavery meant that new forms of dispossession could not be checked. Andrews had nothing to do with the definition of slavery as the violation of moral accountability, and he was dissatisfied with the ordinary economic definition:

[Slavery] is thought to consist in the feature of chattelism, but an

58 Rocker, *Pioneers of American Freedom*, p. 72.
59 Andrews, *The Science of Society* (New York, 1852), No. 1, "The True Constitution of Government in the Sovereignty of the Individual as the Final Development of Protestantism, Democracy, and Socialism," pp. 12, 22.
60 *Liberator*, May 26, 1854, p. 1.

ingenious lawyer would run his pen through every statute upon slavery in existence, and expunge that fiction of the law, and yet leave slavery, for all practical purposes, precisely what it is now. It needs only to appropriate the services of the man by operation of the law, instead of the man himself.[61]

But Andrews was now more concerned with the requisites of a good community: hearts satisfied by religion and love, heads made wise with economic and scientific knowledge. George Fitzhugh, who regarded Southern slavery as the ideal alternative to *laissez-faire*, commended Andrews' critique of Northern economics, even though it was offered as part of the science of antislavery. The anarchist and the proslavery sociologist both hoped that science could mollify sectional conflict and foster reform impulses adapted to particular localities. Science would reconcile freedom and order. Their correspondence and a meeting in New York, however, did not yield the collaboration they had foreseen.[62]

Scientific anarchism, which seemed to afford solutions to the problems of order and authority, could lead into systems of totalitarianism. According to Josiah Warren, "nature demands and will have an *Indiv[i]dual* deciding power in every sphere[;] whether that government is a person, an idea or anything else, it must be an *Individuality* or all will be confusion."[63] Warren preferred the dominance of the principle of the equitable exchange of labor for labor, but this antidemocratic sentiment could be twisted toward authoritarian rule. In Cincinnati one of Warren's followers

[61] Andrews, *Science of Society*, No. 2, "Cost the Limit of Price: A Scientific Measure of Honesty in Trade as One of the Fundamental Principles in the Solution of the Social Problem," p. 124.

[62] Fitzhugh, *Sociology for the South*, in Wish, ed., *Ante-Bellum*, p. 55; Wish, "Stephen Pearl Andrews, American Pioneer Sociologist," *Social Forces*, XIX (1941), 480–481. On Comtean sociology at Modern Times, see L. L. Bernard and Jessie Bernard, *Origins of American Sociology: The Social Science Movement in the United States* (New York, 1943), pp. 161–176, 313–338; and Alfred Owen Aldridge, "Mysticism in Modern Times, L. I.," *Americana*, XXXVI (1942), 555–570.

[63] Josiah Warren, *Practical Applications of the Elementary Principles of "True Civilization," to the Minute Details of Every Day Life* (Princeton, Mass., 1873), p. 20.

dreamed of a renovation of society in which each "circle" of men would choose a "chief," the circle of chiefs in one region would choose a higher chief, and so on nationally and internationally.[64] We may recall Beriah Green's vision that the strongest and wisest man in each area was naturally the king. Stephen Pearl Andrews in his quest for "Natural Order" was eventually dubbed "Pantarch" by his own circle of admiring followers.[65] Additional dangers were forthcoming as individual sovereignty was sometimes merged with versions of spiritualism. It would become possible to claim that obedience to leadership followed from the attractions between spirits which were destined to close affinity; leadership would then be based on a spiritual principle, free of the liabilities of coercion or democratic choice.

The attractions of the spirit, besides their long-range intellectual perils, were the basis of the immediate notoriety of Modern Times: the community became associated with the idea of free love. Warren found free love "more troublesome than a crown of thorns"; in his view Modern Times was invaded by troublemakers who had nothing in common with its original purposes. But Andrews discovered free love to be "the antithesis of enslaved love." His views on the subject were displayed most prominently in a debate with Horace Greeley and the elder Henry James. Marriage, he said, was "neither better nor worse than all other of the arbitrary and artificial institutions of society—contrivances to regulate nature instead of studying her laws." The tendency of the women's rights movement must be toward "the complete emancipation and self-ownership of women" and away from "the legal or prevalent theological idea of marriage." But this was not a rationale for promiscuity: "The lesson has to be learned that order, combining with freedom and ultimating in harmony, is to be the work of science, and not of arbitrary legislation and criminal codes."[66]

[64] *Practical Christian*, Dec. 13, 1846, p. 3.
[65] Wish, "Stephen Pearl Andrews," pp. 481–482; Madeleine B. Stern, *The Pantarch: A Biography of Stephen Pearl Andrews* (Austin, Tex., 1968).
[66] Warren, *Practical Applications*, pp. 16–26; Stern, "Stephen Pearl

It is impossible to be certain how unrestrained this conservative theory became in practice. Two well-known sexual reformers—Thomas Low Nichols and Mary Gove Nichols—moved to Modern Times, and love steadily replaced commerce as the salient concern of the community. Rumors of sexual experimentation soon made the community notorious. Andrews, after initial enthusiasm, was apparently displeased at this change in emphasis, but he agreed with the doctrine of marital reformers that spiritual affinities were surer guides than moral statutes. There is evidence that not even Dr. and Mrs. Nichols were fully reconciled to the practice of sexual freedom: after establishing a new community in Ohio they were advised by the spirit of St. Ignatius Loyola to convert to Roman Catholicism. During the Civil War they were Catholic expatriates in England and critics of licentiousness and radicalism in the union states.[67]

Because marriage could be viewed both as a sentimental source of order independent of state controls and as a worldly form of enslavement sanctioned by human law, it was an institution that seized the attention of antebellum reformers and brought out some of their most ambivalent attitudes. John Humphrey Noyes, who believed in community marriage as the extension of the family among the regenerate, sympathized with the prohibition of sexual relations among the Shakers, but he ridiculed Modern Times. He scorned as "free love" any theories which retained the notion of marital couples while abandoning the institution of marriage or the custom of fidelity. It did not matter whether they were searching for true love matches instead of state-administered marriages.

Andrews and Modern Times," pp. 8–9; Rocker, *Pioneers of American Freedom*, p. 81.

[67] Cf. Moncure Conway's novel, *Pine and Palm*, pp. 226–252; Conway, "Modern Times, New York," *Fortnightly Review*, I (1865), 421–434; Stern, "Stephen Pearl Andrews and Modern Times"; Bertha-Monica Stearns, "Memnonia: The Launching of a Utopia," *New England Quarterly*, XV (1942), 280–295; Stearns, "Two Forgotten New England Reformers," *New England Quarterly*, VI (1933), esp. 78–79; and Philip Gleason, "From Free-Love to Catholicism: Dr. and Mrs. Thomas L. Nichols at Yellow Springs," *Ohio Historical Quarterly*, LXX (1961), 283–307.

Since the 1830s reformers had warned against the dangers of masturbation, prostitution, adultery, and even excessive sexual relations in marriage. In the 1850s there were overtones of sexual permissiveness among reformers; these could be detected in a growing interest in divorce and free choice of marital partners and in occasional defenses of free love. A careful recent study points out, however, that "even the most unconventional sexual theorists of the age"—Andrews, Noyes, the Nicholses, and a host of spiritualists—retained a strong "distrust of sexuality and sexual excitement." Furthermore, Victorian sexual radicalism was no more successful in clarifying the complex interrelationship of freedom and authority than most of the rest of antebellum reform. Many reformers doubted the legitimacy of legal marriage and yet regarded sexual promiscuity as a profanity of the body, akin to masturbation; in some ways it is surprising that more reformers did not venture on the Noyesian path of community marriage. There were other paths to security. If legal marriage was an arbitrary formality, a type of licensed prostitution, then phrenology—or one of various other mental and moral "sciences"—was available to counsel applicants about their natural affinities.[68] Spiritualism likewise promised a natural order of true affinities. Whether proposed remedies were physiological or spiritual, the problem of the proper roles of sex and marriage continued to vex reformers who had never fully resolved contradictions in the various definitions of freedom as self-control or self-fulfillment and the various explanations of sovereignty as arising from God or from individual self-interest.

Abolitionist radicalism was often drawn to the quest to make

[68] On the subject of sexual reform in general, see Stephen Willner Nissenbaum, "Careful Love: Sylvester Graham and the Emergence of Victorian Sexual Theory in America, 1830–1840," unpublished Ph.D. dissertation, University of Wisconsin, Madison, Wis., 1968 (quoted phrases are on p. 259). Charlotte Fowler Wells penciled in this answer to a query from W. H. Channing on how to end licentiousness: "(Not by law, nor suddenly.) True marriages." And how were unsuitable marriages to be prevented? "*Help* from Phren. Spirit. affin." They must be terminated by "*mutual* separations" (W. H. Channing to Mrs. Wells, Sept. 21, 1851, Fowler and Wells Family Papers, Cornell University).

love truly free and yet keep it harmonious with social order. It might even be argued that abolitionists were unusually concerned with sexual excess and self-control as was shown, for example, in their rhetorical descriptions of the South as a great brothel.[69] In any case, several of their habitual ways of thinking—their reliance on abstract definitions of slavery, their determination to uproot unholy forms of authority, and their belief that divine order was regulated through the heart rather than through force— combined to pull them into controversies over marriage. Some versions of "free love" conformed to a paradoxical formula which is familiar in much of antislavery thought: that of escaping anarchy in the bad sense of chaos and enslavement by pursuing anarchy in the good sense of harmony and freedom. Quite apart from questions concerning marriage, the possibility that divine order might be realized through spiritualism or physiological science seemed to offer a way out of some of the antinomian confusion associated with the government of God. The experience of Modern Times, in short, though following from a version of economic anarchism closer to proconstitutional abolitionists like Spooner and Andrews, contained premonitions of more general developments in the careers of many Garrisonians in the 1850s.

iv

One abolitionist withdrew from Modern Times with this protest: "*Wife* with them is synonymous with *slave*, and *monogamy* is denounced as a vicious *monopoly of affection*." He feared invaders from the city of New York, however, more than the true members of the community. Adin Ballou, who felt compelled to distinguish practical Christianity from individual sovereignty, registered his doubts that there were affinities: "appetite itself is involuntary, and asks for that which is adapted to it, as indiscriminately in respect to women as to apples." But he was careful to pay respect to Andrews' intelligence. Unfortunately, in his view,

[69] An argument of this sort was presented by Ronald G. Walters in a paper on "Antislavery and Sexuality" at the convention of the Organization of American Historians, New Orleans, Apr. 15, 1971.

the doctrine of individual sovereignty, no less than despotic or aristocratic or democratic sovereignty, would lead to tyranny by way of human imperfection. The only trustworthy sovereign was God.[70]

Ballou might have assailed free love more forcefully than he did. He may have been reluctant out of shame at the bad grace with which Hopedale had checked its only scandal. Two members of the community, unable to desist from adultery and accused by the moral police of the community, were driven to defend their behavior on philosophical grounds; they took flight to Modern Times. Furthermore, in the witch-hunting atmosphere one of the most valuable members of the community was condemned for not uncovering the crime; she joined Theodore Weld at the Raritan Bay Union in New Jersey.[71] Ballou had additional good reasons for his uncharacteristic restraint in criticism of Modern Times. He was well aware of the excesses to which antislavery was prone when mixed with spiritualism.

Ballou found his own solace in spiritualism—he was compensated for bitter disappointments, was allowed to communicate with his dead son, and given glimpses of beautiful communities of the future. Theologically, for him spiritualism was implicit in belief in the universal restoration of souls. But as the spiritualist movement grew it seemed to compete with the authority of the New Testament by offering new revelations which exaggerated the progress of mankind. For the most part, he stayed away from other spiritualists, although he wrote on spiritualism and Hopedale housed several mediums.[72] Ballou's self-control was not typical of the movement.

[70] George Stearns in *Practical Christian*, Oct. 9, 1852, p. 3; *ibid.*, Jan. 3, 1849, p. 2; Ballou, *Practical Christian Socialism*, p. 585. See also Ballou, ed., *True Love vs. Free Love; Testimony of a True-Hearted Woman* (Hopedale, 1855), and the argument between Ballou and Austin Kent carried in *Practical Christian* throughout the winter of 1854–1855.

[71] *Practical Christian*, July 2, 1853, p. 3; Ballou, *History of Hopedale*, pp. 246–249.

[72] See Ballou's *An Exposition of Views Respecting the Principal Facts, Causes and Peculiarities Involved in Spirit Manifestations; Together with*

Hopedale was quite familiar with John Murray Spear, whose career illustrated some of the tensions connecting antislavery and spiritualism. Spear was brought up in a family close to John Murray, the founder of Universalism. After working in a cotton factory and being trained as a shoemaker, he was called to the ministry. Another famous Universalist, the second Hosea Ballou, helped him get the requisite education. Spear was driven from his first parish because of his radical views on peace, temperance, and slavery; accordingly, like a good come-outer, he announced to his next parish that he would preach the Gospel and leave them to donate whatever they wished. Late in 1844 he was severely injured by a proslavery mob. During a long winter of convalescence, he determined to become a full-time reformer and joined his brother Charles in opposing capital punishment and improving the treatment of prisoners. Both brothers were well-known nonresistants; John Murray Spear actually associated himself with Hopedale's Practical Christian Communion.[73]

This career of straightforward humanitarian reform was diverted when John Murray Spear discovered in 1852 that he was a healer and a medium. A sermon he delivered at Hopedale was supposedly communicated from Benjamin Franklin, who wished to convey his satisfaction with "the rise and progress of a people so *practical*, in respect to all that is necessary to human welfare, morally, intellectually and physically."[74] Soon the spirit of John Murray reminded his namesake how he had cuddled him as a

---

Interesting Statements and Communications (2d ed., Boston, 1853); Ballou, *Autobiography*, pp. 61–62, 98, 149, 374, 379–380, 387, 407, 434, 462; and Field, "Anti-Slavery," *Hopedale Reminiscences*, p. 21.

[73] Mrs. H. F. M. Brown, "Biographical Sketch of John M. Spear," in A. E. Newton, ed., *The Educator: Being Suggestions, Theoretical and Practical, Designed to Promote Man-Culture and Integral Reform, with a View to the Ultimate Establishment of a Divine Social State on Earth. Comprised in a Series of Revelations from Organized Associations in the Spirit Life through John Murray Spear* (Boston, 1857), esp. pp. 10–14; *Non-Resistant*, Apr. 20, 1839, p. 2; *Practical Christian*, Aug. 30, 1851, p. 2.

[74] *Practical Christian*, July 17, 1852, p. 2. Spear often went into a "magnetic state" at Hopedale. See *ibid.*, May 7, 1853, p. 3; Ballou, *Exposition of Views*, pp. 192–203.

child and urged him, now that he was a man, to broaden the message of Universalism. Spear was told that spiritual influences would soon "exert a greater change, in a shorter time, than anything which has before transpired on your earth." The brotherhood of man would prosper on account of the new access to wisdom on high. He was told—as any abolitionist should already have known—that all men were presently enslaved; but now there was the promise that all forms of strife and bondage would shortly be abolished as wisdom was communicated from the spirits.[75]

In November 1852, Spear was informed by a committee in the spirit world that he would be under the care of Thomas Jefferson for a while. A year later, Jefferson, after first discoursing on the evils of slavery, instructed Spear in a needed revolution: the form of government must be changed. He was ambiguous about the means, but the purposes owed a great deal to antislavery and closely resembled disunionism: "Perhaps, in the outset, a half-dozen of the freest States may be selected as the field for the formation of the New Government." These states would provide a haven for fugitives from bondage. The government would renounce war unilaterally; indeed, there would be almost no government, only a company of volunteers. "It is an enterprise which is to spring spontaneously from the heart." Most of Jefferson's plan, though it was plainly antislavery and nonresistant, was very fuzzy. Rather than being arbitrary or coercive, it was to follow natural laws analogous to the bonds of love that unite domestic families or to the principles of hygiene that govern human bodies. What was unmistakable, however, was Spear's desire to find in spiritualism solutions to the problem of authority as it vexed antislavery. This was true in two senses. First, the spirits served as authorities for what was right. Second, they were guides to states of society which would be orderly, just, and uncoercive.[76]

[75] S. C. Hewitt, ed., *Messages from the Superior State; Communicated by John Murray, through John M. Spear, in the Summer of 1852* (Boston, 1853), pp. 45–47, 102–103, 108, 120–125, 137–141.
[76] Adin Ballou, ed., *Twelve Discourses on Government: Purporting to*

The spirits could themselves be challenged as invidious authorities. Ballou, for instance, was impressed with parts of the communications Spear received from the spiritual world; he even edited one of Spear's—or Jefferson's—volumes. But he warned that no one should embrace anything from any authority, spiritual or otherwise, which failed to "commend itself to the soul's highest judgment."[77] Spiritualism itself had to be interpreted in a come-outer spirit and cleansed of the taint of bondage. Spear's followers, echoing controversies over the Bible, denied the "dogma of *plenary verbal inspiration.*" Human communication was always marred with ambiguities, and there was only man's reason to sort truth from error: "If an ANGEL speaks to us, it is to US he must speak, not to anything *less* than *ourselves.* . . . And so, too, is it with the Divine Creator and Father of us all; else how should we *know,* or intelligently and lovingly *believe,* it was our Father's word?"[78] The original antinomies of nonresistance, in which God alone could rule man, could be so transformed that individuals were isolated with only their own affections to guide them toward the truth. It was appealing, therefore, to believe in magnetic cords of understanding and sympathy, existing before souls departed for the spiritual world, which might furnish the basis for earthly communities. Of these cords a new fabric of order and authority might be spun.

Spear was eventually delegated the agent on earth of a heavenly benevolent society, "The Association of the Beneficents," whose members included Benjamin Rush, Benjamin Franklin, Jefferson, William Ellery Channing, John Murray, Swedenborg, Seneca, John Howard the philanthropist, and Lafayette! Spirits, who were free of the bondage of the flesh, could not be accused of enslaving those to whom they delegated responsibility. They fed Spear the knowledge required to end war, competition, and

---

Have Been Delivered in Boston, Mass., December, 1853, by Thomas Jefferson, of the Spirit World; Through John M. Spear, Medium (Hopedale, 1853), *passim.*

[77] *Ibid.,* p. iv.

[78] Newton, ed., *The Educator,* pp. viii–ix; Hewitt, ed., *Messages,* pp. v–vi.

every worldly imperfection. The elaborate diagrams and concentric circles in which this knowledge was expressed might indicate that visions of authoritarianism were imminent. Then under the caption, "Voting Needless," it is stated that "a single leading, sound, central mind" should resolve all disagreements. Though all opinions should be heard, the "leading mind gathers up, focalizes, concentrates the whole." Beriah Green was not the only abolitionist to long for true leaders who would make democratic procedures irrelevant. Through the mediumship of Spear, nonresistance was well on its way to the mythology of mass movements and dictatorship. This was not, of course, his intention. Rather, we may surmise that the government of God, which ruled out human pretensions to govern, was consistent with commands expressed through disinterested, sinless voices from the world of spirits.[79]

In 1854 Spear's spiritual directors, whose numbers came to include Martin Luther and Roger Williams, provided him with all the secrets of a new community which would stand as a city on a hill and reunite mankind. He assumed leadership of spiritualists who founded a city called Harmonia in Western New York. The most outlandish feature of this community was its experiment with technology. A group of scientists in the spiritual world, the "Association of Electric-Izers," headed by Franklin, explained to Spear that perpetual motion existed in reality and taught him how to create a machine which would "draw upon the great reservoir of the magnetic life of nature." Spear returned to the home of the Hutchinson Family Singers in Lynn to build the machine. One of Spear's disciples was informed in a vision that "she was appointed to be 'the Mary of a New Dispensation.'" Then Spear himself was instructed that she should go to the "New Motor." There she experienced pangs of parturition; "her own perception was clear and distinct that through those agonizing throes the most interior and refined elements of her spiritual being were imparted to and absorbed by" Spear's remarkable

79 Newton, ed., *The Educator,* pp. 43–50, 59–63, 467.

contraption. The machine was nurtured, brought to life, and carried to Harmonia, where it was swiftly smashed by a mob of unfriendly neighbors. Spear reflected that, after all, "Garrison was mobbed and Birney's printing press was thrown into the river." In any event, the community soon disintegrated under pressures caused by internal dissensions and outside allegations that free love was being practiced there.[80] Spear's personal reputation seems to have gone into decline. In 1858, after a bizarre trial, he was suspended by the leading, sound, central mind of a cult called the "Order of Patriarchs" in Cincinnati. He was not up to their moral standard; they did not want to be charged with free love.[81]

V

In 1849, John W. Webster, a teacher at Harvard Medical College, murdered the uncle of the historian Francis Parkman over a debt and left his bones in a laboratory vault. Lysander Spooner called the subsequent trial illegal because the judge excused three persons from jury duty on the basis of their conscientious objection to capital punishment. It was not a trial "by the country" but "by that portion only of the country, which has been selected by the government, on account of their having no opinions or feelings different from its own." Henry C. Wright's approach to the case was very different from Spooner's, although he too overlooked the sensational details of the slaying. He argued that Webster, the hangman, and the government all belonged in the same formal category—all assuming the right of one man to kill another in his own interest. In reply to those concerned with law and order he insisted that rapists and assassins acted on the same principle as governments and that only nonresistants exhibited a

[80] See the remarkable account in George Lawton, *The Drama of Life after Death: A Study of the Spiritualist Religion* (New York, 1932), pp. 618–623.

[81] "The World's Great Band; or the 'Order of Patriarchs.' Complaint of Eliza J. Kenney against John M. Spear." Broadside in Adin Ballou, Scrapbook, 1863–1865, Boston Public Library.

better way.[82] Wright, then, never lost his facility with the logic of no-government. In some ways he was the exemplar of the vagaries of antislavery.

"O! the developments made by ANTI-SLAVERY!!" he wrote Nathaniel Rogers. "Little did I once dream that the Clerical Order was the great pillar of support to all that is evil under the sun!" Ministers, that is, condoned the sexual, physical, intellectual, spiritual sins in slavery. Eventually he lumped together slavery, war, marriage, and liquor as forms of licensed sin. Then he distinguished two kinds of free love: the first associated in his mind with bondage, sensualism, concubines, and the Old Testament; the second with the abstract virtues of fidelity, freedom, and progress.[83]

It was not simply the antislavery movement that influenced Wright's development. As a theology student at Andover, he had undergone profound despair when his professors, in teaching him languages, destroyed his reverence for Scripture, and in teaching him logic, annihilated his conceptions of God without supplying a convincing substitute. He finally reached nearly contradictory conclusions. On the one hand, the proof of God's existence was that in his loneliness he could not erase the idea of God from his consciousness. On the other hand, it was futile to conceive of God in terms other than the laws of his physical creation. The first conclusion was conducive to the antinomian formula of nonresistance: no civil or ecclesiastical institution was serviceable between man and God. But the second could also eliminate God from the formula. At Andover he had written in his journal: "We are not bound to obey any command, simply because we suppose it is the command of God, but because we

[82] Lysander Spooner, *Illegality of the Trial of John W. Webster* (Boston, 1850); Henry C. Wright, *John W. Webster, The Murderer, and Joseph Eveleth, The Hangman: The Difference between Them* (Boston, 1855); Edmund L. Pearson, "Webster, John White," *Dictionary of American Biography*, X (New York, 1936), pp. 592–593.

[83] *Herald of Freedom*, May 6, 1842, p. 2; *Liberator*, Nov. 4, 1853, p. 4; May 1, 1857, p. 2.

see it to be right, and in accordance with those laws which He has engraven upon our physical and social and moral constitution." This meant that to discover God's commands we must solicit "the testimony of our own souls."[84]

If his consciousness confirmed the existence of God, it also provided knowledge of human nature. For this reason Wright could not be an experimental scientist; his anthropology consisted of generalizing his own sentiments. The result was a kind of religion of introversion and self-denial in which man was a territory beyond trespass, an "empire in himself."[85] Since no harm could come from loyalty to his own nature, he avoided medical advice and prescribed for himself only cold water.[86] Other consequences were that he rejected the infallibility of the Bible since, for example, no miracle could suspend the law that a body needs food; and yet he subscribed to all of Jesus' teachings since their truth was written on his soul. He too was a spiritualist, and in spiritual conversations with Jesus and Nathaniel P. Rogers he learned that not all of the New Testament was true. Mostly he relied on feeble analogies: just as we know how to avoid burning or drowning by staying out of fire and water, "we know that the only way to be saved from sin, is to stop sinning."[87]

Wright's interest in the laws of the self developed into a preoccupation with marital relations and family love. Marriage, he explained, was a law of nature:

No man can be what he was designed to be, till by marriage, the spirit of a woman has entered into him, to refine, beautify and strengthen his peculiar nature, and assimilate it to the divine. No woman can be

[84] Wright, *Human Life: Illustrated in My Individual Experience as a Child, a Youth, and a Man* (Boston, 1849), pp. 189–201, 220.

[85] Wright, *Anthropology; or, The Science of Man: In Its Bearing on War and Slavery, and on Arguments from the Bible, Marriage, God, Death, Retribution, Atonement and Government, in Support of These and Other Social Wrongs* (Cincinnati, 1850), p. 10.

[86] Wright, *Human Life*, p. 385.

[87] Wright, *Anthropology*, pp. 18–22; *Practical Christian*, Aug. 2, 1851, p. 4.

what she was designed to be, till the spirit of a man has entered into
her, to purify, elevate and adorn her peculiar nature.

He meant not the legal relationship but true love.[88] He did not
defend the right to experiment; he was more concerned with the
right to forbear. After a *man* objected to a resolution at a
woman's rights convention that it was a woman's right to decide
when she will go through maternity, Wright indignantly wrote
Ballou that the mother's "empire" over the child in its "Ante-
Natal history" would become the most important issue of the
age.[89]

To discuss sex did not embarrass him. On the contrary, he
believed children should be taught the nature of the reproductive
system, which he described without much awkwardness. But the
question to which he especially addressed himself was, "WHAT
SHALL WE DO TO BE SAVED?" Religion that looked forward
to a future life neglected the task of developing the conscience
of man. Sexual ignorance impeded the reform and regeneration
of man: "The kingdom of heaven is within those, and only those,
who understand and comply with the conditions of present life
and health to body and soul." Nonresistant virtues were developed in the womb:

If a man were rightly and truly born of woman, he would not need
afterwards to be born of God; for to be rightly born of woman is, in
the truest and highest sense, to be born of God. Those who receive
a healthy and noble creation at first, need no second creation, provided that the first be not deformed by abuse.

He mentioned two deforming factors. First, the soul was sub-
stantial—this was the premise of spiritualism—and must be formed
by the seed of the father and the nutrition of the mother. It was
thus crucial to keep Satan out of the sex act: drunkenness, sor-
row, disease, or lust could blight the conception of the soul and
leave it forever defective. Second, a well-conceived soul could

[88] Wright, *Anthropology*, pp. 28–29.
[89] *Practical Christian*, June 12, 1858, p. 1.

still be ruined in the uterus if the father persisted in "his legal right to sexual intercourse." Presumably souls battered by instances of lust could never become regenerate. Reformers might succeed in controlling sinners born in sin, and the conditions in which they lived might be ameliorated; but perfection would be impossible.[90] For all of Wright's interest in science, his view of sex retained a Calvinistic awareness of human depravity. He questioned, in effect, whether any of the dreams of release and spontaneity, common to nonresistants, perfectionists, and spiritualists, could be attained without the prior self-control of the fathers.

Wright imagined that too many doctors advised men to marry in order to escape the great Victorian curse, "solitary indulgence." Unfortunately, such men, never having conquered themselves, proceeded to victimize their wives and unborn children. In this sense marriage was "*licensed prostitution.*" Government, as every nonresistant knew, could never check vice; man must privately learn self-control.[91] In a long series of fictitious letters between a model man and his wife—Ernest and Nina—Wright's style betrayed his own sentimental evasions. Men were at fault; there was no defect in human nature nor were women ever really guilty. Certainly Ernest addressed his spouse in a tone very different from that in which Wright had earlier called for accuracy about the reproductive system:

Nina! Since we first felt attracted to each other as husband and wife, on no subject have we interchanged our thoughts and feelings so often, so freely, so fully, and so pleasantly, as on the nature, the object, and the power of this element of our being. We have sought to know the fixed, natural laws by which our sexual intercourse was designed to be governed. The effects, on body and soul—on the beauty, the

[90] Wright, *Marriage and Parentage; or, The Reproductive Element in Man, as a Means to His Elevation and Happiness* (6th ed., London, n.d. [1st pub. 1854]), pp. 13–23, iii, 7, 23–45.

[91] *Ibid.*, pp. 33–34. He thought wives should keep their own names and children should bear their mothers' names. Marital disputes should be settled only by private understanding (*Liberator*, Sept. 2, 1853, p. 1).

comfort, the power, the sweet repose and satisfaction of our relation—of *its retention* in my organism, except for offspring, have been deep, vitalizing, ennobling, and intensely joyous and elevating. Deeply and tenderly as we have loved each other, *its expenditure* for sensual pleasure would have changed entirely the tone of our connubial life.[92]

The sentimental opacity of this address obscures what "it" was that brought joy in retention. Perhaps the husband was to avoid all sexual relations "except for offspring." It seems more likely that Wright was favoring coitus reservatus, the form of sexual relations practiced at the Oneida Community, in which the "amative and propagative functions of the sexual organs" were carefully distinguished.[93] That is, to climax sexual intercourse with ejaculation, even after withdrawal, was a form of onanism, a waste of the seed. There was a kind of pleasure, as well as a moral duty, in retention. If this was Wright's meaning, however, he differed from the Oneida perfectionists in two important ways. In the first place, he showed no interest in community marriage, but instead retained and adored the idea of the domestic family. Second, at Oneida this retentive kind of intercourse was only permitted to the regenerate; it was a privilege. Propagation was an even more restricted privilege since the community believed in selective and controlled breeding. For Wright, however, to desire this kind of intercourse with one's mate was itself a sign of perfection; such couples would naturally produce loving and more perfect children. Wright needed no community. For him the family was a kind of monastery for the priesthood of nonresistance who had "come out" of Babylon.

Although Wright is obviously an extreme case, he is important because no one, except possibly Ballou, was more closely identified with nonresistance. The *Liberator,* furthermore, decried the

---

[92] Wright, *Marriage and Parentage,* p. 84. Emphasis added.

[93] Quoted in a long excerpt from the First Annual Report of the Oneida Association in Ballou, *Practical Christian Socialism,* p. 581. Certainly Wright shared Noyes's notion that both the symbolic and the practical significance of original sin rested in the sex act, and so the escape from sin must result in a new sexual procedure.

view that sexual reform was too indelicate to be discussed; on occasion, it seemed to view the struggle against masturbation and licentiousness as equal in importance with antislavery. In fact, abolitionists who favored an extended definition of slavery and hoped for general emancipation from bondage could be charged with hypocrisy if they failed to labor for sexual reform. A correspondent once found the *Liberator* remiss in defending victims of seduction in Northern cities:

I ask Wm. Lloyd Garrison, and all his fellow-laborers, if sin is not a transgression of the law of God? And if he who committeth sin is not the slave of sin, or Satan; thence an object of pity? Or if we incorporate sin with man, and call him the slaveholder who violates God's law, by infringing upon any of his neighbor's rights—who is most guilty, he who, having me in his power, dishonors my body, or he who beguiles my understanding and conscience, and makes me a participator in his guilt? Let me ask, if the violation of the marriage compact is not the putrid fountain, whence flow all the bitter streams of slavery and wrong? And have ye laid the axe to the root of this tree of death? This sin lies at your door. . . . Ye who preach, that the church organizations are worse than any house of ill-fame in the State of Massachusetts, because they help keep the slaves in bondage, do ye not help lock the prisoners in those houses, and carry the key in your pockets?[94]

Extended definitions of slavery might allow quite divergent applications of antislavery to the issues of sex and marriage. In this case, the correspondent was concerned for the sanctity of marriage. Even Wright, who declared that many children born in wedlock were illegitimate, showed little public interest in the potential legitimacy of love children born outside. But once sexual reform and antislavery were equated, it was not a far step for a woman to announce, as happened at the Rutland Convention in June 1858, "I go a step further back, and say it is the marriage institution that keeps woman degraded in mental and moral slavery."[95]

[94] *Liberator*, Jan. 16, 1846, p. 3; March 29, 1844, p. 4.
[95] *Proceedings of the Free Convention Held in Rutland, Vt., June 25th, 26th, 27th, 1858* (Boston and New York, 1858), pp. 52–55.

Reformers had long enjoyed conventions on particular topics, but Rutland was different. It was a "free" convention. All "friends of Free Thought"—that is, all reformers—were called to come and enjoy the freedom to speak on any theme of reform. It was a "free meeting" in the come-outer style, uncoerced but orderly. "That there would be entire harmony of *doctrine* and *symbol* among us is not to be expected, but it is believed that in *purpose,* we should 'see eye to eye,' and it is *purposes,* not *creeds,* that vitalize and harmonize effort." William Goodell came to talk about the Constitution of the United States. Shakers, spiritualists, and communitarians spoke.[96] But the theme of the convention turned out to be free love.

Wright was a key speaker. First he celebrated his own religious isolation: "God, as apprehended in my soul, is the Alpha and Omega, the Great I AM, to me." What the motto, "ALONE WITH GOD," meant was that no external authority could make man feel responsibility. There was accordingly no security and peace in the power of husbands, parents, priests, soldiers, or slaveholders. The effect of absolute power, about which Wright was curiously ambivalent, was that individual convictions would promote rebellions against it. This being unthinkable, the only alternatives were power so oppressive that every impulse of the soul was deadened or no authority whatsoever. Wright turned to the image of a family sustained by the attraction of love. If the government's sole function with regard to marriage were to keep a record, "as it does of births and deaths," there would be no undesired maternity.[97]

Mrs. Julia Branch, another speaker, accused Wright of not going far enough. She decried the cruelty of the ideal of "exclusive conjugal love," whether regulated by government or not. Woman must assert *"her right to bear children when she will and by whom she will."* Otherwise she would remain enslaved, a thing to be purchased on the market. Lucy Stone, according to Mrs. Branch, had told her that the "marriage question" must some day

[96] *Ibid.,* pp. 5–9.
[97] *Ibid.,* pp. 14–23, 71–72.

be discussed, but not until the ballot had been won. This kind of
gradualism was intolerable, however, because the marriage question was, quite simply, a question of slavery. Henry Clapp, the
old no-organizationist, proclaimed her speech the "most touching"
scene he had observed in twenty years, for Mrs. Branch was
braving certain scorn. He summarized her effort as "to insist that
marriage, as now understood, is slavery,—to assert that any institution is false in its nature that employs the element of coercion."
Stephen S. Foster was thoroughly happy with his marriage to
Abby Kelley, but he said he understood that "every family is a
little embryo plantation, and every woman is a slave breeder,—
in the eye of her husband is a slave, and the breeder of slaves,—
and hence comes all the trouble." Thus he sympathized with
Mrs. Branch's remarks and promised to keep his mind open if
other ways of securing the rights of women failed.[98]

Abolitionists who were not present could not bring themselves
to repudiate this connection between antislavery and free love.
In her "just abhorrence of certain features of legalized marriage,"
wrote William Lloyd Garrison, Mrs. Branch might have gone too
far, but with no intentional impurity. Thomas Wentworth Higginson took a broader view, though admitting there had been some
folly. "When I think of the immense value, to myself and many
others, of those strange, miscellaneous, chaotic desultory conventions for all manner of Reforms, held in Marlboro' Chapel and
elsewhere, fifteen or twenty years ag[o],—when 'the soul of the
soldiery of dissent' (in Emerson's phrase) met together,—I welcome their lineal successor, the Rutland Convention, also."[99]

[98] *Ibid.*, pp. 52–57. For Foster's difficulties in reconciling his love of a
woman with his service to God, see Robert E. Riegel, "Abby Kelley,"
New-England Galaxy, VI (1965), 21–26. Riegel makes an interesting comparison to Theodore Weld's confusion in his courtship and marriage.

[99] *Liberator*, Aug. 13, 1858, p. 2; Sept. 3, 1858, p. 3.

VIII

Accommodation to Violence

In 1852 a medium forwarded to William Lloyd Garrison a message from Nathaniel P. Rogers, who in the spiritual state was reflecting on the entire course of antislavery. It now seemed erroneous to have demanded immediate abolition: "While I still loathe the hideous form of slavery, it appears now that that gradual emancipation which must come through the operation of the love principle upon the hearts of all, is far better than to *force* the master—even by words—to relax his grasp upon the heart of his victim, by clutching his own throat; for while, in this case, I could rejoice in the escape of the slave, I should be compelled to weep for the transfer of the same condition to the master, who thence becomes a *slave* to the power which *compels* him to release his slave."[1] Nonresistance required the conversion of slaveholders. However radical its assertions that war and governmental coercion were as evil as slavery, nonresistance obviously meant for the time being a slow pace in the specific attack on the South's peculiar institution. But this implication was conspicuously overlooked. It would have taken more than a medium to let it be heard again.

The preceding chapters have located a variety of manifestations of anarchism in the American antislavery movement: the New England Non-Resistance Society, come-outers, no-organizationists, the Hopedale Community, political secessionists, libertar-

[1] *Liberator*, Dec. 17, 1852, p. 4.

ian deists, individualist anarchists, and followers of spiritual affinities. Much as they differed in theory and practice, sometimes greatly qualifying their anarchism, they all were convinced that force violates the scheme of law that God had laid out for the world. But the nonresistants probably gave this conviction its sharpest statement. This chapter concentrates once more on the nonresistants. We shall seek to understand how they veered away—before the Civil War—from nonviolence and anarchism. Their troubles derived in large measure from their attempt to deny that "immediatism" with regard to individual commitments to a revolutionary principle, such as the abolition of force, might imply gradualism with regard to a particular social reform, such as the abolition of chattel slavery.

Some historians have seen a connection between this veering away from pure nonviolence and anarchism and the excitements of fugitive slave incidents, chaos in Kansas, and the raid on Harper's Ferry.[2] Of course some such connection existed. But we should not assume that abolitionists were abruptly dissuaded from cherished convictions by some clamorous event, nor that they finally found nonresistance inadequate. Instead, they found their doctrine ambiguous enough to condone and even demand violence—usually by other men than themselves. This process was

[2] Merle Curti ("Non-Resistance in New England," pp. 54–55) isolated these causes of the decline of nonresistance in the 1850s: (1) the "extreme character of the cause"; (2) the absorption of its adherents in abolitionism; (3) John Brown's raid and the Civil War, which induced them to alter their principles. A somewhat more subtle analysis by John Demos ("The Antislavery Movement and the Problem of Violent 'Means.'" *New England Quarterly*, XXXVII [1964], 525) suggests these reasons for the "total collapse" of "non-violent abolitionism": (1) the rise of prominent new leaders, such as Henry Ward Beecher, Higginson, Parker, and Joshua Giddings, who advocated force; (2) the impotence of nonviolence when the Fugitive Slave Law brought the evils of slavery home to the North; (3) the inescapable fact of violent conflict in Kansas; (4) the numerical growth of the antislavery movement, now filled with the very men who had once violently opposed it. One might question this last assumption about the growth of antislavery commitment before the war. And it is by no means clear that nonviolence would have been a less effectual response to specific offenses, such as fugitive slave cases, than violence.

discernible almost from the start of nonresistance. Nonresistants did not learn from the provocations of the 1850s that force is more efficient than love or that the state is more reliable than the heart. They were confounded as soon as they were provoked into specifying the immediate implications of their beliefs.

ii

The confusion of the nonresistants was most apparent in their statements about the Negro slave. Out of their confusion on this subject came the first signs of accommodation to the use of force.

It should by now be clear that the attack on slavery by abolitionists, Garrisonian or otherwise, was frequently metaphorical. Abolitionists often identified themselves with the slaves in a mood not so much of compassion as of self-seeking liberation. Furthermore, there was a tendency to impute idealized virtues to the entire race of Negroes as a means of criticizing white civilization. Although abolitionists generally held advanced views on the question of racial equality, they sometimes attributed submissive "feminine" qualities to Negroes. Thus, for example, James Russell Lowell in an argument against racial prejudice presented stereotypes of his own:

We have never had any doubt that the African race was intended to introduce a new element of civilization, and that the Caucasian would be benefited greatly by an infusion of its gentler and less selfish qualities. The Caucasian mind, which seeks always to govern, at whatever cost, can never come to so beautiful or Christian a height of civilization, as with a mixture of those seemingly humbler, but truly more noble, qualities which teach it to obey.[3]

Given these stereotypes concerning government and obedience, it is hardly a surprise that nonresistants could never quite decide on the proper role of the slave in the struggle against slavery.

Garrison himself admired the character of Uncle Tom in

[3] Lowell, *Anti-Slavery Papers*, I, 22; James M. McPherson, "A Brief for Equality: The Abolitionist Reply to the Racist Myth, 1860–1865," in Duberman, ed., *Antislavery Vanguard*, esp. pp. 166, 168; and Frederickson, *Black Image*, pp. 102–117, 163–164.

Harriet Beecher Stowe's novel because of his willingness "to be 'led as a lamb to the slaughter,' returning blessing for cursing, and anxious only for the salvation of his enemies." Here was a glorious example of the "nature, tendency, and results of CHRISTIAN NON-RESISTANCE." But Garrison was wary of the imputations of others: he asked whether Mrs. Stowe considered nonresistance obligatory for whites.[4] Henry C. Wright admitted that he was also moved by much of *Uncle Tom's Cabin*, but he objected to the assumptions that Christianity made a master kind or a slave dutiful. Instead, it should lead a master to release his slaves and a slave to seek his freedom by every right means.[5] These were the questions that plagued nonresistance: Could the doctrine survive in a society which required it solely of the exploited class? Was the Negro who epitomized the doctrine bereft of means to liberate himself?

No abolitionist could be insensitive to the double standard by which white Americans condemned nonresistance in the North as the foulest anarchy and yet expected slaves in the South to bear their sufferings with Christian love. As a result, nonresistants could not restrict their thinking about the Negro to projections of patient dignity. They were compelled to apply to the slave the same standards that were applicable to whites.

As early as April 1841, Henry C. Wright attacked the hypocrisy of Americans who upheld the motto, *"resistance to tyrants is obedience to God";* apparently the motto was meant for whites only.[6] By 1842 Wright was raising the abstract issue of slave revolts to fill out his critique of voting and constitutional government. He argued that slaves who revolted under Nat Turner eleven years earlier were simply imitating Washington and "the revolutionary heroes." How could they be denied the right to take up arms "to free themselves from a bondage, 'one hour of which,' as Jefferson says, 'is fraught with more misery than ages of that which our fathers arose in rebellion to oppose?'" And yet

---

[4] Garrisons, *Garrison*, III, 360–361.
[5] *Liberator*, July 9, 1859, p. 3.
[6] *Herald of Freedom*, Apr. 30, 1841, p. 1.

the government sent troops against them, as the law required. "Who murdered Nat Turner? The voters acted as principals in the bloody tragedy."[7] In condemning the hypocrisy of the politics of union, nonresistants approached a call for patriotic insurrections.

The abstract issue of slave revolts riddled nonresistance in the 1850s. A Nantucket Quaker disavowed the "heathenish" doctrine that ends can justify means, but still insisted that, "as this is the general teaching," slave rebels ought to receive public acclaim as champions of liberty. Observing that the failure of slaves to fight for liberty contributed to racial prejudice, he quoted Frederick Douglass with approval: "My people can never be elevated till they elevate themselves, by fighting for their freedom, and by the sword obtaining it." The audience horrified by this declaration by a black man was simply hypocritical.[8] In this vein nonresistance accepted a narrow list of alternatives: either the slave must meekly await his master's change of heart or he must carry weapons as his master did. An obscure Ohioan defined nonresistance as "Christianity without adulteration" and gave another alternative which might have been expected from his New England counterparts:

A slave is not bound to surrender himself voluntarily to any man, neither is he bound to work without wages; and the truth does not require that he hide himself from his pursuer, but walk boldly forth as a man, preaching the gospel, and earning his living by the sweat of his brow. . . . A few such examples of true piety and moral heroism among the slaves would disarm the slaveholder more completely than all the revolvers Colt ever made.

This procedure might yield a few martyrs, but it was consonant with the "law of nature, that like produces like; and [that] the use of moral power alone can increase the growth of morals."[9] For the most part, this alternative was neglected by nonresistants and slaves alike.

---

[7] *Liberator*, March 25, 1842, p. 4.
[8] Nathaniel Barney, quoted in *ibid.*, Apr. 10, 1857, p. 1.
[9] Micajah T. Johnson, in *Liberator*, July 23, 1852, p. 3.

To be sure, Henry C. Wright repeated the theme that slavery could no more be ended by bloodshed than lying by lying or drunkenness by drunkenness. He claimed that if every slave would at once announce his freedom, slavery would end without much violence. But slaves had not been cultivated with moral power and they had been shown no higher law than that of violence; therefore, they were guiltless in attacks against their tyrants. A good end may be sought by bad means so long as the individual believes the means are right.[10] On the other hand, nonresistance taught that violent means ensured violent consequences. Even as he absolved the slaves of guilt, Wright envisioned the future more starkly than even Rogers in the spiritual state had done:

A baptism of blood awaits the slaveholder and his abbettors. So be it. The retribution is just. Must the slaveholders become the slaves of those whom they have enslaved? History answers "Yes." If slavery goes down in blood, the conquered will be the bondmen and bond women of the conquerors; for the practical teaching of Church and State is, that might makes the right to enslave. Bid American slaveholders beware! Their turn may come, will come, *must* come, to be bought and sold as brutes, and to have their wives and daughters consigned to the negro's harem, unless they willingly and penitently let their slaves go free.[11]

There was a suppressed expectation among abolitionists, who were concerned with their own liberation from sin, that the freedom of the slave ultimately had to be the work of the slave. Thomas Wentworth Higginson, who was not a nonresistant, stated frankly in a private letter: "The great obstacle to antislavery action has always been the apparent feebleness & timidity of the slaves themselves." Had there been more frequent insurrections, he thought, slavery would already have been abolished.[12] Nonresistants held similar sentiments. One of them repeated Lord Byron's often-quoted line, "Who would be free, *themselves* must

[10] *Liberator,* Jan. 30, 1857, p. 4.
[11] *Ibid.,* July 17, 1857, p. 4.
[12] Higginson to Spooner, Nov. 30, 1858, Spooner Papers, BPL.

strike the blow." The antislavery movement could help in removing "the outward forms of bondage," but it was up to the Negroes to raise themselves in the scale of civilization. "The abolitionist can be of little help to them in the struggle for the *highest* emancipation." But this was not pictured as a gradual process; such was the "omnipotent might of non-resistance" that a slave could free himself immediately and just stop behaving like a slave. Even if it required courage to face death, this kind of self-assertion would be the real *"negation* of slavery."[13] Why were the blacks not capable of it? To celebrate individual self-help was completely appropriate to nonresistance's suspicion of outside authority, but it could easily turn toward violence. Adin Ballou was shocked when he read in the *National Anti-Slavery Standard* that blacks must end their captivity by insurrection. But the argument for violence might have been based on his own statement: "To put an end to slavery by emancipation or abolition will not materially elevate the character of the race."[14] Freedom had to be won by struggle. Surely this view of character explains the importance of fugitive slaves in the abolitionist imagination.

It proved impossible for nonresistants, in spite of their passion for self-liberation, to demand nothing of whites in the abolition of slavery. White men, of course, must desist from sinning. As Henry C. Wright journeyed throughout the North in the early 1850s, he thought he saw signs of armed resistance everywhere. In Ohio the Western Anti-Slavery Society was discussing a resolution calling for "DEATH TO KIDNAPPERS." As a nonresistant, he believed that to take another's life was "the greatest crime that man can commit." But "if it ever was right for any men to kill those who seek to enslave them or their wives and children," now was the time to "inflict instant death" on those who chased runaways. His argument grew less conditional: "Every man, who believes resistance to tyrants to be obedience to God, is bound by his *own principles* (not by mine) to arm himself with a pistol or a dirk, a bowie-knife, a rifle, or any deadly weapon, and inflict

---

[13] *Liberty Chimes* (Providence, 1845), pp. 78–80.
[14] *Practical Christian*, March 21, 1857, p. 2.

death with his own hand, on each and every man who shall
attempt to execute the recent law of Congress, or any other law,
made with a view to re-capture and return to bondage fugitive
slaves." In this way, reaction to double standards led not only to
toleration of Negro violence, but also to insistence that murder
could receive adequate sanction from the heart of an individual.
The Fugitive Slave Law, Wright concluded, was actually a blessing. It was a divine test of the capacity of Americans to be true
to their own lights.[15]

It would be misleading to suggest that Wright experienced no
strain in emphasizing the obligation to be true to a violent disposition. On the contrary, as he moved from one scene of potential violence to another, he constantly adjusted his schemes of
evaluation. First, he could see that the "Author of Nature" was
revealing himself in "a new dispensation, that is to look after
man, and only *man,* to regenerate and redeem him."[16] A second
time, he avoided the cosmic approach and, in good Jacksonian
fashion, stressed the futility of political theory when compared to
"the spirit that pervades the people." No new dispensation was
necessary because the people already believed that killing tyrants
was obeying God.[17] Third, he could resort to a calculation of
exceptional necessity. *"Were the means used right?"* he asked
after hearing that doors had been battered down to rescue one
fugitive. One might use violence to save a swimmer from a shark
or an innocent girl from a brutal rapist. No general principle was
at stake.[18]

But there is no denying that nonresistance was proving ambiguous during a time of violence that should have sharpened its
meaning. In 1840 Wright could never have exulted, as he did in
1851, "we are in the midst of a moral revolution—we are on the
eve of a *bloody* revolution." Yet he was confident that all was

[15] *Liberator,* Oct. 4, 1850, p. 3.
[16] *Ibid.,* Oct. 11, 1850, p. 3.
[17] *Ibid.,* Oct. 25, 1850, p. 4.
[18] *Ibid.,* March 28, 1851, p. 3.

for the best.[19] After one of Wright's speeches to the Massachusetts Anti-Slavery Society, Parker Pillsbury said:

One subject has been prominently before this meeting—the subject of violent resistance to the slave power. I have never sympathized fully with the non-resistant idea—I have often feared it might be true; but now, when non-resistants begin to teach, that "resistance to tyrants is obedience to God," perhaps I am a convert, for I certainly believe that.[20]

This accommodation to violent means took place on a highly abstract level. No wave of slave revolts forced revaluations of violence. It is true that black abolitionists were paying greater attention to the possibility of violence in the 1850s.[21] And there were episodes of white resistance to the Fugitive Slave Law, but fewer than the nonresistants hoped. Thousands of Northerners were unfaithful to their convictions that tyranny deserved resistance; that is, they did not share the nonresistants' interpretation of that conviction. Rather than being dragged along by history, nonresistants were in advance of the violence of their times. To account for their accommodation to the use of force, we must inspect the intellectual loopholes in their doctrine.

iii

At the outset of the New England Non-Resistance Society it was impossible to decide whether the authority of the doctrine followed from the command of God or the lessons of human experience. Abolitionists were often attracted to the belief that the relationship between God and man was antinomian—that no intermediary guides or institutions were authoritative. It is evident that men like John Murray Spear and Henry C. Wright could be led into absurdities by this belief, so long as there was ambi-

[19] *Ibid.*, Nov. 29, 1851, p. 4.
[20] *Practical Christian*, Feb. 7, 1857, p. 3.
[21] Howard Holman Bell, "A Survey of the Negro Convention Movement, 1830–1861," unpublished Ph.D. dissertation, Northwestern University, Evanston, Ill., 1953, pp. 111 ff.

guity about the sources of trustworthy authority at either extreme.
Peculiar views of spiritualism or marriage might be tolerated in a
movement whose chief concern was the abolition of slavery. But
the same cloudy antinomian scheme was basic to the process in
which nonresistants came to sanction violence.

The most dramatic conversion, and one which is fully recorded,
was that of Charles B. Stearns. In the mid-1850s he was Kansas
correspondent for the *National Anti-Slavery Standard* and
Liberator. He had few illusions; those who opposed slavery in
Kansas were so prejudiced against Negroes that they would surely
institute their own black code. The emigrant aid movement, in
his opinion, was madness, for it provoked Missourians to try to
take over the territory. It seemed to be founded on a theory that
events in Kansas could lead to civil war and civil war to the
abolition of slavery. He had been robbed and beaten, and his
claim had been jumped, but he was a steadfast nonresistant.
Short of the importation of nonviolent immigrants, the only
course that would benefit the friends of freedom was to imitate
Christ.[22]

In December 1855 he was converted to violence. "When I came
to Kansas," he wrote, "little did I dream of ever becoming a
soldier, but stern fate has driven me into the ranks of the Non-
Resistant *corps de reserve*, who are to fight at the last extremity."
He had refrained from arming himself during ten days of war,
but then had changed his mind "in consequence of becoming
convinced that we had not human beings to contend with."

I always believed it was right to kill a tiger, and our invaders are
nothing but tigers. Christ says, "If a *man* smites thee on the one cheek,
turn to him the other also." These Missourians are not men. I have
always considered that, bad as they were, they had an infinitessimal
[*sic*] spark of divinity in them; but after hearing the screams of the
wife and mother of the murdered Barber, and witnessing his lifeless
form locked in the cold embrace of death, for no other crime than
because he was a Free State man, I made up my mind that our in-

[22] Garrisons, *Garrison*, III, 418–419; *Liberator*, Feb. 1, 1855, p. 3; July
27, 1855, p. 4; Aug. 17, 1855, p. 2.

vaders were wild beasts, and it was my duty to aid in killing them off. When I live with men made in God's image, I will never shoot them; but these pro-slavery Missourians are demons from the bottomless pit and may be shot with impunity.

Yet Stearns admitted that all these monsters had demanded was "the surrender of Sharp's rifles, which they knew, of course, we could not comply with." The shock of death and battle made this fact seem irrelevant, although it might have confirmed his previous dismay at the tactics of the emigrant aid movement.[23]

In Stearns's case, immediate participation in calamity was plainly the occasion for his conversion from nonresistance. Garrison simply noted that "our impulsive friend Stearns has got thoroughly frightened out of his peace principles, as Peter denied his Lord to save himself from impending danger." There was no need for censure: perhaps like Peter he would be inspired to good works by regret of his apostasy. Stearns, having endured a great deal of violence, replied that he was motivated not by cowardice but by reason. Although he reiterated that peace principles were invalid during a siege of "*drunken* ourang-outans," he now found an argument consistent with the Scriptural expositions of nonresistance. Where there was no "law of the land," he wrote, the injunctions of Jesus were irrelevant.[24] Ballou, who might have been pressed to agree that Christianity was more viable under Caesar than in a state of chaos, criticized Stearns for having gone to Kansas in the first place. For a nonresistant, that was as senseless as for an abolitionist to go to New Orleans.[25] (The analogy was suggestive of the inability of nonresistant abolitionism to apply itself directly to the cause of the slave.)

Ballou also observed that Stearns's self-justification involved a strange assumption concerning human judgment. If one could pronounce his neighbor subhuman, then he could kill him and remain a nonresistant. This resembled some justifications of slavery. In addition, previously in his life, Stearns had always

[23] *Practical Christian*, Jan. 26, 1856, p. 4.
[24] *Liberator*, Jan. 4, 1856, p. 2; Feb. 15, 1856, p. 3.
[25] *Practical Christian*, Jan. 26, 1856, p. 2.

vacillated between the unrestricted sovereignty of God and the unrestrained right of private judgment. His opinions on the proper leeway for private judgment had fluctuated erratically, as was so often the case with those who placed themselves under the government of God. But he was always an earnest participant in abolitionist controversies over the problem of authority.

As a student at Oberlin, he had written Garrison that "the truth of the principles of non-resistance has come to my mind with a clearness and force that it never did before." He trusted his own consciousness for direction, since there were few other nonresistants nearby. But he was heartened by "[ac]quaintance with the greatest of all non-resistants, the Lord Jesus Christ; and he understands all about the subject—so that whenever an opposer brings an objection that I cannot see through precisely, I have nothing to do but to go to Jesus, and he makes all plain and clear." He had already been committed to a Connecticut jail for refusal to pay a fine in lieu of militia duty, thus providing one of the few instances of actual civil disobedience in the course of the New England Non-Resistance Society.[26]

In 1844, Stearns was convinced that "this earth's reform is a gone case" because "the doom of America is almost fixed." But Garrison saw steady improvement and chided the "Second Advent notions of our worthy friend." A year later Stearns thought non-resistance should be promoted energetically because he had confidence in "a mighty shower of divine grace to descend in overwhelming torrents." So impressed was he with heavenly commands that he attacked as unchristian one of Ballou's favorite distinctions between harmful force and noninjurious restraint. Human judgment of what constitutes injury was not reliable.[27] As editor of the *Christian Reformer*, Stearns continued to squabble with Hopedale, not only over its justification of nonmalicious types of force, but also over its remuneration of intellectual labor

[26] *Liberator*, Feb. 14, 1840, p. 4; Sept. 17, 1841, p. 3; Sept. 24, 1841, p. 1.
[27] *Ibid.*, Nov. 29, 1844, p. 4; Oct. 10, 1845, p. 4; Oct. 31, 1845, p. 4.

and its faith in intermediaries between man and Christ. Stearns was well on his way to come-outerism. He was delighted with the idea of a convention on the Bible, but he wanted it "spontaneous" and free from the formality of scheduled speakers.[28]

He criticized John Murray Spear and other spiritualists who bridged the antinomies of the human and divine and found a kind of authority of which Stearns now despaired. They repeated "the worst errors of the church." It was especially distressing that the editor of the *Liberator*—which had fought nobly against these errors and "placed on the highest pinnacle of its new spiritual temple, the flag-staff from which floats the banner of 'No Union with Slaveholders' of the mind, as well as of the body"—should give credence to spirit manifestations as otherworldly authorities. Spiritualism contradicted "the fundamental doctrine of 'radical-ism'" inasmuch as it paid attention to statements "*because* of their *supposed* origin." According to Stearns: "All authority, save that of God, is to be hurled from the throne of our mental natures." Because spiritualism claimed that its voices deserved more respect than those on earth, he rejected it "as savoring of slavery."[29] Clearly, this "radical" line of reasoning might also reach the authority of the Bible—in fact, of anyone else's interpre-tation of God's will.

Stearns aroused a storm of protest in 1845 when he wrote to the *Liberator* that not even the God of the Old Testament had any right to take human life vindictively.[30] And in *True Religion and False Religion Compared* (1849), he showed how completely the right of private judgment could overturn the authority of the Bible. There was little more to be said for the Bible than for the visions of Andrew Jackson Davis, the clairvoyant: neither appealed to reason or common sense; neither offered proof of their claims; both pretended to be authoritative because of being

[28] *Ibid.*, Jan. 19, 1849, p. 4; *Practical Christian*, Jan. 8, 1848, p. 3; Feb. 19, 1848, p. 3; Aug. 18, 1849, p. 3.

[29] *Liberator*, Apr. 8, 1853, p. 4.

[30] *Ibid.*, Jan. 2, 1846, p. 4; Apr. 3, 1846, p. 2; Kraditor, *Means and Ends*, pp. 93–95.

touched by the supernatural. But the greatest objection to the Bible was "the barrier that it interposes between our souls and God." Similarly, Stearns had no use for churches and ministers. "We need no mediators between us and God," he wrote; "it is perfectly absurd to suppose that a Moses can bear that glory [of God] better than we can; or that a priest can understand what we cannot."[31] In short, he had become a pure case of anti-nomian immediatism.

His political views were not always so purist. It is a familiar paradox that antinomians, who eschewed earthly intermediaries, were greatly concerned for the rule of law and righteousness. Stearns believed that "the people of this country are not ready for a truly Christian government," and as a nonresistant he could participate in nothing less. But he would have been glad to witness "the faintest resemblance to such an one"; he would have welcomed disunion. "I would like to see all men perfect Christians, but as I do not expect to witness this sight very soon, I am gratified at their becoming anti-slavery, or even temperance men."[32] (Once again nonresistance was separated from abolitionism.) In any case, from the immediatist point of view, slavery was the paradigm of rebellion against the divine government. It violated the principle of moral accountability. Consequently Stearns attacked the Fugitive Slave Law in these terms: "To return a person into slavery . . . is to place him out of the pale of God's kingdom, to reconsign him to heathenism, and is diabolical, or contrary to God's authority."[33] Soon he would interpret the

[31] Stearns, *True Religion and False Religion Compared; or, Christanity in Opposition to the Religion of the Church* (Boston, 1849), esp. pp. 10–26, 62–63.

[32] Stearns, "Cure for the End of Slavery," in *Narrative of Henry Box Brown, Who Escaped from Slavery, Enclosed in a Box Three Feet Long, Two Wide, and Two and a Half High. Written from a Statement of Facts Made by Himself* (Boston, 1849), pp. 66–67.

[33] Stearns, *The "Fugitive Slave Law" of the United States, Shown to be Unconstitutional, Impolitic, Inhuman, and Diabolical* (Boston, 1851), p. 23. For Stearns's discussion of his own Whig upbringing, see his *Facts in the Life of Gen. Taylor; the Cuba Blood-Hound Importer, the Extensive Slave-Holder, and the Hero of the Mexican War!!* (Boston, 1848), pp. 4–5.

Missourians to be demons. When this was the issue, could one hold out for "a truly Christian government"?

In view of his recantation in Kansas, Stearns's reactions to the Fugitive Slave Law are slightly ironic. "Law is not binding on man, only when it is right," he declared. "This doctrine is as old as piety and martyrdom are. It was the exemplification of it, which besprinkled the earth with the blood of the early Christians." He was evidently ready to face martyrdom; commitment to God's law had given Christians strength when confronting fires and lions—and presumably it might encourage them again when confronting tigers and drunken ourang-outans. God's law was the final authority. "The moment a man yields this point, and obeys the laws of man in preference to the law of God, that moment he is a fallen being, and a rebel against Jehovah."[34] But the declaration that law was not binding on man could, of course, have ambiguous meanings. It could come to mean that it was up to private judgments to settle on the methods to be used to achieve the divine rule of peace and emancipation. It could mean that it was appropriate to kill the wild beasts rather than accept martyrdom. This might be especially true where, as in Kansas, there was no law, no system of established intermediaries, to require submission. Slavery was not government, but heathenism. There was no question of obedience to temporal authority; there was only a contest between moral agents in the sight of God. Stearns would later refer to the Kansas conflict as the deliverance of "that 'Garden of Eden' from Slavery's blackened touch."[35]

When we understand the theological outlook with which Stearns went to Kansas, his renunciation of nonresistance appears more complicated than an automatic response to a frightening stimulus. Despite his passion to ascribe absolute authority to God, or perhaps because of this passion, he had failed to locate earthly sources of authority that did not bear the taint of slavery.

[34] Stearns, *The "Fugitive Slave Law,"* pp. 25–26.
[35] Stearns, *The Black Man of the South, and the Rebels; or, The Characteristics of the Former, and the Recent Outrages of the Latter* (New York, 1872), p. 20.

Therefore, truth remained an exercise of private judgment, and, in Kansas, Missourians were judged to be inhuman exceptions to the gospel. Stearns's career illustrates the importance of intellectual loopholes in the demise of nonresistance even in a case where a stimulus-response interpretation might appear quite adequate. It should be stressed that his career typifies the problems of more famous nonresistants who were never exposed to the strains of border warfare.

The right of private judgment was a key phrase of antebellum reform. It was presumed that all Protestants received belief in this right as part of their inheritance from the Reformation. It underlay the enormous importance abolitionists attributed to free speech. Judgments had to be expressed in speech and action; it was hypocrisy for a Protestant nation to hinder that expression. Thomas Low Nichols, after rebounding from free love to Roman Catholicism, warned Englishmen of the prevalence of antimarriage theories in the United States. By defining marriage as an "affair of religion," outside the control of the state, Protestant Americans applied the right of private judgment to the affections. In addition, Nichols doubted that Protestant organizations could equal the successful charitable work of Catholic sisterhoods, for "the exercise of the right of private judgment . . . destroys authority and obedience, the elements of order."[36] Beyond question, this right could reach much further than mere defense of freedom of speech. At the end of the eighteenth century, for example, William Godwin had constructed a clearly anarchistic philosophy upon this very foundation. Unlike physical coercion (which Godwin called "external slavery") or systems of reward and punishment, private judgment made sense of the concept of personal righteousness. From this starting point any form of coercion could be criticized.[37]

The right of private judgment went beyond defense of civil liberties; it suggested a responsibility to live up to private understandings of virtue. It was a corollary of moral accountability and

[36] Nichols, *Forty Years*, II, 44–45, 118.
[37] Krimerman and Perry, eds., *Patterns of Anarchy*, pp. 186–188.

the government of God; as such, it led to the frequent exhortations to "practical Christianity" in the early movement for nonresistance. This usage had been well illustrated by Maria W. Chapman, reporting a meeting of the New England Non-Resistance Society in 1839:

Passive non-resistance is one thing; active non-resistance another. We mean to *apply* our principles. We mean to be bold for God. Action!— Action!—thus shall we overcome the violent. Not by their own weapons . . . but it behooves *us* to preach. We need no body of men to tell us when, and where, and how we may speak, but each one is bound to speak as his own reason and conscience dictate.[38]

There was little disagreement among nonresistants in formulating this basic doctrine. According to Adin Ballou, man "instinctively" reverences "some kind of deity, power, or authority, which to him is supreme, absolute, and irresistible, and which he must submit to and obey or suffer loss." Nor was it only proof of God's existence that lay in human consciousness. Man, as a "responsible moral agent," was impressed with "an essential difference" between right and wrong which he had the "inherent ability" to follow. Class, education, and other advantages were unimportant: man must follow his awareness of virtue "under the divine law of personal responsibility."[39] The cause of nonresistance could be won with the elimination of all forms of authority that were not private.

The doctrine was tinged with enough skepticism about human ability to ascertain truth to allow great latitude of expression. In discussing a convention on the holiness of the Sabbath, Henry C. Wright called for "the *utmost* toleration of opinion. Let no one be moved to indignation if sentiments are avowed *heaven-wide* different from his own." And Garrison, despite his excoriations of government, could encourage the woman's suffrage movement: "It is not for me or any man dogmatically to judge as to what is or what is not a sinful act, or to say to others you shall not

[38] *Non-Resistant,* June 15, 1839, p. 2.
[39] Ballou, *Autobiography,* p. 339.

exercise the right to think for yourselves."[40] But a strong sense of sin limited the range of skeptical toleration, for God, as an absolute sovereign permitting no intermediaries or imitators, demanded strict accountability. Thus one form of expression which Garrisonians tolerated was Stephen S. Foster's disruptive censure of the supposedly proslavery churches. Perhaps these institutions forfeited the protection of the right of private judgment by becoming a corporation and smothering the right for others. In a sense, the right of private judgment was a form of voluntary social control extended only to those who were in league against coercive controls. Hopedale always felt uneasy about Foster's vituperation. But in refraining from judgment of him, they effectively approved his behavior: "Let all be true to the light within, and do cheerfully what the spirit of God dictates, though bonds and imprisonment be the issue."[41]

In struggling to rescue himself from sin, man was on his own. Some of Garrison's critics understood him to mean that Christians could do anything with impunity;[42] but even when advocating sexual reform, abolitionists shied away from this heresy of the free spirit. It was always sinful to be a sensualist or a slaveholder or a governor. The sinfulness of these capacities was precisely their identification with authority and their consequent infringement on the right of private judgment. Garrisonians were not in much danger of being led into licentiousness. They faced a different pitfall. In their fight to vindicate the virtues of voluntarism and independent understanding over the vices of coercion

[40] *Liberator*, Nov. 27, 1840, p. 2; Garrisons, *Garrison*, III, 310.

[41] George W. Stacy in *Practical Christian*, July 23, 1842, p. 3.

[42] Garrisons, *Garrison*, II, 181–182. The Garrisons attribute this charge to William Goodell, who was an astute critic of the loopholes in nonresistance. At the Free Convention, he asked Henry Wright to imagine a man arriving to enslave a child in the audience; "and suppose he should stand up and plant himself on the ground that he knew no rule but his own will, which God had revealed in him, and that he believed in the divinity of slavery." Would not the audience "assert their authority over the man?" The audience yelled that they would and thereby, in Goodell's view, recognized the principle of authority and closed off extreme interpretations of the right of private judgment. See *Proceedings of the Free Convention*, p. 23.

and corporate declarations, their own doctrine allowed wide toleration of *means*.

Nonresistance often resembled a crude prototype of pragmatism: on the supposition that there are indisputably virtuous goals, it asked only about the changing effectiveness of alternative procedures. After his dogmatic nonresistance was modified in Kansas, Charles B. Stearns accepted implications that other nonresistants tried to ignore. "It is hardly becoming in me, whom you consider an apostate from the ranks of Non-Resistance, to undertake to defend that doctrine," Stearns admitted. Nevertheless, he told Garrison that nonresistance was "impregnable" on the grounds of the New Testament; "but, as you say, these sayings are not authoritative, and you have heretofore taught the world the greatest moral lesson of the day, viz., 'that we should call no man master.'" It followed from this liberation that men ought to inquire, "What will be the effect upon the world of such and such doctrines?" Stearns's apostate clarity of mind reveals some weaknesses in Garrison's position. If God's authority were challenged, would men not have to reckon "the practical bearing" of any doctrine?

The question, then, is, "Will Non-Resistance apply to all men, and under all circumstances?" I agree with you, "that a great principle is not to be determined nor set aside as impracticable by a *single* pressing emergency, however perilous." But would not a great number of such emergencies, under whose influence Non-Resistance was seen to be impracticable, go far to show the absurdity of the doctrine in question? . . . It is plain that many of them would, for "godliness hath the promise of the life that now is, as well as that which is to come."

The beauty of the doctrine was that "in nine cases out of ten" it was more powerful than violence against an enemy, but it remained necessary to calculate which tactic would be more effective in particular assaults on "the strongholds of sin." Martyrdom was glorious Christian testimony, "but is it any more so when that martyr refuses to resist than when he dies nobly contending for his rights as long as his arm is able to raise a sword?"[43]

[43] *Liberator*, May 23, 1856, p. 2.

Other nonresistants, who had not been tried in the heat of Kansas, sought to check the relativity of private judgment by appeals to practicability. This was especially evident at a special meeting called to revive nonresistance in 1855. Garrison, explaining that the Bible could settle no dispute, argued that nonresistance was "true in the nature of things"; he cited Hopedale as evidence that it "works well." One of the wealthiest men at Hopedale supplied evidence that nonresistance aided him in bill collecting. As others played on the same theme, Garrison apparently got uneasy. He rose again to say that no one should be a nonresistant because "*it pays today.*" God promised that in general the principle would get results, but it was perfectly possible that a nonresistant might be defrauded. In short, Garrison retrieved just enough divine revelation to forestall the worst damage of an argument "by facts and results." This kept him true to nonresistance for a time, but at the price of a great deal of doctrinal confusion.

At this meeting, Stephen S. Foster took a bolder step. "He was a non-resistant from expediency, and advocated it because it is useful. . . . He did not believe in the inviolability of human life; and he could, therefore, sometimes, consistently call upon men to fight and kill their assailants—judging them by their own standards of duty, and not by his." Henry C. Wright, strangely enough, objected (no one was comfortable when others espoused his views). Foster, who never had liked tactical silence, made it plain that he was not "a *Christian* non-resistant, in the sense of recognizing Christian *authority*." He admired Christ as a kind of Isaac Newton of the moral world, but he believed that "every man should act according to his own convictions, whether he believed in using moral or physical forces." Thus his personal life was "an argument for non-resistance," and yet he was free to urge others to kill kidnappers. Ballou asked Foster to distinguish his views from those of a fighting man like Thomas Wentworth Higginson, who made no profession of nonresistance. "Mr. Foster attempted to do so, when Mr. Higginson humorously suggested that his friend Foster had about as much as he could do to define his own position; and he was quite sure he would not succeed in defining his." It was also hard to distinguish Foster's position from that of other nonresistants. Garrison, Ballou, Wright, and Foster's wife, Abby Kelley, disputed with him all the next day, with only Higginson's mirth to reduce tensions.[44]

In one respect these champions of nonresistance did not adopt Stearns's utilitarian test of truth. None of them would say that a large number of exceptions disproved the doctrine. The use of violence became a question of private judgment or of exceptional utility, but nonresistance remained a more excellent way in other judgments, other circumstances, other dispensations. Therefore we search in vain for many recantations in the 1850s or thereafter. On the other hand, it was a rare nonresistant who was not ready to pay homage to John Brown.

iv

When Parker Pillsbury published his recollections of abolitionism in 1884, he saw great significance in Foster's interruptions of the Sunday congregations. It seemed to him that no other tactic "like it or unlike it, before or afterward, so stirred the whole people, until John Brown with his twenty heroes, marched on Harper's Ferry and challenged the supporters of slavery to mortal combat." The connection sounds peculiar, especially since Pillsbury was praising Foster's nonresistant dignity. But perhaps it is not too farfetched: "One reason that Foster often gave for his extreme action, as well as utterance, was, that ends sometimes justified any means."[45] Few nonresistants went so far as Foster in calling for violence or even political action. For the most part, Garrisonians confined themselves to the assertion that an individual was obliged to apply means that to him seemed right.[46]

[44] *Practical Christian*, Apr. 7, 1855, p. 2; Apr. 21, 1855, p. 2.

[45] Pillsbury, *Acts*, pp. 145–146.

[46] For a good exposition of Foster's views on politics, see his speech at the August First celebration at Hopedale in *Practical Christian*, Sept. 6, 1856, p. 1. He argued that only a nonresistant could practice nonresistance, and meanwhile rising antislavery sentiment was being attracted not to proper abolitionism, but to Sumner and Free Soil. Politics was not "the

But by the time of John Brown's raid they were confronted with the possibility that a high motive could sanctify any course of action.

The issue with John Brown, as one abolitionist noted, was "faith in ideas." Did a man's principles lead him to action?[47] At this point the right of private judgment coincided with the higher law, a phrase with important variations in meaning. The phrase has been much favored by historians, but was not used frequently by nonresistant abolitionists. The higher law could refer simply to the obligations of Christian conscience which prevented compliance with an unjust civil statute (in which case it was a component of the divine government as understood by nonresistants). It could refer to the embodiment of universal, legal morality within the unwritten code of the land (as in Spooner's writings). It could also refer to a Christian standard of politics toward which saints were expected to drive their governments (whether this was a libertarian or authoritarian standard varied among political abolitionists). And in contemporary justification of John Brown it referred to a state of grace in which one man, by virtue of his faith in his ideas, became his own source of law, higher than any government.

Nonresistants may be compared with transcendentalists to clarify different implications of the higher law. With few exceptions, nonresistants believed that there was one grand source of law outside their sphere of understanding: God. Fear of affronting this authority dictated broad leeway of private judgment. It was

---

highest method of action," but it was the duty of abolitionism to provide a political organization that did not "come into existence only to strengthen the system." Garrison debated with Foster on the issue of slave revolts at a Rhode Island convention in 1850 (*Liberator*, Oct. 11, 1850, p. 4). Foster wished slaves would use "the sword of the Spirit," but in any case he urged them to arm themselves. If they knew "no means but the sword of steel," he could not tell them to return to slavery. Garrison simply replied "that he could not recommend to any one to fight; indeed he thought people needed no urging to fight." He, too, would "show to those their inconsistency and hypocrisy who would not use, for the protection of the fugitive slave, the same means they would adopt for their own."

[47] Bradburn, *Memorial*, pp. 197, 199.

clear that intermediate forms of coercion, government, and enslavement violated God's law; the range of options left for private judgment was clearly restricted by God's law. Transcendentalism, generally speaking, assumed correspondence between abstract verities and human impulses, and thus it trusted strictly individual, but nonetheless human, sources of law. Less attention was paid to God the lawmaker. A man had to obey his own nature. Lacking the security of fixed prohibitions, such as that violence and homicide are infractions of the divine law, the transcendentalist might be left in deeper difficulties than the nonresistant by the relativity of private judgment. He might feel unqualified admiration for John Brown as, in Emerson's words, "a pure idealist, with no by-ends of his own," as a man who "believed in his ideas to that extent that he existed to put them all into action; he said 'he did not believe in moral suasion, he believed in putting the thing through.' "[48]

Bronson Alcott, the only one of those ordinarily called transcendentalists who was also a Garrisonian nonresistant, provided one of the most striking examples of nonviolent action in the 1850s. When armed abolitionists were being repelled in their attempt to deliver a Negro fugitive from Boston's court house, Alcott stepped forward and asked quietly, "Why are not we within?" His dignity was unruffled by a response of gunfire, but no one followed him. Though his action did not free anyone, Alcott furnished one of the rare examples of "practical Christianity" or active nonresistance. It is meaningful to say that he excelled other nonresistants on their own terms. We might conclude that, when the law of intuition was made identical with the Christian injunction of nonresistance, the result was proof against even such temptations as the plight of an imprisoned runaway. Alcott did not need to devise categories to exhort other men to violence. But no one else combined nonresistance and transcendentalism. And even Alcott, when he met John Brown, wrote

[48] Emerson, "John Brown," in Atkinson, ed., *Writings of Emerson*, pp. 879–887. See also Gilman M. Ostrander, "Emerson, Thoreau, and John Brown," *Mississippi Valley Historical Review*, XXXIX (1953), 713–726.

ominously in his journal: "This is the man to do the Deed."[49]

Most transcendentalists spurned nonresistance. Brook Farm criticized Hopedale for presuming that divine laws, such as nonresistance, could be generalized in a creed. Orestes Brownson carried transcendentalism into a militant espousal of the interests of labor; in this cause he thought that armed resistance could be a Christian necessity. Although he wished that the world might comply with the principles of peace, he was shocked when nonresistants criticized Bunker Hill, "where Liberty and Slavery once met in the death-struggle."[50] Emerson praised the principle of nonresistance lavishly in his diaries,[51] but these private judgments were part of an inner life, walled off from public action. Adin Ballou could not admire Emerson for this reason. If some of his "transcendental abstractions" were put into practice, they might "regenerate the world. But the fatal hitch with such moralists is that neither they nor their admirers can sail out of the old ship of society as it is." Emerson had told Ballou that his "utmost" would be to guide his own family above the plane of earthly strife.[52]

Theodore Parker did not lay the same priority on private life; he was an active abolitionist. Clear on most subjects, he was ambiguous about nonresistance. Although he respected nonresistants, he stated that the doctrine "never went down with me"—and for a transcendentalist it was what went down with him that counted. He admitted that his private opinions had fluctuated considerably on nonresistance; the Bible was not altogether clear, but he was not in any case "inclined to settle such questions on the authority of Jesus. . . . I could not cast down my own nature and be faithless to my own soul." He did not preach on the question, favorably or unfavorably, because his mind was

[49] Henry Steele Commager, *Theodore Parker* (Boston, 1960), p. 236; Shepard, *Pedlar's Progress*, p. 477.

[50] See Henry Wright's report of a conversation with Brownson in *Liberator* March 26, 1841, p. 4.

[51] Cf. Curti, "Non-Resistance in New England," p. 34; Schuster, *Native American Anarchism*, pp. 77–78.

[52] Ballou, *Autobiography*, pp. 498–500.

not made up, because men needed no urging to fight, and because nonviolence was right in ninety-nine cases out of a hundred. But in being faithful to his own ideas, of course, he was associated with the most violent quarters of antislavery; he was one of the "Secret Six" who conspired with John Brown.[53]

Thoreau deserves special attention since he is often called an anarchist and since his philosophy is sometimes compared to Garrisonism.[54] His views had little in common with nonresistance. Alcott's program for the New England nonresistants was the distillation from their consciences of persuasive simple truths; these were the measures with which he sought to evangelize the coercive world. Thoreau, on the other hand, paid little attention to the existence of universal truths. He placed a somewhat mystical value on particular experiences; he doubted the possibility of universal reform with a Calvinistic vehemence. His few remarks on antislavery, including his praise of John Brown, reveal a violent potential in what often is considered a philosophy of principled nonviolence.

Thoreau was generally critical of the reformers. In 1854, however, after Massachusetts had rendered a fugitive slave back to his owners, he spoke at a protest meeting in Framingham. Much of his time was spent in arguing the superiority of the countryside to the city and in attacking newspapers as bulwarks of slavery. He also used higher law to support arguments already familiar to antislavery—any perceiver of truth must judge the judges, law cannot make men free. But it was necessary for Thoreau to explain how he had gotten onto an antislavery platform in the first place: "I had never respected the government near to which I had lived, but I had foolishly thought I might manage to live here, minding my private affairs, and forget it."

[53] See *Practical Christian*, Dec. 17, 1853, p. 2; Edelstein, *Strange Enthusiasm*, p. 210; and the comment by one of Parker's parishioners, C. K. Whipple, in *Liberator*, July 15, 1859, p. 2.

[54] Lynd, *Intellectual Origins*, p. 125, and *passim*; Wendell Glick, "Thoreau and Radical Abolitionism: A Study of the Native Background of Thoreau's Social Philosophy," unpublished Ph.D. dissertation, Northwestern University, Evanston, Ill., 1950.

Now he was impressed that his life was passing, not through some neutral zone, but *"wholly within hell."*[55]

Even this shock did not mean that he joined organized reform. But he was ready, four years later, to condemn it for failing to equal his admiration for the hero John Brown. "A man of rare common sense and directness of speech, as of action; a transcendentalist above all, a man of ideas and principles," was his conception of Brown. This soldier "had no need to invent anything but to tell the simple truth, and communicate his own resolution." His martyrdom fed Thoreau's hatred of the respectable, commercial world. But Thoreau was not opposed to any government except that which disturbed his peace of mind. He explicitly identified Brown with a government needing no suffrage to establish justice and resist tyranny and occupying a Christian beachhead.[56]

Thoreau brooded over the execution of John Brown and, a year later, he set his reflections down clearly. The martyr had been "the embodiment of principle," and therefore it was irrelevant to pass judgment on his means: "The man who does not recognize in Brown's words a wisdom and nobleness, and therefore an authority, superior to our laws, is a modern Democrat. This is the test by which to discover him. He is not wilfully but constitutionally blind on this side, and he is consistent with himself." Harper's Ferry was a test of personal sanctification; sinners could be discriminated from saints according to the ways in which different persons responded to Brown. As Thoreau proceeded to ridicule the ambitions and even the physical appearance of his neighbors, he spoke in terms of original sin:

It is not every man who can be a Christian, even in a very moderate sense, whatever education you give him. It is a matter of constitution

---

[55] *Liberator*, July 21, 1854, p. 4. For the strongest case that can be made for Thoreau as an abolitionist, see Nick Aaron Ford, "Henry David Thoreau, Abolitionist," *New England Quarterly*, XIX (1946), 359–371.

[56] Thoreau, "A Plea for Captain John Brown," in John L. Thomas, ed., *Slavery Attacked: The Abolitionist Crusade* (Englewood Cliffs, N.J., 1965), pp. 163–168.

and temperament, after all. He may have to be born again many times. I have known many a man who pretended to be a Christian, in whom it was ridiculous, for he had no genius for it. It is not every man who can be a free man, even.[57]

We may judge from this last sentence that not even in his veneration of Captain Brown had Thoreau become an abolitionist.

Brown became Thoreau's personal Christ, a figure of unquestionable authority to liberate him from oppressive visions of authority.[58] In the resulting scheme of law, Brown's importance as a reformer was dismissed; he was simply a vengeful foe of the unregenerate. Thoreau was able to celebrate "Resistance to Civil Government" (this was the original title of his great 1849 essay on civil disobedience). So intent was he on the signs of his private consciousness, however, that he scarcely spoke of sinless alternatives to civil government. It was enough to worship the heroism—the faith in ideas—of Captain Brown.

This brief look at the transcendentalists gives perspective on the vacillations of the nonresistants in the 1850s. Nonresistants may not have measured up very well to their own original standards of pacifism, but they never ventured to proclaim any man a law unto himself. They also kept their minds on the goal of abolishing slavery more clearly than such a worshiper of Brown as Thoreau. But transcendentalists and nonresistants shared the problem of how the validity of principles could be fixed between the sovereign individual and the sovereign God. The transcendentalists decided some men could embody principles and bring them to life. The nonresistant was left with the relativity of private judgment.

Not surprisingly, of all the nonresistants Henry C. Wright took the most extreme stand after Harper's Ferry. In the first of four public letters, he wrote Brown of a Natick meeting which en-

[57] Thoreau, "The Last Days of John Brown," in Louis Ruchames, ed., *John Brown: The Making of a Revolutionary* (New York, 1969), pp. 272–277.

[58] See Carl Bode, "Epilogue by the Editor," *The Portable Thoreau* (New York, 1964), pp. 683–696.

dorsed the rights of slaves to resist their masters and of Northerners to lend their aid. The rhetoric was strongly sectional:
"Wherever the people of the South live . . . they embody death
to liberty. We would stir up the people of the North to embody
death to slavery wherever they live." The importance of Brown's
act lay not in military success but in a symbolic personal confrontation with sin. The formal commitment to nonresistance
remained: "We have wondered that those who hold to armed
resistance to tyrants have not more cheerfully and numerously
gathered around your standard of insurrection against slaveholders." Brown could not expect nonresistants to enlist on his side,
but he need not have feared their criticism.

In a letter to the Richmond *Enquirer*, Wright forgot even the
formalities of nonresistance. Slave insurrections were the devout-
est wish of the Northern people:

The sin of this nation . . . is to be taken away, not by Christ, but by
John Brown. Christ, as represented by those who are called by his
name, has proved a dead failure, as a power to free the slaves. . . .
The nation is to be saved, not by the blood of Christ, (as that is now
administered,) but by the blood of John Brown, which, as administered
by Abolitionists, will prove the "power of God and the wisdom of
God" to resist slaveholders, and bring them to repentance.

In a letter to Governor Wise of Virginia, he was less unchristian,
but still absolved Brown of guilt on the basis of personal sincerity and national standards of morality. The final letter, addressed to Garrison, repeated the old arguments: "MAN-KILL-
ING is the basis of MAN-STEALING," and "Subjection to an
outward, arbitrary authority is the basis of chattel slavery, and
of all oppression." But there were two overriding considerations:
the public was obliged to aid the slaves with whatever means it
deemed right, and the purpose of antislavery was to deplete the
slave's servility, his lack of nerve. Nonviolent insurrections would
be preferable, but the end must come.[59]

---

[59] These letters are reprinted in order in Wright's *The Natick Resolution; or, Resistance to Slaveholders the Right and Duty of Southern Slaves*

Garrison was more circumspect than Wright. In his first hasty notice of Harper's Ferry, he alluded to his well-known opposition to bloodshed and then pointed out that no one who gloried in the legends of the Revolution could deny the right of slaves to revolt. A longer editorial retained this viewpoint on the "well-intended but misguided" raid. Since the slaveowner by his own violence "forfeited his right to live," a harvest of retribution was probably imminent. "O that they might avoid all this by a timely repentance." Without retracting his nonresistance, Garrison soon worked out a way of praising the hero of Harper's Ferry. He emphasized that Brown would not kill unless attacked; thus Brown's gravest sin was advocacy of self-defense. One of the original nonresistants, C. K. Whipple, lauded Brown's nobility of purpose but criticized his reliance on violence. Abolitionists ought to encourage slaves to assert their freedom, but to submit to death rather than slay their oppressors.[60] To Stephen S. Foster, the problem appeared simpler. "I claim to be a Non-Resistant, but not to be a fool," he told a laughing antislavery audience. "I think John Brown has shown himself a *man*, in comparison with the Non-Resistants!"[61]

Harper's Ferry was truly the turning point for nonresistance as an effective voice in reform. A Hopedale medium was inspired to give a lecture praising nonresistance, but said that John Brown was beyond judgment. By being true to his own light he had accomplished what Garrison could not; he had "opened the gates of the nation to let in the bridegroom and bride of the Future." Love and peace would yet have their time to work in the world.[62]

---

and Northern Freemen (Boston, 1859), pp. 3–32. A year later Wright answered critics of this pamphlet with another containing even fewer souvenirs of nonresistance: *No Rights, No Duties; or, Slaveholders, as Such, Have No Rights; Slaves, as Such, Owe No Duties* (Boston, 1860).

[60] *Liberator,* Oct. 21, 1859, p. 2; Oct. 1859, p. 2; *Radical Spiritualist,* II (March 1860), 84–85. See also Whipple's cogent tract on *The Non-Resistance Principle: With Particular Application to the Help of Slaves by Abolitionists* (Boston, 1860).

[61] *Practical Christian,* Nov. 26, 1859, p. 3.

[62] *Radical Spiritualist,* I (Jan. 1860), 69.

But as the violent dispensation prolonged itself through war and reconstruction, it was almost forgotten that this was not what the abolitionists had intended. Garrison's sons were obliged to remind their readers of all the differences between their father and John Brown. But they were eager to show that their father had been in the mainstream of history, and therefore they forgot that the traditional order of dispensations was from violence to peace. Rather unfairly, they said the pacifism of their father had prepared the way for the violence of Brown.[63]

v

By the end of 1859 almost no nonresistant voice remained to be raised against force and violence. What is remarkable about this development is how little it was caused by engagement in exciting circumstances. Had nonresistants been carried away by sympathy for imprisoned fugitives, they might have resorted to pardoning such slips from grace by reference to the passions of the moment. But they made no such excuses.[64] Instead they

[63] Garrisons, *Garrison*, III, 492–493.

[64] Samuel Joseph May provided one possible illustration of this sort of excuse for violence. After the rescue of a fugitive in Syracuse, he wrote Garrison: "Perhaps you will think that I go too far in enjoining it upon all men to act *against* the Fugitive Slave Law as they conscientiously believe to be right, even if it be to fight for the rescue of its victims. But I know not what other counsel to give them. And let me confess to you, that when I saw poor Jerry in the hands of the official kidnappers, I could not preach non-resistance very earnestly to the crowd that were clamoring for his release. And when I found that he had been rescued without serious harm to any one, I was as uproarious as any one in my joy." Garrison's sons attached a footnote saying that their father could not have been alarmed by this counsel, "which resembled his own to the colored people of Boston" (see their *Garrison*, III, 337). But not even May perfectly illustrates this way of pardoning violence, for he also relied on the doctrine that private judgment should determine means and had been among the first to brush against the relativistic borders of this notion. He had told the first anniversary meetings of the New England Non-Resistance Society in 1839: "I find that I place every year less value on organization, as I more clearly discern the power that rests in the individual. This power can be preserved in organizations only by resisting the feeling that leads us to encroach on his right of opinion. It is possible that the widest differences of opinion

stretched their doctrine until it imposed a categorical obligation on those who believed in violence to fight immediately against the slaveholders. And they nearly canonized John Brown for fulfilling this obligation. Once they had criticized men and institutions for relying on the implicit threat of violence; now their criticism was directed at those who did not live up to standards of violence that nonresistants imputed to them.

There was one important exception to this development. Throughout the 1850s Adin Ballou watched in horror as the testimony of nonresistance was silenced, as pacifists urged other men to take up arms. His concern inspired a constantly enlightening commentary on the whole of antislavery. To review this commentary is to draw together most of the themes of this book.

In January 1850, Ballou wrote a sober editorial, "Non-Resistance and Anti-Slavery," in which he decided that of the two reforms nonresistance was "higher and purer." The work of antislavery would be done if the nation repented and declared "the colored people placed on a level with the white population." But nonresistance would still have to calm the continuing hostility between whites and blacks. Furthermore, if nonresistance could reach the slaveholder before antislavery, the blacks would be spared any hostile aftermath. In this eventuality, Ballou expected that freedmen would be loyal to the interests of their former masters and would seek their guidance. "Such slavery would be quite unexceptionable to Anti-Slavery itself." But the reforms were distinct, and it already seemed probable that "Non-Resistance exerts at least a deadening influence on Anti-Slavery zeal, and so is incongruous with it." In making this distinction, he admitted what Garrison, Wright, and the others were never willing to admit: "Anti-Slavery is essentially nothing more than consistent democracy, and . . . democracy contends for political justice and natural rights *merely*—not for the duty of patiently enduring wrongs, submitting to outrage, and forgiving injuries."

---

may exist with the utmost union of heart, and the most uninterrupted affection" (*Non-Resistant*, Oct. 5, 1839, p. 2).

He likewise admitted that it was very hard to agitate for the
end of slavery without sometimes feeling an impulse to fight.
Here was the most extraordinary concession of all: "Anti-Slavery
has a strong natural affinity for political and legal action." What,
then, was the "proper sphere" for nonresistants in the antislavery
struggle?

They can *think, feel, speak, write, publish,* and in a thousand ways
enlighten, purify, and renovate public sentiment. And this, after all,
is the great thing to be done. When this has been accomplished, political, legislative and legal action will follow, as the vane conforms to
the changing wind. . . . In this respect [non-resistance] sustains the
same position to the Anti-Slavery Society, as to all other noble voluntary associations, which are right in their *end,* but liable to err in their
means.[65]

It is uncertain what provoked this editorial. At the end of the
same year, Ballou wrote another, "Pro-War Anti-Slavery," in
which he listed affronts to nonresistance. It was bad enough that
Frederick Douglass and Theodore Parker, who had been understood to favor the doctrine, were calling for the death of kidnappers. It was much more distressing that "devoted and indom-
itable reformers," like Stephen S. Foster and Henry C. Wright,
"though affirming that they themselves are Non-Resistants, declare it to be the duty of such as hold it right to fight to the
death for the poor slave." It resembled the old argument over
defensive war. Could they not see that to justify any fighting
was to open the door to all fighting? Furthermore, was it not obvious that, if slavery were ended by violence, "both black and
white would be subjected to a long series of calamities, moral
and physical, which could never be done away, but by the moral
means we can now employ with fifty times more advantage?"[66]

These were the stakes. In view of the subsequent history of
racial violence and frustrated efforts at reform in the South, they
are not trivial. Ballou's contributions to the debate of the 1850s

[65] *Practical Christian,* Jan. 19, 1850, pp. 2–3.
[66] *Ibid.,* Dec. 21, 1850, p. 2.

were the ideas that by demanding any kind of force abolitionists would forfeit their ability to criticize the violence which would actually occur and that slavery, if ended by force, would leave a legacy of hatred and poverty which even Christian love would have difficulty in overcoming.

Ballou reiterated similar warnings throughout the decade. Non-resistance might be compelled to separate from antislavery. It was understandable, if not excusable, that foes of slavery should get mad enough to fight. But if abolitionists successfully exhorted slave uprisings, they would simply aggravate the racist fear of "black monsters" in the North. In any case, the effective abolition of slavery required a change in the culture and religion of Southerners, white and black.[67]

This testimony came to a head in 1859. A long, troubled editorial on "Practical Christian Anti-Slavery" suggested that secession from the Garrisonian society was probably appropriate for three principal reasons. First, of course, was the predominance of the war spirit among abolitionists. Second was "a growing disposition among our Anti-Slavery Associates to magnify their movement for the abolition of chattel slavery as including the main substance of Christianity, or of a natural religion much purer than Christianity." Third was an increase in the "egotism, extremeism [*sic*], exaggerationism, antagonism and contemptuous personality," of which there always had been too much; it followed from the "absurd doctrine[,] the better a man is the worse he is, or at least the more dangerous, so long as he is not a full saint." In order to come out from antislavery, it was necessary to minimize its importance and reject its utility as a test of sinlessness.[68]

[67] *Ibid.*, Apr. 24, 1852, p. 3; Jan. 28, 1854, p. 3; Nov. 17, 1855, p. 3; Feb. 21, 1857, p. 3.
[68] *Ibid.*, Sept. 3, 1859, pp. 2–3. In ascribing lower importance to antislavery, Ballou anticipated some disputes among abolitionists at the end of the Civil War. "Now we understand the abolition of chattel slavery to be the plain dictate of natural justice. What is proposed? Simply this: to let the enslaved go free and take care of themselves, like the generality of mankind: to abolish all laws, renounce all claims, and cease from all acts,

Both the *Anti-Slavery Standard* and the *Liberator* reprinted this blast, which elicited many comments. George W. Stacy, a fugitive from Hopedale, replied that intolerant "personality" was a crucial weapon, for "there cannot be a *sin* without a *sinner*." Rather inconsistently, he accused Ballou of giving solace to Democratic Conservatives or "hunkers"; one ought to appreciate that in battle some error was inevitable.[69] J. Miller McKim considered it Ballou's duty to stay and persuade others, not to withdraw his influence. Concerning the charge of natural religion he stated: "It is somewhat extraordinary that while orthodox ministers, the 'straitest' of their sect, . . . are now venturing upon our platform, Mr. Ballou, a heretic of heretics, should feel compelled to retire for the very reasons which had before obliged these orthodox men to stand aloof." Surely the cause was not lost: prowar forces were only slightly in the ascendant. It seemed to Ballou, however, that McKim's mild estimate of what was wrong could be explained by his residence among Pennsylvania abolitionists, who generally were Quakers. Ballou collected a mass of evidence that the cause was moving toward violence (most ominously, Wendell Phillips had praised intellectuals for adopting the logic of "valiant old Ossawattamie Brown").[70] This controversy may have encouraged some self-criticism within the antislavery movement. Samuel May, Jr., who frankly opposed violence on grounds of expediency alone, became convinced that the societies had blurred their early testimony. Garrison, who had remained truer than most to nonresistance, commended the excellent spirit in which Ballou's timely criticisms were presented.[71]

---

which regard them as chattels." Antislavery did not call for indemnification, homesteads, education, or even pocket money. "So the Anti-Slavery movement proposes but the simplest justice in behalf of the slave, and that stinted. . . . It does not reach Charity at all, nor insist necessarily on any other great principle of religion, morality or humanity. Consequently Anti-Slavery with all its importance, is but a part of Christianity, or of anything that can be called true religion, and covers but a single point in the vast field of human duty."

[69] *Liberator*, Sept. 23, 1859, p. 2.

[70] *Practical Christian*, Oct. 13, 1859, p. 2.

[71] *Ibid.*, Oct. 29, 1859, pp. 1–3; *Liberator*, Sept. 16, 1859, p. 3.

Then came Harper's Ferry, and there was no turning back. At the outset Ballou tried to dispense with the notion that sincerity makes things right. In the *Practical Christian* he described Brown as neither knavish nor insane, "but an honest milito-religious zealot, who verily believes himself commissioned of God to pray and fight for the liberation of the slaves. Like some other Anti-Slavery zealots he has more self-esteem and combativeness than reason, more zeal than judgment, and really believes that the mass of slaves are ready to strike for their freedom." Actually, Ballou believed that half of the slaves would fight for their masters.[72] Later he argued that force was doomed without the aid of the government, which was constitutionally proslavery. Only Southern secession, he predicted, could lead to the abolition of slavery by arms. Even then, the outcome would not be guaranteed because reason and conversion are not the means by which war proceeds.[73]

But the weaknesses in Brown's plans turned out to be less important than the reactions of abolitionists to his heroism. When Garrison eventually called for meetings to honor Brown, Ballou complained that the effect would be to school the world to trust in might. At a special antislavery meeting in Worcester, he found himself alone among the leaders of the movement in repudiating violent means.[74] When he reviewed comments on Brown in the antislavery press, he criticized Garrison for pretending the hero's intentions had been peaceful and Wright for equating Brown hanged with Christ crucified. Of the wave of panegyrics, he said:

If these laudations had held up John Brown as a devout Calvinist of the old Puritanic, Cromwellian stamp; as a sincere enthusiast . . . ; as a generous, magnanimous, heroic, though unwise, military adventurer for the liberation of the downtrodden slaves, unfortunate in arms; and as a noble-hearted, firm, dignified, soldier-like martyr to his cause; they would have been truthful, just and unexceptionable. But when they characterize his enterprise and conduct as pre-eminently

[72] *Practical Christian*, Oct. 29, 1859, p. 3.
[73] *Ibid.*, Feb. 4, 1860, p. 2.
[74] *Ibid.*, Nov. 12, 1859, p. 2; Nov. 26, 1859, pp. 1, 3–4; Dec. 10, 1859, pp. 1, 4.

Christ-like, and canonize him as a *Christian* saint, and some of them
as a self-sacrificing *redeemer* more to be honored than the Christ of
Calvary, they are untruthful, unjust and utterly absurd.[75]

But some distortion was necessary when men tried to reconcile
the appeal of Brown with their faith in Christian nonresistance.
Garrison criticized Ballou for being too critical of Brown and his
supporters. In January 1860, when Garrison took refuge in the
idea of gradual progress toward nonresistance, Ballou retorted
that ideas cannot progress through war.[76]

As Ballou pondered the record of apostasy, he was not surprised that Wright or Foster deserted the cause of peace. But
Garrison's defection was sorely felt. Ballou observed that the
abolitionists' conversion to the use of force had committed many
of them to the Republicans and "some indefinite conservative
peace policy"; they were unable to sustain their antislavery zeal.[77]
Garrison spoke at Hopedale in 1862, but declined a request for
free debate on the sanctity of the Sabbath, the authority of the
Bible, and the consistency of nonresistance with supporting war.
Therefore only the small Hopedale congregation heard Ballou's
reflections on the course of Garrisonism.

He considered Garrison the leading example of those who
rooted their nonresistance in human nature. Garrison was "pre-
eminently an Individualist rather than a Socialist of any kind."
He accepted no constructive responsibilities, but instead "mag-
nified personal liberty as the right of all men, seeming to think
if this were secured all other blessings would follow as a matter
of course." Ballou believed that unless "high types of individual
and social life" were fostered, mankind would "sink into debasing
irreligion or lawless, irresponsible Nothingarianism." This was
more than a difference of temperament. Garrison pinned nonresistance to human nature, which proved a fickle source of authority, varying its requirements with the appearances of the
moment. Thus he could say: "Although Non-resistance holds hu-

[75] *Ibid.,* Dec. 10, 1859, p. 2.
[76] *Ibid.,* Jan. 21, 1860, p. 2.
[77] Ballou, *Autobiography,* pp. 416–422.

man life in all cases absolutely inviolable by professed Non-resistants yet it is perfectly consistent for them to petition, advise, and strenuously urge a pro-war government to abolish slavery by the war power."

To Ballou this was "to adopt the Jesuitical maxim, 'The end sanctifies the means,' which is false in morals and suicidal in policy." In every kind of law, one is personally responsible for one's agent's actions. Abolitionists, like it or not, were morally stained with the bloodshed of the government.

Ballou had pinned nonresistance to neither of the antitheses—human nature or divine command—but to a typological system in which man humbly tried to discern the substance of the law from the shadows available to him. This proved the more reliable course. He was still able to contrast Garrison's nonresistance to that of Christ, which had not passed away through self-contradiction in emergencies: "His kingdom was not of this world and could not be advanced after the fashion of this world's red revolutionary reformers, but rather by the regeneration of individual men through repentance for sin unto good works, and the love of righteousness whereby they would be brought into true relations with each other—into that state of unity, harmony, and brotherhood in which all should strive together for the universal good and happiness, blessing and cursing not."[78]

It may not be unusual in American history for the approach of war to divide reformers, and finding secure authority for principles has been a recurrent human problem. But it is ironic that the nonresistance movement, which began with certainty in God's government, ended with bitter charges of moral relativism on earth.

[78] These reflections on Garrison may be found in *ibid.*, pp. 444–449.

IX

Survivals and Reconstructions

Originally nonresistance had claimed that the means by which the twin evils of slavery and force were combated held the greatest significance for the millennial aspirations of the country. Since Harper's Ferry was recognized at the time as a prelude to civil war, it might have confirmed the prediction that violence and slavery could not be separated from America's destiny. But for a decade nonresistance had sanctioned the use of violence by celebration of the rights and duties of private judgment. Violence often seemed little more than a matter of personal taste, without national consequences. Thus nonresistants were in no position to see their doctrine vindicated. On the contrary, by evaluating Harper's Ferry solely in terms of individual integrity they helped explode their doctrine, and they could not respond critically as pacifists when the entire nation took to violence.

Having compromised their pacifism, could the nonresistants remain faithful to what we have called their anarchism? By restricting all acts of violence to purely personal significance they postponed an answer to that question. But obviously they could not remain anarchists very long, inasmuch as their indictment of government had always assumed universal condemnation of force. Garrison and Ballou parted ways when the great abolitionist found it possible, as a nonresistant, to ask the government to follow its own light and crush slavery with the war power.

There was a convention in Boston in December 1865 to consider prospects for a new, radical peace movement. Some participants criticized the war, the union, civil government; there were even no-organizationists who disapproved of founding a new reform society because they favored "perfect freedom in all things." Echoes were heard of old-style anarchism, but none of the well-known radical abolitionists, except Adin Ballou, participated.[1] The war had eradicated most traces of antebellum nonresistance.

The Civil War marked a major transformation of American thought.[2] Many of the themes which we have discussed nearly vanished; others assumed new implications. It had not been easy for abolitionists to reverse old commitments and support a war waged by the American government. Not even the right of private judgment could effect such a reconciliation. Instead, it was necessary to conceive of the war as a national judgment, an act of God, for which the guilt of the nation rather than the decision of any man was responsible. Nonresistants shared this conception of the war with most of the rest of the North.[3] It followed from evangelical attitudes toward the sinfulness of slavery and the mission of America which all abolitionists had been teaching the country for years—and which had impassioned some responses to Harper's Ferry. George B. Cheever, writing for William Goo-

[1] Clippings in Adin Ballou, Scrapbook, 1863–1865, Boston Public Library. See also Brock, *Pacifism*, ch. 17, "The Civil War and the Antebellum Pacifists."

[2] Some relevant recent studies are: George M. Frederickson, *The Inner Civil War: Northern Intellectuals and the Crisis of the Union* (New York, 1965); Edmund Wilson, *Patriotic Gore: Studies in the Literature of the American Civil War* (New York, 1966); John Higham, *From Boundlessness to Consolidation: The Transformation of American Culture, 1848–1860* (Ann Arbor, 1969); and William G. McLoughlin, *The Meaning of Henry Ward Beecher: An Essay on the Shifting Values of Mid-Victorian America, 1840–1870* (New York, 1970).

[3] Frederickson, *Inner Civil War*, is sensitive to this theme. See also Robert C. Albrecht, "The Theological Response of the Transcendentalists to the Civil War," *New England Quarterly*, XXXVII (1965), 21–34; and George M. Marsden, *The Evangelical Mind and the New School Presbyterian Experience: A Case Study of Thought and Theology in Nineteenth-Century America* (New Haven, 1970), ch. 10, "The Civil War: The Flag and the Cross."

dell's *Principia*, had preached, for example, that the meaning of
John Brown's raid was that if men failed to end slavery peacefully, God would end it by war. "The storm of God's wrath was
thickening over us," he preached. "Already the big drops began
to fall." Goodell also insisted that, although he opposed the use
of force, Harper's Ferry demonstrated that violence was "the
providential remedy: the permitted remedy, the retributive remedy, when the Divine warnings are unheeded."[4] In the war these
bloody prophecies proved true; abolitionists were able to portray
the war not as the fighting of individuals but as a purifying act
of God. Tallying up the deaths caused by the war, Parker Pillsbury in 1884 reflected that it had not been a rebellion so much
as *"Retribution"*: "From the torture-chambers of the imprisoned
slave our guilt ascended, by silent but sure evaporation, until it
hung in threatening clouds over all the sky, waiting the dread
hour when the Infinite Patience could endure it no longer!"[5]

Even if God's government was vindicated by the nation's afflic-
tion, the war essentially transferred responsibility for abolition
from reformers to human government. The cause became tied to
military decisions and political calculations. Their options severely limited, abolitionists argued bitterly among themselves
over such questions as whether Lincoln deserved their support
and whether abolitionism entailed advocacy of political, social,
and economic rights for Negroes after emancipation. On the
other hand, James M. McPherson has shown that many abolitionists served as dedicated and skillful advocates for these rights
throughout the war and Reconstruction and that the spirit of
abolitionism was still alive in the beginnings of the twentieth
century.[6] Abolitionists undoubtedly contributed to the consecra-

[4] *Principia*, Nov. 26, 1859, pp. 3, 4.

[5] Pillsbury, *Acts*, pp. 70–71. In 1864, Pillsbury claimed that he had re-
quested peaceful change for twenty-three years while no one listened. Now
people were being schooled in the reality of killing. Death and devastation
were harsh teachers, "but we would not learn of any others" (*Progressive
Age*, V [Jan. 1864], 70).

[6] McPherson, *Struggle for Equality;* and "The Antislavery Legacy: From
Reconstruction to the NAACP," in Barton J. Bernstein, ed., *Towards a*

tion to moral purpose with which the war—and the death of Lincoln—have been linked in many Northern minds ever since, to the moral patriotic sentiments beautifully recalled in Robert Lowell's poem, "For the Union Dead" (1964). But except for racial equality—and even that may be questionable—most of anti-slavery radicalism was obliterated by the Civil War. Only a few threads of antigovernmental thought remain to be traced.

ii

Hopedale held firm against all encroachments on nonresistance, but was forced to conceive of the war as an act of divine judgment. The iniquities of the slave power had grown so enormous that they had to be terminated "by the effusion of blood—by the avenging judgment rather than the tender mercy of Almighty God." The "old line Abolitionists" elsewhere succumbed to the crisis, quoted the Old Testament more often than the New, and honored Joshua more than Christ.[7] Ballou condemned these apostasies, but he also interpreted the course of events as a cataclysm out of the old dispensation. Hopedale had been mobilized as a prototype of a new and more merciful way of life. What was its function during a time of justly deserved retribution?

The community's influence began to wane in 1856 when the Draper brothers suddenly decided to withdraw their financial support. They were building a great fortune on the economic basis of the Hopedale Community, and they owned three-fourths of the joint stock. Since no one else could make up this amount, their withdrawal doomed the community as an economic experiment. Nonetheless, the members chose to stay together, in part, as one of them said, because "the cause of Non-Resistance, almost abandoned by her professed friends, urges us to renewed effort and to faithful service."[8] Ebenezer Draper, a devoted abolition-

---

New Past: Dissenting Essays in American History (New York, 1969), pp. 126–157.

[7] Ballou, *History of Hopedale*, pp. 310–312.

[8] *Ibid.*, pp. 289, 302, 351–352. There were desertions, and new residents came who were indifferent to community traditions. In January 1860, the

ist and nonresistant, lost his fortune through unwise investment
in the 1870s.[9] His brother George, who had only come to Hopedale in 1853, prospered in the manufacture of textile machinery.
Eventually the Draper Company developed an improved loom
which, ironically, could be used to greater advantage in the
South, where labor costs were cheap, than in New England.
George Draper doffed his Garrisonian foibles during the war,
subsidized several companies of volunteers, and served on the
Massachusetts advisory board on recruiting. He later turned
staunchly Republican and helped found the Home Market Club,
a leading lobby for the protection of American industry. His son,
William F. Draper, became an officer in the union army and later
a congressman and ambassador (he remembered Ballou as the
highest embodiment of Christianity he ever met).[10] But Hopedale was no longer the center of nonresistance; it was the location
of the Draper Company.

Other Hopedale residents were swept up in the spirit of war:
they waited at the post office for battle news, enlisted to fight,
died in Andersonville. When they fell out of consistency with the
principles of the place, they usually resigned their membership.[11]
Those who remained as members held ambivalent attitudes toward the war, as was evident in a series of resolutions passed by
the community. They explained that they were harmless residents
of the United States, not participating citizens, and thus they

---

Practical Christian Church of Hopedale was formed around a general,
nonresistant creed. The injustice of keeping townspeople outside the
franchise of the community became a source of tension (here was an old
New England issue); and in October 1867, the Hopedale Parish was set
up, without a creed but with Ballou as pastor. While in 1856 the community had about 110 members and about 200 other residents, the Practical Christian Church never exceeded sixty members. See *ibid.*, pp. 305,
331–336, 344.

[9] Ballou, *History of Milford*, pp. 721–722.

[10] Draper, *Recollections*, pp. 4–7, 9, 272–273; Irwin Feller, "The Draper
Loom in New England Textiles, 1894–1914: A Study of Diffusion of an
Innovation," *Journal of Economic History*, XXVI (1966), 320–347.

[11] *Hopedale Reminiscences*, p. 54; Ballou, *History of Hopedale*, p. 312.

should be allowed to remain faithful to their own sense of right. Since their chief duty was to attain Christ's kingdom, they could not join in taking lives. They hated slavery, however, and felt no sympathy for the South and much for the federal government. The war was "a just retribution for national transgressions, to wit: lust of wealth, lust of power, and lust of sensual pleasures, all culminating in the persistent upholding, by law and by force, of the gigantic institution of Africo-chattel slavery." They could not fight, but wanted the war won. They called slavery a national sin, yet prayed for the North to prevail. Some of the ambivalence of these resolutions, in Ballou's opinion, arose from the presence of members who truly supported the war but also respected the faith of older members.[12]

In view of the pacifist and anarchist sentiments that coursed through antislavery before the war, many abolitionists must have been ambivalent about the liberation of the slave by the force of arms. Willie Lee Rose has recounted the marvelous story of how many abolitionists, instead of bearing arms, went to the captured Sea Islands during the war and dedicated their lives to instruction of the Negroes and experimentation with methods of free labor. She called this a "rehearsal for reconstruction," but it may also have been an alternative to military reconstruction. The Gideons bore much the same relation to the army as Christian nonresistants were supposed to bear to Caesar: they were obedient servants in the present who exemplified a superior hope in the future. Three of the most prominent members of the Hopedale Community volunteered to go to Port Royal, South Carolina, to teach freed Negroes, after receiving assurances from the Boston committee in charge that they would not be asked to compromise their peace principles. They were recommended by Senator Charles Sumner. When they got to New York, the government agent required them to swear the soldier's oath of allegiance as well as the civilian's. The leaders of the mission expelled them two days before departure, out of fear that their views would be

[12] *History of Hopedale,* pp. 313–317.

"offensive" in an area where soldiers were trained or that they would rob from the Negroes the "little manhood left them by inculcating the doctrine of non-resistance." With this outlet closed, they returned to Hopedale and collected clothing for the freedmen.[13]

Adin Ballou himself ceased publishing his newspaper in 1860 and became little more than a local minister. His strongest action during the war was to aid one practical Christian in drafting a protest against payment of a commutation fee.[14] After the war there were no reforms he could join. Peace societies were not radical enough; temperance and woman's rights were tied to ballots and legislation. He thought about the "working people's movement," to which other abolitionists, most prominently Wendell Phillips, were lending their support. Right at Hopedale there was a "social Science nucleus" which was concerned with the hours and condition of labor; one of its members, Mary B. Steward, went on to become an important figure in the eight-hour reform movement and the Massachusetts bureau of labor statistics.[15] But Ballou could not support the labor movement:

I found in it little of the spirit of fraternity, of co-operation between the strong and weak; little of the spirit of Christian brotherhood. It sought to level down but not up. Its trust was in legislation and governmental coercion. The sword was its *dernier resort*. It belonged to a moral and social sphere and to a field of reform from which I had withdrawn forever.

Though he wished them well, he disliked their "ways and

[13] *Spiritual Reformer*, III (Apr. 1862), 93; Willie Lee Rose, *Rehearsal for Reconstruction: The Port Royal Experiment* (Indianapolis, 1964), p. 48. A minor flaw in this book, otherwise acutely sensitive to hints of truth in a variety of positions, is that it classifies the Hopedale people as a lunatic fringe best removed.

[14] Ballou, *History of Hopedale*, pp. 308–309, 318; Edward Needles Wright, *Conscientious Objectors in the Civil War* (New York, 1961), pp. 163–164.

[15] David Montgomery concludes that "the idea that the abolitionists as a bloc were hostile to labor reform is pure myth" in *Beyond Equality: Labor and the Radical Republicans, 1862–1872* (New York, 1967), pp. 118, 122–124. See Mrs. Steward's obituary in *Labor Standard*, March 3, 1878.

methods" and retired to "my proper mission," preparing for the age of brotherhood.[16] For the most part, he was a town genealogist and a chronicler of antebellum reform.

Obviously out of phase with the existing dispensation, Ballou himself came to utilize the right of private judgment. In 1879 he preached to the local veterans' organization from the assumption that primitive Christianity took no part in civil government but paid "due respect to civil and military rulers in their sphere." He would therefore judge each man on the moral plane he chose— either the absolute standard of righteousness taught by Christ or the common, relative standard of the times. Though a faithful nonresistant, he commended the veterans for noble service to the state.[17] In 1839 the notion of two planes of morality had been equivalent to the distinction between saints and sinners and had promised the world an escape from servitude. But no longer.

There was a younger generation of nonresistants at Hopedale who were not won over to the war and yet were not lost in bleak resignation. They provide hints of an important continuity from nonresistance. Bryan J. Butts, the leader of the Progressive Group, as it was called, was born in Pompey, New York, in 1826. Most of his relatives were in law or politics, but he trained for the ministry at Meadville Theological School. After several years as a minister, he became interested in socialism and entered the Hopedale Community. In 1858 he married a member with a Rhode Island Quaker background, Harriet N. Greene, "without surrender of name." These details are important because they distinguish the younger group from the less educated, rural New England

---

[16] Ballou, *Autobiography*, pp. 462–463. Herbert G. Gutman of the City College of New York has informed me that at least one element of New England labor reform preached nonresistance. He also kindly supplied a copy of an anonymous article, "Jesus Christ and the Strike," from *The Labor Balance* (Boston), I (Oct. 1877), 3–4, which enthusiastically supports railroad strikers but criticizes the violent methods of both sides. Nonviolent methods of striking and even quitting the scene of oppression (like the old come-outers?), it is argued, would command greater moral influence.

[17] Ballou, *Autobiography*, pp. 481–485.

founders of the community, who were hardly enthusiastic about the effects of spiritualism on marriage. Ballou termed Butts "a Socialist and Progessionalist of the most unfettered, individualistic type." But there is no record of antagonism between the generations. Butts wrote for Ballou's newspaper, used his press to publish his own magazines, and eventually bought him out.[18]

At first Butts and his wife published the *Radical Spiritualist*, many of whose articles appeared in a phonetic alphabet. Its philosophy looked more anarchistic than anything by Ballou. It opposed government not merely for violating Christian injunctions or for being inappropriate to the converted; government was "a positive hindrance to human progress" because it deterred individuals from seeking real moral laws. In consequence, "just so long as the individual depends on the government, or the church, to settle the moral law, so long will slavery of every hue exist." This does not mean the magazine was irreligious or unconcerned with salvation. It conceived it to be "man's business, by inner growth, to show the outer Church and State to be systems of tyranny—that they have no authority whatever to vote a man in or out of the divine government."[19] Here were many of the themes of antebellum reform: the importance of private judgment, the invisible dominion of the elect, the identity of moral law and solitary man. Also, spiritualism was bringing to the fore the idea of progress.

The emphasis of the magazine initially was on sexual life. It attacked those who ransacked the doctrines of spiritualism in order to use the notion of *"new affinities"* to justify free love (it also printed circulars on the horrors of masturbation to be posted in washrooms). Why should reformers assail the evils of church and state while ignoring evils closer to home? Personal and family matters were actually more important: "Man should be a 'law unto himself,' and prove to the world, by a life of truth and virtue, that all outward laws are superfluous." Just as no-government

18 Ballou, *History of Milford*, pp. 609–610.
19 *Radical Spiritualist*, I (May 1859), 3.

had been a philosophy of order, no-marriage was now a philosophy of constancy. It was love in bondage, not love in freedom that led to promiscuity.[20]

With a change of name to the *Spiritual Reformer*, the magazine came out against all creeds and organizations; the soul of the individual was older and worthier of respect.[21] In effect, these young people took the position that had separated Brook Farm from Hopedale. Perhaps it should be stressed that spiritualism was not just a surrogate for nonresistance; this was a spiritualist equivalent of what transcendentalists had considered the permanent source of vitality in Christianity. But it had in common with Ballou's old doctrines a certainty that great public events could be outweighed in significance by exemplary private lives. At any rate, the Progressive Group adhered to nonresistance in the obscurity of Hopedale during the Civil War. Indeed, they circulated a "Standing Protest of New England Non-Resistant Abolitionists" to let the government know who disapproved of the policy of war. They got fifteen signatures, mostly of obscure persons, but among them Stephen S. Foster![22]

The name of the magazine was changed to *Progressive Age*, then to *Modern Age*. These changes of name complied with changes in tone. The commitment to nonresistance became tempered by a belief in shifting dispensations: peace would be possible in some future stage when man's rationality was awakened. Spiritualism usually carried some such belief, and during a prolonged war the belief gained additional relevance.[23] The belief in changing dispensations could be a revolutionary incentive to

[20] *Ibid.*, I (May 1859), 1, 2; I (Sept. 1859), 35; I (Oct. 1859), 43; I (Jan. 1860), 70.

[21] *Spiritual Reformer*, II (Aug. 1860), 28.

[22] *Progressive Age*, IV (Sept. 1862), 40; IV (Oct. 1862), 44; IV (Nov. 1862), 52–53.

[23] *Modern Age*, VII (Nov. 1865), 80. In the view of John Murray Spear, or his spiritual sources, the world was beginning its third dispensation. First came "THE AGE OF POWER"; then after Christ came "the AGE OF LOVE." Spiritualism marked the beginning of "the AGE OF WISDOM" and harmonious relationships. See Hewitt, ed., *Messages*, p. 48.

attempt to turn a corner in history (some had evaluated John
Brown in these terms). For nonresistants during an awful war,
dispensationalism explained why they were out of phase. But the
young "progressionists" at Hopedale did not join Ballou in stubborn resignation. They leveled down the notion of dispensations
and were captivated by essays of Herbert Spencer on "The Development Hypothesis" and "Over-Legislation."[24] Without explicit recognition that they were adjusting their conception of
history, they found in Spencer's philosophy new ways of combining ideas of progress, attacks on legislation, and opposition to the
concept of slavery.

Hopedale, then, was frustrated in its charitable impulses toward the freedmen. Its leading figure, Adin Ballou, was precluded
by his antebellum faith from leadership in the nation renovated
by war. But the community was not completely out of touch with
the new era. It produced one of the most prosperous firms in New
England, and it was a harbinger of social Darwinism.

iii

Like the Progressive Group at Hopedale, Henry C. Wright was
thrilled by the emergence of spiritualism before the war. Spirits
preached the wisdom of teetotalism, antislavery, nonresistance,
and true love matches. In his imagination, they were overthrow-
ing the authority of the clergy. As he beheld the battle he adopted
a tone of millennial destructiveness quite at odds with the
message of peace: "Truth is indissoluble. Error, alone, can be
destroyed. Whatever can be destroyed, in religion or government,
ought to be destroyed, and will be. Every reformer's mission is,
not to bring peace, but the sword."[25] We might expect, therefore,
that he welcomed the Civil War as a process of purification, but
in spite of his unpredictable enthusiasms he was devoted to nonresistance. From his hand came the only significant attempt to
refurbish the doctrine in the midst of the war.

Wright had wandered too far from his original premises, how-

---

[24] *Modern Age,* VII (Aug. 1865), 20–21; VII (Jan. 1866), 99.
[25] *Liberator,* July 29, 1853, p. 4.

ever, to reassert the doctrine in terms of divine commands. Only about five pages of *The Self-Abnegationist*, which he published in 1863, consider religious arguments, and these pages are concerned only with the life of Jesus. The Old Testament was worthless; Jesus by preaching self-denial had conquered the world. Unlike the Progressive Group, Wright avoided schemes of progress. "There is no new truth; all truth is old as Creation, old as God is. . . . Truth is discovered by men, and expressed in words, and to them it is new; but in the age of Creation, there is no age to truth." Examples were Newton and gravity, Galileo and the solar system, the Declaration of Independence and equal rights, Garrison and immediate emancipation. No historical questions about the New Testament mattered: "The record of principles is there, and I am to judge of them without any regard to the question, how they came there." Human nature spontaneously perceived the truth of the preaching of Jesus.[26]

Wright conspicuously failed to use the term nonresistance. Instead he favored "self-abnegation," meaning "SUFFER RATHER THAN INFLICT SUFFERING; DIE, RATHER THAN KILL." This was the great antonym of "self-preservation," meaning "INFLICT RATHER THAN ENDURE SUFFERING; KILL RATHER THAN DIE." By renouncing absolute Scriptural authority he was obliged to stake his faith on human nature. In 1863 he already seemed to feel the threat of the alternative science of human nature known as social Darwinism:

Self-preservation may be the first law of Nature as embodied in sharks and hyenas; but man is not, by nature, a shark, nor a hyena; but a man or a woman, distinct from, and above all animated existencies [*sic*] beneath him; made so more by this one law of his being than by any other attribute. Self-preservation, at the expense of others, is condemned by universal consciousness. . . . Let any man, whatever be his moral or intellectual development, fully understand the meaning of self-abnegation and then enter into the sacred and silent depths

[26] Wright, *The Self-Abnegationist, or The True King and Queen* (Boston, 1863), pp. 49–52.

of his own soul, and he will find this to be an abiding law of his nature, to which he will find his heaven in being obedient.

As though he anticipated the translation of economics into biology, Wright defended self-abnegation in the terminology of "supply and demand." Because God's commands are revealed to man only through the laws of his nature, to obey God perfectly was to sate one's physical and spiritual demands totally. And to sate oneself, in Wright's conception of natural law, was to deny oneself. Wright's "grand secret of all social order and Harmony" was not very different from Adam Smith's (Scottish moral philosophy long before had embraced the paradox that altruism was a form of self-gratification).[27]

As a nonresistant analysis of the war *The Self-Abnegationist* was packed with inconsistencies. For example, John Brown had been praised for his disinterested benevolence. Wright was compelled to include him among the exemplars of self-abnegation. "Not John Brown the warrior, but John Brown the martyr; not John Brown in military array and armed with pike and gun, but John Brown 'WORTH INCONCEIVABLY MORE TO HANG THAN FOR ANY OTHER PURPOSE,' is the hero of Harper's Ferry; a king among men." Moreover, the death of young men on the battlefield could be regarded as a triumph of self-sacrifice: "What grandeur and glory, what kingly and queenly majesty in this self-abnegation of twenty millions of men and women to preserve and perpetuate a government based on the great self-evident truth, that 'all men are created equal' in regard to natural rights!" Wright tried to repair the damage to nonresistance in his argument with a series of modifications. It was unjust to require sacrifice to preserve an institution; it would harm posterity to have complied with the requirement; patriotism contains "the concentrated selfishness of sectarianism." But repair was impossible: "As their highest light assures them that the demand and their compliance are just, the self-abnegation is none the less sublime." This magnanimous judgment was specifically restricted

27 *Ibid.*, pp. 12–14, 23, 25–29.

to the people of the North.[28] Self-abnegation, furthermore, indicated the evil of slaveholding. But it was also possible to respect the slave as an epitome of self-abdication. Not surprisingly, therefore, Wright's restatement of nonresistance is mainly silent on the subjects of the war and slavery.

Since war and slavery failed to fit his categories, what was left for Wright to discuss in these years of conflict? He dwelt on episodes of personal heroism, the sailor vigilant for the welfare of infants, and Grace Darling, the lighthouse keeper's daughter risking her life for victims of a shipwreck.[29] He returned adoringly to images of family life. Though he briefly criticized civil marriage, his chief purpose was to honor the tenderness of parents and children for one another. And he made this significant admission:

In contemplating the relations of human beings, in the family, or in the general society, I instinctively and of necessity, think of the relation of man to woman, and of woman to man, and never of man to man, nor of woman to woman; of the relation of husbands and wives, fathers and daughters, mothers and sons, brothers and sisters; not of father and sons, mothers and daughters, and sisters and sisters. Relations between those of the same sex have an influence, but never so endearing, so refining, so ennobling, nor so potential, as those that exist between persons of the opposite sex.[30]

Surrounded by the manly horrors of war, Wright was trying to live the conventional fantasies of the sentimental novel. Surely he was not alone in drowning out the war with sentiment, but he could not reassert nonresistance from such a viewpoint. There had always been a sentimental quality to Wright's thought, alongside his obedience to the divine government. Now, however, sentimentalism helped him to accept the havoc of earthly warfare.

Wright's sentimental evasions, in other words, prevented him from a consistent intellectual reaction to public issues. He was

[28] Wright, *Self-Abnegationist*, pp. 95–96, 112–113.
[29] *Ibid.*, pp. 92–94.
[30] *Ibid.*, p. 56.

able to join Garrison in demanding the use of the war power against slavery. Once he had urged secession from the supposedly proslavery Constitution; now that the South found the union a threat to slavery, he was willing to take his cues from their suspicions. "THE CONSTITUTION AND ABOLITION—ONE AND INSEPARABLE," was his new motto.[31]

Since Lysander Spooner had championed the Constitution as an antislavery weapon and had plotted armed assaults on the South, he might have been in his glory during the war. Senator Charles Sumner, for instance, while advocating the amendment that outlawed slavery, insisted that the institution had always been unconstitutional. Sumner's premises could all have been taken from Spooner's prewar writings: the absence of the word "slave" in the document; the purposes established in the preamble; and the guarantee of republican liberty in the Fifth Amendment. The way in which the courts applied the Constitution was crucial to Sumner's antislavery program, as it had been to Spooner's. Sumner argued for a new amendment on the grounds that republics need great calamities to purify them and carry them back to their "baptismal vows"; here was no new departure.[32] But Spooner could not abide this program, for all its resemblance to one that he had formerly championed. As Henry C. Wright advanced toward the constitutional purposes of the North, Spooner retreated.

He remained silent until the question arose of the treason of the people of the Confederacy. The war had been waged, in his opinion, "not to liberate the slaves, but by a government that had always perverted and violated the Constitution, to keep the slaves in bondage; and was still willing to do so, if the slaveholders could be thereby induced to stay in the Union." Consequently there was only one principle at stake in the war: "That men may rightfully be compelled to submit to, and support, a government that they do not want; and that resistance, on their part, makes

[31] *Liberator*, Nov. 15, 1861, p. 3.
[32] Charles Sumner, *No Property in Man* (New York, 1864), pp. 3, 5, 7, 15, 19.

them traitors and criminals." This principle Spooner would gladly
see defeated. "If it be really established," he complained, then
"the number of slaves, instead of having been diminished by the
war, has been greatly increased; for a man, thus subjected to a
government that he does not want, is a slave." Political and
chattel slavery alike deprived men of ownership of their persons
and placed their economic productivity at the discretion of others.
Before the war, he had thought American government to be
admirably free in theory, if not in practice. The war jeopardized
even its theoretical innocence.[33]

Spooner went to great lengths, therefore, to reassert the theory
of free government as distinct from political slavery. The necessary basis of freedom was consent, *"the separate, individual consent of every man who is required to contribute, either by
taxation or personal service, to the support of the government."*
The notion of treason referred only to deceit with regard to
specific contracts between a person and a government. In this
view, government occupied the status of a firm, or a church, or
one of the antebellum reform societies:

All governments, the worst on earth, and the most tyrannical on earth,
are free governments to that portion of the people who voluntarily
support them. And all governments—though the best on earth in other
respects—are nevertheless tyrannies to that portion of the people—
whether few or many—who are compelled to support them against
their will. A government is like a church, or any other institution, in
these respects. There is no criterion whatever, by which to determine
whether a government is a free one, or not, than the single one of its
depending, or not depending, solely on voluntary support.

Government had been so conceived before the war by abolitionists as diverse as Wendell Phillips and Nathaniel P. Rogers. But
now Spooner contended that the United States was committed to
this radical concept by its revolutionary origins. Having acted on

[33] Spooner, *No Treason,* No. 1 (Boston, 1867), pp. iii-iv. In his *Address
of the Free Constitutionalists to the People of the United States* (Boston,
1860), Spooner had denounced the Republican Party for its limited understanding of liberty.

the proposition that government required the consent of the governed, the nation could never breach the promise it had made. There was no way to close off the open-endedness of the proposition.[34]

As he pursued this logic further, this erstwhile vindicator of the Constitution concluded that it had "no inherent authority or obligation." Through a belabored application to the Constitution of the technicalities of the law of contracts, he attempted to show that no one is properly authorized as an agent of any of the people of the United States. The relationship between the government and the people, therefore, was precisely that of master and slave. The war was, at best, an insane effort to impose on others a form of subjugation that the people of the North ought in their own self-interest to resist. As far as the pretense of fighting against slavery was concerned:

If their object had really been to abolish slavery, or maintain liberty or justice generally, they had only to say: All, whether white or black, who want the protection of this government, shall have it; and all who do not want it, will be left in peace, so long as they leave us in peace. Had they said this, slavery would necessarily have been abolished at once; the war would have been saved; and a thousand times nobler union than we have ever had would have been the result.

In a sad, brief appendix Spooner remembered that, although the Constitution had never properly been adopted as a contract among the framers or their contemporaries, let alone their posterity, he once had believed the document intrinsically commendable. But did it really matter whether it was as good as he had thought? Either it authorized the tyranny which now held power "or has been powerless to prevent it. In either case, it is unfit to exist."[35]

[34] Spooner, *No Treason*, No. 1, p. 11; No. 2 (Boston, 1867), pp. 12–13, and *passim*.

[35] Spooner, *No Treason*, No. 6, *The Constitution of No Authority* (reprint ed., Larkspur, Col., 1966), esp. pp. 53–55. This number was first published in 1870; according to the introduction by James J. Martin (p. 4), numbers 3–5 never appeared.

The ironies in this development may easily be overdrawn.[36] Even when he promoted the idea that slavery contravened the law of the land, Spooner had refused to associate himself with the political parties of abolitionism. He had favored judicial attacks on slavery and other self-regulating antislavery activities that did not involve expansion of governmental power. Moreover, he had appealed to the law of the nation in the same way he might indicate to a Mohammedan the good in the Koran. At most Reconstruction taught him to retract this concession to the right of private judgment. Like Henry C. Wright, he believed ballots to be deadly substitutes for bullets and preferred the workings of what he called natural law. But Wright, in wandering close to Spooner's type of deism, had fallen into sentimental incoherence. Spooner, in the end, tightened up his philosophy so that it was at least consistent with itself. Though a great deal of general influence cannot be claimed for him, he did become one of the patrons of the postbellum anarchist movement in America.[37]

[36] Thus Martin (*ibid.*, p. 57n.) juxtaposes Spooner's previous support of the Constitution with his sharp "assaulting" of it and explains that he may have been "influenced" by his "fellow townsman William Lloyd Garrison," who considered it a covenant with death. Frederickson (*Inner Civil War*, pp. 188–189) characterizes Spooner as a "moderate" when he believed in the unconstitutionality of slavery and then as "a radical of the Garrison type" whose renunciation of the Constitution signified awareness that history had bypassed his generation. These kinds of misinterpretation have been fostered by the oversimplified treatments of the schism in the American Anti-Slavery Society discussed in Ch. 6, above.

[37] Spooner corresponded with many Southerners after the war and tried to promote interest in voluntary economic institutions, particularly banks, as the basis of Reconstruction. See, for example, K. Raynor to Spooner, Raleigh, N.C., May 4, 1867; John A. Thomson to Spooner, Summit Point, West Virginia "so called," Sept. 7, Sept. 30, 1871; Dec. 17, 1877, Spooner Papers, NYHS. The issue between Spooner and other abolitionists was clearly defined in a letter to him from Elizur Wright (Boston, Apr. 10, 1866, *ibid.*). Wright favored a vigilant army and the attraction of capital; Spooner favored an end to occupation and the emergence of local institutions.

iv

If older nonresistants were baffled during war and excluded from the reforms afterward, one nonresistant in the 1870s was at the center of New England labor reform. He was Ezra H. Heywood, another inspiration to the anarchist movement. As soon as he was graduated from Brown University, Heywood had joined the Garrisonian wing of antislavery. He quickly became president of a local society as well as a touring lecturer. He also advertised his desire for lyceum engagements to pay debts incurred in his education; his topic would be "Individualism and Institutionalism," and he was recommended by Harriet Beecher Stowe and Wendell Phillips. Before long he was general agent of the Massachusetts Anti-Slavery Society.[38]

Heywood forthrightly took the side of those who opposed political involvement, especially with the Republican Party. He favored the old argument that, since politics can never transcend the prejudices of the people, true reform could hardly be political. No matter how few its adherents, the business of a reform was to circulate ideas. And abolitionism inherited mighty ideas. "The Anti-Slavery enterprise," he told his audiences, "is the lineal and legitimate descendant of Plymouth Rock, the youngest born of Martin Luther. 'No Union with Slaveholders' is the inevitable corollary to 'All men are created free and equal.'" The downfall of slavery promised to be a grand lesson in "the omnipotence of ideas." Both the Reformation and the Revolution already had displayed the power of seceding from evil in the name of great ideas. Similarly empowered, abolitionists could trust in "the religious sentiment of the masses, in a redeemed, regenerated public opinion, in the *vox populi* converted into the *vox Dei*." The fear of free speech "in the dovecotes of authority" attested to the power of this weapon for reform.[39] Here was a remarkable exception to the tendency of enthusiastic young abolitionists in the 1850s to favor physical force.

[38] Pillsbury, *Acts*, p. 490; *Liberator*, Oct. 22, 1858, p. 3; Nov. 5, 1858, pp. 1, 3; Nov. 12, 1858, p. 3.
[39] *Ibid.*, Feb. 4, 1859, p. 2; July 15, 1859, pp. 2–3.

Even more remarkably, Heywood remained loyal to nonresistance throughout the war. He cheered Hopedale with a speech on "Moral Agitation" in April 1861 and again, after two years of respectful silence, when the *Liberator* published his address on the "War Method of Peace."[40] He was troubled that nonresistance was a forgotten phrase. Frankly revering Garrison as the greatest name since Luther, Heywood still could not see how the war could advance the purposes of antislavery. It was inevitable— slavery or not—that the states should separate; this would facilitate economic progress everywhere. But the cause of the Negro needed the moral influences that nonresistants had once advocated. Of course, he was speaking in vain. Garrison simply noted that "there is 'a time to keep silent,' as well as 'a time to speak,' and . . . while the whirlwind, the earthquake and the fire of civil war are in full operation it is not possible for 'the still, small voice' of non-resistance to be heard." George W. Stacy, who once had been a leader at Hopedale and then one of its severest critics, attacked Heywood for delighting the "hunkers." Abstractly nonresistance was correct, but "if man in an unregenerate state will fight, can we refrain from the desire that they will fight on the side of freedom?"[41]

By this time Heywood was veering close to Spooner's viewpoint. The people at Hopedale, he said, were wiser than advocates of the war power; they knew that "war is impolitic and unnecessary because it is sinful and unchristian." But perhaps even they did not go far enough. "Are they aware that this effort to force government on unwilling states, this making a desolation of the South to call it peace, is also politically wrong and inexpedient? The true basis of democracy, 'self-evident' in '76, is the consent of the governed." The right of secession was consequently basic to all other rights.[42] It was this belief that marked Heywood off from his nonresistant predecessors. In their infatuation with

[40] *Spiritual Reformer,* III (May 1861), 7; *Progressive Age,* V (Sept. 1863), 34.
[41] *Liberator,* July 17, 1863, pp. 2, 4; July 31, 1863, p. 4.
[42] *Progressive Age,* VI (Sept. 1864), 37–38.

disunionism and their discussions of the Constitution, their moral separatism provided no reliable political insight. The argument for a Northern republic contained no principle for them to apply to the prerogatives of the South.

Heywood's role in antislavery has largely been overlooked. He was, in fact, a direct link between Garrisonism and postwar radicalism; he was also a link with other antebellum traditions. He was turned in new directions by the visit to Boston in 1863 of Josiah Warren, the prewar anarchist.[43] About the time that Heywood was dissociating himself from war-power abolitionists, the individual sovereigns of Modern Times sailed from Long Island to South America to escape the evils of fighting, taxation, and conscription.[44] But Heywood remained to reinterpret Warren's message, which he took to be a restatement of the Declaration of Independence. Most important, he became devoted to the organization of workingmen; he was the principal instigator of the New England Labor Reform League. Heywood's chief historical notoriety, however, derives from the fact that as his newspaper, *The Word,* got increasingly involved in free love he became a leading target of the Comstock laws. His rights were defended by such varied reformers as Elizabeth Cady Stanton, Andrew Jackson Davis, and Theodore Dwight Weld, but after much litigation he served two years in prison. Although Heywood's career after the war is intrinsically interesting, it is sufficient for our purposes to list the organizations, besides the labor reform leagues, in which he was a guiding figure: American Anti-Usury Society, Universal Peace Union, American Spiritualist Association, Boston Eight-Hour League, American Free Dress League, New England Anti-Death Society, and New England Free Love League.[45]

The wave of violent railroad strikes in 1877 impressed Heywood much as the Civil War had overwhelmed other abolitionists. In *The Great Strike,* he revealed the extent to which he was still governed by the ideas of the antislavery movement. Before he

---

[43] Martin, *Men against the State,* p. 110.
[44] Conway, "Modern Times, New York," p. 434.
[45] Martin, *Men against the State,* pp. 117–118, 122–124, 136n.

had carefully studied "the property question," he explained, "George L. Stearns, a prominent anti-slavery merchant of Boston, . . . startled me by remarking: 'There is nothing more to be said for capital than for slavery.' " Whatever ideas he had gained from abolitionists, his rhetoric owed a great debt to antislavery evangelism ("Labor Reform is simply an anti-theft movement; all it asks is that people have intelligence enough to know what stealing is, and character enough to keep their hands off of other people's property"). Repeatedly he tried to identify the similarity of slavery and capitalism. To be sure, labor was "bound by subtler chains than of old," but the compulsions created by monopoly control of land, transportation, currency, and government meant that slavery was still the prevailing system of labor. "What whips, revolvers, and blood-hounds were to chattel bondage, usurped control of raw materials and the means of exchange . . . is to the profit system." Just as slavery was called the natural condition of Negroes, poverty was considered inevitable for working people. But "when the laws which gave whites State-force to hold their vassals were nullified, negroes became anti-slaves," and in a new conflict poverty would also be exposed as an artificial condition.[46]

This reinterpretation of slavery, however, had little to do with nonresistance. In fact, Heywood now admitted that the war ended slavery, as he once had denied was possible. He proceeded to exonerate the destructiveness of rioters by pointing out that adjacent private property was scrupulously respected while wicked corporation property was burned. Here was a case, like the Boston Tea Party and John Brown's raid, of "moral discrimination guiding a retributive tornado." He was personally a nonresistant; he belonged to organizations which opposed strikes, legislative action, and "trades-union monopolies of labor" and preached that reforms could never be advanced by force. Nonresistance had been born out of disputes over defensive war. But

[46] Heywood, *The Great Strike: Its Relations to Labor, Property, and Government* (Princeton, Mass., 1878), pp. 2, 4–5n.

Heywood now took advantage of the logic Garrison employed after Harper's Ferry: "Impartial observers recognize the Pittsburgh strikers as morally lawful belligerents, and concede to them all the rights of defensive warfare." The very idea that Garrison in wrongly combating secession freed four million slaves made it seem plausible that the strikers in wrongly demanding a kind of monopoly might be on the side of progress. But one suspects that Heywood trembled at his own accommodation. He writes vaguely of "the Logic of Events," inscrutably using John Brown or the Mollie McGuires to suit its purposes. And he praised any militiaman refusing to fire on the rioters as the *"Non-Resistant soldier."*[47]

Other American anarchists had interesting connections with antislavery. Dyer Lum, who took over the *Alarm* from Albert Parsons during the Haymarket tempest, was descended from the Tappan family. He reformulated a familiar argument: exploitation, in place of slavery, was the image of strife; and anarchism, in place of abolitionism, was the secret of peace.[48] William B. Greene, educated at West Point and the Harvard Divinity School, "mercilessly opinionated" according to his classmate Thomas Wentworth Higginson, and representative of "Demonic Man" to his friend Bronson Alcott, developed a theory of unregulated banking and found a French authority for it when he met Proudhon. Like Spooner, Greene illustrates how anarchism combined the concerns of abolitionism with those of the banking controversy of the 1830s. It is worth noting that Garrison, who related money shortages to a border ruffian government, in 1857 had commended Greene's theories.[49] And, of course, Stephen Pearl Andrews and Lysander Spooner, two of the most prominent individualist anarchists, had both labored in the abolition move-

[47] *Ibid.*, pp. 13–15, 20.

[48] Voltairine de Cleyre, "Dyer D. Lum," *The Freethinkers' Magazine*, XI (1893), 497–501. Lum was also Samuel Gompers' secretary; see Schuster, *Native American Anarchism*, p. 168n.

[49] Higginson, *Cheerful Yesterdays*, pp. 106–107, 174–175; Shepard, *Pedlar's Progress*, p. 240; Rocker, *Pioneers of American Freedom*, p. 102; *Liberator*, Nov. 20, 1857, p. 2.

ment. All this evidence notwithstanding, the country after the war wanted to believe that anarchism had no native roots.

v

There can be no doubt that American anarchism, even if we ignore foreign-language movements, drew heavily on European sources. By the end of the nineteenth century, the philosophical spokesman for the movement, Benjamin R. Tucker, referred often to Proudhon, Stirner, or Tolstoy and almost never to Garrison. Born in 1854, Tucker was barely exposed to the excitement of antislavery. Yet in his sketch of his own character he chose to emphasize his boyhood in New Bedford, "a community noted for the important part that it played in the long struggle for the abolition of slavery." He heard "very radical" preaching in the Unitarian church, and at the lyceum his mind was stirred by Phillips, Garrison, Emerson, and Anna Dickinson. The newspapers of Horace Greeley and Theodore Tilton also figured in his wanderings among atheism, materialism, evolutionism, prohibitionism, free trade, the eight-hour day, woman's suffrage, and antimarriage before he reached the age of eighteen. Then "a lucky combination of influences" straightened out his enthusiastic confusion, and he became "the consistent anarchist that I have remained unto this day." For one thing, he chanced to meet Josiah Warren. Perhaps more important, he was seduced by Victoria Woodhull, the beautiful lecturer on free love to whom he came as a youthful admirer.[50]

We have been observing continuities from abolitionism in the most rational, primarily economic thought of anarchism. The career of Victoria Woodhull[51] fulfilled the more exotic potential of the anarchistic ideas in antislavery. Furthermore, she seems to

[50] Emanie Sachs, *"The Terrible Siren": Victoria Woodhull (1838–1927)* (New York, 1928), pp. 239–266; Charles A. Madison, *Critics and Crusaders* (New York, 1947–1948), pp. 194–195.

[51] I have followed Sachs, *"The Terrible Siren,"* throughout the following paragraphs, except where otherwise noted. See also Johanna Johnston, *Mrs. Satan: The Incredible Saga of Victoria C. Woodhull* (New York, 1967).

have linked together most of the strains of anarchism in mid-Victorian America. Her speeches were written by Stephen Pearl Andrews, and Tucker met her through Ezra H. Heywood.

She came out of the Midwest as a touring spiritualist after the war, with her equally beautiful sister, Tennessee Claflin. Under the patronage of Cornelius Vanderbilt, the sisters became New York's most notorious stockbrokers. Soon Victoria went to Washington to tell a congressional committee that the amendment enfranchising the black man had also enfranchised women. Of the legislators she persuaded only Ben Butler, but she captivated the woman's rights movement. For a time she officiated at both feminist and spiritualist conventions, as part of her unending campaign to be elected President of the United States (Frederick Douglass was supposedly her running mate). Theodore Tilton, an important abolitionist editor, fell wildly in love with her, gave her a fantastic biography, then regretted his headlong behavior. When she learned that Henry Ward Beecher, the nation's most famous minister, carried on an extramarital romance with Tilton's wife, she tried to blackmail Beecher into introducing one of her speeches on free love. In 1872 her newspaper, *Woodhull and Claflin's Weekly*, featured the delicious story, diagnosing Beecher as a great man rightly impelled by amativeness. One of the most spectacular trials in American history ensued.[52]

The theme with which Victoria Woodhull mesmerized postwar America was: "I would rather be the labor slave of a master, with his whip cracking continually about my ears than the forced sexual slave of any man a single hour." That is, the only sexual crime is "sexual intercourse obtained by force," either in prostitution or in marriage. To this theme she added bizarre promises that in "a perfected sexuality shall continuous life be found." Therefore the "mission of spiritualism" was identical to "the sexual emancipation of woman, and her return to *self-ownership*."

[52] On the Tilton-Beecher scandal, see Constance Mayfield Rourke, *Trumpets of Jubilee: Henry Ward Beecher, Harriet Beecher Stowe, Lyman Beecher, Horace Greeley, P. T. Barnum* (New York, 1927), pp. 191–225; and Robert Shaplen, *Free Love and Heavenly Sinners* (New York, 1954).

If this message was sometimes incoherent (she contrasted materialism and spirituality in love), audiences must have preferred it that way. In any event, she was speaking in a familiar idiom. Though we may suspect her practice from her seduction of Tucker, her theory repudiated promiscuity: "Freedom does not mean anarchy in the social relations any more than it does in religion and politics." Would there be an increase in the number of illegitimate children? "You are shouldering on free love the results that flow from precisely its antithesis, which is the spirit, if not the letter of your marriage theory, which is slavery and not freedom." She had the candid respect of many of her antagonists, while Henry Ward Beecher, who was adjusting Christianity to the findings of science, had their contempt. One of Beecher's brothers wrote during the trial: "In my judgment Henry is following his slippery doctrines of expediency, and in the cry of progress and nobleness of nature, has sacrificed clear, exact integrity. . . . Of the two, Woodhull is my hero, and Henry my coward. . . . I was not anti-slavery; I am not anti-family."[53]

As if her time did not pass spectacularly enough, Victoria Woodhull organized an American section of the International Workingmen's Association. In this endeavor her chief ally was William West, a land reformer who before the war had dismissed abolitionism as an inadequate response to the general problem of enslaved labor, but who had hailed Nathaniel P. Rogers as the "advocate of the freest speech."[54] Their section of the International advocated woman's suffrage and sexual freedom as well as Stephen Pearl Andrews' pet theories of universal language and "pantarchical" order. To other American sections it was an embarrassment, a bourgeois travesty. In 1872 Karl Marx was troubled by the prospect that the Bakuninists might dominate the movement in Europe. The surest safeguard was to remove international headquarters from London to New York, a strategy de-

[53] Quotations in Sachs, *"The Terrible Siren,"* pp. 129, 133, 189, 219.
[54] *Herald of Freedom,* July 18, 1845, p. 1. For West's views on slavery and nonresistance, see *Liberator,* Sept. 25, 1846, p. 4; Aug. 28, 1846, p. 4.

Epilogue

In working on this topic, I have frequently been aware of possible analogies between the materials I have been studying and developments in the contemporary "new left." Friends and colleagues, differing widely in their political opinions, have remarked on the timeliness of the study. A thoughtful review of recent writing on abolitionism, in commenting on a series of articles pursuing the theme of nonviolence, speculated that the authors "have not been unaware of the several tactical choices available to contemporary civil rights advocates."[1] Moreover, at least one recent study of antebellum radicalism frankly described its purposes as partly "unhistorical." Staughton Lynd has admitted his desire to show that the "characteristic concepts of the existential radicalism of today have a long and honorable history"; he has expressed hope that awareness of this tradition may "help in sharpening intellectual tools for the work of tomorrow."[2]

Though I have been aware of analogies, they have shifted dramatically over the past few years. At first they concerned the emergence of nonresistance and related versions of anarchism in abolitionism—in other words, the first half of this book. In the mid-1960s, it sometimes seemed that much of the left was heading toward nonviolent anarchism. This might have been an offshoot of the pacifistic tactics taught by Martin Luther King; there

[1] Merton L. Dillon, "The Abolitionists: A Decade of Historiography, 1959–1969," *Journal of Southern History*, XXXV (1969), 511.

[2] Lynd, *Intellectual Origins*, p. vii.

was also evidence of a "modest upsurge of interest in Anarchism" on the part of young radicals in the North.[3] Much of the rhetoric, if not the motivation, was religious; and all forms of coercion were regularly denounced as forms of slavery. The term "anarchist," which had dropped out of common speech, became once again so emotion-laden that one presidential candidate in the 1968 election widely proclaimed his intention to run over the first anarchist who lay down in front of his automobile. More recently, however, it has been the second half of this study that has seemed to have echoes in our own times. The anarchism and pacifism of the new left have yielded to acts of symbolic violence, intellectual toleration of violence, and vague apocalyptic rhetoric. It is tempting to see the analogue of spiritualism in psychedelic drugs and consciousness expansion. And it is easy to find parallels to the cries for sexual reform and the emancipation of women which arose from some quarters of abolitionism in the 1850s.

Like most analogies, these comparisons between abolitionism and the new left have some explanatory value, but they overlook aspects of past experience which have no modern counterpart. In short, they underestimate the importance of historical change.

It would be difficult to ignore analogies between the tribulations of the abolitionists and those of our time. To ignore them would require an insensitivity and lack of curiosity that would hinder historical understanding rather than assist it; there can be no question that commitments to the civil rights and antiwar struggles of the 1960s—though not necessarily uncritical commitments—helped to inspire a number of historians to conduct a major re-examination of the purposes and achievements of the abolitionists. It is not unlikely that the unfolding agony of the American left may continue to suggest new perspectives on reformist and radical groups before the holocaust of the Civil War.[4]

[3] Martin B. Duberman, "Anarchism Left and Right," *Partisan Review*, XXXIII (1965), 610–615. See also Jack Newfield, "The Question of SNCC," *Nation*, CCI (July 19, 1965), 38–40.

[4] See John Rosenberg, "Toward a New Civil War Revisionism," *American Scholar*, XXXVIII (1969), 250–272.

Nevertheless, I am wary of the notion of an intellectual tradition of American radicalism, and I question the authenticity of intellectual connections between present-day and antebellum radicals. Mythological needs may be served in making such connections, but historical accuracy may well be forfeited.

In important ways radicals have been bound by the prevailing ideals and values of the cultural period in which they lived and which furnished their vocabularies. Even when rejecting some of the assumptions of their contemporaries or improvising creatively in the vocabularies they received, they have sometimes confined their options and defined alternatives for themselves in ways that have had none of the binding force of tradition for subsequent radicals. In any case, the radical abolitionists seem to me culturally quite remote from most of the new left.

Of course, there have been important continuities in the cultural values of Americans. But there have also been important periods of transformation, one of which surrounded the Civil War. Radical antislavery is more valuable for the clues it holds for an understanding of the time in which it occurred than for delineating a tradition of American radicalism. If any tradition was involved, it was one which scarcely survived its own era. Most of what survived either underwent extensive revision or began to seem conservative and fundamentalist in later times.

ii

The cultural remoteness of the abolitionists from the modern left should be apparent from even a brief recapitulation of the principal themes in the preceding chapters. One thing we may learn, I believe, from almost any successful study in intellectual history is simply to appreciate the freedom of our choices in the present as we gain insight into the ways in which other men and women have limited their options in the past. Knowledge of this kind may perhaps aid radicals in sharpening their intellectual tools for the work of the future, but its relevance is not restricted to radicals. It is human knowledge.

To recapitulate, then, it was argued at the outset of this book

that abolitionists tended toward anarchism because of their opposition in principle to slavery. Again and again, we have seen that
when abolitionists took an anarchistic position they tended to
argue in this form: whoever does not go all the way with us is,
in effect, in league with slavery. Slavery became a paradigm of
human authority, of any state in which the standing of one man
with respect to another was secured by force. The only consistent
antislavery, then, was anarchism. Even in this abstract analysis,
however, there appeared one important source of ambivalence.
In one sense slavery was wrong because it was the government
of man by force, but in another sense it was wrong because it
was a government of insufficient force. That is, government by
force did not work. It did not keep the peace. It led to the multi-
plying use of force, not to anarchism in the good sense of harmonious self-government but to anarchy in the bad sense of lawlessness and pandemonium.

This ambivalence becomes more understandable when we
study the New England Non-Resistance Society. Originating
within an antiwar movement, this society insisted on the Christian doctrine that violence should never be resisted with violence. Just as anarchism alone consistently opposed slavery, it
was said that no opposition to war would be consistent and uncompromising unless it repudiated all manifestations of force. It
does not seem strange that it was the abolitionists, of all the
opponents of war, who seceded into anarchism. But the origins
of nonresistance were slightly more complicated. In the background were millenarian and perfectionist strains of thought
within revivalism that had been best articulated by John Humphrey Noyes. When they broke out from the narrowness of the
peace movement, abolitionists were responding to the perfectionist claim that any human government was a challenge to the
commanding authority of God. To end war and slavery—to end
anarchy in the bad sense of lawlessness—the guiding strategy was
to abolish human government and to institute the government
of God. The precept of nonviolence had been construed narrowly
by the Quakers as they moderated the ecstasies of the Reforma-

tion; now that same precept had led others back into its radical past.

In a word, nonresistance was millennial. The millennium, variously as it may be conceived in detail, is the government of God. It has also been useful to call nonresistance antinomian in order to indicate that its view of the progress of the millennium precluded support for intermediary authorities between God and the individual moral agent. Attacks on governors, soldiers, and religious officials were not extraneous to the attack on slaveholding, as Garrison's critics charged, once it was felt that the true objective was the millennium. All human authorities were extraneous to that exalted period to come.

The most important source of ambivalence, then, was this antinomian emphasis on the pre-emptive sovereignty of God. Until the time of the millennium, it could reasonably be asked, would not the renunciation of human authorities contribute to that very lawlessness to which the millennium was theoretically opposed? There were a few coherent answers to this question—particularly in Adin Ballou's faith that the means of introducing the millennium must not contradict the end for which they were supposedly designed. But the point is that such answers were few and were disregarded. For the most part, nonresistant abolitionism sought to be both a harbinger of the millennium and a secular reform movement. When come-outers and no-organizationists pursued the antinomian argument to what appear to be quite logical conclusions, the leading Garrisonians were appalled. In the ensuing struggle the heart of New England abolitionism was rent, but the errors of the no-organizationists could not be explained. Faced with the possibility that a temporal reform movement, however dedicated to ending slavery in the South, might well be a violation of God's authority over individuals, the Garrisonians assailed those who brought the possibility to light. At this point a potential contradiction was made real and irremediable. Thereafter abolitionists were less certain of their attitude toward human authorities, and the millennium came to seem less imminent.

In the 1850s the anarchistic denunciation of force was silenced,

I have argued that the silencing was due less to influences outside the movement than to internal contradictions—the very contradictions just summarized. In the first place, a secular reform
concerned with slavery had to assign some role to the slave. From
a millennial perspective it might have been possible to argue that
perfect love would vanquish the masters, that an immediate assertion of liberation would loose little tactical violence, or that
in this vale of woes chattel slavery was no worse than any other
bondage. But these viewpoints were not accessible to a secular
reform movement: the problem was that whites owned Negroes,
not that man was alienated from his true ruler. When nonresistance turned to the subject of the rights and duties of the slave,
it doffed any pretense of millenarianism. It exonerated the slave
of guilt in possible acts of violence, and ultimately it exhorted
him to violence thus excused.

Second, and more significantly, the sovereignty of God implied
the right of private judgment on the part of every individual
moral agent. And this right entailed responsibility to act out
whatever was privately judged to be true and holy. The right of
private judgment theoretically did not extend to goals (these
were still tacitly assumed to be millennial, insofar as anything
made sense any more); it extended only to the choice of alternative means. Nevertheless, the general goal of ending force became
less important than the specific goal of ending one manifestation
of force: slavery. In terms of the antislavery struggle this meant
that nonresistants could beseech others to take up arms in the
cause of the slave. They could finally solicit the government to
obey its best lights and to end slavery by force, which had once
seemed a contradiction in terms. Now antislavery entered into an
awkward, contradictory partnership in that very work.

In foreshortened form, this is the argument that unifies this
book. Comments on other movements, distinct from nonresistance
but related to antislavery, serve to fill out the argument. Come-
outerism and no-organizationism clarified the paradox of antinomian abolitionism: law and order could be established only by
terminating human efforts to enforce these virtues. Political aboli-

tionism, on the other hand, feared the antinomianism of the Garrisonians. But the fact that it was political did not mean that it compromised principles or believed in governmental coercion as the remedy for sin. On the contrary, it agreed with the Garrisonians that an effective end to slavery had to be voluntary. It prized independent political action chiefly as a method of registering individual moral commitments. Independent parties and local congregations were, in other words, vanguards of the millennium, exerting moral influence but eschewing secular compulsions. Political abolitionists, then, yearned to build some institutions in the vastness between man and the divine sovereign. But although they feared antinomianism, they drew many of the same conclusions from evangelicalism as did the Garrisonians.

We have also seen that not all of the anarchistic aspects of antislavery got lost in the right of private judgment. There is evidence that the desire to supersede human authority led to receptiveness to the authority of spiritualism. Here was a way of introducing superior authorities that did not ostensibly rely on human force. Often this tendency appeared to be a mad reaction to the bewildering void between self-sovereignty and divine sovereignty. We may guess that this alternative grew more attractive after the Civil War wrote an end to anarchism; at least one might believe in a gradual spiritualistic progress of civilization toward peace.

Whether this alternative was followed or not, anarchism seemed a complete failure in its own time. The Civil War was taken to be hideous proof that nonresistance was out of phase with reality. God waged the Civil War; maybe thereafter would come a dispensation when men could bring on the millennium by ending war and government as well as slavery. Of course that time did not come. By the century's end, Tolstoy was frustrated to discover that scarcely an American remembered that any abolitionists had been anarchists.

iii

Anarchism among the abolitionists inherited much from evangelicalism, Puritanism, and the Reformation. But it left almost no

legacy to the generations who followed. We have noticed a few
continuities—but those left by failure, evasions and drastic revisions. Abolitionism as a whole may be counted as a failure in
regard to its dream of racial equality in America;[5] but it was not
without some influence on the religious hagiography of the Civil
War, for example, or on the continuing efforts of groups of whites
to aid and educate Negroes, or even on the agitation of white
workers for an end to "wage slavery." But little of the anarchistic
tendency to champion the government of God and denounce all
human coercion can be followed beyond Harper's Ferry. Although
we can find partial analogies between antislavery radicalism and
certain controversial aspects of the new left in the 1960s, I doubt
that we can speak of a legacy or tradition. There is no evidence
that anarchistic beliefs were handed down from one generation
to the next; and there is little evidence of modern anarchists
seeking to recover a legitimate, anarchistic tradition in the history
of abolitionism.

Perhaps American culture has generally been fertile ground for
anarchistic styles of radicalism. American anarchists have often
maintained that their beliefs were derived from native traditions.
They have been compelled to state this conviction because anarchism has often been attacked for being un-American, for being
the product of alien ideologies, for being the mania of immigrant
assassins. Consequently anarchists have been anxious to stress
the native traditions supporting their beliefs, but almost never
have they mentioned the antebellum abolitionists. Instead they
have invariably gone back to the American Revolution—and particularly to Thomas Jefferson. In 1893, Benjamin R. Tucker explained that anarchists were "simply unterrified Jeffersonian Dem-
ocrats."[6] In 1901, Henry Bool wrote an *Apology for His Jeffersonian Anarchism.*[7] In 1914, Voltairine de Cleyre published a

[5] See Merton L. Dillon, "The Abolitionists as a Dissenting Minority," in
Alfred F. Young, ed., *Dissent: Explorations in the History of American
Radicalism* (DeKalb, Ill., 1968), pp. 83–108.

[6] Tucker, *Instead of a Book, by a Man Too Busy to Write One* (New
York, 1893), p. 14.

[7] *Henry Bool's Apology for His Jeffersonian Anarchism* (Ithaca, 1901).

thoughtful essay on "Anarchism and American Traditions," which praised much of the political thought of the Revolution; she was attracted by the beliefs in democratic consent, small government, and the rights of states and local communities. Like Tucker, she suggested that Jeffersonian principles had been compromised by fear: "The sin our fathers sinned was that they did not trust liberty wholly. They thought it possible to compromise between liberty and government, believing the latter to be 'a necessary evil.' "[8]

Throughout the twentieth century some libertarian figures have continued to applaud the republicanism of the founding fathers and regret its demise in the course of American history. A recent study of Albert Jay Nock and "the Anarchist Elitist Tradition in America" has called Nock "an unreconstructed Jeffersonian in an un-Jeffersonian age."[9] Paul Goodman, a modern community anarchist, traced the ideals of community initiative and decentralism back to the eighteenth century, but regarded them as in eclipse after the Jackson period. It is only with the Populists of the 1890s that he found revivals of political attitudes favorable to anarchism.[10] The point is that individualist, elitist, and community anarchists have all claimed ancestry in the Jeffersonian tradition. They have said nothing about the abolitionists.

Regardless of how anarchists have interpreted their lineage, students of the American past have detected several tendencies hospitable to anarchism. It may be well to enumerate these tendencies. Perhaps the first would be the image of an unrestrained, uncoerced, uncommercialized, harmonious, paradisiacal existence which prospered in the earliest descriptions of the New World and recurrently confused westward migration with a search for

[8] Alexander Berkman, ed., *Selected Works of Voltairine de Cleyre* (New York, 1914), pp. 121, 131.

[9] Michael Wreszin, "Albert Jay Nock and the Anarchist Elitist Tradition in America," *American Quarterly*, XXI (1969), 165.

[10] Goodman, "The Sentiment of Powerlessness in American History," in *People or Personnel: Decentralizing and the Mixed System* (New York, 1965), pp. 28–49.

utopia.[11] Second would come the evangelical emphasis on individual striving for grace and the related de-emphasis on secular and collective institutions; from this value system followed a suspicion of earthly intermediaries which has been discussed at length in this study. Third, we should mention the persistence of the Jeffersonian idea that the best government is the smallest government, an idea which for a long time reflected the reality of weak, dispersed political institutions. The Jeffersonian heritage was ambiguous and was used for a great variety of changing and contradictory purposes;[12] one of these uses was to confer legitimacy on anarchistic thought. A fourth relevant tendency is literary rebellion against the values of the genteel tradition. Once again, there has been considerable ambiguity, but literary nonconformity has yielded attacks on all the restraints of civilization. Huck Finn and Jim, on the raft and on the shore, are the best example of tension between freedom and civilization which has run through much of American literature.

A fifth tendency should be added to this list: the tendency of Americans to believe that "individualism" was the secret of their institutions, the factor that made their land unique and exemplary. In Europe, we learn from two recent studies, "individualism" was a pejorative term referring to selfish, antisocial impulses, but it began to acquire new values after Alexis de Tocqueville used it to describe the ideal of behavior celebrated by Americans of the Jacksonian period. As Yehoshua Arieli explains:

Although individualism as a historical and sociological concept was elaborated in Europe, its value-content changed completely with its transplantation to America. The term, which in the Old World was almost synonymous with selfishness, social anarchy, and individual

[11] Cf. Howard Mumford Jones, *O Strange New World; American Culture; The Formative Years* (New York, 1964), ch. I; Arthur K. Moore, *The Frontier Mind* (New York, 1963); R. W. B. Lewis, *The American Adam: Innocence, Tragedy, and Tradition in the Nineteenth Century* (Chicago, 1955).

[12] See Merrill D. Peterson, *The Jefferson Image in the American Mind* (New York, 1962).

self-assertion, connoted in America self-determination, moral freedom, the rule of liberty, and the dignity of man. Instead of signifying a period of transition toward a higher level of social harmony and unity, it came to mean the final stage of human progress.

John William Ward relates the revalution of individualism to a belief in a natural law of society, independent of artificial rules, which permitted celebration of the individualistic, asocial hero.[13] Individualism, as is well known, could excuse indifference to social problems and even cruelty on the part of the rich and powerful, but it could also reveal anarchistic implications. Arieli points out, for example, that the individualistic anarchism of Josiah Warren and his followers was "consciously based on the main tradition of American thought."[14]

No doubt the list could be extended; some of these tendencies, on the other hand, overlap or are stated at different levels of abstraction. It is clear enough that anarchism is not foreign to American thought. Nor is it hard to understand why fear of anarchism has been a recurrent theme in American history. The abolitionists may be taken as a good illustration of the susceptibility of American reformers to anarchism. But only one of the tendencies we have enumerated had much to do with the currents of anarchist thinking among the abolitionists. Each of the tendencies could be shown to have some passing relevance, but only evangelicalism was directly related to key terms and concepts found in the vocabularies of the abolitionist radicals. When abolitionists spoke as anarchists, they seldom referred to paradise, Jeffersonian political theory, the stultifying effect of civilized values, or individualism. But the theological problem of divine sovereignty, as it related to civil government and individual self-government, was of the greatest importance in their thought. The abolitionists represented a significant prebellum attempt to find religious alterna-

[13] Arieli, *Individualism and Nationalism*, p. 189; and Ward, *Red, White, and Blue: Men, Books, and Ideas in American Culture* (New York, 1969), pp. 235–236.

[14] Arieli, *Individualism and Nationalism*, p. 292.

tives to the amoral, Jacksonian cult of popular democracy. Their beliefs unwound into the religion of humanity and the toleration of human coercion even before the war had come.

Echoes of the controversies which surrounded abolitionists may still be heard among theologians. In 1966, for example, the *New York Times* reported on Billy Graham's concern that the World Council of Churches and other Protestant groups have forgotten that social change can proceed only from the "redemptive witness of the Gospel."

The famed evangelist holds that the error being made by many churchmen in trying to cure the ills of society lies in their approaching the task as if society were already made up of "truly Christian men." He does not deny that there are injustices on all sides but holds that they can never be righted as long as men themselves remain spiritually unchanged.

Like many of the Garrisonians, Billy Graham "regards it as naive to expect governments to legislate 'Christian behavior' while hearts go untouched." He points out that Paul passed slaves on the streets while he preached a message that would eventually lead to their freedom. Billy Graham's critics, on the other hand, emphasize that slavery persisted under Christian auspices 1800 years after Paul:

"If Paul had a chance to lobby for an anti-slavery law, I'm pretty sure what he would do," one opponent of Dr. Graham's position said. "I don't think Paul would say, 'Let them stay slaves and in 1500 years or so, we'll get the message across that slavery is bad.'" Another said: "Paul couldn't get away with telling slaves to obey their masters today. Nor can we."[15]

It is curious that the dispute over the Christian remedy for slavery continues long after the abolition of slavery. But the Garrisonian position has come to appear conservative while political recourses appear radical. Billy Graham's views in some ways resemble those which Adin Ballou upheld even in wartime, but he

[15] *New York Times*, Sept. 4, 1966, sect. 4, p. 12.

is so far from being an anarchist that he has become the religious arm of the Nixon administration.

There may not be any anarchistic traditions in American thought; perhaps there have been only a number of traditions which can be mined for anarchistic potential when it suits the needs of reformers who face changing problems. It remains chilling, however, to recall in a period of racial strife that some abolitionists predicted that if a racist society ended slavery by war the result had to be new forms of slavery and prolonged violence. Their legacy is not a set of beliefs passed down to radicals, but a definition of problems which we are still trying to escape. It is sobering to reflect that they canceled out their own testimony as one of the prologues to a cruel civil war.

Appendix

European Anarchism and the Idea of Slavery

In the second chapter I offered the generalization that European anarchism characteristically defined itself by attacking slavery. The purpose of this appendix is to support that generalization by pursuing the meaning of slavery in the thought of four quite different anarchists: Pierre-Joseph Proudhon, Michael Bakunin, Max Stirner, and Leo Tolstoy.

In one respect Proudhon resembled the American abolitionists: he phrased his ideas in terms of shocking metaphorical comparisons which seem less metaphorical the more closely we examine them, for they actually carry the argument. Both Proudhon and the abolitionists, for example, assert that there is no difference between slavery and man-killing; otherwise their moral categories lose effectiveness. But Proudhon was not interested in America's peculiar institution. He wanted to find out why the French people during the Revolution, "when seeking liberty and equality . . . fell back into privilege and slavery." The answer, he concluded, was that they retained private property. To clarify the notion of a free economy, devoid of slavery or privilege, he ruled out the instances of a Negro forfeiting his person, a civilized laborer motivated by fear of starvation, and a consumer governed by irrationality or habit. Economic exchanges were free only where power was evenly divided. Most commonly, transactions were not free because one party controlled property on which the other depended. It followed that "what political economy, speaking in the name of eternal justice, calls *producing by his capital,—producing by his tools*," ought to be called *"producing by a slave,—producing as a thief and a tyrant.*" It was no longer necessary to own a man, or to rub out his official existence, in order to take all he had.[1]

Proudhon relied heavily on the labor theory of value, in its socialist usage of explaining the injustice of one man having power over another's products. He illustrates the ease with which the metaphor of slavery suited that theoretical account of injustice: the value being robbed was in the man who made something, not in the thing itself and not in whatever capital was required. In this way he anticipated the Marxist appeal for workers to unshackle themselves. However, slavery was not simply a metaphor. To define slavery, Proudhon turned to history and the idea of progress: before the establishment of property rights all producers were slaves. The introduction of some property rights made slavery impossible, and serfdom took its place. A further extension of property rights was the triumph of the *bourgeoisie*. And the next stage, the farthest removed from slavery, would be the recognition of every man's possession of what he produces.[2] It is only this last stage that Proudhon evaluated differently from the Marxists. They regarded the possessionary rights to which he looked forward as a vestige of property and slavery. He replied that mass ownership was a fiction; in reality the state would be the grand property holder. And this would "secure universal servitude."[3]

In a sense, then, the first dispute between anarchism and Marxism turned on different understandings of the relationships of property, liberty, and slavery. The importance of the concept of slavery in European radicalism was already established. Both Proudhon and the Marxists spoke of slavery as a timeless metaphorical category and also as an historical bench mark in surveying the failure of previous revolutionary movements. Anything resembling slavery was in fact as odious as slavery.

Michael Bakunin, the anarchist par excellence, discussed slavery even more extensively than Proudhon. It was, in his opinion, the state of nature:

"Man becomes man in reality, he conquers the possibility of a develop-

[1] Proudhon, *What Is Property? An Inquiry into the Principle of Right and of Government,* trans. Benjamin R. Tucker (New York, n.d. [1890]), pp. 36, 133, 210.
[2] *Ibid.,* pp. 352 ff.
[3] Quoted in James Joll, *The Anarchists* (Boston, 1964), p. 81.

ment and internal perfection provided only that he breaks, to some extent at least, the slave-chains which Nature fastened upon its children. Those chains are hunger, privation of all sorts, physical pain, the influence of climate and seasons, and in general, the thousands of conditions of animal life which keep the human being in absolute dependence upon his immediate environment; which in the guise of natural phenomena threaten him on all sides; the perpetual fear which lurks in the depths of all animal existence and which dominates the natural and savage individual to such an extent that he finds within himself no power of struggle or resistance; in other words, not a single element of the most absolute slavery is lacking."

We may sometimes imagine anarchism to have been bent on demolishing civilization so that a primitive Eden might resurrect itself. But Bakunin, at least, viewed civilization as man's endeavor to escape slavery and "to win and realize his freedom to the full."[4]

Bakunin ridiculed Rousseau's "state of innocence" as a period of universal brutality out of which man had advanced only through "progressive intelligence," through a positivistic analysis of "real things and facts" and "their inherent laws." Every stage in this advance was a flight from a new kind of slavery. Thus intelligence first delivered man materially from the slavery of nature. But it delivered him into the hands of religion, which in turn "condemns him to absurdity, and, misdirecting his steps, makes him seek the divine instead of the human." As a result, "peoples who have scarcely freed themselves from natural slavery in which other animal species are deeply sunk, forthwith relapse into a new slavery, into bondage to strong men and castes privileged by divine election." Freedom from this outward form of slavery will be difficult, for there is "a natural inner yoke which man must also learn to shake off." Uneasily aware that his nature is divided, partly still brutal and partly growing toward humanity, man is too prone to make an abstraction of himself. Then he is fettered by his own conceits. The only method of "struggling against this inner slavery," however, is the same scientific objectivity that worked out his material deliverance.[5]

Bakunin's attack on dualism, the inner slavery, is clarified by his

[4] G. P. Maximoff, ed., *The Political Philosophy of Bakunin: Scientific Anarchism* (New York, 1964), p. 87.
[5] *Ibid.*, pp. 90–91, 120–121.

analysis of original sin. He recognized that the idea of innate depravity was essential to the defense of government. The church deceitfully located paradise in the past, when man must in reality have been a beast. This trick subverted every aspiration for freedom, the capacity for which was said to have been lost at the fall. Actually limited by incomplete victory over his past brutality, man was taught to regard his internal visions of freedom as externally forfeited. Thus religion understood and exploited the inner slavery:

"A contradictory being, inwardly infinite as the spirit, but outwardly dependent, defective, and material, man is compelled to combine with others into a society, not for the needs of his soul, but in order to preserve his body. Society then is formed by a sort of sacrifice of the interests and the independence of the soul to the contemptible needs of the body. It is a veritable fall and enslavement for the individual who is inwardly free and immortal; it is at least a partial renunciation of his primitive liberty."

Socialization, in religious doctrine, is not part of man's liberation, but a divine penalty. Saints have to be portrayed as asocial creatures, hermits divorced from their own humanity.[6] But in truth society conforms to the humanization of man, who is rather a fugitive from slavery than an exile from paradise.

The point should be emphasized: although he attacked the idea of original sin, Bakunin did not believe human nature to be perfect. He so distrusted human nature for retaining traits from the bestial past that he insisted any inequality of power leads to corruption and bondage.[7]

Like Proudhon, Bakunin sometimes abandoned his historical sense of slavery and regarded it instead as a timeless category of evil. Then he seemed to fight, as a Catholic critic has charged, against a God in whose existence he really believed.[8] For example, he criticized idealistic philosophy for "linking up two terms which, once separated, cannot be conjoined without destroying each other." Their fault lay in

[6] *Ibid.*, pp. 163, 160–161, 143.

[7] See Irving Louis Horowitz, ed., *The Anarchists* (New York, 1964), p. 128.

[8] James Hogan, "Anarchism and the Spanish Civil War," *Studies: An Irish Quarterly Review*, XXV (1936), 552–553.

saying " 'God and the liberty of man,' or 'God and the dignity, justice, equality, fraternity, and welfare of men,' " without realizing that the existence of God condemned these other virtues to nonexistence. *"For if God is,"* Bakunin argued, "he is necessarily the eternal, supreme, and absolute Master, and if such a Master exists, man is a slave." And justice, equality, fraternity, and prosperity are as unknown as liberty to a slave. Nor was it any help to attribute to God a gentle love of human liberty, for a master is always a master. Regardless of his intentions, a master's existence "will necessarily entail the slavery of all those who are beneath him." Bakunin concluded that "if God existed, he could render service to human liberty in one way only—by ceasing to exist."[9] In this formulation, anarchism equaled antislavery which equaled atheism.

Since anarchism has been deeply involved in disowning slavery, it has been obliged to seek out the essence of slavery. For Proudhon it was a traditional code allowing for economic expropriation. Sometimes Bakunin reiterated this historical understanding. Both men subscribed to versions of the idea of progress. But in his analysis of the "inner yoke" and man's tendency to make an abstraction of himself Bakunin more closely resembled another precursor of the 1840s: Max Stirner. What Bakunin only hinted at, however, had been the substance of Stirner's anarchism.

What Stirner primarily attacked, even more than government, was fixed ideas which dominate human decisions. Partly he saw them as the springs of compulsive behavior familiar to the insane asylum. But he thought that ideas of faith, patriotism, virtue, and morality similarly rigidified the assumptions of men at large and made the world a madhouse. He attacked the self-renunciation of both holy and unholy men, for he feared that unselfishness was "the article of fashion in the civilized world." Unselfishness begins when a personal objective ceases to be *"our* end and our *property,* which we, as owners, can dispose of at pleasure."[10]

What Stirner advocated defies paraphrase, but here is a typical statement: "I am not unselfish so long as the end remains my *own,*

[9] Maximoff, ed., *Political Philosophy,* pp. 62, 130–131; Bakunin, *God and the State* (Indore, India, n.d.), p. 29.

[10] Stirner, *The Ego and His Own,* trans. Steven T. Byington (New York, 1963), pp. 43, 60–61.

and I, instead of giving myself up to be the blind means of its fulfill-
ment, leave it always an open question. My zeal need not on that
account be slacker than the most fanatical, but at the same time I
remain toward it frostily cold, unbelieving, and its most irreconcilable
enemy; I remain its *judge*, because I am its owner." In ordinary English, he was maintaining that whatever a man is bound to do he cannot do freely.[11]

Plainly with Stirner the metaphor of slavery is inseparable from his
meaning. He ridiculed the liberation movements of his time in Europe:
"The man who is set free is nothing but a freed man, a *libertinus*, a
dog dragging a piece of chain with him." The only effective freedom
is self-liberation. In the end, Stirner disavowed freedom itself as a
Christian obsession, not subject to self-control and ultimately frustrat-
ing. He borrowed the lexicon of slavery to contrast his goal with freedom. "I am free from what I am *rid* of, owner of what I have in my
power or what I control." The sole escape from being property is self-
possession, and to make this point he seldom ventured far from his
central figure:

"Under the dominion of a cruel master my body is not 'free' from
torments and lashes; but it is *my* bones that moan under the torture,
my fibres that quiver under the blows, and *I* moan because *my* body
moans. . . . My leg is not 'free' from the master's stick, but it is *my*
leg and is inseparable. Let him tear it off me. . . . He retains in his
hand nothing but the—corpse of my leg!"

Stirner even insisted that the freedom of a people always subdues the
individual. His anarchism called not for revolution but for insurrection,
not for a new society but "a working forth of me out of the established." His purpose was not political and social but *"egoistic."*[12]

Stirner was not primarily interested in economic problems, but on
that subject the antislavery overtones of his philosophy resounded most
clearly. He maintained that government means everything in the end
is insured by the state. Therefore the worker, who has nothing, would
lose nothing if the protection of government were suspended. In fact,
the state guarantees that he will not be protected in the production
of his labor. Otherwise property rights would be worthless and the
state would have a hold on nobody. Therefore labor disturbances are

[11] *Ibid.*, p. 62.
[12] *Ibid.*, pp. 168, 156–158, 214, 316.

always potentially anarchistic. "The State rests on the—*slavery of labor*. If *labor* becomes *free*, the State is lost."[13]

Of course Stirner was by no means as colorful a figure in European history as Bakunin. But his writings drew out strange implications of the metaphor of slavery in anarchist literature. Since most anarchists have wanted to broaden the meaning of slavery to indict any compulsory behavior, it is not surprising to find one of them seceding from the social notion of morality. Most philosophical outlooks sort out good or bad conventions; in Stirner's view anything conventional represents the enslavement of the individual by society.

There is one more anarchist whose study of slavery calls for attention. Leo Tolstoy, as was noted in the first chapter, entitled an important book *The Slavery of Our Times*. He insisted that he did not mean slavery in a metaphorical sense:

"If between the slaves and slave owners of to-day it is difficult to draw as sharp a dividing line as that which separated the former slaves from their masters, and if among the slaves of to-day there are some who are only temporarily slaves and then become slave owners, or some who, at one and the same time, are slaves and slave owners, this blending of the two classes at their points of contact does not upset the fact that the people of our time are divided into slaves and slave owners as definitely as, in spite of the twilight, each twenty-four hours is divided into day and night."

His book pleads for a moral revolution, revoking so-called economic laws, enabling society to accept technological change "without keeping our brother men in slavery."[14]

As did Proudhon, Bakunin, and Stirner, Tolstoy blamed modern slavery on unequal bargaining power and other imperfections in a supposedly free market. He stressed this obstacle to freedom: "Luxurious habits" adopted in the process of economic change induce men to sell "their labour and their liberty."[15] Self-renunciation, which was Stirner's chief target, was therefore a key to Tolstoy's anarchism.

But Tolstoy's argument was more involved in morals than in economics. The means of alleviating poverty, he warned, "must consist in this: . . . in admitting that among us slavery exists not in some fig-

13 *Ibid.*, pp. 115–116.
14 Tolstoy, *The Slavery of Our Times* (New York, n.d.), pp. 78, 73–74.
15 *Ibid.*, pp. 78–79, 87–88.

urative, metaphorical sense, but in the simplest and plainest sense; slavery which keeps some people—the majority—in the power of others —the minority." In other words people must admit that "the essence of slavery" lies in "the fact that legislation exists" rather than in specific bad laws. The presence of legislation ensures economic inequality, whether the thrust of laws be to retain chattels, to monopolize land, or to entrench the division of labor. Because laws distribute power unevenly, "people can only be freed from slavery by the abolition of governments." Moreover, governments must be abolished peacefully— by conversion—for violence is the basis of law and will reorganize itself into government.[16]

We may conclude, then, that European anarchism depended on the concept of slavery. We may be able to make sense of Proudhon's possessionary rights, Bakunin's progressive intelligence, Stirner's self-ownership, or Tolstoy's faith in conversion without alluding to slavery. But they could not. The concept of slavery does not simply illustrate their philosophy; it informs it. We may not conclude, however, that all anarchists supported the North in the War for Southern Independence. It is sufficient to remember that Proudhon firmly supported the South, in part because he thought the obliteration of states' rights would make the Negroes into proletarians and thus ensure their further enslavement.[17] None of these thinkers influenced abolitionist thought.

[16] *Ibid.*, pp. 83–84, 114, 147–148.
[17] Joll, *Anarchists*, p. 77.

Bibliographical Note

Texts which have been useful to me and other bibliographical references are indicated in the notes. It may be helpful, however, to mention some of the books and articles that might interest readers who wish to look further into antislavery radicalism.

I should begin by recommending three excellent and more general bibliographical essays. In order of publication, they appear in Louis Filler, *The Crusade against Slavery, 1830–1860* (New York: Harper Torchbooks, 1960), pp. 281–303; James M. McPherson, *The Struggle for Equality: Abolitionists and the Negro in the Civil War and Reconstruction* (Princeton: Princeton University Press, 1964), pp. 433–450; and Bertram Wyatt-Brown, *Lewis Tappan and the Evangelical War against Slavery* (Cleveland: Press of Case Western Reserve University, 1969), pp. 347–357. Two informative historiographical essays are Merton L. Dillon, "The Abolitionists: A Decade of Historiography, 1959–1969," *Journal of Southern History*, XXXV (1969), 500–522; and Aileen S. Kraditor, *Means and Ends in American Abolitionism: Garrison and His Critics on Strategy and Tactics, 1834–1850* (New York: Pantheon, 1968). The latter work is much more than an essay on historiography; it is one of the most provocative books on abolitionism—one of the most sympathetic to the radicals—to appear in this century.

Among general scholarly accounts of abolitionism, the one giving the most adequate consideration to pacifism and anarchism is Louis Filler, *The Crusade against Slavery, 1830–1860* (cited above); on these subjects its viewpoint is fairer and more reliable than that of Dwight Lowell Dumond, *Antislavery: The Crusade for Freedom in America* (Ann Arbor: University of Michigan Press, 1961). Gilbert Hobbs Barnes, *The Antislavery Impulse, 1830–1844*, has been reprinted with a valuable introduction by William G. McLoughlin (New York; Harcourt, Brace & World, 1964); though it is strongly biased against Garrison and is silent on the late 1840s and 1850s, the student of antislavery radicalism will still find it stimulating. A sampling of essays by recent scholars on abolitionism may be found in Martin Duberman, ed., *The Antislavery Vanguard: New Essays on the Abolitionists* (Princeton: Princeton University Press, 1965); most relevant to our subject is John L. Thomas, "Antislavery and Utopia." One of the fairest and most incisive accounts of all the factions in abolitionism was written by a participant in the movement: William Goodell, *Slavery and Anti-Slavery: A History of the Great Struggle in Both Hemispheres* (New York: William Goodell, 1855). One of the most rewarding approaches to abolitionism is through Gilbert Hobbs Barnes and Dwight Lowell Dumond, eds., *Letters of Theodore Dwight Weld, Angelina Grimké Weld, and Sarah Grimké, 1822–1844,* 2 vols. (Gloucester, Mass.: Peter Smith, 1965).

Some of the best work on abolitionism has taken the form of biographical studies. The student of antislavery radicalism should look closely at two recent studies of Garrison: Walter M. Merrill, *Against Wind and Tide: A Biography of Wm. Lloyd Garrison* (Cambridge: Harvard University Press, 1963); and John L. Thomas, *The Liberator: William Lloyd Garrison* (Boston: Little, Brown, 1963). Thomas, in particular, has taken great pains to understand Garrison's radicalism, though he is unmistakably hostile to the subject. Bertram Wyatt-Brown, *Lewis Tappan and the Evangelical War against Slavery* (cited above) is an illuminating biography; its scope is more general than its title suggests. Another successful and relevant biography is Tilden G. Edelstein, *Strange Enthusiasm: A Life of Thomas Wentworth Higginson* (New York: Atheneum, 1970). The latest and most scholarly biography of John Brown is Stephen B. Oates, *To Purge This Land with Blood: A Biography of John Brown* (New York: Harper & Row, 1970); the reader may wish to look at the thoughtful review by Willie Lee Rose, and the sometimes bitter exchange that followed, in the *New York Review of Books,* Dec. 3, 1970, Feb. 11, 1971, and Apr. 22, 1971. Two additional biographies, focusing on different aspects of antislavery radicalism, are Carol Ryrie Brink, *Harps in the Wind: The Story of the Singing Hutchinsons* (New York: MacMillan, 1947); and Madeleine B. Stern, *The Pantarch: A Biography of Stephen Pearl Andrews* (Austin; University of Texas Press, 1968).

Tensions between Negro abolitionists and white radicals are discussed in Leon Litwack, "The Emancipation of the Negro Abolitionist," in Martin Duberman, ed., *The Antislavery Vanguard* (cited above); and Benjamin Quarles, *Black Abolitionists* (New York: Oxford University Press, 1969). A significant black radical movement is traced in Howard Holman Bell, *A Survey of the Negro Convention Movement, 1830–1861*, a 1953 Northwestern dissertation which has recently been published (New York: Arno Press, 1970). A useful volume on Negro abolitionists is John H. Bracey, Jr., August Meier, and Elliott Rudwick, eds., *Blacks in the Abolitionist Movement* (Belmont, Calif.: Wadsworth Publishing Company, 1971).

On the social and intellectual origins of abolitionism, the reader should consult two superb and widely acclaimed studies of the 1960s: David Brion Davis, *The Problem of Slavery in Western Culture* (Ithaca, N.Y.: Cornell University Press, 1966); and Winthrop D. Jordan, *White over Black: American Attitudes toward the Negro, 1550–1812* (Baltimore: Pelican Books, 1969). These books deal with earlier periods than that of the present study, but they have raised the general level of discussion of abolitionism, and they will reward the student of any aspect of the history of slavery and antislavery. Professor Davis' book is the first of a promised multivolume study; he has already contributed "The Emergence of Immediatism in British and American Antislavery Thought," *Mississippi Valley Historical Review*, XLIX (1962), 209–230. Also of interest on early antislavery thought is Merton L. Dillon, *Benjamin Lundy and the Struggle for Negro Freedom* (Urbana and London: University of Illinois Press, 1966). A controversial study of slavery and antislavery, which criticizes most of abolitionist thought for being too immoderate and anti-institutional, is Stanley M. Elkins, *Slavery: A Problem in American Institutional and Intellectual Life* (2nd ed., Chicago and London: University of Chicago Press, 1968). In general it identifies abolitionist thought too closely with transcendentalism.

There are numerous books and articles on American radicalism, few of which are illuminating in regard to abolitionism. For a helpful selection of scholarly essays on radicalism, one may consult Alfred Young, ed., *Dissent: Explorations in the History of American Radicalism* (DeKalb: Northern Illinois University Press, 1968). An intelligent popular survey of radicalism, including abolitionism and anarchism, is Charles A. Madison, *Critics and Crusaders* (New York: Henry Holt, 1947–

1948). Staughton Lynd, *Intellectual Origins of American Radicalism*
(New York: Vintage Books, 1969), is a stimulating essay with much
to say about abolitionism, although it is flawed by failure to observe
differences between the Garrisonians and transcendentalists as well as
by an attempt to uncover a single radical tradition following from
Jefferson to the present. There are important works on pacifism which
no student of antislavery radicalism could afford to ignore. Peter Brock,
*Pacifism in the United States from the Colonial Era to the First World
War* (Princeton: Princeton University Press, 1968), is indispensable
on nonresistance. Merle Eugene Curti gave sympathetic scholarly attention to pacifism in several studies, including *The American Peace
Crusade, 1815–1860* (Durham: Duke University Press, 1929); and
"Non-Resistance in New England," *New England Quarterly*, II (1929),
34–57. Also relevant is John Demos, "The Antislavery Movement and
the Problem of Violent 'Means,'" *New England Quarterly*, XXXVII
(1964), 501–526. Staughton Lynd, ed., *Nonviolence in America: A
Documentary History* (Indianapolis: Bobbs-Merrill, 1966), is a good
anthology.

The history of American anarchism has mostly been written by
anarchists. The soundest volumes deal primarily with individualist
anarchism after the Civil War: Rudolf Rocker, *Pioneers of American
Freedom: Origin of Liberal and Radical Thought in America*, trans.
Arthur E. Briggs (Los Angeles: Rocker Publications Committee,
1949); and James J. Martin, *Men against the State: The Expositors of
Individualist Anarchism in America, 1827–1908* (DeKalb: Adrien
Allen Associates, 1953). More attention is paid to antebellum anarchism in Eunice Minette Schuster, *Native American Anarchism: A
Study of Left-Wing American Individualism* (New York: DaCapo,
1970; 1st pub. 1932), which is serviceable but by no means definitive.
Corinne Jacker, *The Black Flag of Anarchy: Antistatism in the United
States* (New York: Charles Scribner's Sons, 1968), is derivative and
frequently inaccurate. On anarchism outside the United States, study
may be begun with James Joll, *The Anarchists* (Boston: Little, Brown,
1964); and George Woodcock, *Anarchism: A History of Libertarian
Ideas and Movements* (Cleveland: Meridian Books, 1962). Some of
the themes of the present essay may be pursued in Leonard I. Krimerman and Lewis Perry, eds., *Patterns of Anarchy: A Collection of
Writings on the Anarchist Tradition* (Garden City, N.Y.: Anchor
Books, 1966).

Antislavery radicalism was connected with diverse other movements. The best approach to its connections with communitarianism is still John Humphrey Noyes, *History of American Socialisms* (Philadelphia: J. B. Lippincott, 1870); one may also consult Donald Drew Egbert and Stow Persons, eds., *Socialism and American Life* (Princeton: Princeton University Press, 1952). On Southern thought, I recommend Eugene D. Genovese, *The World the Slaveholders Made: Two Essays in Interpretation* (New York: Pantheon Books, 1969); William Sumner Jenkins, *Pro-Slavery Thought in the Old South* (Chapel Hill: University of North Carolina Press, 1935); and C. Vann Woodward's edition of *Cannibals All* by George Fitzhugh (Cambridge: Harvard University Press, 1960). There are a great many studies of antebellum reform. Some of the best scholarship is brought together in David Brion Davis, ed., *Ante-Bellum Reform* (New York: Harper & Row, 1967); and what may be the obverse side of radicalism is delineated in Clifford S. Griffin, *Their Brothers' Keepers: Moral Stewardship in the United States, 1800–1865* (New Brunswick, N.J.: Rutgers University Press, 1960). Abolitionists sometimes shared in various cults, foibles, and fads of antebellum popular culture, although abolitionism should not be too loosely compared to the more bizarre movements of the period. Some sense may be made of this subject by reading E. Douglas Branch, *The Sentimental Years, 1836–1860* (New York: Hill & Wang, 1965); Alice Felt Tyler, *Freedom's Ferment: Phases of American Social History from the Colonial Period to the Outbreak of the Civil War* (New York: Harper Torchbooks, 1962); and a successful anthology, David Grimsted, *Notions of the Americans, 1820–1860* (New York: George Braziller, 1970).

My approach to antislavery radicalism is heavily dependent on readings in American religious and intellectual history; it would be folly to attempt here any kind of comprehensive listing. All intellectual historians are indebted to the splendid works of Perry Miller, of which the most relevant here are the posthumous *Life of the Mind in America: From the Revolution to the Civil War* (New York: Harcourt, Brace & World, 1965); and *The Transcendentalists* (Cambridge: Harvard University Press, 1966). Particularly relevant studies in religious history include: Timothy L. Smith, *Revivalism and Social Reform: American Protestantism on the Eve of the Civil War* (New York: Harper Torchbooks, 1965); Robert Allerton Parker, *A Yankee Saint: John Humphrey Noyes and the Oneida Community* (New York: G. P. Put-

322 Bibliographical Note

nam's Sons, 1935); Whitney R. Cross, *The Burned-Over District: The Social and Intellectual History of Enthusiastic Religion in Western New York, 1800–1850* (New York: Harper Torchbooks, 1965); H. Richard Niebuhr, *The Kingdom of God in America* (New York: Harper Torchbooks, 1959); William G. McLoughlin, "Pietism and the American Character," *American Quarterly*, XVII (1965), 163–186; and Anne C. Loveland, "Evangelicalism and 'Immediate Emancipation' in American Antislavery Thought," *Journal of Southern History*, XXXII (1966), 172–188. There are scores of relevant works in literary and intellectual history, but the reader should surely not miss Yehoshua Arieli, *Individualism and Nationalism in American Ideology* (Cambridge: Harvard University Press, 1964); R. W. B. Lewis, *The American Adam: Innocence, Tragedy, and Tradition in the Nineteenth Century* (Chicago: University of Chicago Press, 1955); William R. Taylor, *Cavalier and Yankee: The Old South and American National Character* (Garden City, N.Y.: Anchor Books, 1963); F. O. Matthiessen, *American Renaissance: Art and Expression in the Age of Emerson and Whitman* (London, Oxford, and New York: Oxford University Press, 1941); George M. Frederickson, *The Inner Civil War: Northern Intellectuals and the Crisis of the Union* (New York: Harper & Row, 1965); and John L. Thomas, "Romantic Reform in America, 1815–1865," *American Quarterly*, XVII (1965), 656–681.

Finally, of writings by abolitionist radicals themselves, William Goodell's excellent history, *Slavery and Anti-Slavery*, has previously been mentioned. In many ways the best source for antislavery radicalism is Garrison's newspaper, *The Liberator*. There are copious quotations from *The Liberator* in Wendell Phillips Garrison and Francis Jackson Garrison, *William Lloyd Garrison, 1805–1879: The Story of His Life Told by His Children*, 4 vols. (New York: Century Company, 1885–1889); in addition, a brief, readable selection may be found in Truman Nelson, ed., *Documents of Upheaval: Selections from William Lloyd Garrison's* The Liberator, *1831–1865* (New York: Hill & Wang, 1966). Of the many volumes of post-Civil War reminiscences, several are especially revealing on the subject of abolitionist radicalism: *Autobiography of Adin Ballou*, ed. William S. Heywood (Lowell: Vox Populi Press–Thompson & Hill, 1896); Parker Pillsbury, *Acts of the Anti-Slavery Apostles* (Boston: Cupples, Upham & Co., 1884); and two by Thomas Wentworth Higginson, *Cheerful Yesterdays* (Boston and New York: Houghton, Mifflin, 1898), and *Contemporaries* (Boston and New York: Houghton, Mifflin, 1899).

Abolitionist radicalism may not have produced any literary masterpieces, and most of its writings were ephemeral tracts and newspaper columns. But it may be useful to enumerate a dozen of its more successful, characteristic, or ambitious statements. The two most important works on nonresistance were Adin Ballou, *Christian Non-Resistance, in All Its Important Bearings, Illustrated and Defended* (Philadelphia: J. Miller M'Kim, 1846); and Henry Clarke Wright, *Defensive War Proved to Be a Denial of Christianity and of the Government of God* (London: Charles Gilpin, 1846). Wright was a prolific author; his works included an unusual autobiography, *Human Life: Illustrated in My Individual Experience as a Child, a Youth, and a Man* (Boston: Bela Marsh, 1849), and an important treatise on sexual reform, *Marriage and Parentage; or, The Reproductive Element in Man, as a Means to His Elevation and Happiness* (6th ed.; London: John Heywood, n.d. [1877?]). The best writing of the come-outer movement appears in *A Collection from the Miscellaneous Writings of Nathaniel Peabody Rogers*, ed. John Pierpont (Manchester, N.H.: William H. Fisk; Boston: Benj. B. Mussey, 1849); and the most cogent exposition of come-outerism is William Goodell, *Come-Outerism: The Duty of Secession from a Corrupt Church* (New York: American Anti-Slavery Society, 1845). One of the most interesting documents of disunionism is Wendell Phillips, *Can Abolitionists Vote or Take Office under the United States Constitution?* (New York: American Anti-Slavery Society, 1845). Two significant statements of the radicalism inherent in political abolitionism are Beriah Green, *Belief without Confession* (Utica: R. W. Roberts, 1844); and William Goodell, *The Democracy of Christianity; or, An Analysis of the Bible and Its Doctrines in Their Relation to the Principle of Democracy*, 2 vols. (New York: Cady & Burgess, 1849, 1852). No one was more radical than Lysander Spooner, whose legal theories were expressed forcefully in *The Unconstitutionality of Slavery* (Boston: Bela Marsh, 1860), and *An Essay on the Trial by Jury* (Boston: Bela Marsh, 1852). A neglected document of the era—and yet one which provides important insights into radical antislavery thought—is the *Proceedings of the Free Convention Held at Rutland, Vt., June 25th, 26th, 27th, 1858* (New York: S. T. Munson; Boston: J. B. Yerrinton and Son, 1858).

Index

Abolitionism: and come-outerism, 95, 104–113, 178–182; and eccentricity, 13–16; historical backgrounds of, 8–12, 43, 95; in historical writing, 6–7, 166–170, 295–296; and quest for personal liberation, 16–17, 105–106, 110; and religion of humanity, 112, 116, 121–122, 180, 195, 305–306

Accountability, individual: and government of God, 45, 53; and sin of slavery, 48–51

Addams, Jane, 2

Alcott, A. Bronson, 78, 81–87, 103, 253–254, 290

American Anti-Slavery Society, 11, 51, 56, 69, 89, 143, 158, 161, 166–169, 181

American Colonization Society, 9, 48–50

American Peace Society, 58, 59–62

Anarchism, 2, 20–26, 31, 54, 150, 182–183, 199, 209–213, 285, 290–291, 293–294, 295–296, 302–303, 309–316, 320

Andrews, Stephen Pearl, 28, 29, 210–216, 290, 292, 293

Antinomianism, 16, 36, 47–48, 58–59, 66, 83–84, 88, 149, 220, 223, 244, 299

Arieli, Yehoshua, 304–305, 322

Bakunin, Michael, 310–313

Ballou, Adin, 62, 74, 159, 163, 193–194, 216–217, 220, 241, 247, 250, 254, 299, 306, 322, 323; during and after Civil War, 269, 271, 274–275; early life of, 134–139;

leads Hopedale Community, 139–157; secedes from abolitionism, 261–267; speech of, at 1839 nonresistance meetings, 130–133; and Tolstoy, 4

Barnes, Gilbert Hobbs, 93, 167, 170, 317–318

Barry, Francis, 192

Bassett, William, 109–111

Beach, Thomas Parnell, 108–109, 119

Beecher, Edward, 66, 175

Beecher, Henry Ward, 292–293

Beecher, Lyman, 68, 128

Benevolence societies, 40–42, 128

Bible, 59, 93, 95, 99–100, 111–112, 121–122, 130, 133, 152–155, 160, 220, 224, 243–244, 279

Birney, James Gillespie, 12, 129, 172, 175

Bloom, Morgan, 144

Bool, Henry, 302

Bourne, George, 95

Boyle, James, 65, 72

Bradburn, George, 138n, 185, 198, 199–200, 203, 252

Branch, Julia, 229–230

Brock, Peter, 62, 320

Brook Farm, 102, 140–141, 254

Brown, John, 122, 184, 194, 204–207, 251–253, 254, 255–260, 265–266, 270, 280, 289–290, 318

Brownson, Orestes, 87, 138n, 140, 254

Bryan, William Jennings, 1–2

Butts, Bryan, 275–278

Calhoun, John C., 27

RADICAL ABOLITIONISM

Designed by R. E. Rosenbaum.
Composed by York Composition Company, Inc.,
in 10 point linotype Caledonia, 3 points leaded,
with display lines in monotype Bulmer.
Printed letterpress from type by York Composition Company
on Warren's 1854 text, 60 pound basis,
with the Cornell University Press watermark.
Bound by Vail-Ballou Press
in Columbia book cloth
and stamped in All Purpose foil.

Library of Congress Cataloging in Publication Data
(for library cataloging purposes only)

Perry, Lewis.
    Radical abolitionism.

    Bibliography: p.
    1. Slavery in the United States—Anti-slavery
movements. 2. Abolitionists.   3. Anarchism and
anarchists.   I. Title.
E449.P46   322.4′4′0973   72-12913
ISBN 0-8014-0754-0